Okanagan Trips & Trails

A Guide to the Backroads and Hiking Trails of British Columbia's Okanagan – Similkameen Region

New Edition –Fully Updated and Revised

Judie Steeves & Murphy Shewchuk

Fitzhenry & Whiteside

All inquiries should be addressed to:
Fitzhenry and Whiteside Limited
195 Allstate Parkway
Markham, Ontario L3R 4T8

In the United States:
311 Washington St.
Brighton, Massachusetts 02135
www.fitzhenry.ca godwit@fitzhenry.ca

Fitzhenry & Whiteside acknowledges with thanks the Canada Council for the Arts, and the Ontario Arts Council for their support of our publishing program. We acknowledge the financial support of the Government of Canada through the Canada Book Fund (CBF) for our publishing activities.

Library and Archives Canada Cataloguing in Publication
Steeves, Judie
Okanagan trips & trails : a guide to backroads and hiking trails of British Columbia's Okanagan-Similkameen region / Judie Steeves & Murphy Shewchuk.
Includes index.
ISBN 978-1-55455-267-2
Data available on file

United States Cataloguing-in-Publication Data
Steeves, Judie.
Okanagan trips & trails : a guide to backroads and hiking trails of British Columbia'ss Okanagan-Similkameen region / Judie Steeves ; Murphy Shewchuk.
Originally published: Merritt, BC, Canada : Sonotek Publishing Ltd., 1999.
ISBN 978-1-55455-267-2
Data available on file

Designed by Kerry Designs
Cover photo by Murphy Shewchuk is of Okanagan Lake.
Printed and bound in Canada

10 9 8 7 6 5 4 3 2 1

I'd like to dedicate this updated and revised edition to my nephew and godson David Charles Steeves, who was born Oct. 19, 1967 and died too young on Oct. 24, 2003. In the intervening years, he touched many lives. With his love of the outdoors he explored many of the fishing lakes and trails described in this book from his home base in Kelowna.

Special thanks go to hiking partners Sharon Coleman, Winnie Schlyter, Rick Simpson, Carol Ulm, daughters Gillian and Emily and their friends, and my husband Dennis Vergnano.

— Judie

I would like to dedicate this edition to my parents, Murphy & Julia Shewchuk of Keremeos, BC. Their backyard orchard has served as a shady haven and an impromptu campground on many occasions.

I would also like to add my heartfelt thanks to my wife Katharine. Without her note-taking skills and knowledge of the flora and fauna of the region, my portion of this book would not have been possible.

—Murphy

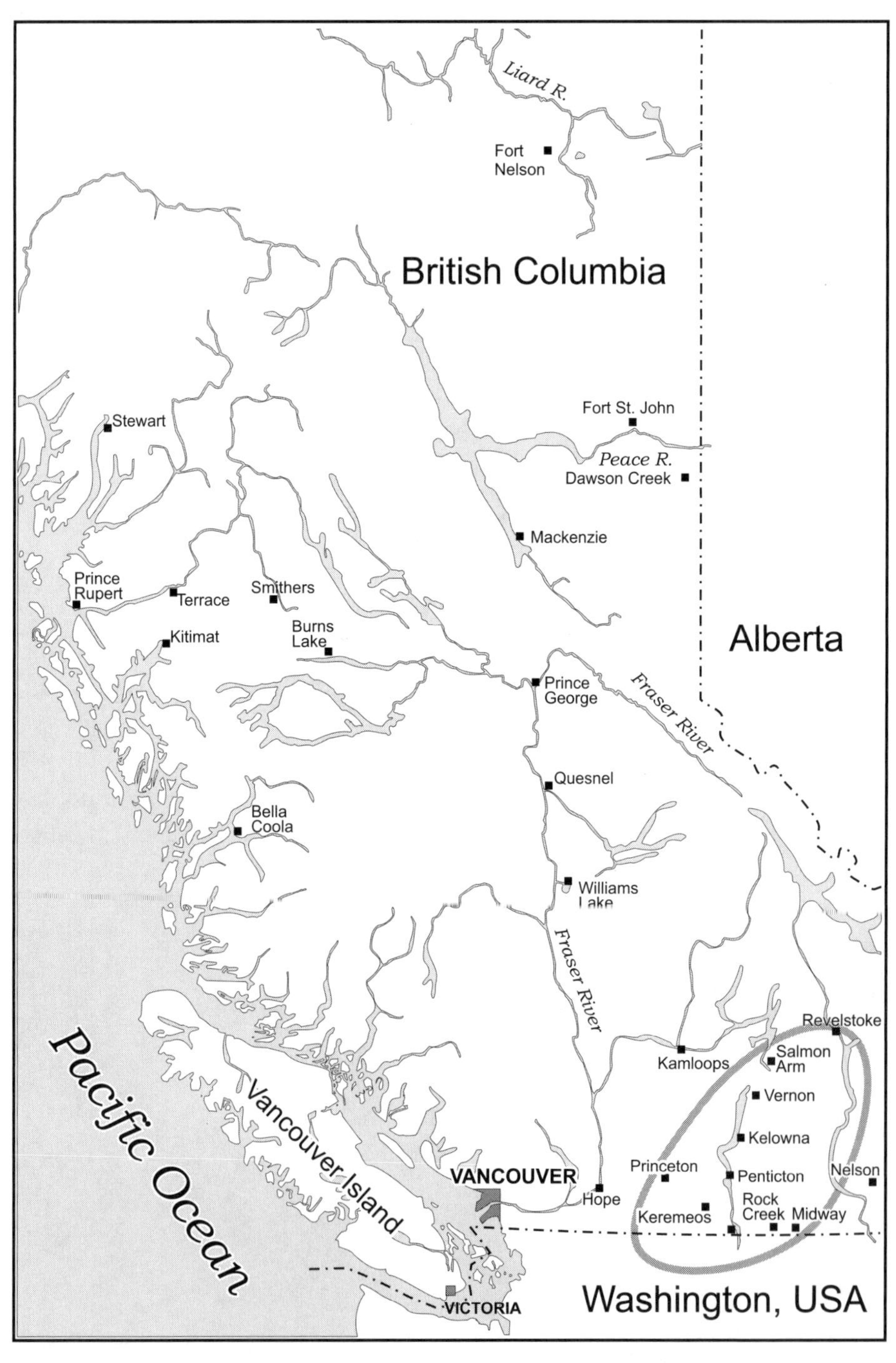
Liard R.
Fort Nelson
British Columbia
Fort St. John
Peace R.
Dawson Creek
Stewart
Mackenzie
Prince Rupert
Terrace
Smithers
Burns Lake
Kitimat
Alberta
Prince George
Fraser River
Quesnel
Bella Coola
Williams Lake
Fraser River
Revelstoke
Kamloops
Salmon Arm
Vernon
Pacific Ocean
Vancouver Island
Kelowna
Princeton
Penticton
Nelson
VANCOUVER
Hope
Rock Creek
Keremeos
Midway
VICTORIA
Washington, USA

CONTENTS

I North Okanagan & Shuswap

II Central Okanagan

III South Okanagan, Similkameen & Boundary

List of Maps

Introduction

British Columbia is the custodian of some of the most spectacular wilderness remaining in the world, including the unique ecosystems of the Okanagan basin.

However, there has been and continues to be degradation of these precious wild areas even by those who revere them. As more and more of us discover the wonders of our natural environment, it becomes increasingly important that each of us ensures that our natural surroundings are protected and preserved so our children may also know the same wonders of this incredible region.

Keep this in mind as you head out on the backroads and byways. Educate yourself to protect and preserve our natural areas, even as you enjoy them. Remember to protect yourself as well, by learning—beforehand—about the nature of the area in which you plan to explore. Arm yourself with up-to-date maps (see the "Topographic Maps" section), a compass (and the skill to use it), water, some sustenance, and suitable clothing.

Always let someone know where you plan to go and when you'll be back. And don't travel alone.

Water and Waste

Although it's essential to life, water can also harm life as well. No open body of water should be considered safe to drink without first treating it for invisible parasites and microorganisms which can cause mild to acute illness.

One of the most common causes of illness is the Giardia lamblia cyst, which multiplies in the intestinal tract of warm-blooded animals such as humans, and causes an illness often called beaver fever. The cysts are spread in water contaminated by the feces of infected animals or people and are present in more than 70 percent of our watersheds.

To be safe, either boil your water for one minute before cooling and drinking it; treat it with four drops of iodine tincture per litre or four drops of pure household bleach per four litres of water, up to double that if cloudy; or filter it with a special system available in outdoor stores.

If using the iodine or bleach method, make sure you stir it in and let it sit for at least half an hour before drinking.

Cryptosporidium, a microscopic parasite, is found in soil, food, water, or surfaces

that have been contaminated with infected human or animal feces. It is resistant to chlorine, but water can be treated by heating to a rolling boil for at least one minute, or by the use of a filter that has an absolute pore size of at least one micron or one that has been NSF rated for "cyst removal."

We can help prevent the spread of such internal infections by being responsible about disposal of our waste in the outdoors.

Never use streams or lakes as a bath, toilet or sink.

Use the proper facilities provided whenever possible, but otherwise when hiking or camping in the backcountry, the ideal solution is to carry out all human waste.

If that goes further than your commitment to preserving the natural environment, do ensure you never urinate or defecate within one hundred metres of open water. Instead, dig a small hole and replace the sod after you're through.

When camping, wash water should be disposed of in a hole, 25-30 centimetres deep, at least one hundred metres from any body of water.

Create as little waste as possible. Always pack out what you pack in.

In wilderness areas, tread lightly in both the figurative and the literal sense, leaving no trace of your presence behind you. That way, both you and those who follow will enjoy fields of wild flowers, trees alive with birds and forests full of wildlife.

Leaving no trace begins with good planning before you depart, eliminating leftovers and reducing the garbage produced while on your trip.

Wild Ways

Wherever possible, use existing trails. Do not detour around muddy sections since the added traffic will break down the trail edge and widen it, or cause multiple trails which scar the natural areas that are the reason you go hiking.

Where trails don't already exist, select a route over the most durable terrain such as gravel creek beds, sandy or rocky areas. Whenever possible, avoid steep, loose slopes and wet areas.

Keep in mind that many plants die if they're stepped on and some soils will erode even after being trampled lightly.

When camping in a wilderness area, select a site that would be least damaged by your stay. Choose either high use sites already damaged, or pristine sites in durable areas such as on rocky terrain, or a gravel bar, rather than the forest floor or sites with low growing shrubs.

Do not cut trees for firewood, furniture or boughs for beds. If you must have a fire, use an existing fire ring if possible, built on rocky or sandy soil away from trees, dry vegetation or roots. Use only as much dry dead wood as you need.

Burn your fire down to ash before pouring water on it. The extinguished fire should be cold enough for you to lay your bare hand on it. Leave no sign of your fire.

Remember: When you enter the wilderness you are entering the homes of wild animals. Respect their space and minimize your intrusion on their lives. View them from enough distance so they are unaware of your presence.

Leave your pets at home.

Trail Etiquette

Trails are often traversed by hooves, feet, and wheels, but by using common sense, communication and courtesy, conflict, danger and damage can be avoided.

Trail protocol suggests that the most mobile yields the right-of-way, but there are exceptions to this rule. Ideally, cyclists yield to everyone, and hikers yield to horses. A loaded string of horses going uphill always has the right of way, and a cyclist climbing steeply will appreciate the same courtesy.

Hikers: If you encounter horse riders, your group should step off to the same side of the trail, the lower side if possible, allowing two to three metres for them to pass. If you come up on horses from behind, greet the riders before you pass so they're aware you're there. Otherwise you might startle either the animal or rider.

Mountain Bikers: Always anticipate a horse or hiker around a blind curve. Prevent the possible sudden, unexpected encounter from a bike's quick and silent approach. Yield to hikers and equestrians. Get off the bike and move to the lower side of the trail to let horses pass. When approaching from behind, speak so they know you're there. Learn to minimize damage to trails with techniques such as riding and not sliding, and cycle on designated trails. Bicycle tires easily damage meadows. Stay off trails when they're wet and muddy. Otherwise, they'll become pathways for water erosion.

Horse Riders: Use an experienced, steady mount, and give clear directions to other trail users on how you would like them to stand clear. In steep, rough country, downhill traffic yields to uphill travellers, but use common sense. Whoever can pull off easiest should. Avoid soft and muddy trails.

Warn others of wire, potholes and boggy areas.

Above all, respect private property, "No Trespassing" signs, and leave gates as you found them.

Acknowledgments

The seed for a book on hiking trails and backroads in and around the Okanagan Valley was planted in the summer of 1997. Judie Steeves had been working on a series on hiking trails in her weekly "Trail Mix" outdoor column for the *Kelowna Capital News* and Murphy Shewchuk and his wife Katharine had been spending a lot of time exploring the Okanagan backroads for his regular features in *BC Outdoors* magazine.

A chance meeting brought the two together early in 1998, when Murphy was touring the Okanagan, promoting the recently-released second edition of his *Coquihalla Country* guidebook.

Both seemed headed toward an Okanagan outdoors book featuring trails and backroads, so it seemed natural to work together on such a project. The result was the first edition of *Okanagan Trips & Trails* released in 1999.

This revised edition is the culmination of continuing research and a close watch on developments in outdoor recreation in the region. It includes a much expanded section on the Kettle Valley Railway / Trans Canada Trail. It also has expanded information on bird watching and a special section on bird watching "hot spots" in each region by Chris Charlesworth.

A number of groups and individuals deserve thanks for their invaluable assistance in the development of this second edition. They include the staff in the Central Okanagan Regional District Parks Department; John Donnelly and the staff at the Ministry of Forests; Mike Ladd of BC Parks; City of Kelowna Parks Department; Penny Gubbels and Isabel Pritchard of the Friends of the South Slopes; Jan and Ken Walden of the Friends of Fintry; Kelowna Capital News photographer Gordon Bazzana; Marilyn Hansen of the Summerland Trans Canada Trail Society; The Gellatly Nut Farm Society and many others.

Topographic Maps

All topographic maps cited in this book are on a scale of 1:50,000. Below is a list of maps covering the region.

Ashnola River, BC 92 H/1
Aspen Grove, BC 92 H/15
Bankier, BC 92 H/9
Beaverdell, BC 82 E/6
Creighton Creek, BC 82 L/2
Gates Creek, BC 82 L/9
Greenwood, BC 82 E/2
Hedley, BC 92 H/8
Kelowna, BC 82 E/14
Keremeos, BC 82 E/4
Mabel Lake, BC 82 L/10
Malakwa, BC 82 L/15
Manning Park, BC 92 H/2
Mount Fosthall, BC 82 L/8
Osoyoos, BC 82 E/3
Oyama, BC 82 L/3
Paradise Lake, BC 92 H/16
Peachland, BC 82 E/13
Penticton, BC 82 E/5
Princeton, BC 92 H/7
Revelstoke, BC 82 L/16
Salmon Arm, BC 82 L/11
Shorts Creek, BC 82 L/4
Shuswap Falls, BC 82 L/7
Summerland, BC 82 E/12
Tulameen, BC 92 H/10
Vernon, BC 82 L/6
Wilkinson Creek, BC 82 E/11

The 1:50,000 maps referenced here are part of the Canadian Topographic Maps series. See: http://maps.nrcan.gc.ca/topographic.html — from Natural Resources Canada. Although they are among the best topographical maps available to the casual user, unfortunately some of them are also out-of-date and do not show the latest backroads.

These topographic maps are available from map dealers across Canada. To find map dealers in your area, please consult the Yellow Pages under "Maps."

In the Okanagan, you can also contact:
Mosaic Books
411 Bernard Avenue,
Kelowna, BC V1Y 6N8
Tel: (250) 763-4418
Toll-free: 1-800-663-1225
E-mail: orders@mosaicbooks.ca
Web: www.mosaicbooks.ca

The 1:50,000 Canadian Topographic Maps are also available in digital format on CD-ROM. Used with a GPS and a computer program such as OziExplorer, they can be an invaluable tool for backcountry exploring. OziExplorer is available in "Windows" format as well as a format that will work on many pocket computers or PDAs. With care and experimentation, a hand-held moving-map arrangement can be built that will help you track your every move — whether by bicycling, hiking or driving. For more information on digital maps, contact:

Spectrum Digital Imaging
#4–1145 North Park St.
Victoria, BC V8T 1C7
Tel: (778) 440-4851
Fax: (866) 524-2865
E-mail: spectrumdigital@shaw.ca
Web: www.mapsdigital.com

At the time of writing, Spectrum Digital Imaging's following CD-ROM contained all the required maps and more: Cat. 1002 Vancouver / Okanagan, BC (80 Maps).

There are also map books which cover the area, although they are usually of a higher scale. One source is the Backroad Mapbook series published by Mussio Ventures Ltd. These are available from many bookstores and book racks. For additional information, visit: http://www.backroadmapbooks.com.

There is also a quickly growing online mapping resource.

Google Earth (http://www.earth.google.com) is a source of aerial and satellite images of the region. Although they may be several years old, detailed BC government aerial photos are part of the free Google Earth service. Open Street Map (http://www.openstreetmap.org/) is a collaborative effort that you can use and contribute your GPS tracks and information. Other sources of digital maps include Garmin's MapSource TopoCanada and Ibycus Topo.

Abbreviations Used

B & B	bed and breakfast
cm	centimetre
CPR	Canadian Pacific Railway
elev.	elevation
FOSS	Friends of the South Slopes
FS	Forest Service
FSR	Forest Service Road
GNR	Great Northern Railway
GPS	Global Positioning System
ha	hectare
hwy	highway
JS	authored by Judie Steeves
km	kilometre
KVR	Kettle Valley Railway
LRMP	Land and Resource Management Plan
m	metre
MS	authored by Murphy Shewchuk
rd	road
RV	recreational vehicle
stn	station
TCT	Trans Canada Trail
topo	topographic or topographic map

Symbols Used

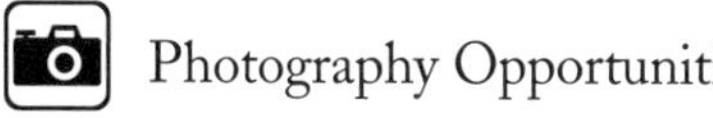
Photography Opportunities

Wildlife Viewing

Bird Watching

Wildflowers

Interpretive Trail

Point of Interest

Viewpoint

Picnic Site

Open Picnic Shelter

Enclosed Picnic Shelter

Sleeping Shelter

Wilderness Campsite

RV Park

Campground

Campfire Ring

RV Sani-Station

Public Washrooms

Amphitheatre

 Accommodations

 Meal Service

 Fuel

 Public Telephone

 First Aid Station

 Hospital

 Museum

 Airport

 Information Centre

Marina

 Swimming Beach

 Angling

 Ice Fishing

 Boat Launch

 Canoe Portage

 Canoeing & Kayaking

 Sailing

 Motor Boating

 Windsurfing

 Hiking Trail

 Rock Climbing Route

 Golf Course

 Rockhounding

 Shooting Sports

 Horse Riding

 Bicycle Trail

 Mountain Bicycle Trail

 Motorcycle Trail

 Four-Wheel-Drive Road

 Winter Sports

 Alpine Ski Hill

 Nordic Ski Trail

 Snowshoe Trail

 Sledding Hill

 Ice Skating

 Snowmobile Trail

 Chairlift

 Gondola Lift

 Cave

 Tunnel

 Recycling

 Radio Observatory

 Wheelchair Access

 Parking

North Okanagan & Shuswap

It is hard not to sound like a tourist brochure or a travel commercial when describing British Columbia's North Okanagan and Shuswap region. If water is your weakness, it has lakes of every size that include over a thousand kilometres of lakeshore, hundreds of sheltered bays and sandy beaches. Moving waterways range from placid rivers to white-water streams to roaring creeks and spectacular waterfalls. If you prefer to keep your feet on or close to the ground, the inventory includes paved highways, gravel backroads, abandoned rail grade, alpine trails, and white-knuckle cliffs.

If you can't decide whether you're a party animal or a hermit, you can satisfy the requirements of either indulgence and go from one extreme to the other in a matter of an hour or two. Wine festivals abound. The bird watching is spectacular. You can turn wildflower photography into art. Hiking, cycling, horse riding, backcountry exploring, cross-country skiing, and alpine skiing are just a few ways you can keep fit.

The Land and the Details

The North Okanagan forms a transition zone between the hot, dry southern reaches of the Okanagan Valley and the wetter, more moderate Shuswap region. The physical division between the two drainage basins, however, is barely perceptible. If it were not for a geographical marker alongside Highway 97A north of Armstrong, most travellers would not notice the change.

The North Okanagan region offers many unique recreational opportunities. Silver Star Ski Resort ranks among the best in British Columbia and western North America. The skiing and snowmobiling trails here become hiking, biking and horse riding trails in mid-summer, presenting opportunities to explore subalpine forests and alpine meadows. South of Vernon, less than an hour from Silver Star, the semi-desert rocky ridges and emerald green bays of Kalamalka Provincial Park present a sharp contrast to the forested alpine. With sheltered, sandy beaches and 10 kilometres of trails through the grasslands, it is an attractive recreation destination.

Somewhere between the two climatic extremes lay several other parks. Ellison Provincial Park, southwest of Vernon on Okanagan Lake, also has rocky bluffs, sheltered bays and sandy beaches, but it has a few more trees to keep it a touch

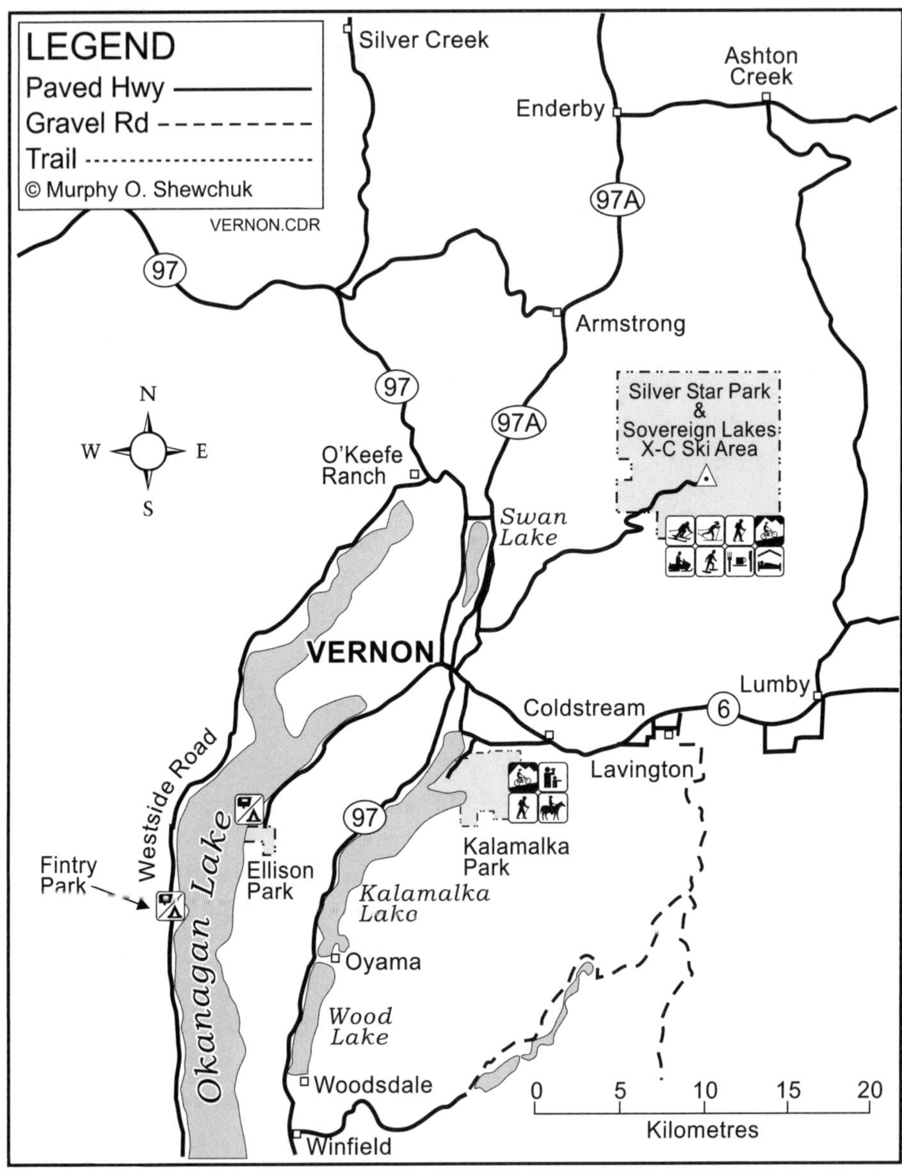

Vernon and area parks.

cooler in mid-summer. Mabel Lake Provincial Park, higher and farther into the Monashee Mountains, north of Lumby, has sandy beaches and clear water in the heart of the forest. Monashee Provincial Park, still farther to the east, is dominated by 2,697-metre-high Mount Fosthall, part of the rugged Monashee Range of snow-capped peaks.

When you've had your fill of strenuous activity, the historic O'Keefe Ranch, northwest of Vernon, is open all year round for a glimpse of the area's colourful past. If you are interested in a bit of culture, the Caravan Farm Theatre near Armstrong presents unique plays in an outdoor setting year round. The museum in Vernon, the Armstrong Fair and a host of other diversions will also keep you enjoyably occupied.

While researching and writing this book, it quickly became apparent that the Vernon region could easily fill a book of its own, thus what we offer here is only a brief glimpse at what lies off the beaten track. May it whet your appetite long enough to keep you exploring until that book is written.

May we meet along the way?

CHAPTER 1

Ellison Provincial Park

Statistics	For map, see page 2
Distance:	16 kilometres from the junction of Highway 97 and Highway 6 in downtown Vernon
Travel Time:	One half hour
Condition:	Paved throughout
Season:	Park open year round; campground open April 1 - October 31
Topo Maps:	Vernon, BC 82 L/6 Oyama, BC 82 L/3
Communities:	Vernon and Okanagan Landing

Located just 16 kilometres from downtown Vernon, on the north-eastern shore of Okanagan Lake, 200-hectare Ellison Provincial Park is a land of rocky, forested headlands and sheltered, sandy bays. The diverse terrain, combined with the North Okanagan's relatively dry climate (less than 40 centimetres of precipitation per year) and abundant sunshine, make it a favourite for a wide range of recreational activities.

Okanagan Landing Road

To get there, take 25th Avenue west from the junction of Highway 97 and Highway 6 on the south side of downtown Vernon. Follow 25th Avenue as it becomes Okanagan Landing Road, and continue south along the east shore of Okanagan Lake to the end of the road at the park.

Seventy-one private, yet spacious campsites (eight are double sites), suitable for most types of camping units, are tucked into an attractive natural forest setting with toilets and firewood nearby. A children's playground is located in the large grassed playing field near the amphitheatre. For additional security there is a resident park contractor. A campground host is also on site from May through September to answer questions.

A view of Okanagan Lake from the trail on the rock bluffs. *© Murphy Shewchuk*

Easy walking trails provide access to the lakeshore where rocky headlands separate two beautiful bays, with coarse sandy beaches. Here, scattered under the shade of the forest canopy, are more than 50 picnic tables with fire pits. Drinking water is nearby and the large change house includes flush toilets and showers. The various trails across the rocky headlands provide some boulder-climbing excitement for young explorers and an opportunity to bird-watch or photograph the scenery and wildflowers.

The gradually sloping bottom and the warm water make the three main beaches very popular during summer months. For safety reasons, swim buoys at South Beach closely follow the edge of an underwater shelf. Watch for steep drop-offs outside the buoys and anywhere along the rocky cliff edges. Please remember that there are no lifeguards on duty. Don't swim alone and watch your children whenever they are near or in the water.

Diving and Snorkeling

Scuba diving / snorkeling buoys in Otter Bay mark the boundaries of western Canada's first freshwater dive park, sponsored by the Vernon Scuba Club and BC Parks. Sunken artifacts add to the variety of fascinating plant and animal life that thrive in the bay's warm waters.

Abundant fish life, including carp, burbot, kokanee, and trout is attracted to the rocky outcroppings and vegetation along the lakefront. The best fishing is in the deeper waters offshore anywhere along the north arm of Okanagan Lake. A BC angling licence is required.

While there isn't a boat launch at the park (the closest is six kilometres to the north), water skiing, cruising, and fishing are popular park activities. Mooring buoys offshore in South Bay and Otter Bay are part of a marine park system sponsored by the Okanagan's yacht clubs. Houseboats can pull ashore at Sandy Beach. The standard park camping fee is charged for overnight use by boaters. When staying in the campground, you can leave your boat pulled up on the beach, but please remove all life jackets and other equipment for safekeeping.

Printed guides are available for more than six kilometres of walking trails that provide access to many of the park's natural features and scenic viewpoints. A one-hour return walk on the nature trail will take you up and down the undulating benches typical of this portion of the Thompson Plateau. Most of the park is dominated by ponderosa pine and Douglas-fir stands with grassy open areas and rocky outcroppings along the headlands. Porcupine and Columbian ground squirrels are commonly seen near the nature trail.

Excellent Base

Ellison Provincial Park can also save as an excellent base from which to explore the North Okanagan. The region's climate has made this a prime fruit growing and ranching area since the mid 1800s. Cycling the rolling hills past orchards, farms, and ranches can be an excellent family activity. Historic O'Keefe Ranch, northwest of Vernon, is open all year and is well worth exploring. (See *Westside Road* for more information.)

Kalamalka Provincial Park, just east of Vernon, has broad, sandy beaches and 10 kilometres of trails through the grasslands. Mabel Lake Provincial Park, 23 kilometres north of Lumby, has beautiful sandy beaches, open grassy playing fields and great fishing. The 81-unit Mabel Lake campground is not quite as busy mid-week during July and August.

Echo Lake Provincial Park, off Highway 6, 47 kilometres east of Vernon, has picnicking and fishing with boat launch facilities, a store and fishing equipment rentals. Echo Lake Resort in Echo Lake Provincial Park has housekeeping cabins and a campground. Reservations are preferred.

Silver Star Provincial Park, 22 kilometres northeast of Vernon, has chairlift operations for summer mountain biking and hiking the alpine meadows, with alpine and Nordic skiing in winter. (See *Silver Star Resort* for details.) —MS

Additional Information:

BC Parks
For up-to-date information visit the BC Parks website at:
www.BCParks.ca or
www.env.gov.bc.ca/bcparks/index.html

CHAPTER 2

Kalamalka Provincial Park

Statistics	For map, see page 9
Distance:	7.6 kilometres, Highway 97 in Coldstream to parking lot
Travel Time:	Less than 10 minutes, on paved streets
Season:	Year around
Topo Maps:	Vernon, BC 82 L/6
	Oyama, BC 82 L/3
Communities:	Vernon and Coldstream

Located on the northeast side of beautiful Kalamalka Lake, Kalamalka Provincial Park encompasses an 4209-hectare remnant of the natural grasslands that once stretched from Vernon to Osoyoos. Access is easy. If you are travelling from the south on Highway 97, you can turn right on College Way in Coldstream and follow it and then Kickwillie Loop down to Kalamalka Lake. Swing left and follow Westkal Road to Kalamalka Road, keep right past the public beach to Kidston Road (3.8 kilometres from Hwy 97). Turn right on Kidston Road and follow it another 3.8 kilometres to the parking lot. Access from Highway 6 is via Kalamalka Road and Kidston Road.

Kalamalka Provincial Park has all-season appeal. Easy walking and horse riding trails wind through the grassland slopes and along forest ridges. Many scenic viewpoints overlook a shoreline indented with bays and tiny coves. The spring wildflowers are truly spectacular. In summer, the beaches attract boaters and swimmers wanting relative seclusion. The golden hues of autumn have appeal all their own. In winter, cross-country skiers enjoy the park's wild beauty and rolling hills.

Wide Range of Activities

To quote the BC Parks website, this park offers a variety of day-use activities

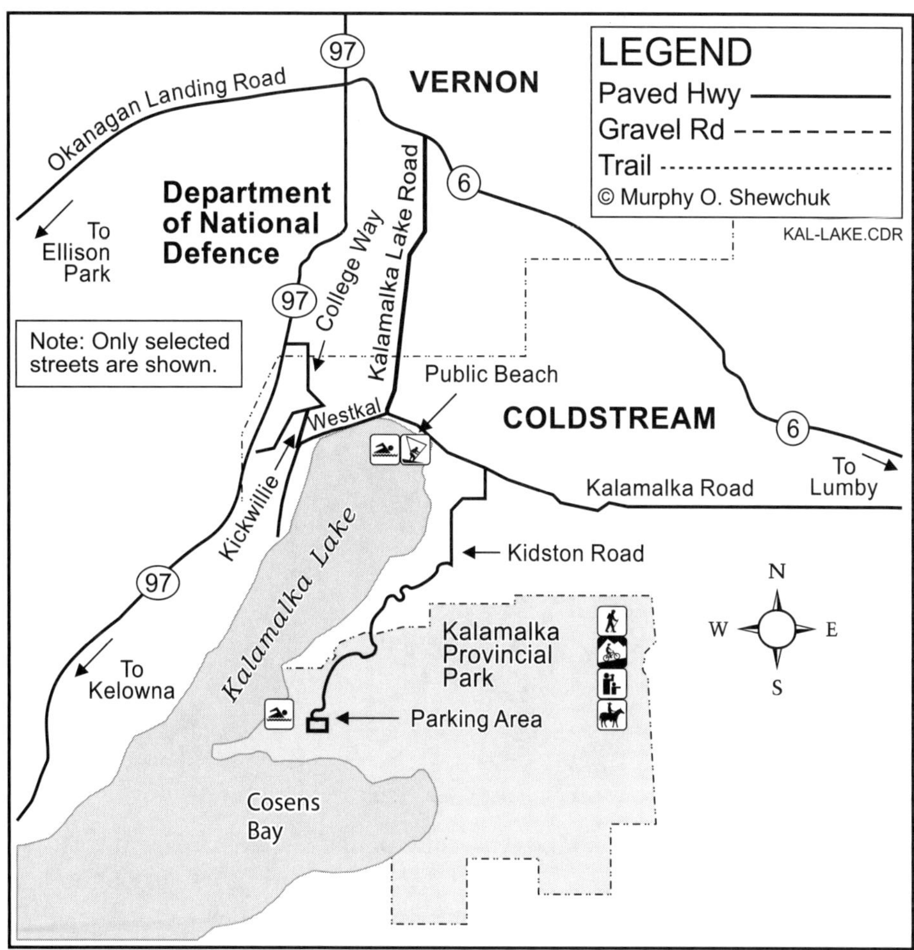

Vernon and Kalamalka Provincial Park area.

accessed from three main parking areas: Red Gate, Cosens Bay and, largest of the three, the parking lot at the trailhead to Jade and Juniper Bays.

Red Gate has a gravel pullout with parking for roughly six vehicles, though there are often more parked along the side of the road on busy weekends. There is an information shelter just inside the gate. Trails from here access the upland portions of the park; they also loop around to both the Cosens Bay parking and Jade / Juniper parking areas. The trail to the other two parking areas is wide and easy to follow. Other trails are less developed.

Cosens Bay has a large gravel parking lot for around 20 vehicles. There is an information shelter and a pit toilet. Access to the Okanagan High Rim Trail is from this parking lot. A gravel road enters the park and runs through the grass-

Beware of the shy Pacific rattlesnake in Kalamalka Prov. Park. *© Murphy Shewchuk*

lands. This is an access road for private cabins on the east side of Cosens Bay and does not go down to the public beach. Hikers should park at the lot and walk to the beach since there is no parking along the road. Cosens Bay has a large beach of coarse sand which extends into the water, making swimming a treat. Picnic tables are situated along the beach, beside the fringe of cottonwood trees that separates the beach from surrounding grasslands. There are pit toilets where the trail reaches the beach.

Jade and Juniper Bays are very popular summer destinations. Two large gravel parking lots can hold up to 160 cars. There are two information shelters, one beside the trail to the bays, and one beside the trail that splits (one way) to follow the height of land to Rattlesnake Point (and the other way) to Cosens Bay. There is one wheelchair accessible pit toilet beside the trail down to Jade and Juniper Bays. A 600-metre paved trail runs down to Juniper Bay. The slope is gradual and there is a bench along the way. The trail leads down to sloped, irrigated lawns shaded by a few large ponderosa pines. There are 11 tables on cement pads spread out across the lawn in three clusters. There is a BBQ stand beside one of the tables. The tables and lawns overlook the large beach of fine sand. The sheltered bay is a great spot for swimming. Thick shrubs and wild trees cover the small rocky headland at one end of the bay. Also situated on the headland just off the lawn is a stone and concrete interpretive display with information on native vegetation and wildlife.

The trail to Jade Bay splits from the paved trail about 20 metres from the parking lot. This is a wide gravel trail with a moderately steep slope. It is about 500 metres to the beach. The trail passes through ponderosa pine with a thick understory of young Douglas-fir and shrubs. There is a pit toilet beside the trail 50 metres before the beach. A narrow pebbly beach is rimmed by grass, on which are four picnic tables. The beach is smaller than the one at Juniper Bay. A short trail along the lake links both day use areas.

Dryland Plants and Animals

Kalamalka Park and the surrounding area have a diversity of wildlife although none is particularly abundant. You might see coyote, deer, or black bear but are more likely to observe Columbian ground squirrels and yellow-bellied marmots. Pacific rattlesnakes, shy creatures that only wish to be left alone, are an important part of this fascinating ecosystem. For botanists, there are four distinct plant associations — arid grasslands, woodland, forest and wet areas — with more than 430 species of vascular plants so far identified in the park (10 of these are rare in British Columbia).

Please be aware that this is a natural environment protecting one of the few remaining habitats for Pacific rattlesnakes. Practice safe hiking procedures when in rattlesnake country — stay on the trails and watch where you are putting your hands, feet and seat. These animals usually strike only when threatened. If a bite does occur, try to stay calm and seek medical aid at the Vernon Hospital.

Stay on the Trails

There is another reason to be aware of where you sit. This area was used as a military target range during the Second World War and unexploded bombs are still working their way to the surface.

From a safety perspective, please keep close watch on children: there are no lifeguards in attendance. Deep drop-offs exist outside the buoyed swim areas and along the lakeshore. Cliff jumping can be extremely hazardous because of projecting rock shelves and debris just below the surface. Other regulations concerning pets, parking, and noise are posted in the park. —MS

Additional Information

BC Parks
Web: www.env.gov.bc.ca/bcparks

Up-to-date maps are available on the BC Parks website at: www.env.gov.bc.ca/bcparks/explore/parkpgs/kalamalka_lk

CHAPTER 3

Silver Star Mountain Resort / Sovereign Lake Nordic Centre

Statistics	For map, see page 2
Distance:	22 kilometres, from Highway 97 in Vernon
Travel Time:	One half hour
Condition:	Paved throughout
Season:	Year round
Topo Maps:	Vernon, BC 82 L/6
Communities:	Vernon

There are a few who think that mountains have no personalities — that they are mere piles of rock held together by the moss and trees that cover their slopes. These non-believers have obviously never skied the mountains of British Columbia's Okanagan region.

Take Silver Star Mountain Resort, for example. This ski resort has a warm, western personality produced, in part, from the resort staff and the friendly residents of nearby Vernon. First impressions are lasting impressions. And should you arrive in the evening, the first impression at the start of your Silver Star ski vacation is of an 1890s Old Canadian West village.

Former Silver Mine

Silver Star Mountain comes by its Old West theme quite honestly. Some sources suggest the mountain, originally named Aberdeen Mountain, received its present name from the star-like appearance of the peak on a moonlit winter night and the silver deposits that were discovered near the 1,915-metre summit in the 1890s. Silver Star was a mining hotspot in 1896 when a quartz vein containing silver, lead and gold was discovered. A forestry lookout was built near the top in 1914, and skiing began in the early 1920s. An access road was built into the area in 1939, setting off a chain of events that led to today's modern development.

A skier at the Black Prince cabin. *© Murphy Shewchuk*

Ski to Your Door

Today, the scene on your evening arrival from Vernon is of well-lit ski slopes, a cozy hotel complex and the mellow lighting of the pedestrian square. Everything is true ski-to-your-door at Silver Star. Night skiing on the lower slopes and a lighted five-kilometre cross-country loop trail are only a few steps from any of the hotels. Daylight broadens the picture. The hotels look bigger — big enough to accommodate more than 1,850 people. The mountain looks bigger — in fact, with the Putnam Creek addition, it's twice as big as it was a few years ago. And the service is even friendlier.

Silver Star offers a blend of skiing under near-perfect conditions. Fine slope grooming often means an earlier start and a longer spring skiing season than other ski resorts. The original Vance Creek area of Silver Star Mountain offered plenty of variety. But recent additions have increased the skiing and snowboarding area to 1,135 hectares, adding considerable intermediate and expert terrain. The addition also makes Silver Star the second largest ski area in British Columbia. For those interested in specs, the mountain now has a vertical difference of 760 metres and an average snowfall of over 700 centimetres! It also has, at last count, more than 100 runs served by 12 lifts capable of conveying 14,000 skiers / boarders per hour.

If you brought your skinny skis, you will be particularly pleased with the range of cross-country ski trails on Silver Star Mountain. A low-cost lift ride takes you to the top of the Summit Chair and the beginning of a well-groomed loop that brings you back to the hotel complex — with plenty of diversions. These include some 55 kilometres of trails that are part of the Silver Star Mountain Resort complex and another 50 kilometres of trails in the Sovereign Lake network in adjacent Silver Star Provincial Park.

Sovereign Lake Nordic Centre

The Sovereign Lake ski trails are operated by the Sovereign Lake Nordic Club in cooperation with BC Parks under a park use permit. A fee is charged for trail usage to help offset maintenance costs. A day lodge, ski lessons and equipment rentals are available.

The Nordic trails are groomed double-wide with plenty of variety. You can practice your skating style in comfort or tackle a bush trail where strong legs and backcountry skis are the order of the day.

Mountain Bike in Summer

Silver Star doesn't shut down in summer. From late June until Labour Day, you can ride the Summit Chair Lift to the alpine, then mountain bike the trails through alpine meadows, lush forests, grasslands, and orchards to the city of Vernon. If a two-wheeled rush down the mountain is too wild for you, take your time and your camera and explore the mountain trails on foot or horseback.

Wine Festival

Silver Star Mountain Resort is also host for the Annual Okanagan Summer Wine Festival held during the second weekend in August — an intimate weekend of wine education, arts, music, and mile-high outdoor recreation. The Summer Wine Festival offers unique wine seminars, great evening entertainment, a foot stomping musical, outdoor wine tasting, and wonderful presentations by local artists. For more information, see the listing for the Okanagan Wine Festivals' Society below.

To get to Silver Star, turn east off Highway 97 on 48th Avenue (Silver Star Road) in north Vernon and follow the signs for 22 kilometres to the ski village. Good snow tires are necessary in winter. —MS

Additional Information:

Okanagan Wine Festivals' Society
1527 Ellis Street
Kelowna, BC V1Y 2A7
Tel: (250) 861-6654
Fax: (250) 861-3942
E-mail: info@TheWineFestivals.com
Web: www.thewinefestivals.com

Silver Star Mountain Resort
PO Box 3002
Silver Star Mountain, BC V1B 3M1
Tel: (250) 542-0224
Fax: (250) 542-1236
E-mail: star@skisilverstar.com
Web: www.skisilverstar.com

Sovereign Lake Nordic Centre
PO Box 1231
Vernon, BC V1T 6N6
Tel: (250) 558-3036
Fax: (250) 558-3076
E-mail: info@sovereignlake.com
Web: www.sovereignlake.com

CHAPTER 4

Three Valley to Enderby via Mabel Lake

Statistics	For map, see page 2 and page 18
Distance:	Approximately 90 kilometres, Three Valley Lake to Enderby
Travel Time:	Two to four hours
Condition:	Some rough gravel; may be closed in winter
Season:	July through October
Topo Maps:	Revelstoke, BC 82 L/16
	Malakwa, BC 82 L/15
	Mabel Lake, BC 82 L/10
	Salmon Arm, BC 82 L/11
Communities:	Revelstoke, Sicamous and Enderby

If you're looking for an excuse to get off the pavement while on your way from the Rockies to the Okanagan, this British Columbia backcountry road is a few kilometres shorter than the regular route via Sicamous. But like most backroad shortcuts, the Mabel Lake Shortcut will probably take you twice as long as Highway 1 and Highway 97A.

There are, however, two major reasons to make a mid-summer meander through the heart of the Monashee Mountains. The first is to get away from the hell-bent-for-destruction crowds that seem intent on turning the Trans-Canada Highway into a training ground for crash-test dummies. The second reason is actually much more positive than negative — unless you happen to be a fish: the route provides relatively easy access to quiet recreation sites on Wap Lake, Mabel Lake and several other off-the-road lakes.

And please take note that this is a mid-summer excursion. The north end of this route passes through the heart of the Monashee rain forest and ease of access depends on logging activity and the prerequisite road maintenance. Washouts and late-season snowdrifts are common on the section between Three Valley Lake and

Three Valley to Enderby via Mabel Lake

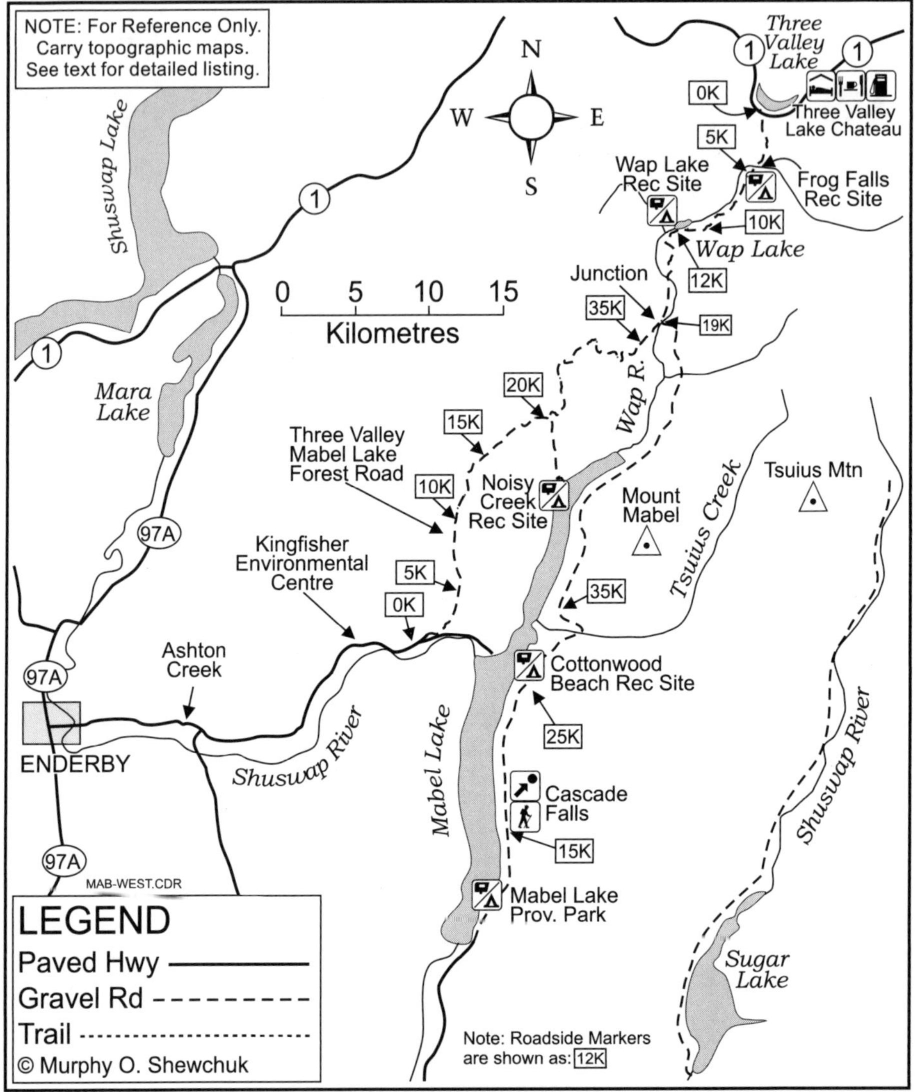

North Okanagan and Shuswap area — Enderby to Three Valley Lake.

Wap Lake, so a full fuel tank, a shovel and lots of time are definite requirements before heading south. These items, plus a chainsaw or a good swede saw and an axe should be part of any backroad explorer's kit anyway.

The Mabel Lake Shortcut hasn't gone unnoticed. There were rumours more than two decades ago that the government was considering routing a brand-new four-lane highway through here in a direct link from Revelstoke to the Okanagan Valley and then to the Coast via the Okanagan / Coquihalla Connector. The arguments then — and now — are that this route, if continued down the west side of Okanagan Lake, would bypass most of the congestion and development of the Shuswap, Okanagan and Thompson Valleys. I have no idea if this route is still being considered and I don't intend to ask anyone. It's much more fun to speculate based on true ignorance than on inside knowledge.

We've made the Mabel Lake Shortcut several times during the past dozen years. The first was in mid-August, 1986, and washouts and questionable bridges were common. By August 1988, a rotting bridge across the Wap River had been replaced by a steel structure and most of the washouts had been re-routed or rebuilt with larger culverts. By the late 1990s, the road, though narrow and rough in spots, was easily passable by cars or light trucks with fair clearance. Logging was active in the area and logging trucks could be expected at any time. Although logging activity changes from year to year, it is probably safest to travel this route on weekends or evenings. Better yet, contact the BC Forest Service Okanagan Shuswap Forest District office at Vernon — (250) 558-1700 — for up-to-date information.

A Logging Railway

For the purpose of this backroad trip, km 0 is the junction of the Trans-Canada Highway and Three Valley-Mabel Lake Forest Service Road, 20 kilometres west of Revelstoke near the west end of Three Valley Lake. The grade is easy here, with smooth wide corners hinting that this is not your average logging road. A bridge at km 1.3 that looks remarkably like a railway bridge confirms the suspicion that

A chipmunk feeds near Wap Lake. *© Murphy Shewchuk*

other methods of transportation may have been used here before the rubber-tired vehicle became king of the backroad.

The late David Stewart, himself a king of the backroads, had a plausible explanation in *Okanagan Backroads Volume 2,* published by Saltaire in 1975 and long out of print. "The valley of the Wap has an interesting past," wrote Stewart. "Around the turn of the century, an English firm with headquarters in London built a logging railroad from Three Valley, on the CP mainline, in past Wap Lake. Until two or three decades ago, traces of the old railway could be seen, along with a steam donkey engine and the big old stumps left by the loggers of that far-away time. In 1948 I stumbled on several racks of steel rails not far west of Wap Lake (we called it Frog Lake those days). Presumably this steel is still hidden in the dense underbrush: the logging railway it had been intended to extend having disappeared over the intervening four decades."

Gordon Bell, owner of the Three Valley Lake Chateau at the east end of Three Valley Lake, had the good fortune of meeting one of the descendants of the original operators. According to his information, the logging railway once extended as far south as Mabel Lake, with spur lines up many of the side valleys. The company operated one of the largest sawmills in western Canada at the west end of Three Valley Lake with, says Gordon, three planers, a post office and the Bell House hotel (no relation). The hotel was later dismantled and moved to the top of Mount Revelstoke where it became the Mount Revelstoke Chalet until Parks Canada tore it down around 1970. Note: Gordon Bell passed away in November, 2007.

Giant Cedars

Giant cedar stumps, some still with clearly visible spring-board notches from the hand logging of a previous era, surround the Frog Falls Recreation Site at km 4.4. Nearby Wap River starts in the southeast on the slopes of Mount Begbie, and after a northward rush, swings south here as it twists and tumbles down to Mabel Lake. A wide trail leads from the recreation site to the crest of the 25-metre-high two-step Frog Falls.

The trail to the falls passes, buried in the mountainside, what was until recently, one of the largest private hydroelectric plants in BC. Faced with an estimated $450,000 tab from BC Hydro to run lines from Revelstoke or Malakwa, to his resort at Three Valley Gap, Gordon Bell set out to build his own power plant using the 30-metre head developed at Frog Falls and two additional run-of-the-river dams farther upstream. After obtaining the necessary permits from seven different bureaucracies, Bell went ahead with construction.

The Three Valley Gap system is unusual in two ways. First, it uses water pumps operating as turbines to drive the 150,000-watt electric generator, instead of more expensive, specially designed turbines. Second, it is a constant load system, using an electronically controlled load distribution system to maintain a steady AC supply while heating and lighting the complete resort. Bell's system cost almost what Hydro would have charged, but his real saving is the elimination of an enormous monthly energy bill.

Wap Lake Recreation Site

The road south of the recreation site and the Wap River bridge follow the old railbed near the valley floor. Several side roads lead to left into the high country and some maps hint that there may be a route to Sugar Lake through here, but I haven't yet confirmed it. Water lily marshes near km 10.5 are the first hints of Wap Lake, but it is almost two kilometres farther along the old railbed before you reach the small Recreation Site at the west end of the lake.

Wap Lake Recreation Site. *© Murphy Shewchuk*

South of the lake, the road swings away from the river for several kilometres, skirting a knoll before crossing under a 500,000 volt power line near km 16 and again crossing the river half a kilometre farther along. The BC Hydro power line links the Revelstoke hydro plant with the rest of the system at the Ashton Creek substation near Enderby.

A junction near km 19 marks the beginning of a climb away from the valley floor. On one trip through, a small sign on the road to the right signalled the start of the Kingfisher Forest Service Road. On our latest trip, this road appeared to be a continuation of the Three Valley-Mabel Lake Forest Service Road.

The road to the right leads to Enderby, while the road to the left (Mabel Lake Forest Service Road) again crosses Wap River, and with a little luck and good planning, could take you all the way to Lumby.

Mabel Lake, looking south from Noisy Creek. © Murphy Shewchuk

Noisy Creek Recreation Site

Three Valley-Mabel Lake Road climbs steadily, reaching an elevation of about 850 metres before it crosses into the Noisy Creek drainage. Sideroads lead into several old log cuts (and a few newer ones) where wild blueberries, raspberries, huckleberries and moose are plentiful. The roadside markers begin a countdown as you continue south. Another junction just south of the 21K marker (36 kilometres from Three Valley Lake) marks the route down to Noisy Creek FS Recreation Site at Mabel Lake. It's a five-kilometre drive down to the lake, but the large recreation site and excellent beach are well worth the trip. In fact, the site is actually two quite different campgrounds split by Noisy Creek and its delta. The south campground looks down the lake, with a few waterfront campsites and a larger number sheltered in the trees. The campground north of the delta gets the morning sun and could be better protected in case of storm. Although the road is somewhat rough, it is usually passable by truck campers and a variety of other vehicles. According to some of the campers we talked to, this has been a popular site for at least 30 years. Firewood is usually in short supply, so plan on bringing wood with you, or collecting it off the ground from the old logged areas on your way down.

Note that Noisy Creek is a "Managed Recreation Site" under the recently introduced recreation site program; daily fees are charged from May 1 to September 30.

Mabel Lake Road

Beyond the Noisy Creek junction, Three Valley-Mabel Lake Road crosses into the Danforth Creek drainage. Rough sideroads lead west into Mount Mara and the Hunters Range and east into Stony, Holiday and Noreen Lakes. Then the backroad parallels Kingfisher Creek valley before making a long, winding descent to Mabel Lake Road and the Shuswap River, approximately 56.5 kilometres from Three Valley Lake.

Kingfisher, at the western outlet of Mabel Lake, is a small resort community that comes alive during the summer. Located where the pavement ends 37 kilometres east of Enderby and about five kilometres east of the junction with Three Valley-Mabel Lake FS Road, Kingfisher may offer your last chance for supplies if you are following the Wap Lake route north.

Shuswap River Canoe Route

The 36-kilometre route west to Enderby passes through a peaceful pastoral valley with several access points to the Shuswap River. Canoeists favour the river, and except for the Skookumchuck Rapids near the outlet of Mabel Lake, it is considered "rather tranquil and a large breeding ground for Canada Geese." The newly proclaimed 71-hectare Skookumchuk Rapids Provincial Park has been established to protect the rapids.

The Kingfisher Environmental Interpretive Centre, approximately 10 kilometres west of the Three Valley-Mabel Lake Road junction, is a good spot to spend an afternoon.

Three Valley to Enderby via Mabel Lake

A junction near the Ashton Creek General Store, 10 kilometres east of Enderby, presents another backroad detour south through the Trinity Valley to Lumby. But if Enderby and Highway 97A is your destination, continue west through the broad Shuswap River Valley and you'll soon be back at civilization. — MS

Additional Information:

Kingfisher Environmental Interpretive Centre
2550 Mabel Lake Rd.
Enderby, BC VOE 1V0
Tel: (250) 838-0004

Okanagan Shuswap Forest District
2501 – 14th Ave.
Vernon, BC V1T 8Z1
Tel: (250) 558-1700
Fax: (250) 549-5485
Toll-free (via Enquiry BC) 1-800-663-7867
Web: www.for.gov.bc.ca/dos

Three Valley Lake Chateau Ltd.
Box 860
Revelstoke, BC V0E 2S0
Tel: (250) 837-2109
Fax: (250) 837-5220
Toll-free: 1-888-667-2109
E-mail: hello@3valley.com
Web: www.3valley.com

CHAPTER 5

Mabel Lake Road (East Side)

Statistics	For map, see page 26
Distance:	110 kilometres, Lumby to Highway 1 at Three Valley Lake
Travel Time:	Four to five hours minimum
Conditions:	Partly paved, some rough gravel sections
Season:	Dry weather; north portion may be closed in winter
Topo Maps:	Shuswap Falls, BC 82 L/7
	Mabel Lake, BC 82 L/10
	Malakwa, BC 82 L/15
	Revelstoke, BC 82 L/16
Communities:	Lumby, Vernon and Revelstoke

I've been especially attracted to the Mabel Lake region ever since I flew over the area in a helicopter more than three decades ago. The long, narrow lake looked particularly inviting, partly because of its beauty but more important, because of its isolation. Time often has a way of passing without allowing us to follow our dreams, but fortunately we have been able to explore the area on several occasions. Initially, topographic maps presented conflicting information and our usually reliable sources weren't much better. Except for the warning about frequent washouts north of Wap Lake and rumours of a beautiful waterfall on Cascade Creek, we were basically on our own.

Our initial trip was "interesting." We had to negotiate rotten bridges and skirt some ridiculous washouts, yet we made it through. Each subsequent trip has been better. On a recent August excursion through the area (from north to south), we met little traffic and no obstacles.

However, next year could be different so be prepared for adventure. Before you set out to explore this route, check with the Forest Service office in Vernon — (250) 558-1700 — and be sure to have enough fuel and supplies to travel double the 110-kilometre distance.

Mabel Lake Road (East Side)

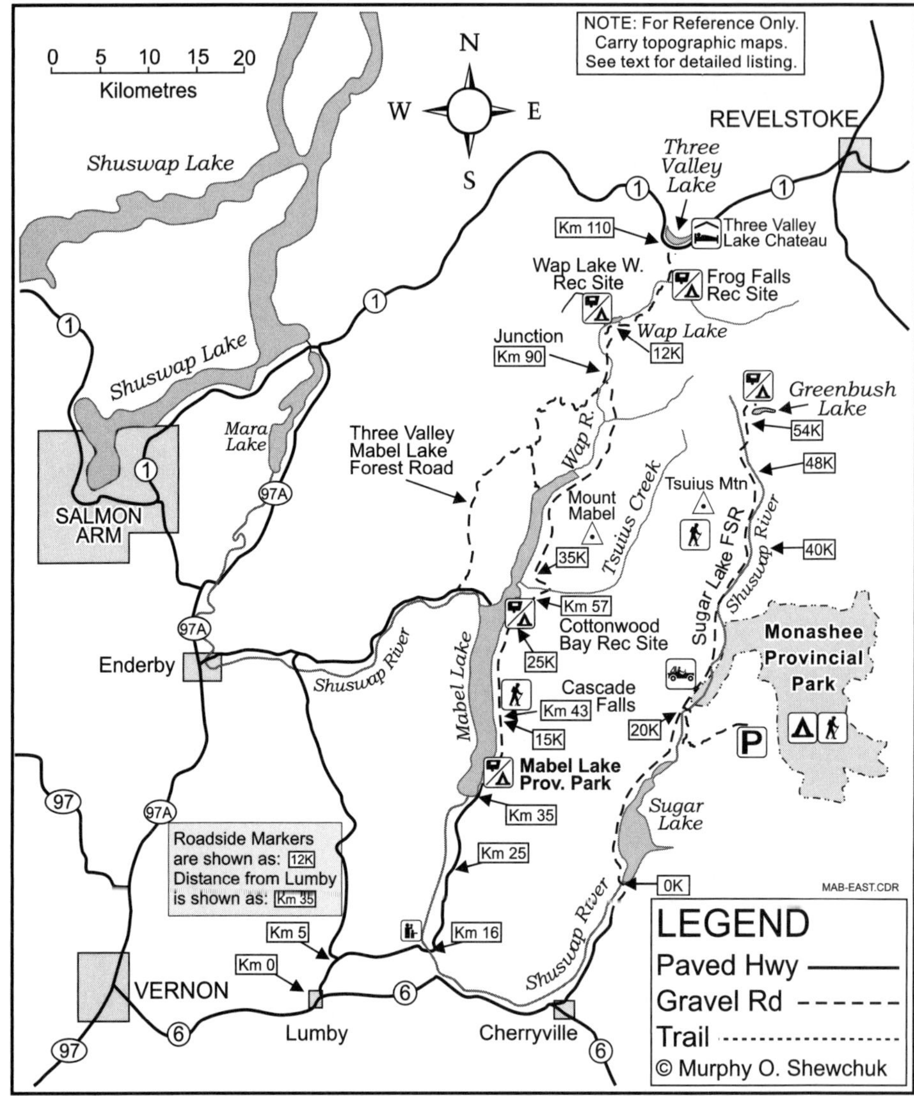

North Okanagan and East Shuswap area — Vernon to Revelstoke.

Lumby Starting Point

Set your odometer to zero at the corner of Highway 6 (Vernon Street) and Shuswap Avenue in Lumby. Then, as you head north on Shuswap Avenue, the Trinity Valley Road, near km 5, becomes the first point of diversion. This road to the left follows Vance Creek and Trinity Creek northwest through Trinity Valley to Ashton Creek. Then it is a short drive on to Enderby, providing a scenic route to the heart of the south Shuswap. The road to Mabel Lake continues east down Bessette Creek to Shuswap Falls, passing through bottomland rich with hay, corn and livestock. Rawlings Lake Road, near km 11.5, provides an alternate route to Highway 6, east of Lumby.

This backroad route crosses the Shuswap River near km 16. The river rises in the heart of the rugged Monashee Mountains, north of Sugar Lake, before looping south to Cherryville. Dams at Brenda Falls at the foot of Sugar Lake and at Shuswap Falls, near km 16.8, harness the flow of the river to generate electricity. Here at Wilsey Dam, BC Hydro has created a recreation area with trails to the falls and canyon. Paddlers on the Shuswap River use the wide trails to portage around the falls and rapids.

Mabel Lake

The paved road swings north near Shuswap Falls, climbing away from the river. Near km 35, an opening in the timber provides the first glimpse of the south end of Mabel Lake (and the last glimpse of pavement).

Mabel Lake Provincial Park, at km 37.8, is a welcome sight on any summer afternoon. On more than one occasion, we've had our choice of sites and were able to camp near the beach and playground. The beach gets the afternoon sun, and the lake's long, undulating shoreline, ensures that it never seems particularly crowded.

A Pioneer Storekeeper and a Pioneer Lumberman

On one particularly beautiful afternoon, after a swim and supper, I settled down to read *Grassroots of Lumby: 1877-1927,* a hardcover book I acquired earlier at the Lumby information centre. From it, I learned that the surrounding land first belonged to Reginald Sadler, a young Englishman who came to Canada around 1900. T.A. Norris, Lumby's first schoolteacher, later bought the lakeshore property and lived here for some time before selling it in the 1930s. Will Shields, who spent much of his life as a storekeeper in Lumby, and Henry Sigalet, a pioneer lumberman, bought the property, and built comfortable summer homes near the lake.

Born in Ontario in 1884, Shields came to Lumby about 1910 and retired to the Vernon area in 1956. Henry Sigalet was born in Alberta in 1899 and came to the Okanagan Valley two years later. In the midst of the Depression, Henry Sigalet built a lumber mill in nearby Squaw Valley, and in 1940 opened a mill in Lumby. Both Shields and Sigalet died in 1972, not long after completing negotiations on the sale of the property for the Mabel Lake Provincial Park site.

Cascade Falls, approximately 5.7 km north of Mabel Lake Park. *© Murphy Shewchuk*

The majority of park development took place from 1978-80, but there have been recent additions to facilities. The 81-unit campground has an attractive 2,100-metre-long shoreline with an excellent beach. The park has a large day-use / picnic area extending from Trinity Campground to the boat launch. The lawns are level, open and spacious providing the opportunity for a variety of games. There are picnic tables among cottonwood trees that separate the lawn from the beach. Hemlock, red cedar, and birch shade much of the property — a visible contrast to the sagebrush, bunchgrass, and scattered pine nearer Vernon.

Cascade Falls Trail

The gravel road, now known as Mabel Lake Forest Service Road, winds along the mountainside well above the lake as it continues north of the park. Logging roads offer the occasional diversion, as do roaring creeks. A small, decaying roadside sign on a corner near km 43.0 (about 5.7 kilometres north of the park entrance and just beyond the 15K marker) indicates the start of the trail to Cascade Falls, which certainly lives up to its name. It resembles an ever-broadening veil as it tumbles down the steep rocky slope. The 300-metre switchback trail to the foot of the waterfall will require some caution but otherwise is not difficult. If you enjoy photography, a tripod and wide-angle lens will help when photographing the falls. A close-up or macro lens will also prove useful for the many fungi, berries and wildflowers along the trail.

Cottonwood Bay Recreation Site

As you continue northward, Torrent Creek, a boulder-strewn waterway near km 51, marks the first return to Mabel Lake since leaving the provincial park. The occasional logging road climbs to the right, away from the main track, but otherwise Mabel Lake Road follows the timbered benches. If the provincial park campground is full, you might want to consider exploring the Cottonwood Bay Forest Service Recreation Site near km 56.8. The beach and campground are about two kilometres off the main road.

In general, this backroad continues north, except for a loop east to avoid the canyon of Tsuius Creek. If Three Valley Lake is your destination, keep left at the major junctions.

The road climbs high above the lake, offering some spectacular views as it winds through the timber. Then it begins to descend, presenting a last brief glimpse of Mabel Lake through the trees at km 77. Some maps suggest that the old road once crossed Wap River near the north end of the lake. However, the present route to the west side of the lake is still another 10 kilometres to the north.

From the north end of Mabel Lake to the Wap River crossing near km 89, the route varies from a good gravel logging road to a somewhat narrow, lumpy backroad. The barren, boulder-strewn creekbeds reveal the terrific force of flash floods that can occur almost any time of the year. The forest roads that veer east off the main road often appear better and more used. This can be deceiving — a point brought home when one ends up in a log landing.

Reflections on Wap Lake, south of Three Valley Lake. *© Murphy Shewchuk*

Alternate Route to Enderby

The junction near km 90, a short distance north of the Wap River Bridge, is the first left turn to ignore in your relentless search for Three Valley Lake. Three Valley-Mabel Lake Road to the left (west) climbs steadily to a high valley paralleling the west side of Mabel Lake and then continues south to the Shuswap River outflow of Mabel Lake. (See the *Three Valley to Enderby via Mabel Lake* section for details.)

The road straight ahead again crosses the Wap River near km 93, after traversing a few sandy sections. The road passes under a 500-kilovolt power line a short distance beyond the bridge and swings left through the timber.

It may not be apparent at first, but the gravel road and the Wap Lake West Recreation Site, at km 97, sit on what was once a railway bed. A logging railway, built near the turn of the 19th century, carried timber from as far south as Mabel Lake north to the Canadian Pacific Railway at Three Valley Lake. (See the *Three Valley to Enderby via Mabel Lake* section for additional information.)

Wap Lake is unusual in that the railway bed allows good casting from the shoreline as well as providing several places to launch a canoe or car-top boat. Camping is limited, with a few spaces at the Forest Service recreation site and a wide spot or two along the road. On one trip, while I tried casting from shore, the rest of the motley crew picked huckleberries and blueberries for dessert. A tasty frying-pan upside-down cake compensated for my usual lack of trout reserved for that very same frying pan.

Beyond Wap Lake, the backroad skirts the colourful lily-dotted marshes and the river, bouncing over several rough sections that could be difficult in spring or after wet weather. This is the section that has occasionally been almost impassable in the past and is most likely to present a problem in future. The steel-framed bridge across the Wap River, near km 105, is a sign that you have survived the worst and that the rest of the road to the Trans-Canada Highway should be a cinch.

Frog Falls

An old sign in a tree just north of the bridge points to an overgrown trail leading upstream to Frog Falls. Giant cedar stumps stand like guards at the hidden trail entrance. However, a few hundred metres beyond the bridge, a sideroad leads into an excellent Recreation Site and a wider trail to the crest of the falls.

Beyond Frog Falls Recreation Site the much-improved road begins a steady descent to Three Valley Lake and Highway 1. After following South Pass Creek and the old logging railway bed, it reaches pavement approximately 110 kilometres from the heart of Lumby. If you are attempting to travel this route southward, look for the "Three Valley-Mabel Lake Forest Service Road" sign on the south side of Highway 1 (the Trans-Canada Highway), approximately 21 kilometres west of Revelstoke.

Three Valley Gap

If you've had enough of camping and your own cooking, why not stop in at the Three Valley Lake Chateau at the east end of the lake. With hard work and ingenuity, Gordon Bell has turned an old railway whistle-stop into a fine hotel and unique heritage destination. In addition to the hotel, restaurant and gift shop, there are numerous restored pioneer buildings and railway cars. — MS

Additional Information:

BC Parks
Web: www.env.gov.bc.ca/bcparks

Lumby & District Chamber of Commerce
1882 Vernon Street
PO Box 534
Lumby, BC V0E 2G0
Tel/Fax: (250) 547-2300
E-mail: lumbychamber@shaw.ca
Web: www.monasheetourism.com

Okanagan Shuswap Forest District
2501 - 14th Ave.
Vernon, BC V1T 8Z1
Tel: (250) 558-1700
Fax: (250) 549-5485
Toll-free (via Enquiry BC) 1-800-663-7867
Web: www.for.gov.bc.ca/dos

Three Valley Lake Chateau Ltd.
Box 860
Revelstoke, BC V0E 2S0
Tel: (250) 837-2109
Fax: (250) 837-5220
Toll-free: 1-888-667-2109
E-mail: hello@3valley.com
Web: www.3valley.com

CHAPTER 6

Sugar Lake Road

Statistics	For map, see page 18 and page 43
Distance:	73 kilometres, Highway 6 at Cherryville to Greenbush Lake
Travel Time:	Three to four hours minimum
Conditions:	Partly paved, some rough gravel sections
Season:	Dry weather; north portion may be closed in winter
Topo Maps:	Creighton Creek, BC 82 L/2
	Shuswap Falls, BC 82 L/7
	Mount Fosthall, BC 82 L/8
	Gates Creek, BC 82 L/9
	Revelstoke, BC 82 L/16
Communities:	Vernon, Lumby and Cherryville

Monashee Mountain Escape

This backroad into the heart of the Monashee Mountains begins at the junction of Highway 6 and Sugar Lake Road 25 kilometres east of Lumby and less than an hour east of Vernon. In dry summer weather, you should be able to drive north some 73 kilometres to Greenbush Lake. If you have a suitable vehicle and suitable conditions, there are plenty of opportunities for side trips. In addition to spectacular Monashee Provincial Park, there are numerous forest roads and a network of trails on mountain ridges that separate the Shuswap River from Mabel Lake.

Cherryville Junction Start

Chasing down the history of a region is both intriguing and fraught with danger. Recorded names of individuals are subject to the vagaries of memory, spelling and handwriting. Names of communities and common landmarks change when the broader perspective of the country is applied and duplicates are eliminated. Researching the history of Cherryville revealed the evolution of the place name

Rainbow Falls on Spectrum Creek. *© Murphy Shewchuk*

and inconsistencies in spelling of names of some of the pioneers.

The history of Cherryville dates back to the early 1860s — not significant when compared to the recorded history of the rest of Canada, but still early in the settled history of British Columbia.

While it would be convenient to say that the cherries the Okanagan Valley is famous for were the original focal point, it was instead gold that drew William Peon and Louis Christien to the region in 1863. In *The History of Cherryville*, produced by the Cherryville and Area Historical Society, the editors write: "In 1863, Mr. W.C. Young, then stationed in Osoyoos, was instructed by Governor Douglas to visit Okanagan gold strikes. Two miles from the mouth of Cherry Creek he found a budding and as yet, unnamed settlement, consisting of two houses and another building being built. One mile further along the creek was a cabin and the discovery claim of partners, Pion [Peon] and Louis. They reportedly earned $93.00 in four days with a rocker. Between 1863 and 1895, the original town that we know of as Cherryville, was merely a small mining camp located deep within the canyon walls of Cherry Creek. It boasted a population of more than 100 people, half of which were Chinese miners. Every possible method of extraction was tried to get the gold and silver from the area (It had been calculated that over $125,000 worth of gold was extracted from Cherry Creek). By today's gold prices, the same amount of gold would bring in over $7,250,000. Most of the gold was less than 720 fine, but nuggets weighing 1/2 to 1 ounce were quite common."

The original "Cherry Creek" was likely named after the wild chokecherries that still grow on the dry hillsides, not the luscious cherries that the Okanagan Valley is famous for. When it came to naming the community Post Office, the bureaucrats in Ottawa chose "Cherryville" from the selection presented by pioneer Post Mistress, Olava Hanson.

Head Northeast

Sugar Lake Road (well-marked with Monashee Provincial Park signs) leaves Highway 6 about 25 kilometres east of downtown Lumby. The main centre of rural Cherryville is a few kilometres to the east and a short drive off the main highway. The paved secondary road crosses Cherry Creek about 2.5 kilometres from the highway and continues northeast, winding through a broad valley filled with scattered farms and small ranch holdings. The pavement ends at kilometre 13.5 and the road soon descends to Sugar Lake, with a junction to the Kate Creek Road just before the crossing. Kate Creek Forest Service Road (FSR) and its branches can, according to reliable sources, take you more than 20 kilometres into the mountains to the east of Sugar Lake.

Pioneer Hydroelectric Dam

The upper Shuswap River was first harnessed to generate electricity when the West Canadian Hydro Electric Corporation constructed the Wilsey Dam and generating station at Shuswap Falls in 1929. The dam and falls are easily accessible about 16 kilometres north of Lumby on Mabel Lake Road.

The concrete Wilsey Dam was built at the site of the original 21-metre-high Shuswap Falls while the spillway channel was blasted through solid rock immediately to the north. Initially, the facility used only water available in the Shuswap River, without a storage reservoir (known as run-of-the-river). The Shuswap River flows powered this 4,000-horsepower (HP) generating unit.

Sugar Lake Road

In 1942, a second dam was constructed at the outlet of Sugar Lake to create storage and increased generating potential. This new dam allowed for another 4,000-HP generating unit at Shuswap Falls, which translates to another 5.2 megawatts (MW) of capacity. From 1929 to 1951, the Shuswap Falls facility provided most of the electric power for the North Okanagan region. As BC's power demands increased, new dams were built on the Bridge and Peace Rivers, lessening reliance on the Shuswap system. During this evolution, the West Canadian Hydro Electric Corporation was succeeded by the BC Power Commission, which in turn, became BC Hydro.

Shuswap River Recreation Area

Sugar Lake is the upper end of the busy Shuswap River Recreation Area, supported in large part by BC Hydro. Facilities at the Shuswap Falls Recreation Areas include 10 picnic tables, a 40-car parking lot, landscaped areas, viewing platform, canoe pull-out, launch and portage trail, hiking trail, drinking water, and two toilets. Facilities at the Shuswap River Picnic Area (just west of Cherryville) include a 30-car parking area, wheelchair-accessible trail from the parking area, eight picnic tables, picnic area and portage, two toilets, trail and chute portage (two kilometres downstream). Sorry, no drinking water. Facilities at the Sugar Lake Dam Viewpoint include one parking stall, four picnic tables, viewing area, and one toilet. Again, no drinking water.

Fraser Lodge

British Columbia history is literally being written on the walls as we recognize those who have helped develop the province and the special character of the people who live here. The mural, painted or plastered on public and private buildings, is now gaining popularity throughout the region.

A little bit of Sugar Lake history is located on the side of Frontier Video in Lumby. The Schunter mural, developed by artist Lorreen Norman Chambers, shows the Schunter family crest and Bill Schunter Sr. in front of his truck at the ramp to a barge on Sugar Lake.

William Frederick Schunter was born in 1900 in Bracebridge, Ontario. He moved with his family to Vernon in 1905 then homesteaded in Cherryville in 1907. William and his brother Frederick formed Schunter Bros. Logging in 1921 and started cutting in the Chase and Nelson areas. In 1923 William and Frederick came back to the Cherryville area and built, for Bell Pole, the road from the start of Sugar Lake to the Fraser Lodge (near the 8K marker). The men continued to log and ranch in the area until their deaths in the last quarter of the century.

William Schunter's descendants continue to live in the Creighton Valley area.

Sugar Lake Access

Sugar Lake FSR stays well above the lake before dropping down near the 10K marker (26 kilometres from Highway 6). Spice Road, to the west at km 28, and Fraser Trail, near Fraser Lodge, present an opportunity to explore Park Mountain and the Silver Hills. As in any serious backroads exploring, take along your maps, compass and GPS. The appropriate 1:50,000 topographic map for the area is Shuswap Falls, BC 82 L/7. Make sure you know how to use your GPS, and that you carry spare batteries for it.

Monashee Provincial Park

The next major detour off Sugar Lake FSR is a minute or two past the 20K marker (37.4 kilometres from Highway 6). If the alpine meadows of Monashee Provincial Park are your chosen destination, then take Spectrum Creek Forest Service Road to the right. (See *Monashee Provincial Park* for details.)

Go North, Young Man

For the sake of continuity (and my sanity), we will continue this description north on Sugar Lake FSR. For the sake of your safety, be aware that the Forest Service signs show that this road is not maintained. In our mid-August sojourn up the valley, there were a few narrow and a few rough sections, but nothing we couldn't handle with a pickup truck and camper — and perhaps other types of conveyance judging by the variety of vehicles we met along the way. However, as in any adventure of this sort, proceed with caution and at your own risk.

North of the Spectrum Creek FSR junction, the Sugar Lake road climbs away from the meandering oxbows and marshland of the Shuswap River. You'll pass several logging roads, some still used and some de-activated, but keep to the right at all the major junctions. If you enjoy scenic photography, you can stretch your legs and try a long shot of the Lindmark Creek valley and the Cranberry Mountain icefields near the 45K marker. If you would rather wield a fishing rod or a gold pan, the road drops back down to river level near the 47K marker.

Tsuius Mountain Trails

The Tsuius subalpine hiking area in the Sawtooth Range is difficult hiking, and is recommended for experienced hikers only! (Caution, this is grizzly country.) There are trailheads at Tsuius Creek (off Mabel Lake FSR), Tourmaline Creek, and this access, considered the most popular, near the 48K marker on Sugar Lake FSR.

Greenbush Lake, looking east. *© Murphy Shewchuk*

The rough road and trails head southwest to Mirror Lake at about 1,950 metres above sea level.

Although the hike to the lake may be considered strenuous, the Vernon Outdoors Club rates the rest of the scramble to the 2,460-metre summit of Tsuius Mountain as a Level 3. The editors of *Hiking Trails Enjoyed by The Vernon Outdoors Club* explain: "While this is a rocky peak, technical equipment is not necessary to make the climb to the summit. Two and one half hours from Mirror Lake should put you on top to enjoy the limitless view of the mountains and snow fields."

Greenbush Lake

If you are determined to limit your exercise to flailing the water with a fly line or popping a few pull-tabs, then ignore the rough road to the west near the 48K marker and continue northwest along the mountainside for a few more kilometres. This backroad crosses the Shuswap River near the 52K marker (about 69 kilometres from Highway 6) and then, for the first time since Sugar Lake, takes a left turn at the junction a couple hundred metres farther along. Continue north for 2.7 kilometres to another junction, then follow the rough road right (east) for little over a kilometre to the Greenbush Lake Recreation Site.

Protected Area

The 2,820-hectare Greenbush Lake Protected Area was recommended by the Okanagan-Shuswap Land and Resource Management Plan (LRMP) in 2000 and formally established as a protected area in April 2001. It takes in much of the Greenbush drainage basin to the southeast and east of the lake, but excludes the recreation site and access road. The protected area was established to preserve prime habitat for grizzly bear and mountain caribou. In addition to a variety of other mammals, the old-growth forests provide habitat for a wide variety of birds including pileated woodpeckers and several species of owl.

At the time of writing, a questionable road continued up the Shuswap River northwest of the final junction to Greenbush Lake. Some sources suggest that this was built to access forest fires in the area, and our maps suggest that there is a route through Joss Pass to the Wap River, but it will have to wait for another exploration trip. — MS

Kilometre Quick Reference Table

Dist. from Highway 6	Forest Road Ref.	
0.0		Junction of Highway 6 and Sugar Lake Road.
13.5		End of Pavement.
16.5	0	Bridge across foot of Sugar Lake.
24.2	8	Junction to Fraser Lodge.
37.4	21	Junction: Spectrum Creek FSR
		Monashee Provincial Park to right (east).
64.5	48	Tsuius Mountain Trails.
68.5	52	Shuswap River bridge.
73	56.5	Greenbush Lake Forest Rec. Site.

Additional Information:

BC Parks
Web: www.env.gov.bc.ca/bcparks

Cherryville
Web: www.cherryville.net/

Lumby & District Chamber of Commerce
1882 Vernon Street
PO Box 534
Lumby, BC V0E 2G0
Tel/Fax: (250) 547-2300
E-mail: lumbychamber@shaw.ca
Web: www.monasheetourism.com

Okanagan Shuswap Forest District
2501 - 14th Ave.
Vernon, BC V1T 8Z1
Tel: (250) 558-1700
Fax: (250) 549-5485
Toll-free (via Enquiry BC): 1-800-663-7867
Web: www.for.gov.bc.ca/dos

CHAPTER 7

Monashee Provincial Park

Statistics	For map, see page 43
Distance:	51 kilometres, Highway 6 at Cherryville to Spectrum Creek Parking Lot
Travel Time:	One to two hours
Conditions:	Partly paved, some rough gravel sections
Season:	Dry weather; north portion closed in winter
Topo Maps:	Creighton Creek, BC 82 L/2 Shuswap Falls, BC 82 L/7 Mount Fosthall, BC 82 L/8 Gates Creek, BC 82 L/9
Communities:	Vernon, Lumby and Cherryville

A Little Bit of Everything and a Lot of Wilderness

While Monashee Provincial Park doesn't offer the civilized services that we see in many other provincial parks, it does offer a significant variety for the self-reliant backcountry explorer determined to leave most of the "madding" crowds behind.

Spectrum Creek footbridge.

© Murphy Shewchuk

To start, there is no official vehicle campground. There are a few almost flat spots in the trail-head parking lot halfway up Spectrum Creek. There is also a biffy or pit toilet and two nearby creeks where you can fill your canteen although the routine "boil your water" advice applies. The first designated camp-

Hiker at Peters Lake. *© Murphy Shewchuk*

ground is at Spectrum Lake, a two-hour, six-kilometre "easy" walk from the Spectrum Creek parking lot. (Easy is a relative term. If you are part of the over-50 crowd and the thermometer is pushing 30°C in the shade, you might just want to add another hour to the trip.)

East of Spectrum Lake, the next designated campsite is at Little Peters Lake. Although the distance from Spectrum Lake to Little Peters is a bit shorter, the distance is made up by a significant elevation gain. While it easy enough to do a day hike into Spectrum Lake, it would be much wiser to plan on spending two or more nights if you hope to explore the high country surrounding Peters Lake.

Valley of the Moon

With designated wilderness campsites at Little Peters Lake, Peters Lake and Margie Lake, there are several base camp options. There are also several trails to explore, with varying levels of difficulty. If you are looking for a ramble after the scramble up from Spectrum Lake, the five-kilometre trail from Peters Lake to Margie Lake should suit you. On the other hand, if you're after a challenge, the climb to the 2,697-metre summit of Mount Fosthall should keep you occupied for most of a day. In between these two is the 5.5 kilometre hike to the Valley of the Moon. Aside from a few patches of green shrubs and white snow, the glacier-

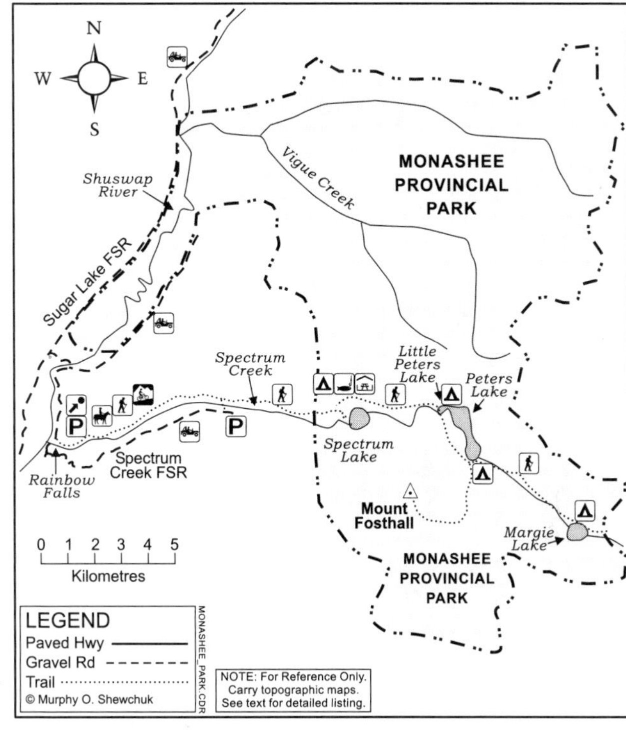

carved landscape does indeed resemble a moonscape.

Horses and Bicycles

Bicycles are not permitted in the park except for the Spectrum Creek trail between Rainbow Falls and Spectrum Creek parking lots. Horses are permitted in the park.

Getting There

Monashee Provincial Park straddles the height of the Monashee Mountains about 40 kilometres northeast of Cherryville. However, as is usual in the mountains, getting there is a bit more circuitous. Take the Sugar Lake Road northeast of Cherryville for approximately 37.4 kilometres, then take Spectrum Creek FSR east, south and then east again as it loops down along the east side of the Shuswap River and then up Spectrum Creek. Keep right at a junction approximately 1.4 kilometres from Sugar Lake Road and right at another junction marked Rainbow Falls. Keep left at the next few junctions (follow the "Monashee Park" signs) and you should reach the Spectrum Creek parking area about 51 kilometres from Cherryville, or 13 kilometres from Sugar Lake Road.

Note that the park is closed in winter and that the road can be slippery any time of the year. Good tires are essential and a four-wheel-drive vehicle is a definite asset. — MS

Additional Information:

BC Parks

Web: www.env.gov.bc.ca/bcparks

CHAPTER 8

Westside Road

Statistics	For map, see page 45
Distance:	64 kilometres, Highway 97 at O'Keefe to Highway 97 at West Kelowna
Travel Time:	One to two hours
Condition:	Mostly paved, with narrow, winding sections
Season:	Year round; may be slippery in winter
Topo Maps:	Vernon, BC 82 L/6 Oyama, BC 82 L/3 Shorts Creek, BC 82 L/4 Kelowna, BC 82 E/14 Peachland, BC 82 E/13
Communities:	Vernon, Kelowna and West Kelowna

If you are looking for a scenic drive that will not rattle the fenders off the old auto, you might want to take a close look at Westside Road. There are plenty of reasons to recommend it — and a few reasons to consider an alternative route. If you have lots of time, the pluses, such as historic O'Keefe Ranch, Fintry Provincial Park, Okanagan Lake Resort, Bear Creek Provincial Park and numerous sideroads and lakeside viewpoints and campsites make it well worth it. However, if you are in a hurry, consider staying on Highway 97. Westside Road really is not conducive to hurrying at any time of the year.

Access is from Highway 97, between downtown Westbank and Kelowna, or Spallumcheen, northwest of Vernon. I have chosen to describe Westside Road in a north-south direction, beginning at Highway 97 near the O'Keefe Ranch.

Historic O'Keefe Ranch

O'Keefe Ranch had its beginning in 1867 when Cornelius O'Keefe and Thomas Greenhow drove a herd of cattle from Oregon to the North Okanagan. A year

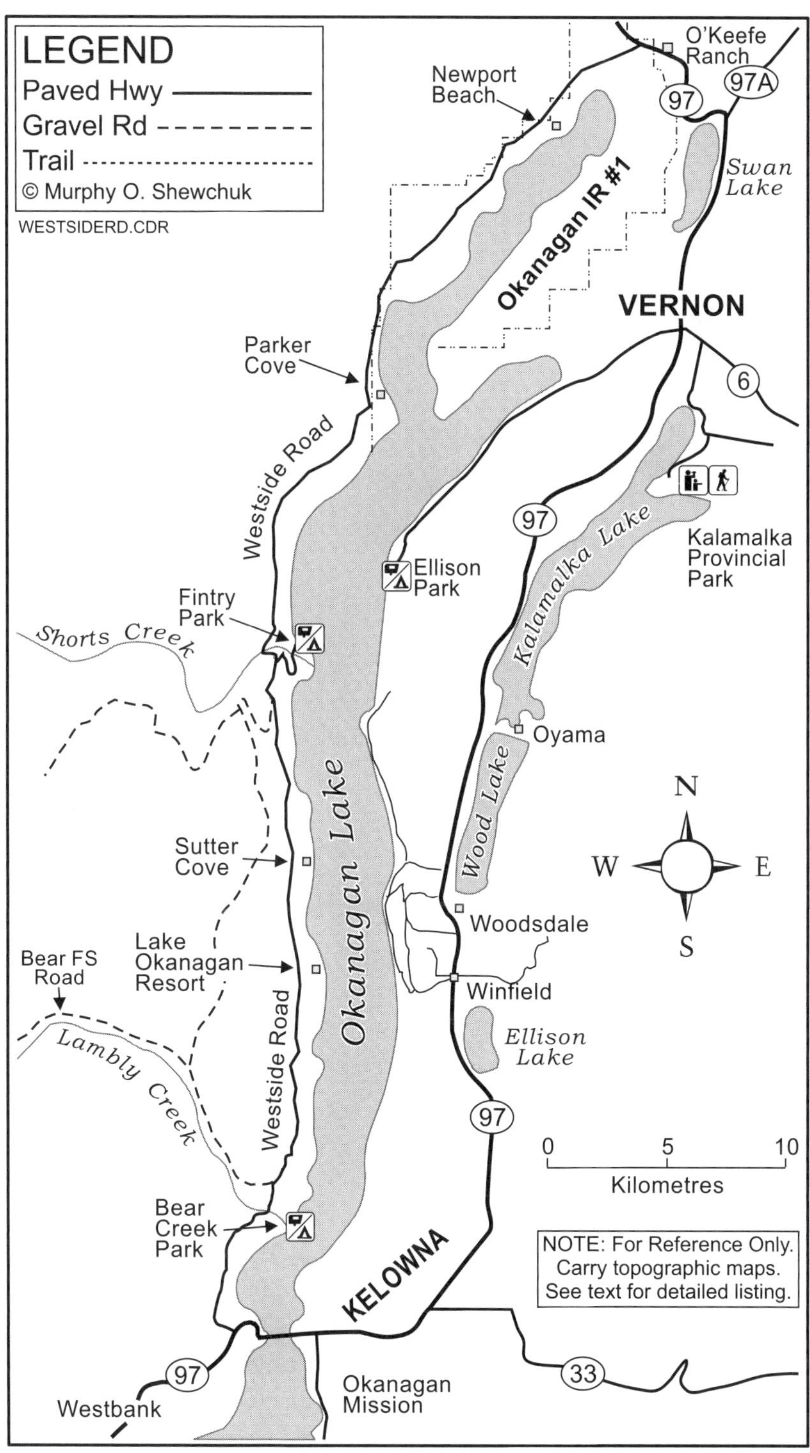
LEGEND
Paved Hwy
Gravel Rd
Trail
© Murphy O. Shewchuk
WESTSIDERD.CDR
O'Keefe Ranch
Newport Beach
97
97A
Swan Lake
Okanagan IR #1
VERNON
Parker Cove
6
Westside Road
97
Kalamalka Lake
Kalamalka Provincial Park
Ellison Park
Fintry Park
Shorts Creek
Oyama
Wood Lake
N
W
E
S
Sutter Cove
Okanagan Lake
Woodsdale
Bear FS Road
Lake Okanagan Resort
Winfield
Lambly Creek
Westside Road
Ellison Lake
97
0
5
10
Kilometres
Bear Creek Park
KELOWNA
NOTE: For Reference Only.
Carry topographic maps.
See text for detailed listing.
97
33
Westbank
Okanagan Mission

St. Ann's Church at the O'Keefe Ranch was built in 1889 and is still in excellent condition. *© Murphy Shewchuk*

later, O'Keefe homesteaded 65 hectares nearby, and within 40 years his cattle were grazing over 6,000 hectares of the North Okanagan's prime grasslands. O'Keefe gradually built up one of the largest cattle empires in the Okanagan Valley, establishing his own community to serve the ranch and its employees. It had a store, post office, blacksmith shop, and church.

The living ranch museum has preserved many of the original buildings and much of the period farm equipment. To complement the ranch setting, the historic O'Keefe Ranch has a restaurant and other attractions and is usually open from mid-May to Thanksgiving. For a small entry fee, you can explore the old buildings, many of which contain original furnishings. In the summer months, you can also ride around the ranch aboard a horse-drawn hay wagon.

St. Ann's Church, a notable landmark alongside Highway 97, stands on its original site near the ranch house. The oldest Catholic Church in the BC Interior, it was built in 1889 and is still in excellent condition.

Okanagan Indian Reserve

With the junction of Highway 97 as km 0, follow Westside Road south through the Okanagan Indian Reserve. The dry hills alongside the road appear quite barren in late summer, but in April and May they are a mass of colour as a wide variety of wildflowers compete for spring rains.

The sunny, dry climate has also attracted a growing number of hobby farms, retirement communities, and beach resorts. Newport Beach Recreational Park, near km 5.3, offers a full campground and marina facilities. Newport Beach is also one of the northernmost accesses to 110-kilometre-long Okanagan Lake. Newport Beach marina could be your launching point for an extended boat trip to Penticton.

The Native community at Six-Mile Creek (km 13.3) is home to the Sn-qt-pas-xn-c'utn, the Six-Mile Creek Education Centre, complete with a state-of-the-art, multimedia computer network and an extensive reference library. Westside Road leaves the reserve near km 21.5, just south of the Parker Cove community.

Evely Recreation Site, at km 23.5, has 50 campsites along Okanagan Lake. It was formerly known as Okanagan Lake rec site, but was renamed in honour of the late Glen Evely. There's a swimming beach and small boat launch, picnic tables, and firepits.

The Killiney Beach area, near km 27, also offers access to the lake with a five-hectare regional park with picnic tables and a swimming beach. No dogs. There are some excellent viewpoints south of Killiney. Be careful when you pull off the narrow road.

Fintry Delta Road

Fintry Delta Road, near km 34, marks the access to the mouth of Shorts Creek and one of the oldest communities on the west side of the lake — and also, one of BC's newer provincial parks.

There are also several lake accesses, including a wharf and boat launch at the end of Fintry Delta Road and a lake access left off Fintry Delta Road onto Shorts Road. Dogs aren't welcome at either. See the *Fintry Provincial Park* chapter for more information on the history of the delta and Fintry Provincial Park.

Lake Okanagan Resort

Lake Okanagan Resort, near km 47, is a first-class facility that is attracting attention — and guests — worldwide. If "roughing it" at Fintry Provincial Park doesn't turn your crank, you might consider the luxurious three-bedroom chalets and one-bedroom suites, complete with kitchenettes, as a replacement for your tent. Add a half-dozen tennis courts and an executive par 3 nine-hole golf course, and you have a suitable get-away from the rat race.

If you decide not to stop at the resort, you can pull over at an excellent viewpoint near km 52 or detour down to Okanagan Lake at Traders Cove Marine Park, a regional park with a boat dock, swim area, covered picnic area, and playground near km 56. The park entrance is opposite Bear Forest Service Road (a.k.a. Bear Main Road or Bear Road). If you are looking for a little more excitement, you could follow Bear Road southwest into the high country and join the Okanagan Connector just west of the Pennask summit. See the *Bear Forest Service Road* chapter for more information.

Bear Creek Park

Bear Creek Provincial Park, near km 57, is also well worth a stop. Westside Road acts as the boundary between two quite different natural environments that attract a wide-ranging diversity in the park. To the west, Lambly (Bear) Creek has cut a spectacular steep-walled canyon in its final descent from the rugged 1,800-metre-high Pennask Plateau. To the east the fan-shaped delta in Okanagan Lake has been developed into a fine camping and picnic area with excellent beaches and a boat launch. See *Bear Creek Provincial Park* for more details.

As you continue south from Bear Creek Provincial Park, you'll find a little grassy lakefront regional park called Raymer Bay with a swim area, playground, and covered picnic area.

Watch the lakeshore nearer Highway 97 for remnants of the docks that once served the Okanagan Lake ferry, prior to construction of the floating bridge in 1958. The 1958 bridge was replaced by the new five-lane William R. Bennett Bridge which opened on May 25, 2008.

The junction of Westside Road and Highway 97 (km 64), a few minutes southwest of downtown Kelowna, is the southern terminal of this scenic backroad.

Do you turn left and cross the floating bridge to Kelowna or turn right to Westbank and points south? The decision is yours! — MS

Additional Information:

BC Parks
Web: www.env.gov.bc.ca/bcparks

Friends of Fintry Society
Provincial Park Society
7655 Fintry Delta Rd.
Kelowna, BC V1Z 3V2
Tel: (250) 542-4031
E-mail: info@fintry.ca
Web: www.fintry.ca

District of West Kelowna
2760 Cameron Road
West Kelowna, BC V1Z 2T6
Tel: (778) 797-1000
Web: www.districtofwestkelowna.ca

CHAPTER 9

Top Five Okanagan Birding Locations

by Chris Charlesworth — Avocet Tours

Introduction

The Okanagan Valley is a popular destination for bird watchers because of its vast variety of birds and habitats. A birder can climb from the arid valley bottom, through four major biogeoclimatic zones, and into the alpine meadows in less than an hour by vehicle.

Each habitat type brings its own birdlife with the Okanagan Valley hosting over 330 species of birds, more than 200 of which breed here. Nearly 15 species of birds found in the Okanagan can not be found, or are very difficult to find, elsewhere in Canada. Included in this list of birds are canyon wrens, gray flycatchers, and flammulated owls.

Below you will find my top five birding locations for the Okanagan Valley, between the U.S. border and Armstrong. I have chosen these sites for their abundance and variety of birds, variety of habitats, and accessibility. Most birders visit the Okanagan during the breeding season between May and August. However,

A Bohemian Waxwing swallows a Mountain Ash berry in mid-January.

© Murphy Shewchuk

great birding can be found even in the dead of winter. The descriptions below will emphasize those birds found during the breeding season, but winter species will also be briefly discussed.

Okanagan River Oxbows

Directions

From the intersection of Highways 3 and 97 in Osoyoos, travel north on Hwy 97 for 7.7 kilometres to Road 22.

Site Guide

Between the towns of Osoyoos and Oliver, the Okanagan River carves a straight path through the valley bottom. Although the river was channelled in the early 1950s, many oxbows, the remnants of a meandering river course, still remain. Though much of the valley bottom habitat along the Okanagan River has been converted for agricultural purposes, extensive marshes and riparian bottomlands still exist and provide excellent habitat for birds.

Immediately after turning off the highway, you will find interesting birding. On the north side of Road 22 you will find a mid-sized cattail and bulrush marsh. From April to July look and listen for flashy yellow-headed and red-winged blackbirds. Marsh wrens and common yellowthroats, two tiny wetland songsters, are regular summer residents that can often be seen and heard singing loudly perched atop a cattail. Hiding deep in the marsh are soras and Virginia rails. Both rails are common during summer, but only the Virginia attempts to spend the winter. Tape recordings of their calls may lure these birds into view. Just east of the marshes on Road 22, you will find open hayfields, home to bobolinks from mid-May to August. Males often perch on irrigation wheels and fence posts while singing their bubbly songs. Listen also for the soft, buzzy song of the Savannah sparrow and the high-pitched

An Evening Grosbeak watches from a branch in late March. *© Murphy Shewchuk*

trills of the eastern kingbird in the fields.

About one kilometre from the highway, you will come to a small bridge crossing the Okanagan River Channel. Gravel roads are on either side of the channel. Sometimes these roads are closed by locked gate, but one or two are always open. You may drive along these roads, respecting pedestrians and cyclists. By turning south along the river, you can explore marshes and riparian bottomlands between the bridge and Osoyoos Lake. Most songbirds are easily found from mid-May to July; and an early morning trip along the dykes south of Road 22 can be a memorable experience for any birder. Among the most common birds found are western wood-pewees, willow flycatchers, Bullock's orioles, house wrens, black-headed grosbeaks, yellow warblers, red-winged blackbirds, gray catbirds, tree swallows, and eastern and western kingbirds.

About half a kilometre south of the bridge you will find a large cliff swallow colony nesting on the concrete dam structure crossing the river. These swallows build their gourd-like mud nests below overhangs and almost always nest in large colonies. It is a marvel to watch them travel en masse, swirling and swooping over the river. With luck you may find a yellow-breasted chat along the river channel during breeding season. Chats are the largest members of the warbler family. Their cacophony of songs can often be heard deep among the green foliage. There are excellent views of ospreys along the dykes in summer. Naturalists erected several nesting platforms in the Road 22 area and one is very visible in a large field about one kilometre south of the bridge on the east side of the river. Once you reach the south end of the road you will see Osoyoos Lake to the south. If there are sandbars present at the river's mouth, scan them for sleeping gulls and ducks. Be sure to explore the road on the north side of the bridge as well, where no doubt, other surprises await.

During winter the dykes are comparatively quiet, but some interesting birds are always present. On the river, watch for ducks such as common and Barrow's goldeneyes, bufflehead, hooded merganser, and gadwall. Common redpolls feed on birch seeds during eruption years, and mixed flocks of white-crowned sparrows and song sparrows are common. Be sure to search through these flocks for rarities such as Harris's, American tree, Lincoln's, and white-throated sparrows. Patrolling field edges are northern shrikes and American kestrels, while sharp-shinned and Cooper's hawks hunt in the trees. Merlins, generalists that can exploit almost any habitat type, are often seen pursuing prey over fields and forests.

Close to Road 22 is the Haynes Lease Ecological Reserve. Continue east on Road 22, over the bridge and follow the road's curve to the north. At this point, Road 22 becomes Black Sage Road. Only a short distance after this curve, turn right on Meadowlark Lane. This short, but very steep road ends in a parking area at the base of a spectacular cliff locally known as the "throne." Sagebrush flats and rocky cliffs are the main habitat types to explore here via trails. During the breeding season you should find nicely patterned lark sparrows, western meadowlarks, western bluebirds, and Say's phoebes scattered in the sage. Be sure to watch for cactus and listen for rattlesnakes while exploring this fabulous area. On the cliffs, watch and listen for canyon and rock wrens, chukars, and Lewis's woodpeckers. Prairie falcons nest sporadically on the cliff and can often be seen soaring overhead.

Vaseux Lake

Directions

From the town of Okanagan Falls, travel south on Highway 97 for about five kilometres. Your first point of exploration could be the boardwalk at the north end of the lake. You will see a sign with binoculars on it on the east side of the road. This indicates wildlife viewing. Pull into the large gravel parking area and begin your explorations here. The boardwalk runs north through marshes and riparian thickets to a two-storey viewing platform. The walk takes less than 10 minutes and is usually worth the effort. Be sure to take your scope if you have one. Look for typical marsh and riparian birds like marsh wren, red-winged blackbird, American coot, American goldfinch, black-capped chickadee, yellow warbler and black-headed grosbeak. From the platform you might see hundreds of ducks, geese, and swans.

Strolling the Vaseux boardwalk. *© Murphy Shewchuk.*

Once you've finished with the boardwalk, continue south along Highway 97 a very short distance to MacIntyre Creek Road on the left. Take this road to explore the rugged cliffs famous for canyon wrens and white-throated swifts. This is a good area for rattlesnakes, so watch where you step. Both canyon and rock wrens sing from these cliffs, especially early in the morning. With luck you'll find chukars among the boulders at the base of the cliffs. Lewis's woodpeckers nest here and can be seen sallying out for insects on warm summer days. Arriving in April, white-throated swifts chatter amongst the swallows high above the cliffs. The swifts' long, narrow wings and faster flight differentiate them from the slower swallows. You may continue up this road, but be aware much of it runs through private property so limit your birding to the road. You will need a four-wheel-drive vehicle with good clearance to complete the road, or you could spend the day hiking up it in search of birds. Typical birds of the ponderosa pine forest can be found year round along this road; they include pygmy nuthatches, mountain chickadees, Townsend's solitaires, and hairy woodpeckers. During the summer check pockets of live trees for dusky flycatchers, western tanagers, Nashville warblers, Cassin's vireos, and western bluebirds. Gray flycatchers can be found near the top of the road (which runs approximately eight kilometres from top to bottom). Once you reach the top you will pop out on the Shuttleworth Creek Forest Service Road. You may either turn right and head higher up into the forest, where you might find interesting woodpeckers, thrushes and owls, or you can turn left and return to Okanagan Falls (about eight kilometres). No matter which way you turn be on the lookout for logging trucks.

Kelowna's Mission Creek Greenway

Access to Mission Creek

For the birder, some access points to Mission Creek are better than others. The most productive access is along Casorso Road, which can be found by turning south off Highway 97 on Cooper Road adjacent to Orchard Park Mall. From the end of Cooper Road turn right onto Benvoulin Road. Continue along Benvoulin past the intersection with KLO Road and you will soon come to the bridge. The only parking area is on the west side of the road, on the south side of the bridge. Once you park, walk north over the bridge, cross Casorso Road and follow the path upstream.

Other worthwhile access points can be found along Mission Creek where Gordon Drive, KLO Road and East Kelowna Road each intersect the creek.

Site Guide

A ribbon of cottonwoods line the meandering banks of Mission Creek as it slices through the urban sprawl of Kelowna. The Mission Creek Greenway, an ever-expanding trail system along the banks of the creek, offers walkers, cyclists, horse-back riders, and wheelchair-bound enthusiasts alike the opportunity to explore the cottonwood bottomlands of a riparian forest. Though the trails are often busy, the trees and sounds of the creek can make you forget you are in the heart of the Okanagan's largest city. The birding is most exciting on summer days early in the morning. Songsters such as northern waterthrush, veery, warbling vireo, winter wren, Bullock's oriole, and American goldfinch produce an enchanting dawn chorus. Flocks of turkey vultures roost in cottonwood snags along Mission Creek and one can often see them sunning in the trees about half a kilometre upstream from Casorso Road. This area is also great for woodpeckers, including the prehistoric-looking pileated woodpecker, the largest such bird in North America. This species is a denizen of old-growth forests. It is quite spectacular to watch as it goes about its daily life in the trees along Mission Creek. Other common woodpeckers include the tiny black-and-white downy woodpecker (found all year), the ubiquitous northern flicker and, in the summer, the red-naped sapsucker.

Winter birding along Mission Creek is also productive. American dippers can

A Killdeer stands guard over her eggs in early June. *© Murphy Shewchuk.*

be found feeding in the rapids near most bridges, but especially upstream from Casorso Road and at the East Kelowna Bridge. Small flocks of common and Barrow's goldeneyes display along the creek as well. Flocks of roaming black-capped chickadees can sometimes contain a ruby-crowned kinglet or brown creeper. All three accipiters — northern goshawk, sharp-shinned hawk, and Cooper's hawk — are regular in winter.

Crepuscular excursions along Mission Creek may produce owls if you are lucky. Year round, great horned and western screech owls can be found along Mission Creek. The best location for the western screech owl is along the west side of the creek, about half a kilometre upstream from the KLO Road Bridge. Be sure to watch overhead for flocks of common nighthawks on summer evenings. During the winter, northern pygmy owls, the smallest Canadian owl, and great gray owls, the largest, have been seen, especially near the viewing deck upstream from Casorso Road. Long-eared owls and barn owls have also been seen near the Gordon Drive Bridge.

Glenmore Valley to Beaver Lake Road

Directions

This route makes for a very productive day trip from Kelowna. It is best done from May to September. The starting point is at Highway 97 and Spall Road in Kelowna. From Highway 97 turn north onto Spall Road (which becomes Glenmore Road) and continue for 6.2 kilometres, then turn right onto Scenic Road. Continue along Scenic for a short distance then turn left onto Valley Road. Follow Valley Road for one kilometre to Robert Lake. The only vantage point is the small fenced pull-off with an information sign on the left where Valley bends right to go around the lake. The rest of the road is private, as is much of the lake and the land around it. Property owners may confront you if you walk or drive down the road. From Robert Lake retrace your route to Glenmore Road and continue north. You will first pass by the Kelowna Landfill and soon after, two small ponds on the right. These ponds are Bubna Slough and Slater Pond. Continuing north along Glenmore Road you will eventually find yourself in Winfield. Once you come to the light at Highway 97 continue east straight through the light onto Beaver Lake Road.

Site Guide

Robert Lake is an outstanding birding location during most years. During dry spells the alkaline lake evaporates and becomes a dust bowl; and during the win-

A Hairy Woodpecker in mid-November.
© Murphy Shewchuk

ter it always freezes over, making birding slow. In late March and early April the first waterfowl begin arriving. Large flocks of northern pintail, mallard, gadwall, American wigeon, green-winged teal, and Canada geese are easily seen. May brings the first shorebirds such as killdeer, least sandpiper, American avocet, black-necked stilt, long-billed dowitcher, Wilson's snipe, and red-necked and Wilson's phalaropes. Yellow-headed blackbirds breed here as do red-tailed hawks and Say's phoebes. Many ducks use the lake for nesting during the summer, including uncommon ruddy ducks and eared grebes. Late summer is the most productive time at Robert Lake. Flocks of shorebirds feast on the mudflats from July to October and one can often find up to 15 shorebird species in a day. Be sure to visit in the evening instead of a sunny day so the sun's glare off the lake won't blind you. You can expect lesser yellowlegs, greater yellowlegs, and least, semipalmated, western, pectoral, Baird's, spotted, and solitary sandpipers. Also look for long-billed dowitchers, Wilson's phalaropes, red-necked phalaropes, killdeers, semipalmated plovers, and Wilson's snipes. Late September and October are good months for black-bellied plovers and American golden-plovers. During winter there is very little worth seeing, other than possibly northern harrier and northern shrikes.

Continuing north along Glenmore Road from Scenic Road for three kilometres, you will come to the Kelowna Landfill on the east side. For gull-watchers, birders are permitted to visit the dump as long as you register at the drive-up window near the dump entrance. Common birds include herring, California, ring-billed, Thayer's and glaucous-winged gulls. Glaucous gulls are annual in small numbers as are mew gulls. Watch also for good numbers of wintering bald eagles and occasional golden eagles.

You will come to the first of two small ponds one kilometre north of the dump on Glenmore Road. The first, Bubna Slough, is home to a small breeding population of ruddy ducks and eared grebes. You will undoubtedly find other ducks here as well. The second pond, Slater Pond, is 2.9 kilometres farther to the north. This pond is less attractive to ducks, but is more attractive to migrant shorebirds in spring and fall.

Continue north following Glenmore Road as it meanders through suburban Winfield to Highway 97. Once you cross the highway you will be on Beaver Lake Road. This is a popular birding route with local and visiting birders alike. The well-maintained road climbs from the valley bottom to Beaver Lake for 16 kilometres. A multitude of habitats are easily explored along Beaver Lake Road. The first kilometre or so will take you through industrial wastelands, but between km 2 and 6, picturesque rolling hillsides covered in grasslands dominate. Many birds can be found here from April to August, the most noteworthy are breeding western and mountain bluebirds. These birds nest in the boxes along a busy bluebird trail beside Beaver Lake Road. Western meadowlarks, eastern and western kingbirds and Lazuli buntings sing from exposed perches in these grasslands. Watch for rough-legged hawks during winter. The forest dominates from km 6 onwards. You will first travel through Douglas-fir / ponderosa pine woods where dusky flycatchers, yellow-rumped warblers, western tanagers, and red-breasted nuthatches are common breeders. As you enter the lodgepole pine and western redcedar habitats, be on the lookout for Townsend's warblers high in the canopy, Swainson's thrushes, and possible northern pygmy owls. Near the lake, Engelmann spruce and subalpine fir are the dominant tree species. High-elevation birds like pine grosbeak, red crossbill, gray jay, boreal chickadee, Arctic three-toed woodpecker, and common raven can be found. The lake itself often has common loons, ospreys, mallards, and sometimes migrant Bonaparte's gulls. The Two Loons Restaurant at Beaver Lake is an excellent place for a coffee and to watch Steller's jays and Clark's nutcrackers feed on seed.

Swan Lake

Directions

Swan Lake is located along the west side of Highway 97 in the north end of Vernon. It is a small, fairly shallow body of water lined with cattail marshes; it is also easily accessed. The best vantage points include Meadowlark Road (halfway along the lake, off the west side of Highway 97) and Highland Road (at the north end of Swan Lake, follow the signs toward Kamloops; soon after the interchange turn left (south) onto Highland Road and continue for a short distance until you can see the lake).

Site Guide

Swan Lake is an important breeding and staging area for waterfowl. Spring brings flocks of Canada geese, mallards, northern pintails, American widgeons, grebes, and loons to the rich waters of Swan Lake. A small number of western grebes once nested here, but now they are just regular summer visitors, with at least a few present most days. Also present are red-necked grebes and in fall and early spring,

A Black-capped Chickadee in mid-November. *© Murphy Shewchuk*

horned grebes. Despite its name, swans are not common on Swan Lake. During the fall large flocks of common mergansers gather to feed before heading south. Scan through them for the rarer red-breasted merganser. The extensive reed beds around the lake are home to typical wetland species, such as marsh wren, common yellowthroat, yellow-headed blackbird, red-winged blackbird, and song sparrow. Be sure to scan through the swallow flocks in May to July for black swifts, which are fairly common over Swan Lake. Winter usually finds Swan Lake covered in snow and ice, but open patches may hold some waterfowl. —CC

Additional information:
Chris Charlesworth
Avocet Tours
725 Richards Road
Kelowna, BC V1X 2X5
Tel: (250) 718-0335
E-mail: info@avocettours.ca
Web: www.avocettours.ca

Central Okanagan

Kelowna has grown at such a rapid pace in recent years that a newcomer may initially be struck by its urban sprawl. However, with further exploration there is a world of quiet places to be found. Kelowna and its surrounding area offer many outdoor recreation opportunities if you take the time to look beyond (and sometimes between) its hotels, shopping centres, and housing developments.

Knox Mountain Park, for example, can be quiet early in the morning before the sounds of the city start to drift upward. Woodhaven Nature Conservancy, at the end of Raymer Road in Okanagan Mission, can be quiet — or noisy — any day of the week. It depends on whether you consider the frantic chatter of a squirrel part of the quiet, or part of the noise. The pathways in Mission Creek Regional Park are seldom devoid of people, but it is easy to let the burble of the water flowing through the kokanee spawning channels carry you away from your surroundings.

The trails into the north slopes of Okanagan Mountain Provincial Park can also be quiet and uncrowded — even in mid-summer. Access to the park is off Lakeshore Road from Kelowna, by boat across Okanagan Lake, or via the Chute Lake Road, north of Naramata. This is a wilderness park, so facilities are minimal throughout.

Bear Creek Provincial Park, on the west shore of Okanagan Lake, has full facilities, but the spectacular canyon and waterfalls encourage wild birds and animals — and satisfy the need for free space demanded by the wild animal within all of us. Hardy Falls Regional Park in Peachland has a canyon and waterfall, although on a much smaller scale. It is also much more accessible for those with limited mobility.

If you have that urge to get mobile, backroads lead up into the hills from Peachland, West Kelowna, and Kelowna where you will find places to golf, trek, cycle, fish or camp in summer — or ski, snowmobile or ice-fish in winter. These backroads can also provide alternative routes to other parts of the Okanagan Wonderland.

CHAPTER 10

Public Gardens in Kelowna

Statistics:	For map, see page 62
Distance:	All within the City of Kelowna core
Travel Time:	Allow half a day or so to wander around
Condition:	Wheelchair accessible; level paths
Season:	Year round

These rambles in four public gardens in Kelowna will take you from the formality of the beds of colourful Dutch tulips at Veendam Garden, to the controlled serenity of Kasugai, a Japanese walled garden. A short drive away you may stop and wander around the Edwardian garden surrounding historic Guisachan House, then complete your garden tour with a visit to the xeriscape demonstration garden at Benvoulin Heritage Park, located between a lovingly restored heritage church and home.

Dutch Colour Dots the Green

Veendam Way in Kelowna's City Park is lined with gardens that are brilliant with colour in spring from the masses of tulip bulbs planted to honour Kelowna's sister city, Veendam, in the Netherlands. That colour continues through spring, summer and fall with both annuals and perennials maintained by Kelowna's park staff. The blooms are sheltered by mature trees that shade those who wander on the grass or along the lakeshore.

However, in 1997, brutal winds decimated the big trees in City Park, ripping out the old cottonwood trees by the roots and damaging a number of other specimen trees. Although new trees have been planted, it's a more open park than it was before that sudden, devastating storm.

An adjacent rose garden is another feature of City Park. There's also a children's water park, concession, tennis courts, and a lawn bowling green.

City Park is bounded by the lake, the Okanagan Lake Floating Bridge,

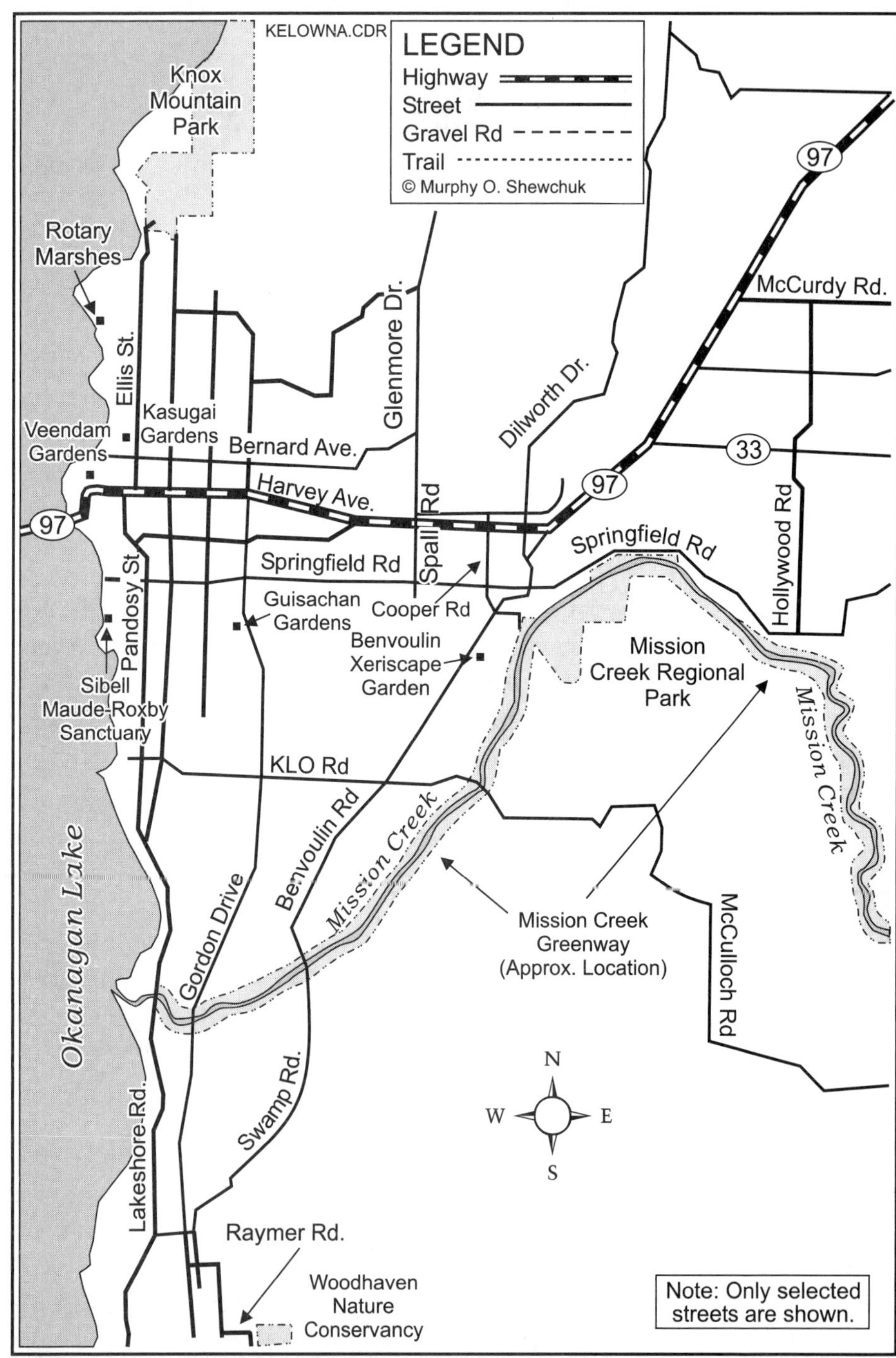

Kelowna's public gardens and Mission Creek Regional Park.

Highway 97, Abbott Street, and the foot of Bernard Avenue where the Sails sculpture by R. Dow Reid stands. The entrance to Veendam Way is 0.3 kilometres from Highway 97 north on Abbott Street.

Statuary in Kasui Gardens © *Judie Steeves*

A Peaceful Enclave in a Bustling Downtown

Kasugai Gardens was opened in 1987, a tribute to Kelowna's other sister city, Kasugai, Japan. Entering this carefully-manicured walled garden is like entering a different world from the bustling transit mall and busy city core outside.

Even the noise is muted by the thick walls and green growth, and by the restful sound of trickling water from the stream that flows through this well-maintained garden. Ducks perch on the rocks, staring at the large carp that inhabit the waterfall-fed pond. A bridge arches over the water to take strollers from one path to another. Sculptured pines, Japanese statuary, topiary and patches of colourful flowers greet the eye in little vignettes all around this tranquil retreat. It's a perfect setting for family photos, a quiet contemplative stroll, or a discreet discussion.

Unlike the brash boldness of the Bennett clock sculpture outside the walls, inside is all peace and serenity. Outside, the clock sculpture towers over the low garden walls, set in a fountain of constantly flowing water. The clock was built by the public to honour former BC Premier W.A.C. Bennett, a Kelowna resident who governed the province from 1952 to 1972. He died in February 1979.

The entrance to this garden is 0.4 kilometres north of Highway 97 (Harvey Avenue), at the foot of Pandosy Street on Queensway, just behind Kelowna City Hall.

Step Back in Time

Guisachan House was built in 1891-1892 for the Earl and Countess of Aberdeen. It was designed in the Indian colonial bungalow style, and became the focal point of a 194-hectare ranch. It was named after Lady Aberdeen's childhood home in Inverness-shire, Scotland. Lord Aberdeen was Governor-General of Canada from 1893 to 1898.

W.C. Cameron purchased the property in 1903, after he'd moved his family from the prairies.

After serving overseas in the First World War, his son Paddy Cameron married Elaine Hopkins in 1919. The couple took up residence in what is now known as Guisachan House.

Paddy's son Bill, still a resident of Kelowna, says his grandfather lived in the house for 84 years, purchasing the part of the farm with the "summer house" in 1925 when he and his brother Alister split the family property.

Bill remembers Guisachan House as cold and drafty in winter because it had no insulation. Nevertheless, he lived there for 22 years until he left to marry Shirley Cope in 1947.

The Edwardian gardens were established at Guisachan House by Bill's mother, Elaine Cameron. Many of the trees and gardens surrounding it date from as many as 100 years ago.

Guisachan was purchased by Aberdeen Holdings in 1964. The deal required that just over one hectare be donated to the City of Kelowna for a historic site and park, including the house and gardens, which were then restored by the Central Okanagan Heritage Society.

Bill Cameron says, while not missing the irony, that when the house was first built in 1892 it cost $8,000, but a restoration with public money nearly 100 years later cost approximately $300,000.

You won't be the first if you hear the mysterious clump of horse hooves and the creak of buggy wheels emanating along the 100-year-old cedar-lined avenue on a night bright with a full moon.

The gardens feature a rose arbour and rose garden with more than 100 varieties arranged in formal beds, each labelled. They begin to bloom in late May, and continue through to the first heavy frosts in November. Many are fragrant. The gardens also include a new rose bed with the winter-hardy Prairie Series developed at the Morden, Manitoba federal agricultural research facility.

A rhododendron and a shade garden are special features of the perennial and annual beds which are defined by the walkways that run through Guisachan Gardens.

McDougall House, built by John McDougall in 1886, The Milk Shed gift shop, a remnant of the era when this was a dairy farm, and an elegant restaurant in Guisachan House, operated under the eye of gold medal-winning Master Chef Georg Rieder, are other features in the park. The Central Okanagan Heritage Society manages the one-hectare-plus Guisachan Heritage Park. To reach this garden, drive 1.8 kilometres south of Highway 97 (Harvey Avenue) on Gordon Drive and turn right onto Cameron Avenue just past the traffic lights at Guisachan. And you're there at 1060 Cameron Ave.

Benvoulin Xeriscape Garden and McIver House.

© Judie Steeves

A Heritage of Native Plants

Xeriscape, from the Greek xeros, meaning dry, and scape, meaning scene, is gardening with the natural conditions of the environment, to create a landscape that needs little or no supplemental water.

Benvoulin Xeriscape Garden, an early example of this technique, opened in 1998. It is located at 2279 Benvoulin Road, between McIver House, which was built in the early 1890s, and the Benvoulin Church, a picturesque Gothic Revival-style building which was constructed in 1892. Both of these historic buildings were restored and are owned by the Central Okanagan Heritage Society. The church is now a unique community facility used for public, cultural and family events.

The heritage garden includes traditional shrubs and flowers that have survived in this arid climate. From the early-blooming, native spring sunflowers and Saskatoon bushes, to summer's golden gaillardia, hardy roses and purple Echinacea, to the red sumac leaves and yellow rabbit brush of autumn, Benvoulin Xeriscape Garden illustrates that there's lots of colour in drought-resistant plants.

To get there, follow Cooper Road south from Highway 97 (Harvey Avenue) to Benvoulin Road, and then turn right. Watch for the Heritage signs and the garden on the left (east).

The UnH2O Garden

One of Kelowna's newest public gardens opened in 2010. It is a 4,000 square foot xeriscape demonstration garden located in front of the city's H2O Adventure & Fitness Centre. Called the UnH2O Garden, it was the brainchild of local xeriscape specialist Gwen Steele. It was created by volunteers of the Okanagan Xeriscape Association with help from the local landscape industry and financial assistance from the Government of Canada's Department of the Environment, the City of Kelowna and the Okanagan Basin Water Board.

The UnH2O demonstration garden is located at 4075 Gordon Drive, beside the Capital News Centre and Thomson Marsh, where a public walkway is always noisy with the song of birds. Kelowna's Mission Recreation Park Arboretum, which features 56 different varieties of trees, each selected for its drought and pest tolerance, beauty and landscape value, can also be enjoyed along the pathway.

The goal of the xeriscape garden is to show the beauty and range of garden styles that can be achieved with a view to encouraging people to convert existing water-hungry landscapes and conserve water. All plants are labelled and a brochure is available that includes a list of the 77 drought-tolerant plants planted there. The Okanagan Xeriscape Association's website (www.okanaganxeriscape.org) also includes a detailed database of appropriate plants.—JS

Additional information:

City of Kelowna
1435 Water Street
Kelowna, BC V1Y 1J4
Tel: City Hall – (250) 469-8500
Parks Info Hotline: (250) 71-PARKS
Fax: (250) 862-3339
E-mail: ask@kelowna.ca
Web: www.kelowna.ca

CHAPTER 11

Birding Walks in Kelowna

Statistics: For map, see page 62 and page 68
Travel Time: Allow an hour or so for each
Condition: Well-maintained
Season: Year round
Topo Maps: Kelowna, BC 82 E/14
Communities: Kelowna

From the dramatic towering osprey snag at Rotary Marshes in downtown Kelowna to the relative serenity of the Sibell Maude-Roxby Bird Sanctuary south along the lakeshore; from the aquatic life around Robert Lake to the well-hidden Woodhaven Nature Conservancy — bird watchers could spend the better part of a day behind their binoculars right here in the city.

Each of these little spots of wilderness inside the city boundaries has been either saved or restored from human efforts to alter the natural landscape.

Build It and They'll Find It

Restoration of the two- or three-hectare marshland only began in 1995, but Rotary Marshes has already been discovered and adopted by the birds it was intended to attract.

Located adjacent to a high-rise condominium development and Kelowna's more-formal Waterfront Park, this rebuilt wetland is now home to a family of ospreys who were quick to make use of the community-funded high-rise tree trunk on which they nest.

Re-creation of this marsh is a joint effort of local Rotarians, the city, senior governments, local foundations, corporations, and volunteers. Their efforts transformed a bit of lakeshore from an unattractive pile of dirt and fill to the vibrant marsh it used to be. Decades ago, this was the wetland where Brandt Creek filtered through the bulrushes before entering Okanagan Lake.

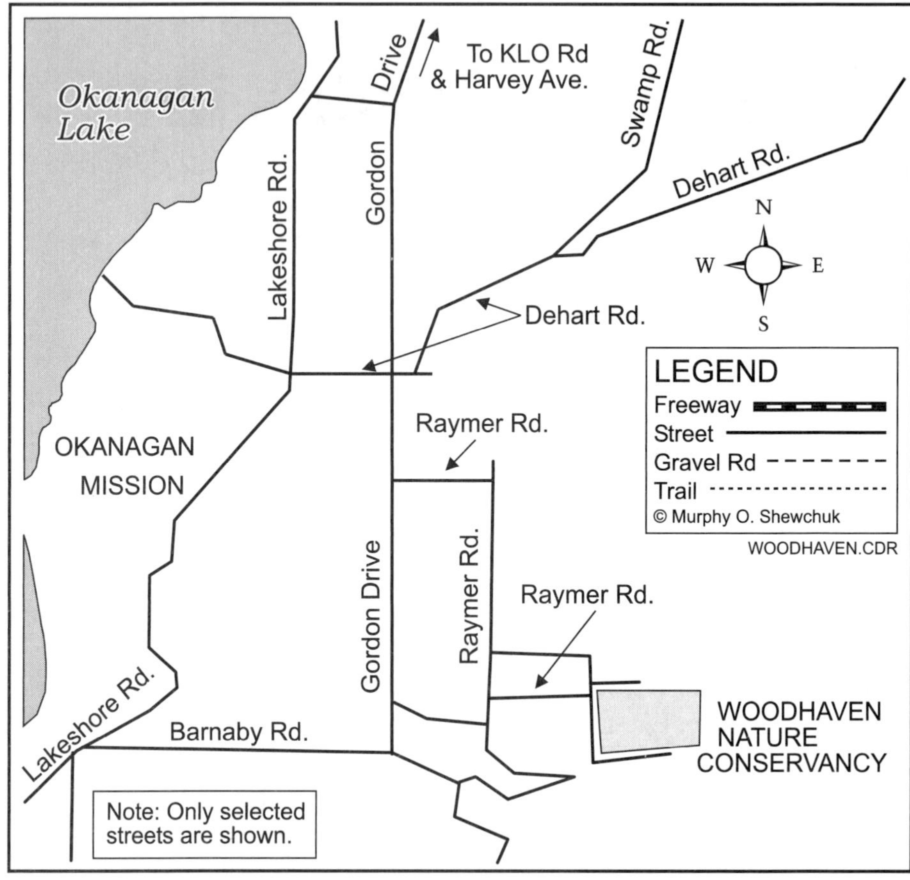

Okanagan Mission and the Woodhaven Nature Conservancy.

A wooden walkway on stilts now allows human families to see into the living rooms of winged families — with only minimal disruption to the wild things.

To reach Rotary Marshes, turn north off Highway 97 (Harvey Avenue) onto Water Street, a block from the Okanagan Lake Floating Bridge. Follow Water Street across downtown Kelowna's main street, Bernard Avenue, past the city hall, community theatre, courthouse, art gallery, a resort hotel and Waterfront Park, to Sunset Drive.

Turn left onto Sunset and almost immediately you'll see the entrance to the marsh on your left, 1.7 kilometres from the highway.

There's also an interpretive walk along Brandt Creek beginning across Sunset Drive from the entrance to Rotary Marshes.

Kelowna's Tolko Industries mill can be seen at the end of the street.

A Flourishing Memorial

The Sibell Maude-Roxby Bird Sanctuary is a more-established wetland preserve, named for a woman who lobbied unsuccessfully for the protection of this marshy area in the 1940s.

It wasn't until 1988, two years after her death, that restoration actually began with a joint project of the Central Okanagan Heritage Society and the Central Okanagan Naturalists Club.

Prior to this, the marsh had been filled in with garbage, grass clippings, and dirt. The water had been drained and diverted.

The site had to be dredged, a groundwater pump system installed, and islands re-created to restore the vital wildlife habitat that Sibell, and her husband Victor, had recognized decades earlier.

This sanctuary is the last remaining foreshore marsh in the central Okanagan. It too features a series of raised wooden walkways so human feet can tramp through the marsh without destroying the fragile plant life and disturbing the delicate balance that keeps this little ecosystem working.

Waterfowl, shorebirds, insects, aquatic mammals, reptiles, and fish such as carp now make their homes among the two-metre-high cattails, towering cottonwoods, and dense willow thickets.

The sound of traffic swarming over the Okanagan Lake Floating Bridge murmurs in the background as you walk through this misty marshland. However, the

Display panels in the Sibell Maude-Roxby Bird Sanctuary. © *Murphy Shewchuk*

foreground is full of the seasonal sounds of the marsh, whether it's the mating noises of mallards, the call of the red-winged blackbird, or the splash of migrating waterfowl taking off from the water as they make their way south after a rest.

The sanctuary is found at the foot of Francis Avenue, near Kelowna General Hospital.

Turn south off Highway 97 onto Abbott Street near the east end of the Okanagan Lake Floating Bridge, and follow it for 1.7 kilometres as it twists and turns. Turn right onto Francis Avenue and park. You're at the lake. Just walk down to the sandy beach and turn right into the marsh.

Kinsmen Park, which includes a playground, beach and grassy area, is to your left.

Woodhaven — A Secret in the City

Surrounded by a chain link fence, Woodhaven Nature Conservancy is an island of wildland situated smack in the middle of the blacktop and concrete of Mission district.

Within this nine-hectare haven of wilderness are three distinct biogeoclimatic zones that you can explore along several kilometres of trails that loop through this Central Okanagan Regional Park.

It features not only the dry grasslands and ponderosa pine that is typical of the Okanagan's Dry Interior Zone, but also a sharply contrasting mature stand of cedars more typical of the Wet Interior Zone.

Take a self-guided tour with the aid of interpretive map brochures, available near the little parking lot inside the entrance to Woodhaven. Please respect the privacy of the caretakers, whose rustic home nestles inside the park among the trees.

In 1973, this unusual area of mature and diverse woods was threatened by development, with the first two acres bought and tree clearing begun before the efforts of Kelowna naturalists, the late Jim and Joan Burbridge.

The two convinced civic politicians that the plot of wilderness warranted preservation for the edification and enjoyment of future generations. They raised funds from the Nature Trust of BC and the Nature Conservancy of Canada to purchase the land.

Now, it's home to dozens of species of birds, from the colourful western tanager and yellow warbler to the familiar American robin and Oregon junco, the noisy Steller's jay and magpie.

Trail features range from the old black cottonwoods clustered along the creek trail, to the fragrant western redcedars that allow only shafts of sun to reach the ground through the thick canopy that covers the cedar trail. Ponderosa pine dot the hillside along the flume trail.

Watch the open hillsides for patches of prickly pear cactus which can attach themselves to your leg as you pass by.

Reach this peaceful little oasis by turning south off Highway 97 (Harvey Avenue) onto Gordon Drive at the Capri Centre Mall. Follow Gordon Drive for 7.2 kilometres, then turn east on Raymer Road. Follow Raymer Road for 1.8 kilometres to the gate of Woodhaven Nature Conservancy.

A female Redwing Blackbird watches from the top of a cattail. *© Murphy Shewchuk*

A Lake That's Not a Lake

Robert Lake is not officially a lake because it has been known to dry up and has neither water inflow nor outflow. Instead, it's the result of rain and meltwater. This means Robert Lake embodies a unique ecosystem particularly prized by a wide variety of birds, including the elegant American avocet, an endangered bird known to nest in only two regions of BC.

Situated in Glenmore's Dry Valley, this little lake is a good example of an alkali playa or salt flat, with dry and mineralized mud flats left when seasonal accumulations of water evaporate. The result is ideal habitat for water and shorebirds.

A small parking spot and viewing areas have been built and users are asked not to venture farther afield; it is mostly private land around the lake and visitors are expected to view, not disturb, the birds and other wildlife.

This two-hectare regional park was acquired in partnership with the Central Okanagan Parks and Wildlife Trust in 1998 through private donations, including contributions from the Lunam family. Interpretive signs have been installed with the assistance of the Central Okanagan Naturalists' Club and TD Friends of the Environment Foundation.

No dogs, overnight camping, or open fires permitted.

Reach it from downtown Kelowna by taking Gordon Drive north from Highway 97 to High Road where you turn right. Follow its twists and turns to

Glenmore Road. Continue through at the light, where it changes to Summit Drive. Turn left almost immediately onto Valley Road and follow it all the way to Robert Lake.

Alternatively, you could access it by turning west at Sexsmith Road off Highway 97 and following Sexsmith to Curtis Road. Make a right until it runs into Valley Road and continue right, to Robert Lake.

Chichester Wetland

The call of the wild is one of the first things you notice as you begin your walk into the Chichester Wetland: at all seasons of the year, Chichester is alive with the voices of birds.

This is a small City of Kelowna natural park in Rutland. It's just four hectares in size, but may expand in future to the west along Francis Brook.

There's a small path along the outer edge of the bulrushes and reeds, then a bridge across the pond at the end.

Committed birders have counted 180 species of birds in this little marsh, and it's on the radar of migrating birds, so unusual species are often spotted here.

For instance, golden-crowned sparrows, widgeons, and black-necked stilts have been found here as well as a variety of more common ducks, and the bright red-winged and yellow-headed blackbirds.

You can reach Chichester Wetland by turning east off Highway 97 at Finns Road and turning right onto Fitzpatrick. After a couple of blocks, turn right onto Chichester Court and go to the end and park. —JS

Additional information:

City of Kelowna
1435 Water Street
Kelowna, BC V1Y 1J4
Tel: City Hall – (250) 469-8500
Parks Info Hotline: (250) 71-PARKS
E-mail: ask@kelowna.ca
Web: www.kelowna.ca

Chapter 12

Kopje, Kaloya & Reiswig Parks

Statistics: For map, see page 103
Distance: Five to six kilometres from Highway 97
Travel time: 15 minutes
Condition: Excellent
Season: All but winter
Communities: Lake Country

Lake Country comes by its name naturally. The following are a trio of regional parks which will give visitors a taste of three lakes in the community: Okanagan, Kalamalka and Wood Lakes. Each features swimming opportunities, and great facilities for family fun.

Kopje Regional Park

On Okanagan Lake, Kopje Regional Park in historic Carr's Landing is a lovely lakefront property featuring a heritage house that's now a museum. In all, there are 3.2 hectares where you can picnic, swim, and enjoy field games such as baseball. You can also tour the Gibson Heritage House during the summer months on weekends when it's open, or by appointment. Park-run interpretive programs are available for school and community groups who would like to learn about the local cultural history.

The annual Gibson Heritage House Strawberry Tea event takes place every June.

George Gibson came to the Okanagan from England in 1906, rode his horse along what is now called Carr's Landing Road overlooking Okanagan Lake, and made the decision to buy land and settle here. He built the house in 1912 and it's been part of the park since 1987. As a museum, the Gibson House takes visitors back to the early days of the Okanagan Valley and sets them down on an orchard homestead in the early 1900s when the fruit growing industry in the valley was

Bald Eagles can be frequently seen near the lakes and ranchland in spring. © Murphy Shewchuk

just taking off.

The stately beach home was rebuilt from photographs and with help from Gibson's daughter, Joan Shaw, and grandchildren Rosemary Carter and Mick Wentworth. The house has been entirely restored and refurnished by community donations and grants. It includes local historical information and artifacts from the 1910s to the 1930s.

To Get There

Turn east off Highway 97 in Lake Country onto Oceola Road, which runs into Okanagan Centre Road. Follow it to Carr's Landing Road and turn right. Continue to the park at 15480 Carr's Landing Road.

At the intersection, if you continue along Okanagan Centre Road, you will come to the Okanagan Safe Harbour where there's a boat launch, beach, and a museum nearby. Along the way, you'll pass Camp Road which will take you up the hill to Gray Monk Estate Winery, and Arrowleaf Cellars. Follow the signs for both, and enjoy a meal overlooking Okanagan Lake at Gray Monk, as well as tours and tastings of local VQA wines at both wineries.

Kaloya Regional Park

While you're in the area, you might want to visit the 3.7-hectare Kaloya Park, which offers swimming, boating, picnicking, and trails.

This park is on Kalamalka Lake. It features a lily pond with pink water lilies blooming much of the summer, a covered picnic area and gazebo, as well as a playground, boat beach, and a wedding arbour. This is a family park, but it's also a great spot for a bit of bird watching as there is good waterfowl habitat about. In fact, grebes can be spotted during breeding season.

Kaloya Park is closed in winter and dogs are not welcome.

To reach it, turn east off Highway 97 onto Oyama Road, then left onto MacLaren Road and follow it to the parking lot at the end.

Reiswig Regional Park

Reiswig is another local regional park that is great for the family. It has a beach on Wood Lake, a running track and field for year round sports activities. There's also a small natural area with mature poplar trees which provide waterfowl habitat and attract ospreys that nest in the canopy.

Reiswig is a 2.7-hectare regional district park adjacent to the District of Lake Country's Beasley Park.

To get there, take Woodsdale Road east from Highway 97 in Winfield, at the last traffic light. The park is on the left side of the road. — JS

Additional information:

Regional District of Central Okanagan
1450 KLO Road
Kelowna, BC
Tel: (250) 763-4918
Fax: (250) 763-0606
E-mail: info@cord.bc.ca
Web: www.regionaldistrict.com

Pinnacle Rock, near the base of Layer Cake Hill, is a remnant of ancient volcanic activity. © *Gordon Bazzana*

Chapter 13

Mission Creek Greenway

Statistics:	For map, see page 62
Distance:	16.5-kilometre greenway, with plans for growth; plus 12 kilometres of hiking trails
Travel Time:	Depends on your mode of travel
Condition:	Excellent: Greenway is hard-packed gravel, mostly on the level Trails are easy, except for the occasional section upstream from the park
Season:	Year round
Topo Maps:	Kelowna, BC 82 E/14
Communities:	Kelowna

Designated one of BC's Heritage Rivers in 1998, Mission Creek begins at the junction of the Shuswap / Kettle and Okanagan watersheds, and drops from an elevation of 1,829 metres to the floor of the Okanagan Valley as it winds its way over 43 kilometres. On its way down, it boils through narrow canyons, thunders over waterfalls, gurgles through forested glades, and spreads out over flatter land before spilling into Okanagan Lake.

This little creek contributes a third of the total amount of water dumped into the valley's main lake. It is also home to the largest single spawning grounds for the Okanagan Lake kokanee (a land-locked sockeye salmon) population.

Mission Creek is not only a vital link in the natural world; it has also played a key role in the human history of this area as well. It provided a Native peoples fishery; supplied irrigation water for farming settlers; and even supported gold-mining operations as recently as the 1940s. Mission Creek still serves a large agricultural area covering 4,054 hectares.

The Native name for Mission Creek was N'wha-kwi-sen, which means smoothing stones. French settlers named Mission Creek Rivière de L'Anse au

Sable, or Sandy Cove River. It was renamed Mission Creek in honour of the Oblate Mission established in 1859-1860 by Father Charles Marie Pandosy.

Significant local features include Layer Cake Mountain, which rises 108 metres above the floor of the canyon near Gallagher's Canyon Golf Course, and a spectacular waterfall near the City of Kelowna boundary.

Gold was discovered in Mission Creek in 1861 by William Pion (Peon), and in 1898 Dan Gallagher (Gallagher's Canyon) preempted land on the creek. He passed away in 1950. As much as $80,000 worth of gold was mined, all downstream from Gallagher's Canyon.

Community Created It

From 1996 through 1997, a grassroots community fundraising effort led to creation of a public streamside corridor, maintained as a regional park, called the Mission Creek Greenway. In 2004, a second community effort resulted in the extension of this linear park in a second phase to take in the 89.4-hectare Scenic Canyon Regional Park, a wilderness area of notable geological formations and natural beauty, adjacent to the Gallagher's Canyon Golf Course.

The first phase of the trail is between three and four metres wide along the north side of the creek, from Lakeshore Road, 7.3 kilometres to Ziprick Road in Mission Creek Regional Park. The second phase continues from Ziprick Road for a further 9.2 kilometres to the KLO Creek corridor at Field Road (just beyond Gallagher's Canyon Golf Course). The most recent extension includes three bridges across Mission Creek and was officially opened May 1, 2005, in conjunction with the City of Kelowna's centennial celebrations. A future third phase is also planned that will add another six kilometres along Mission Creek to Mission Creek Falls.

This is a joint-use creekside trail through the City of Kelowna for walkers, joggers, cyclists, wheelchair users, and equestrians; note, however, that it is not suitable for standard wheelchairs from the South Hollywood Road trailhead. Consideration and cooperation is essential among the different users on such trails in order to prevent conflicts.

With its ancient cottonwoods often meeting overhead, and dense undergrowth below, this trail offers a cool, refreshing walk on a hot Okanagan summer day. Viewing platforms and interpretive signs point out features such as swampy areas where dramatically different ecosystems support birds, reptiles, and plant growth quite different from that in most of this arid valley. Although it is a natural corridor, this pathway is city-style, not a wilderness hike. With large numbers of feet, wheels, and hooves tramping the trail, no green growth has a chance to mar its surface, but the creek burbles and rushes alongside you all the way.

In the newest phase of the greenway, upstream from Mission Creek Regional Park, are some of the Okanagan's most extraordinary geologic formations, including Layer Cake Hill, in which folded beds of siltstone, sandstone, and conglomerate sandstone 50 to 60 million years old are visible.

The newest extension to the Mission Creek Greenway includes some spectacular rock formations. © Gordon Bazzana

Pinnacle Rock soars into the air separate from the rest of Layer Cake Hill, a phenomenon that puzzles even geologists. Deep in Scenic Canyon is an ancient grove of cedar trees beneath a towering 70-metre rock face carved out over millennia by natural forces. Those same forces created intriguing shapes in the soft sandstone cliffs of Scenic Canyon. It's an awe-inspiring place to visit.

For background on the formation of the Okanagan Valley and other particular landmarks, have a look at the Kelowna Geology Committee's book, Okanagan Geology, edited by Murray Roed and John Greenough.

Start at Either End

To walk upstream, begin by driving south off Highway 97 (Harvey Avenue) in Kelowna at Pandosy Street. Continue past the Kelowna Regional Hospital, a total of 4.8 kilometres to Mission Creek. Don't be alarmed if you suddenly find you're

A runner on the Mission Creek Greenway. © Judie Steeves

on Lakeshore Road after crossing KLO Road. It's just a street name change. Rather than crossing over Mission Creek on Lakeshore Road, make a left turn across the road, and park at the entrance to the 19-hectare Mission Creek Greenway.

There's an interpretive kiosk at the entrance with information about the greenway, how it came to be, and what it features. You can walk from here to Gordon Drive and back, or arrange to be picked up there. You can continue farther along to Benvoulin Road; or hike the whole distance to Mission Creek Regional Park or the Field Road trailhead. You could also begin your trip either way on the greenway from the park, by turning east off Highway 97 at Leckie Road, and following Leckie a couple of blocks directly into Mission Creek Regional Park.

Or, you could begin at the other end, taking McCulloch Road out of Kelowna, past Gallagher's Canyon Golf Course to Field Road. Turn left at Field Road to the traihead.

Watch the Kokanee Spawning

Mission Creek Regional Park is one of the largest parks (92-hectares) in Kelowna, although it's a Central Okanagan Regional District-maintained facility. Autumn features interpretive tours of the kokanee spawning channel that was built adjacent to Mission Creek. The channel is an attempt to provide ideal habitat for the little fish to lay their eggs so that the most fry survive. Expect the red-flushed kokanee to be fighting their way back upstream to spawn beginning around September 10 most years, and continuing for about a month. The freshwater salmon die after laying their eggs, usually in their fourth year of life.

There's also an environment educational centre in a new log building in the park, with displays specific to the park and the valley. And there's a composting education garden too. The park has a picnic area, playground, grassy areas, and an informational kiosk. It also has a network of trails beyond the Mission Creek Greenway.

In fact, there are seven hiking routes, ranging from less than one kilometre to over four kilometres long, providing a total of more than 12 kilometres of easy hiking. Check the information available at the kiosks near the parking lot. All are on the south side of the creek, so you must cross the bridge spanning the creek to begin your hike. You may choose the perimeter loop trail of 3.5 kilometres; the lookout trail loop of 1.8 kilometres; the four-kilometre upstream loop; 1.3-kilometre downstream loop; the 2.3 kilometre pond loop; or the spawning channel loops. During your walk, take the time to watch for some of the park's 130 bird species, and some of the complex aquatic ecosystems. Beware of poison ivy.

Cycling is permitted on the greenway, the main trail from Hall Road to the dike and along dike surfaces, but not on other trails. Dogs must be kept on a leash at all times while in the park, and their owners are expected to clean up after them. — JS

Additional information:

Regional District of Central Okanagan
1450 KLO Road
Kelowna, BC
Tel: (250) 763-4918
Fax: (250) 763-0606
E-mail: info@cord.bc.ca
Web: www.regionaldistrict.com

CHAPTER 14

Knox Mountain Park Trails

Statistics	For map, see page 62
Distance:	Three-kilometre drive-up access road
Travel Time:	Trail lengths vary
Condition:	Variable
Season:	Access road closed to vehicles in winter
Topo Maps:	Kelowna, BC 82 E/14
Communities:	Kelowna

Knox Mountain Park is a near-wilderness area smack in the middle of the City of Kelowna with panoramic views out over the city, up and down Okanagan Lake and the Okanagan Valley. Within its 235 hectares there are hiking and cycling trails, two lookouts, ponds and mountain tops, grasslands and forest, lakeshore and sage-dotted hills. Access is by a three-kilometre paved road to a lookout with picnic facilities and the glorious new rock and wood beam Pioneer Pavilion overlooking the lake some 246 metres below.

The pavilion was constructed with money from a trust fund set up by Kelowna pioneer S.M. Simpson who started Kelowna's first sawmill as a one-man operation in 1913. The sawmill is now owned by Tolko Industries Ltd., and is situated at the base of the mountain on the shore of Okanagan Lake.

Kelowna's first physician, Benjamin Furlong Boyce, who died in 1945, donated property for this valuable downtown park. A cairn at the summit is dedicated to his memory.

The City of Kelowna recently completed negotiations with the owners of adjacent properties to add peaceful Kathleen Lake and the surrounding mountaintop to the city-owned park. Several community groups were also lobbying the city to purchase and add wilderness shoreline immediately north of the park. The property-owners were proposing a residential development instead.

Bridget strides along a trail at the summit of Knox Mountain. *© Murphy Shewchuk*

A Network of Trails

If you're a person who wants more than just nature on your hikes, you won't be alone in this park. The trails here are used by a wide variety of people who are looking for a good cardio-vascular workout, or are training for an event. Some hike up the trails to the top while others run up the road.

Others take along their canine companions, on leashes of course.

Fitness buffs say that a couple of hours on these trails can provide better exercise than a couple of hours spent at the gym.

Several routes in the trail system that criss-cross the park begin at the pavilion, and make a series of loops in several directions. They vary from well-developed and maintained trails to intermediate trails and rough footpaths. Some are used by mountain bikers, while others are unsuitable for bikes. Portions of the park are too steep for anything but billy goats and beard's tongue penstemon.

Much of the park is very fragile, with just a thin layer of soil over bedrock, which is easily disturbed and destroyed. In summer, delicate bitterroot, rock rose, or Lewisia rediviva flower briefly on the exposed hillside.

In order to protect the mountain's delicate ecosystem, please stay on the trails.

Short trails include: a 1.2-kilometre hike from Apex Lookout to the parking lot near the city reservoir, part-way up the mountainside; a half kilometre hike from the lookout to a meadow; and a 0.8-kilometre trail from there down to the road near Crown Lookout.

Several trails wind up the mountain to the Pioneer Pavilion and from there you can strike off on a one-kilometre trail to Magic Estates, a residential subdivision.

From there, walkers can continue on into a network of trails that wind their way through the North Glenmore area of Kelowna. These trails can also be accessed through neighbourhood parks such as Millard Glen Park. They include a walk along Brandt Creek in Glenmore.

Paul's Tomb

There's an easy 2.6-kilometre walk to Paul's Tomb along the lakeshore. It begins at the Crown Lookout. It is a wide, well-used gravel path with sweeping views. You can also access the Paul's Tomb area via a more difficult, twisting pathway down the mountainside from the summit, that includes a series of old stone steps, and some lovely views.

Paul's Tomb is the resting place of an early Kelowna settler, Rembler Paul, a fairly well-off man who is remembered as a colourful eccentric. He and his wife are still entombed on the site. He owned the property and had the tomb built about 1910 for 12 coffins, but the rest of the family declined to have their caskets laid there.

In recent years, it was closed up because of vandalism. However, the couple remain buried there in what is probably the only such tomb in the whole Okanagan Valley. Today only the curved top of the door remains visible above the ground with the date 1910 engraved above it.

Clumps of spring-blooming lilacs in the area are a reminder that this was once someone's home.

There is a large picnic area with a lovely view out over the water adjacent, and a delightful little cove with a beach of smoothed stones below. From that peaceful vantage point we watched a pair of horned grebes in winter plumage one brisk, sunny November day.

Reach Knox Mountain Park's access road by turning north off Highway 97 (Harvey Avenue) onto Ellis Street, and driving 2.4 kilometres through the downtown area of Kelowna. The access road, because of its steepness, is closed in winter.

Visitors must keep their dogs on leash as there are deer in the park, as well as coyotes, porcupines, raccoons, marmots, and the occasional cougar.

There are public washrooms (open seasonally) at the Pioneer Pavilion and a caretaker on site. — JS

Additional information:

City of Kelowna
1435 Water Street
Kelowna, BC V1Y 1J4
Tel: City Hall – (250) 469-8500
Parks Info Hotline: (250) 71-PARKS [717-2757]
E-mail: ask@kelowna.ca
Web: www.kelowna.ca

CHAPTER 15

Lower Myra-Bellevue Trails

Statistics	For map, see page 87; detailed trail map available at Kelowna outdoor stores.
Distance:	Vast network of trails.
Travel Time:	Varies, depending on trails taken.
Condition:	Most trails are well-maintained, but the park is still very wild in places.
Season:	Dependent on elevation
Topo Maps:	Kelowna, BC 82 E/14
Communities:	Kelowna

You can embark on this network of trails at several points, depending on the season, your appetite for exercise, your fitness level, and whether you want to spend a few hours, a whole day, or a weekend hiking, cycling, or horseback riding. This is a wilderness park but it was dramatically affected by the 2003 Okanagan Mountain Park wildfire. Since then, the Friends of the South Slopes have done considerable hazard tree removal and trail restoration and have installed new bridges across streams. Some of this work was with the assistance of government programs and local school programs. Some involved professionals, while much of it was strictly volunteer labour.

Lower Myra-Bellevue Trails

The trails vary from open grassland to dense forest; dryland ecosystems to moist or swampy areas; rocky and austere landscapes to lush, green pockets, often found along streams or ponds or in glens along the way.

All trails in Myra-Bellevue Provincial Park are for non-motorized use only.

You may wish to arrange for pick-up at an alternate access point so you don't have to return on the same trail you set out on, although several trails provide a loop so you can always find new scenery around the bend.

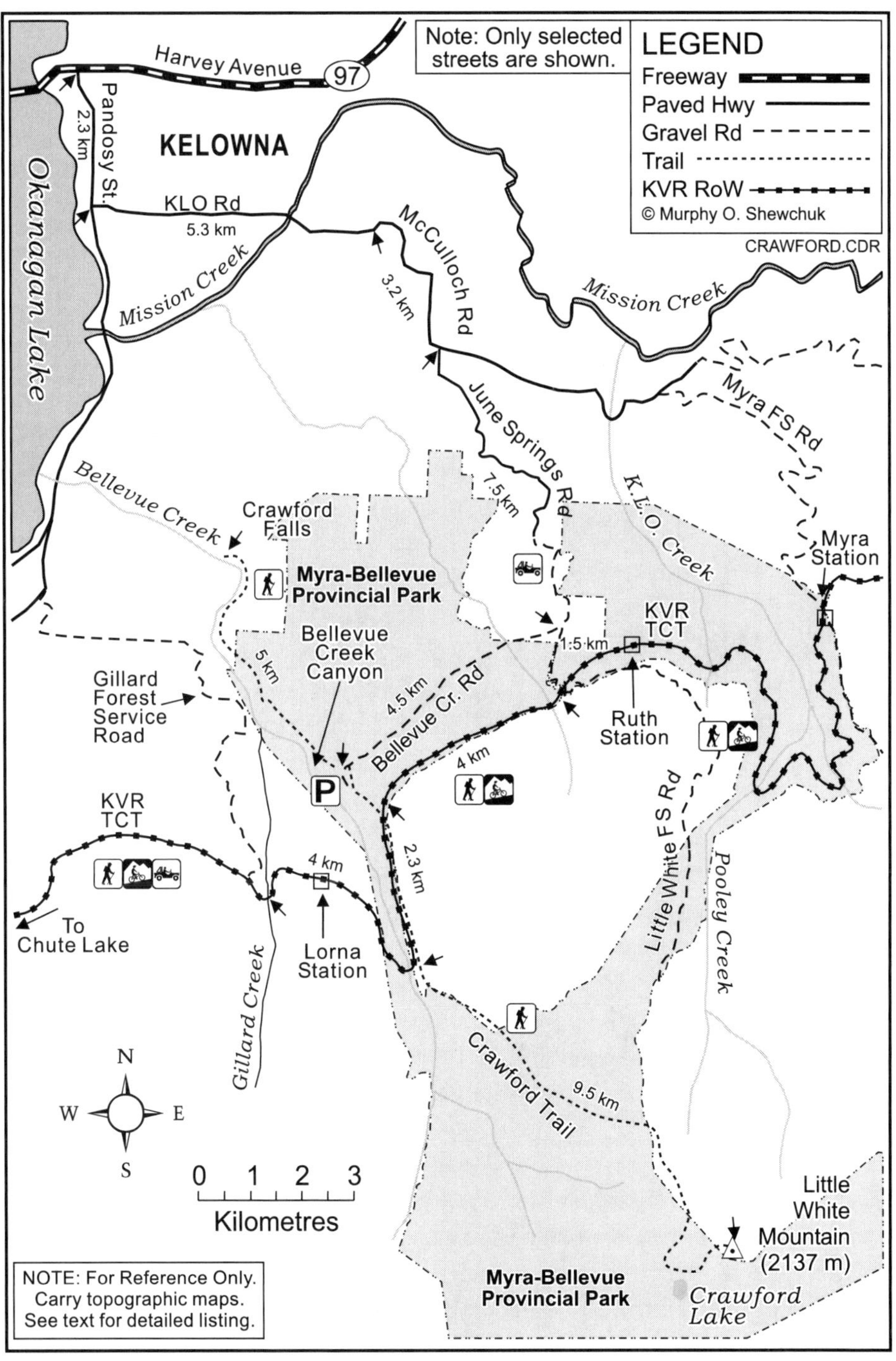

Crawford trails and Myra-Bellevue Provincial Park.

On the Crawford Trail. *© Judie Steeves*

These trails get a lot of use from mountain bikers and backcountry horsemen as well as hikers, so it's important that everyone observe good trail etiquette. There are also competitions held in the area, but race dates are usually posted.

To access these trails take Gordon Drive south off Highway 97 at the Capri Shopping Centre in Kelowna. Drive south on Gordon Drive, then turn left on Casorso Road. When you reach the roundabout at the intersection with Benvoulin Road, take the first exit to continue on Casorso Road and cross Mission Creek. There's another roundabout here, and you take the second exit to continue on Casorso Road, driving past the Kelowna Fish and Game Club facility on your left.

At the next intersection, stay to your left and it becomes Bedford Road. At the four-way stop at Saucier Road, go straight ahead. You're on Stewart Road East. Pass under the power lines to the parking lot and the main trailhead, where there are washrooms and interpretive signs, including a trail map.

From here on, it's your decision what trails you take and the scenery you'll enjoy. Some of the major trails include the Fairlane Trail, which traverses the lower end of this trail network, and which can also be accessed from Harvard Road, Ball Court off Balldock Road and Luxmore Road. There's also the Lost Lake Trail, which circles around to meet up with the KVR, an elevation gain of more than 500 metres, but with lots of up and down along the way. At Teddy Bear Junction, you could choose the Pink Highway which intersects with the Lookout Trail at Obelisk Junction.

Historic Crawford Trail

Or, you could take the historic Crawford Trail, on the west side of the park, via the Upper Bench Trail or Earring Trail. However, the Crawford Trail really begins from the Stewart Road West access where there's a small parking lot. To get there, take Gordon Drive south off Highway 97 at the Capri Shopping Centre in Kelowna. Drive 7.3 kilometres south to DeHart Road and turn left onto DeHart, which makes a right turn uphill after several long blocks. Turn right onto Saucier Road, which becomes Stewart Road West, and follow it to the parking lot. Historically, the Crawford Trail went all the way from Kelowna to the top of Little White Mountain, crossing over the Kettle Valley Railway in the process, but the upper portion has been de-commissioned.

On the lower slopes, there are panoramic views across steep canyons to Okanagan Lake far below. At the beginning of the trail, you'll hear Bellevue Creek as it falls 20 metres through a narrow, rocky gorge. In the middle, stately mariposa lilies dot the hillsides; chipmunks scour the pathway for tidbits, and grouse will startle you with their sudden awkward flight into the bushes.

The trail to Crawford Lake near the top of Little White Mountain was constructed at the turn of the century. It provided access to an open flume system used to carry irrigation water to the Crawford fields far below. Until the Okanagan Mountain Park fire of 2003, sections of the old flume still lay rotting in the underbrush along the canyon rim. Growth of a different kind has now sprouted in the Crawford fields. Asphalt and concrete and the stately homes of Crawford Estates have replaced the flora of earlier decades at lower elevations.

Be aware that the first part of this old trail goes over private land before it enters the provincial park.

You'll hear the waterfall far below, where Bellevue Creek gushes out of the steep canyon to the floor of the Okanagan Valley, before it flows into Okanagan Lake. The canyon is 150 meters or so below the trail; and it's a steady climb along the canyon rim to the Bellevue Lookout where Gillard Creek Canyon comes into Bellevue Creek Canyon. The trail climbs from the 510-metre elevation of the trailhead to 1,050 metres, where it intersects with the Bellevue Access, a former forest service road. Allow two or three hours for this hike.

It's a further 2.3 kilometres along the KVR at an elevation of 1,220 metres, after you turn south (right) along this section of the Trans Canada Trail, to the Bellevue Creek Trestle. At the curving Bellevue Canyon steel trestle on the KVR, the Crawford Trail once continued up to Little White Mountain, at an elevation of 2,165 metres at its summit. However, due to the constant intrusion of people on dirt bikes and in 4x4 vehicles who caused almost-irreparable damage to the sensitive alpine area, the access has now been de-commissioned by B.C. Parks.

This section of the trail once served as a horse trail up to a fire lookout tower on Little White Mountain and it was historically the route for the telegraph line to the tower.

You can also access the Crawford Trail from the KVR. The trail intersects the KVR between the Ruth and Lorna Stations, about four kilometres from the Little White Forest Service Road, more than six kilometres from the site of the former KVR Lorna station.—JS

Additional Information:

Friends of the South Slopes (FOSS)
Box 28011 RPO East Kelowna
Kelowna, BC V1W 4A6
E-mail: info@foss-kelowna.org
Web: www.foss-kelowna.org

BC Parks
Web: www.env.gov.bc.ca/bcparks

CHAPTER 16

Angel Spring Trail

Statistics	For map, see page 87
Distance:	5.7 kilometres, return
Travel Time:	Three hours, average
Condition:	Well-maintained, but some steep sections
Season:	Much is shaded, so late spring, summer and early fall are best
Topo Maps:	Kelowna, BC 82 E/14
Communities:	Kelowna

If not for the well-organized and determined efforts of the Friends of the South Slopes (FOSS), the trail to Angel Spring would today likely be obliterated by a road built to cart out the natural geological formations of tufa created by this mineral spring over centuries.

A mining company staked claims to the area during negotiations for a Land and Resource Management Plan (LRMP) for the Okanagan-Shuswap, but the claims were eventually expropriated by the government and the area included in what officially became Myra-Bellevue Provincial Park in May 2004.

Tufa is a rough-textured, porous deposit formed underwater when the calcium-rich warm spring meets cooler water rich in carbonates. Calcium carbonate, or limestone, is precipitated out by the chemical reaction.

It's prized as a landscaping material by gardeners, who like to plant in the hollows of the rock. But because of its scarcity, many now use a man-made product called hypertufa.

As tufa forms it encompasses the plants, mosses, invertebrates, and even tree trunks around it so they are often preserved as fossils within the tufa. As water from the spring flows over the benches of tufa, new layers are continually formed.

In geologists Murray Roed's and John Greenough's *Okanagan Geology*,

Installing trail signs in Myra-Bellevue Provincial Park.
© Penny Gubbels

Greenough writes that the reddish-orange colour in the spring comes from the growth of algae and a precipitate from iron-bearing minerals. It adds a surreal look to the area.

He speculates that the water's warmth comes from a fault that lies along the ravine in the ancient gneiss outcroppings, allowing water from deep in the earth to follow the fault to the surface. Since the springs themselves erupt above the trail, the water cools as it flows downhill, and it mixes with cooler water, so that by the time it crosses the trail you'd never know it came from a warm spring.

The terraces of tufa are visible in the gloom of the deep canyon and the towering canopy of ancient cedars that mark the spring. In season, the platter-sized leaves of prickly devil's club contribute to the darkness of the spot, making it virtually impossible to take photographs of the spring itself.

Visitors are asked to stay in the observation area of the spring to avoid damaging the delicate ecosystem. Tufa is easily eroded.

Trail Re-routed

As a result of the Okanagan Mountain Park wildfire in August and September of

2003, parts of the historic trail in to Angel Spring were destroyed by fireguards built in an effort to stop the flames.

In 2004, Friends of the South Slopes volunteers re-routed the trail along an old logging road avoiding areas where the worst of the damage was done to the original trail, and work crews funded by the federal government restored the trail in to the spring.

To reach the trailhead from Highway 97 in Kelowna, set your odometer at Gordon Drive and turn south, travelling for 2.6 kilometres. Turn left on KLO Road, crossing over Mission Creek at the 5 kilometre mark and turning right on McCulloch Road at 6.6 kilometres. Follow McCulloch, then turn right onto June Springs Road before Gallagher's Canyon. Follow June Springs Road to the sign announcing the entrance to Myra-Bellevue Provincial Park, at the 16.2 kilometre mark.

Continue just past the one kilometre marker on Little White Forest Service Road and watch for the sign for the Angel Spring trailhead, on your left. There's parking on your right.

Start Walking

The trail begins at an elevation of 930.5 metres, and gradually ascends for about 1.3 kilometres through dry pine and fir forest, with rocky outcroppings; then a trail veers off to the left. Straight ahead the trail is called the Myra Bailout; here it is a steep switchback to the old Kettle Valley Railway above. Cyclists mainly used this part of the trail.

Continue to Angel Spring by taking the trail that angles to the left. The trail levels out and goes through a wetland where the habitat includes more cedars than pines and is altogether wetter as you round the hill.

The trail crosses the fireguard, then meets the original Angel Spring trail, where the descent to the spring begins. There's a warning sign here that you're entering a particularly sensitive ecosystem, and mountain bikers are asked to dismount and walk their bicycles from here on. Now, the trail is carved out of the side of the hill and winds down 0.95 kilometres into the all-day twilight of the canyon where the spring comes up from underground and becomes the source of Angel Creek, which runs into KLO Creek.

In many places along this part of the trail, the face of the burned-over canyon slope across the gully is visible. It's in sharp contrast to the green forest you're walking through, because it escaped the fast-flying wildfire of 2003.

The highest point on the trail is 1,081.9 metres, and it is 987.1 metres in elevation at the spring.

No motorbikes, campfires or wood cutting is permitted, and users are asked to respect the environment by leaving no trash behind and keeping the trail in good condition. — JS

Additional Information:

Friends of the South Slopes (FOSS)
Box 28011 RPO East Kelowna
Kelowna, BC V1W 4A6
E-mail: info@foss-kelowna.org
Web: www.foss-kelowna.org

BC Parks
Web: www.env.gov.bc.ca/bcparks

CHAPTER 17

McCulloch Road

Statistics	For map, see page 96
Distance:	40 kilometres, Highway 33 to downtown Kelowna
Travel Time:	Up to one hour
Elev. descent:	Approximately 925 metres
Condition:	Gravel road with some steep sections
Season:	May be closed in winter, slippery when wet
Topo Maps:	Kelowna, BC 82 E/14
Communities:	Kelowna, Rutland, and East Kelowna

If you're looking for some fishing, backroad exploring and beautiful scenic views — with the option to explore a few Kettle Valley Railway (KVR) trestles or strap on the cross-country skis, McCulloch Road is the answer. The upper or east end of McCulloch Road begins at Highway 33 in the West Kettle Valley, 40 kilometres southeast of the junction of Highway 97 and Highway 33 in Rutland, or six kilometres south of the junction to the Big White Ski Resort. (See *Big White Ski Resort* for details.)

With the junction of Highway 33 and McCulloch Road as km 0, the first major sideroad is less than one kilometre to the northwest. The well-maintained Okanagan Falls Forest Service Road to the south will take you past Haynes Lake and Idabel Lake Resort. If you follow it far enough, you can descend to the Okanagan Valley at Penticton or Okanagan Falls with opportunities to fish, hike and explore along the way. However, as this is an active logging road it would be wise to restrict your exploring to weekends. (See *Okanagan Falls FS Road* for details.)

Staying on McCulloch Road, a junction at km 4.5 marks a short sideroad lead-

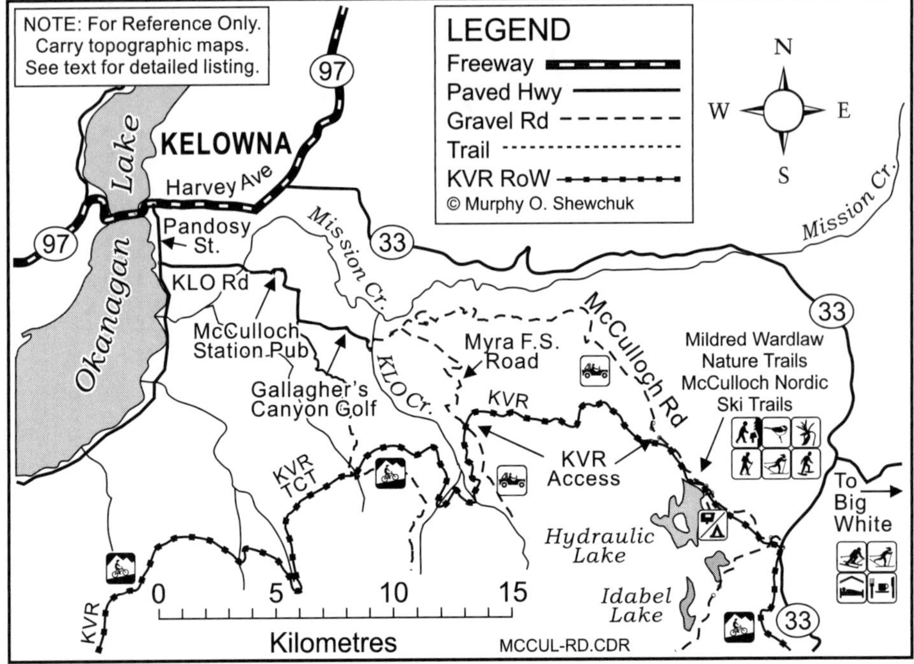

McCulloch Road and the Kettle Valley Railway near Kelowna.

ing south to the Hydraulic (McCulloch) Lake reservoir and several small recreation sites. Fishing, cycling and cross-country skiing are the main pursuits in the area (see *Mildred Wardlaw Nature Trails*). The lakes serve as reservoirs for the residents and orchards of Kelowna.

The trackless remains of the KVR parallel the road for a short distance before continuing their descent to Naramata and Penticton, via Chute Lake. McCulloch Station, near km 6, served as the KVR station for Kelowna. Stage coaches and freight wagons made the hair-raising trips to and from the orchard community on a regular basis. See the *West Kettle Route — Highway 33* section for more information on Andrew McCulloch and the KVR.

A rough sideroad near km 8.5 leads south to the KVR right-of-way and Myra Canyon (see *Myra Canyon KVR Corridor*).

Remnants of wooden irrigation flumes can be seen as the road descends into the Okanagan Valley. A rough sideroad leads through the trees to an opening near km 21. Here you'll get an excellent view of East Kelowna with basalt columns in the foreground and Mount Boucherie in the distance.

Beyond the viewpoint, the road descends through a mix of grasslands and light timber. Switchback turns provide a bit of excitement for those unfamiliar with mountain roads, but good brakes and extra caution are all that is really needed to make the descent.

The basalt columns that were far below at the viewpoint a few minutes earlier are now just across a narrow valley near km 24. A short distance farther along, the road crosses Hydraulic Creek as it carries whatever water hasn't been used for domestic and irrigation purposes.

Viewpoint for Valley

In 1890, in what was probably the first move toward irrigating the dry benches above Kelowna, the Lequimes built an irrigation ditch from what was then called Canyon Creek, near km 28, to the upper bench that is now East Kelowna. The Kelowna Land and Orchard Company (KLO), formed in 1904, bought up the Lequime estate and the irrigation system. The water system is now part of the South East Kelowna Irrigation District.

The gravel of McCulloch Road gives way to pavement and farther down the road, vineyards soak up the sun on the slopes.

A viewpoint of the city of Kelowna (km 33) with its orchards and a backdrop of hills to the west present still another reason why this is the largest community in the Okanagan Valley. McCulloch Road ends a short distance farther along, but if you wish to continue down toward Kelowna and Highway 97, follow KLO Road west after crossing Mission Creek.

First known as Riviere L'Anse du Sable, Mission Creek took its present name from the settlement first established in 1859-1860 by Father Pandosy. The Priests' ranch at Okanagan Mission is believed to be one of the first in the area to use irrigation, with water rights on Mission Creek issued in April 1874.

Mission Creek Regional Park, in the centre of greater Kelowna, is well worth a side trip. The 92-hectare park contains more than 12 kilometres of hiking trails, a children's playground and a kokanee spawning channel — all in a mixed forest and river setting. To get there, turn north on Benvoulin Road and then east on Springfield Road (see *Mission Creek Greenway*).

Turn left (south) on Benvoulin Road, km 37, to explore the Pandosy Mission grounds near the corner of Benvoulin Road and Casorso Road. Casorso Road winds northwest to join KLO Road, which in turn runs into Pandosy. After exploring the Pandosy Mission, you can also turn north on Benvoulin Road to Highway 97, a distance of about four kilometres. If you continue on KLO Road at the Benvoulin Road junction, turn right on Pandosy and it will take you to Harvey Avenue (Highway 97). If you are now totally confused, before heading for the hills stop for a city map at the Kelowna Chamber of Commerce office on Harvey Avenue. — MS

Additional information:

Kelowna Nordic Ski Club
P. O. Box 22089, Capri Centre
Kelowna, BC V1Y 9N9
Snowphone: (778) 478-3595
E-mail: admin@kelownanordic.com
Web: www.kelownanordic.com

CHAPTER 18

Mildred Wardlaw Nature Trails / Nordic Ski Trails

Statistics For map, see page 96
Travel Time: You can decide
Condition: Well-maintained
Season: Ski here in winter; hike in summer
Topo Maps: Kelowna, BC 82 E/14
Communities: Kelowna

More than 100 wildflower species have been documented on the Mildred Wardlaw Nature Trail system which winds through the forest near McCulloch Reservoir (Hydraulic Lake) east of Kelowna. The Kelowna Nordic Ski Club, Central Okanagan Naturalists' Club, and Canada Trust's Friends of the Environment Foundation opened phase one of the Mildred Wardlaw Nature Trails in July 1999. Phase three opened July 17, 2002, which includes interpretive signs about the flora and fauna of the area.

Mildred Wardlaw was the daughter of Emily and Dave Wardlaw. Dave was employed by the South East Kelowna Irrigation District in the 1930s. Mildred, who died in 1995, was steward of the nearby Brown Lake Ecological Reserve.

The 70 kilometres of ski trails and 75 kilometres of snowshoe trails vary in length from half a kilometre to several kilometres. There are also 28 kilometres of K-9 trails. The trail is at an altitude of 1,280 metres, so after the snow melts, the biggest show of flowers is usually in early summer rather than spring.

In 2004, the club built a new 44.6 square metre warming cabin on the Log Cabin Trail, just 15 metres from the previous one, which was a leftover from the horse logging days back in the early 1900s. The warming hut on the outer trail has also been updated.

All Roads Lead There

The Nordic Ski Trails are located near the intersection of McCulloch Road, Highway 33 and the Okanagan Falls Forest Service Road. They can be reached from Kelowna via either Highway 33 off Highway 97, or along McCulloch Road via KLO Road and Gordon Drive off Highway 97 in Kelowna. Parking and the trailhead are off McCulloch Road across from the McCulloch Lake Resort. There are two fairly primitive Recreation Sites for camping adjacent to Hydraulic Lake, and near Minnow Lake. There are more than eight lakes in the area, most stocked with rainbow trout. On the south side of McCulloch Road, trails loop from Idabel Lake Resort on Idabel Lake, to the Kettle Valley Railway (KVR) line, and along Haynes, Minnow, and Hydraulic Lakes. As well there is a canoe route from the McCulloch Forest Service Recreation Site around a couple of the islands on Hydraulic Lake, to a portage between it and Pear Lake. From there you could cross Pear Lake to another short portage to Haynes Lake, then across a corner of that lake to Minnow Lake, and back to the recreation site.

Diversity's the Key Here

The Ministry of Forests calls this an integrated use area because it's managed for a diversity of values. Hydraulic Lake is the McCulloch Reservoir providing water to residences and farms in the southeast area of Kelowna. The ski club has created a series of trails and maintain the area for public use all seasons of the year. The KVR corridor, now part of the Trans Canada Trail, provides world-class opportunities for cyclists, and there are other outdoor recreation uses as well. There is recreational fishing at several of the lakes in the area, and there's ample wildlife viewing opportunities, as well as good hunting. Rangeland permits are let by the ministry to local ranchers, which allows them to graze their cattle on some of the Crown-owned land in this area. The ministry manages the timber harvest on Crown-owned land in the area. It also manages replanting, thinning, and other silviculture practices. The Central Okanagan Regional District operates the two Recreation Sites.

There's a strong link between BC's settlement and economic history, and the section of Kettle Valley Railbed that cuts through this area. Andrew McCulloch was the chief engineer during the construction of the KVR in the early part of the 1900s, and a nearby station on this rail line, as well as the road and reservoir, were named after him. — JS

Additional information:

Kelowna Nordic Ski Club
P.O. Box 22089, Capri Centre
Kelowna, BC V1Y 9N9
Snowphone: (778) 478-3595
Web: www.kelownanordic.com

Regional District of Central Okanagan
1450 KLO Road
Kelowna, BC V1W 3Z4
Tel: (250) 763-4918
Fax: (250) 763-0606
E-mail: info@cord.bc.ca
Web: www.regionaldistrict.com

CHAPTER 19

Grizzly Hill / Dee Lakes Loop

Statistics	For map, see page 103
Distance:	Approximately 100 kilometres from Highway 97 in Rutland to Highway 97 in Winfield
Travel Time:	Allow one day, minimum
Conditions:	Mostly gravel; portions closed in winter
Season:	Best in dry weather — June to October
Topo Maps:	Kelowna, BC 82 E/14 Oyama, BC 82 L/3
Communities:	Kelowna, Lavington, and Winfield

If you are looking for an opportunity to explore the Okanagan Highlands and try some serious fishing, there are more than two dozen lakes on the plateau surrounding Grizzly Hill, northeast of Kelowna. And these just might fill the bill. If you are planning an overnight jaunt, there are two fishing resorts and more than a dozen recreation sites that can accommodate you.

Some of the lakes have roadside access while others may require you to pack your canoe or belly-boat a short distance. Not all lakes or access roads are well-marked. A little bush-sense will be necessary, but if you are willing to explore, you may just find your own private hideaway, even on a busy summer weekend.

A couple of important points to note: First, if you are looking for pristine wilderness, this isn't it. Much of the area has been logged — some of it so long ago that it might seem that the loggers have been back for a second time. Second, many of the lakes are dammed. These serve as domestic water reservoirs for communities in the Okanagan Valley. With this in mind, there are often special fishing restrictions, including bans against gasoline motors. It is important to check up-to-date fishing regulations.

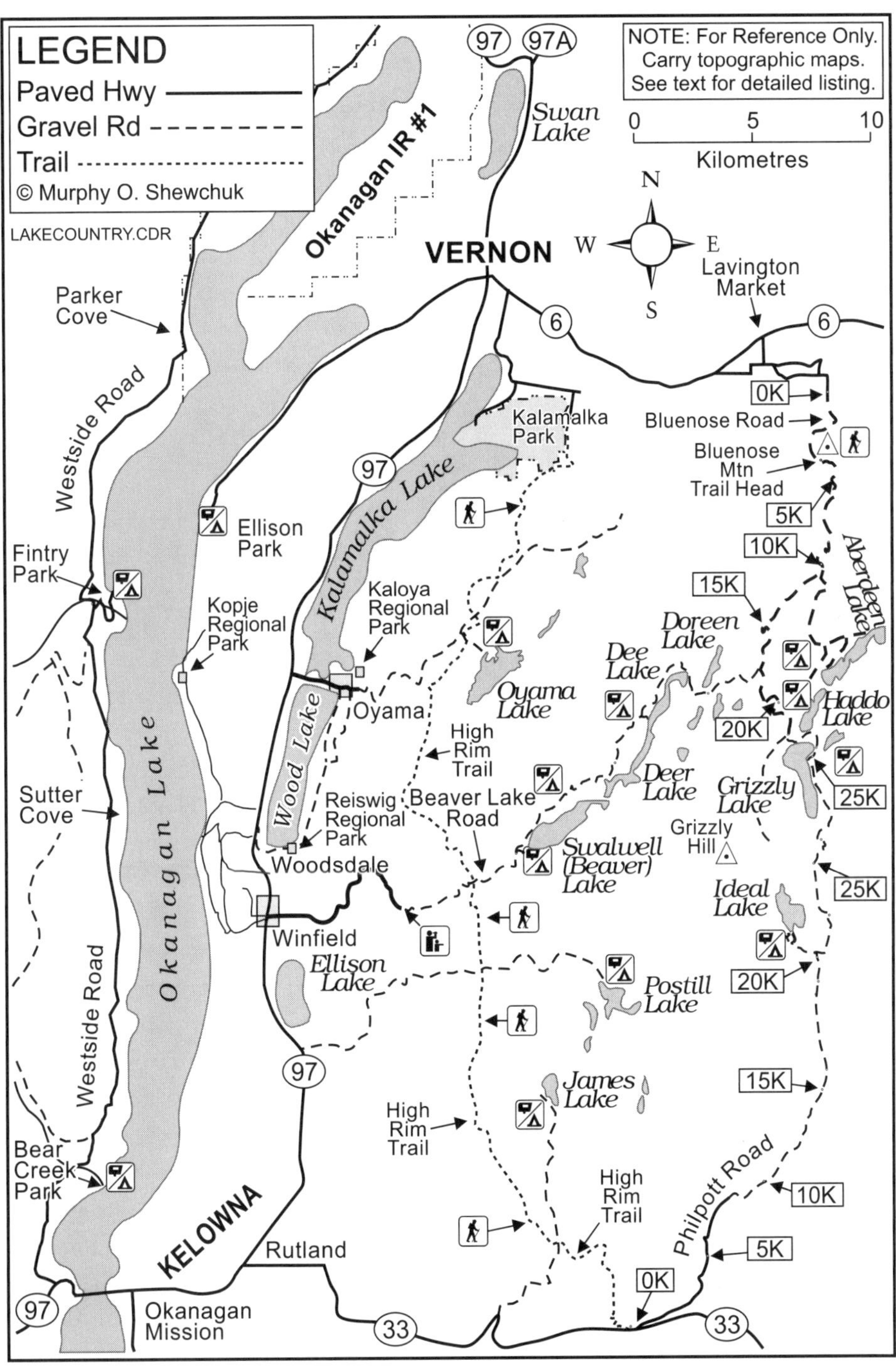

Grizzly Hill / Dee Lakes area.

Rutland Starting Point

In dry weather, two-wheel-drive access is possible from the Rutland area of Kelowna, or from Winfield or Lavington. During the "wet" season, which some Okanagan residents suggest hardly ever happens, a 4x4 may be required to safely negotiate some of the steeper hills.

While there are at least three ways in, the route from Rutland (a community within Kelowna) via Highway 33, appears to have the fewest steep grades on the gravel sections. With the junction of Highway 97 and Highway 33 as your reference, follow Highway 33 eastward as it climbs across the foot of Black Knight Mountain and then follows Mission Creek upstream. Look for Philpott Road, approximately 20.5 kilometres from Highway 97.

High Rim Trail

A sign at the junction of Highway 33 and Philpott Road marks the first of many possible diversions. If you are interested in some serious hiking, you may want to take a close look at the Okanagan Highlands High Rim Trail. The trail starts here at Philpott Road at an elevation of about 860 metres and climbs steadily to about 1,145 metres elevation at Cardinal Creek. It generally stays near the 1,250-metre elevation zone as it meanders some 50 kilometres north across the mountainside before descending to Kalamalka Provincial Park, near Vernon.

On the Bluenose Mountain Trail.

It is important to note that this is a wilderness hiking trail not suited for bicycles or horses. It will require skill, endurance, and proper equipment.

Ideal Lake

If you are going to leave the hiking for another trip, reset your odometer and take Philpott Road north up the Belgo Creek valley. The pavement ends in a gravel pit about 6.5 kilometres from Highway 33. Then you are on Philpott

Forest Service Road as you climb up onto the Okanagan Highlands. The road levels off near the 18K marker at an elevation of about 1,220 metres. The junction just past the 20K marker presents the option to explore Ideal Lake or continue north. Take Ideal Lake FS Road to the left and stay on it for another two kilometres to the Belgo Dam (Ideal Lake) Recreation Site.

Belgo Dam is really three dams on the south end of this 146-hectare lake. Ideal Lake is an excellent family lake that can provide budding anglers with their limit of smaller rainbow trout. The large 30-vehicle recreation site is spread throughout the trees with car-top boat launching available at two of the dams.

Older maps show the road continuing north around the west side of the lake, but when we last tried it, this route was blocked by windfalls.

Grizzly Swamp

If you are interested in continuing north to explore more of the highland lakes surrounding Grizzly Hill, backtrack about 1.5 kilometres to the junction near the 20K marker. The road was marked "Hilda Creek" at one time, but was unmarked in the fall of 2004. It cuts off at right angles from Ideal Lake FS Road and climbs eastward for about half a kilometre before swinging north on what was labelled Philpott Main but may now be Aberdeen-Grizzly FS Road. (At the time of writing, the Forest Service was updating and consolidating their road naming.)

If you reset your odometer at the junction to Ideal Lake, watch for access roads to "Grizzly Swamp" near km 9 and a road across one leg of it at km 10. Although this 190-hectare lake has the telltale marks of a reservoir, including dead trees on the fringe, it also has an excellent fishery for rainbow trout to 45 centimetres.

According to one source, Grizzly Swamp was an excellent source of rainbow trout before it was turned into a reservoir in 1978. In the following years the fishery declined until the lake was completely drained in 1987. Subsequent stocking of Pennask / Beaver rainbows has resulted in a renewed fishery for large trout.

There are no formal recreation sites at Grizzly Swamp, but there are several places where self-contained campers can set up to try the fishing. There is also a recreation site at Specs Lake, about one kilometre north of the crossing.

Beyond Specs Lake, the road crosses the upland valley at the foot of the Grizzly Swamp dam. A major junction about 2.3 kilometres from Specs Lake (km 13.2) provides another opportunity to explore the uplands. Wollaston and Treen lakes lie in separate hollows four to five kilometres to the south. In the past they were both best considered walk-in lakes as the mud holes in the final few hundred metres would swallow most vehicles — even in dry weather.

Haddo Lake

Fortunately the road to Haddo Lake (km 13.4) doesn't fit into the same category. Although narrow in places, it does have a solid bottom and should not pose any serious difficulty for a vehicle with decent clearance. Beyond the turn-off to Haddo Lake, the road winds down to Duteau Creek and then climbs up the west side of the valley. Junctions at km 18.1 and km 18.9 will take you west to Dee Lake and then south past Swalwell (Beaver) Lake to Winfield.

Bluenose Mountain and Lavington

However, before we give you the blow-by-blow description of that route, let's continue 22 kilometres north. If you have been watching the roadside markers, you may have noticed that they are counting down. A junction to the right near the 11K marker presents the opportunity to explore Aberdeen and Nicklen lakes. At 254 hectares, Aberdeen is one of the larger lakes on the uplands. It is reported to produce wild rainbow trout to one kilogram.

The road (marked Aberdeen Lake FS Road) begins a steady descent at the 9K marker. Watch for signs marking the Bluenose Mountain Trail near the 5K marker. If you are interested in a spectacular view of the Lavington area, take a hike up the Bluenose trail. It will take one to two hours' return to navigate the switchback trail to the north peak. Keep left at a junction near the saddle between the peaks and watch your step at the top.

Beyond the Bluenose Mountain Trail parking area, it's about 9.5 km to Henry's Café and the Shell station at the junction of Highway 6 and School Road in Lavington. If you are planning to return to the Highlands, this would be a good place to re-stock your larder and fuel tank.

Dee Lake

Meanwhile, back at the Dee Lake junction, if you choose to wind your way southwest to Winfield, you'll have plenty of opportunity to explore more lakes and recreation sites. Doreen Lake, about four kilometres from the junction (near the 20K marker) is just off the road with good access. Fishing regulations list it as "artificial fly only," so double-check before you drag out the "Ford Fender" or the worms.

Beyond Doreen Lake, the road swings northward around the end of Dee Lake before continuing southwest. If you aren't ready for another night at a recreation site, Dee Lake Wilderness Resort (a.k.a. Dee Lake Lodge) will offer you a few more comforts. Approximately 1.7 kilometres farther south, a side road leads a short distance to the Island Lake recreation site. Another 5.5 kilometres and you should be close to the Beaver Lake recreation site. While there may have been five

Wollaston Lake, southwest of Grizzly Lake. *© Murphy Shewchuk*

(or more) distinct bodies of water in this chain before humans started messing around, the reservoir dams have changed all that. In high water, you can paddle and portage your canoe from the north end of Dee Lake to the south end of Swalwell (Beaver) Lake.

Beaver Lake

Canada must be full of Beaver Lakes. The name must be used darn near as often as Loon, Round, and Green. Fortunately, the map makers seem to have given this lake a more distinctive name. Unfortunately, Swalwell does not seem to have met with the approval of the local gentry and Beaver is the recognized name everywhere except on the map.

Beaver Lake Mountain Resort (a.k.a. Beaver Lake Lodge) is a fishing camp with a difference. The well-built cabins and the colourful playground filled with rambunctious kids are a sharp contrast from the pre-World War II beginnings of this camp. In addition to the "fishing experience," the resort offers canoeing, cycling, and hiking in the summer. There is also winter access to the area from Winfield, and from Christmas to March you can add snowmobiling, cross-country skiing, and snowshoeing to the ice fishing possibilities.

Beaver Lake Road

The road begins a steady descent to Winfield shortly after passing Beaver Lake Lodge. If you look closely, you may notice the "High Rim Trail" markers about three kilometres from the lodge. This is one of several points where the trail crosses regular access roads, making it possible to hike smaller sections of the trail using a two-car system.

Wrinkly Face

Forty-three hectare Wrinkly Face Provincial Park can be reached by a 1.5 hour hike north along the High Rim Trail. The park is at an elevation of 1,360 metres and includes the south-facing cliff made up of ridges of volcanic rock and basalt, topped with rich meadows. The meadows are known to provide habitat for a number of red and blue-listed species of wildflowers, including the red-listed, delicate Needle-leaved Navarretia (Navarretia intertexta), which Judie has personally found there. An added feature is the panoramic view of the Okanagan Valley including Duck Lake and Okanagan Lake.

The cliff was first identified as Wrinkly Face on Feb. 7, 1922 by the federal government from a label on a 1916 topographic map of the "Okanagan Lake Valley." On Feb. 7, 1951, the name was changed to Wrinkly Face Cliff. As a result of recommendations by the Okanagan-Shuswap Land and Resource Management Plan (LRMP), on May 20, 2004 a new provincial park was created to protect this outstanding feature.

Motorized vehicles are not permitted in the park, in order to protect its natural ecosystem. Hikers are encouraged to stay on the established trail through the park.

After another 12 kilometres of brake-burning descent, you should be rolling through the heart of Winfield and approaching Highway 97.

Now, wasn't that more fun than the direct route from Rutland to Winfield — even if it will be difficult to explain to your "significant other" why you spent an extra day and drove an extra 80 kilometres to travel the usual 16. — MS

Additional Information:

Beaver Lake Mountain Resort
6350 Beaver Lake Rd
Winfield, BC V4V 1T5
Tel: (250) 762-2225
E-mail: info@beaverlakeresort.com
Web: www.beaverlakeresort.com

Dee Lake Wilderness Resort
10250 Dee Lake Rd
Winfield, BC V4V 1T5
Tel: (250) 212-2129
E-mail: info@deelakeresort.com
Web: www.deelakeresort.com

CHAPTER 20

High Rim Trail

Statistics	For map, see page 103
Distance:	50 kilometres, Kelowna to Vernon
Travel Time:	Several days, in all; less to hike a section
Condition:	Seasonal; high altitude wilderness hiking trail
Season:	Spring, summer and fall without snowshoes
Topo Maps:	Kelowna 82E/14
	Oyama 82L/3
Communities:	Kelowna, Vernon

The High Rim Trail was conceived and constructed by local volunteer members of the Western Canada Wilderness Committee. It joins up with the Okanagan Highlands Trail, another high elevation wilderness trail. It is a cool, green, clean alternative to spending a hot summer day baking on a beach in the Okanagan Valley bottom.

Although the steepest parts of this highland wilderness hiking trail are at both ends, some sections are recommended for experienced hikers only. It is not suitable for horses, trail bikes, or mountain bikes. There are no formal campsites, garbage cans, or toilets along the trail.

This is a very wild trail cut through dense forest in places, and traversing wet areas in others. It also includes wide-open spaces with excellent panoramic views of the central Okanagan Valley. For the bird watcher or nature photographer, the trail passes through some excellent wildlife habitat representative of the various elevations in BC's southern interior.

Some sections of the High Rim Trail are used fairly regularly, but other sections may be in disrepair, particularly the Postill Lake to Goudie Road section. Be warned that there is no guarantee of regular trail maintenance.

Easy Access

The northern trailhead access is from Vernon off Cosens Bay Road through Kalamalka Provincial Park. Access to the southern part is from Kelowna by turning east off Highway 97 onto Highway 33. Drive through the Rutland area to Philpott Road, 20.5 kilometres east of the junction of Highways 97 and 33. This initial section has been nicknamed "Cardiac Hill," so be warned.

There are eight other points where the trail can be accessed, mainly from secondary gravel roads. This allows you to hike individual sections of the trail rather than the whole 50 kilometres at once. By leaving your vehicle at one of these points, you can hike to the next access point and arrange to be picked up there. This way you don't have to retrace your steps along the trail.

Watch for pink-and-black striped trail ribbons and trail markers high in the trees.

James Lake Road

On a south-to-north basis, another access, 6.7 kilometres north along the James Lake Road, avoids the steep initial climb up the trail from Philpott Road. James Lake Road branches off Highway 33 about 13 kilometres east of Highway 97. The next access north along the trail is 12.1 kilometres along the Postill Lake Road from Highway 97. The Beaver Lake Road out of Winfield presents another access possibility, 12.9 kilometres from Highway 97.

You could also reach it 12.6 kilometres along the Oyama Lake Road from Oyama. There have been reports that the trail is difficult to follow in the clear cuts on the Goudie Plateau, but with a compass and care, observant hikers can make their way through.

Hikers from Oyama and Vernon cross a log bridge on the High Rim Trail. © Mary Bailey

On Beaver Lake Road drive about 12 kilometres to where the trail crosses it. The trail is fairly clear from the Postill Lake Road to the Beaver Lake Road.

Diverse Country

The Okanagan High Rim Trail provides an opportunity to see the valley from a different angle — above. You will cross canyons and creeks over bridges that consist of a large log, with matching handrails. You'll walk through fallen logs that have been separated by only 50-centimetre cuts, which allow you to walk through without scratching your shoulders – but at the same time, discourage passage of ATVs and dirt bikes. You'll also feel your way through waist-high fields of fireweed in clearcut areas and meadows.

At the Philpott Road trailhead on Mission Creek, your starting point is about 860 metres in altitude. There are six stations along the trail, with postings of measurements such as the altitude, kilometres, and name of the station. The first station is Cardinal Creek, and it is about 1,145 metres in altitude. Here a 25-metre-long tree was felled to span the canyon about four metres above the creek. The Cardinal Canyon Bridge is the tree, with a 26-centimetre-wide de-barked walking space, and a handrail attached to one side. It is simple and unsophisticated, but it works.

Kalamalka Provincial Park

Most of the trail north is at the 1,250-metre elevation, until you approach Kalamalka Provincial Park at Vernon, and descend into the valley.

The trail traverses Crown-owned forestland along the rim of the valley, on the eastern fringe of the Thompson Plateau. Some important features of the trail include viewpoints, lakes, Wrinkly Face Cliff, and The Monolith.

On the 50 kilometre section between Philpott Road to Kalamalka Park, you pass through widely diverse habitat, ranging from sagebrush and grasslands to marshes, and from ponderosa pine to lodgepole pine and Engelmann spruce. Bear and deer, cougar and smaller mammals abound, along with the full range of wildflowers, birds, and bushes commonly seen in the interior, and a few that are rarer.

Go Prepared

Before embarking on the High Rim Trail, be sure you are properly equipped with suitable boots and hiking clothes, including a hat. Take water, food, and emergency supplies. Take and understand how to use your map and compass. A GPS is invaluable. And for those dire emergencies, a cellular telephone, with a spare fully charged battery, could be an asset. Most important of all, never hike alone. — JS

CHAPTER 21

Graystokes Provincial Park

Statistics	For map, see page 113 and page 116
Distance:	Approximately 50 kilometres from the junction of Highways 97 and 33 to Graystoke Lake
Travel Time:	Depends on your goal
Condition:	High elevation wilderness park
Season:	All
Topo Maps:	Kelowna, BC 82E/14 Damfino Creek, BC 82E/15
Communities:	Kelowna

This is a new provincial park established on April 18, 2001 when it was identified by the round table negotiating a Land and Resource Management Plan (LRMP) for the Okanagan's and Shuswap's Crown-owned lands.

The 11,958 hectare park was established because it contains a number of biogeoclimatic areas which are representative of the North Okanagan Highlands.

The park includes an extensive complex of swamps, meandering streams, and meadows which provide ideal habitat for moose, mule deer, and white-tailed deer.

There is a ban on use of motorized vehicles, including off-road and all-terrain vehicles except on the few roads, although snowmobiles are permitted during winter months.

Access from Kelowna is off Highway 33, reached from Highway 97 north of Kelowna's downtown area. Follow Highway 33 for 22 kilometres through Rutland's town centre, then the Joe Rich Valley, past the Eight Mile Ranch and Philpott Road to Three Forks Road. Turn left off the highway on Three Forks Road. It is about 28 kilometres to Graystoke Lake. It is advised that you use a vehicle with good clearance as the road can get pretty rough in spots. Topographic maps, a compass, and GPS are also necessary tools when exploring the backcountry.

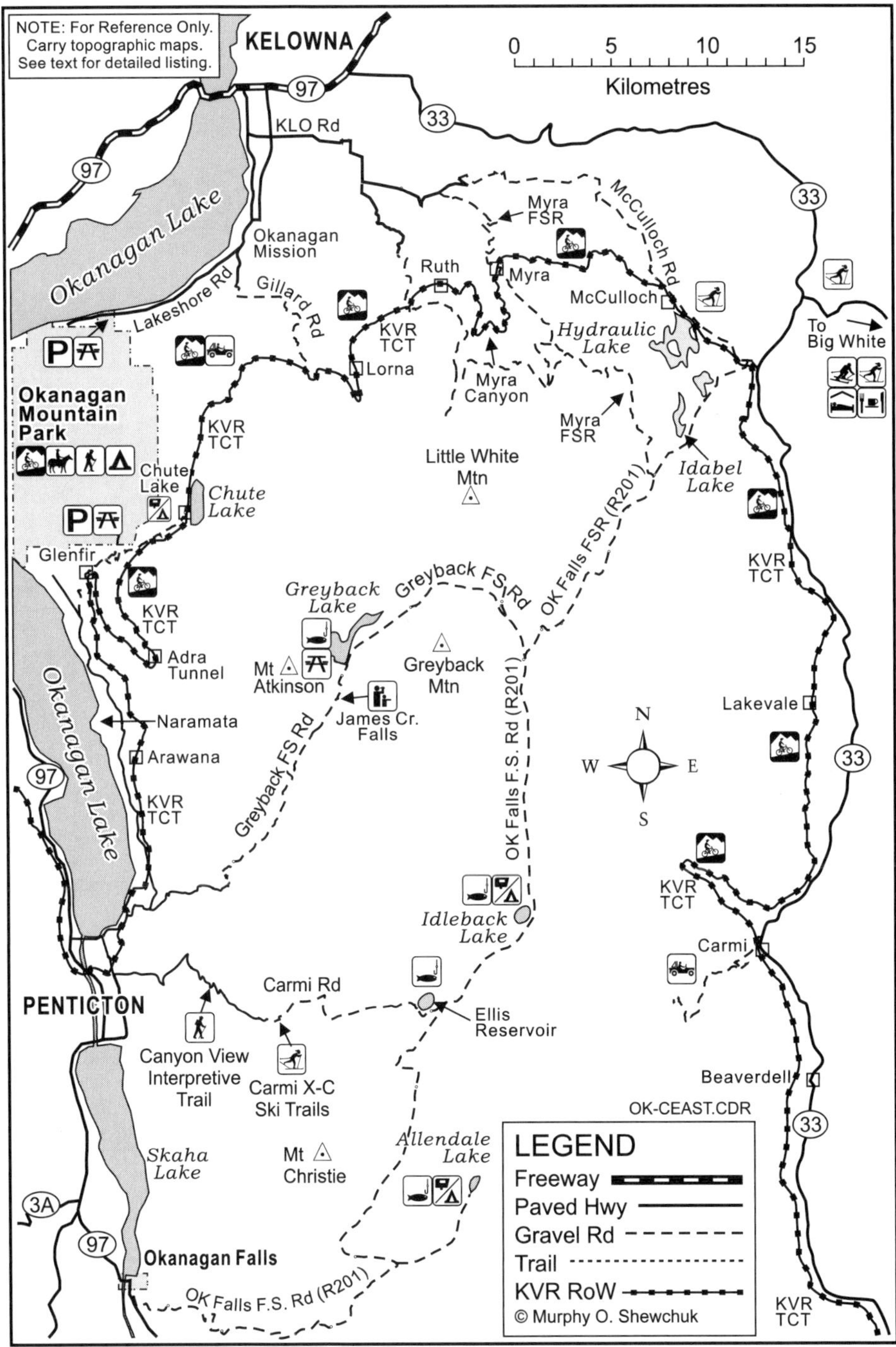

The Okanagan Highland, east of the Okanagan Valley.

Graystokes Provincial Park

Park past the snowmobile chalet near Long Lake and follow the trail up to the top of Jubilee Mountain, which is at an elevation of 2,100 metres; apparently there's a great view. It's about a 10 kilometre round trip, or 24 kilometres if you continue on to Mount Moore as well. Be warned there are swampy spots.

Because of the alpine area this trip accesses, the wildflowers in July are spectacular, but it would be easy to get lost as this is not a well-marked trail. — JS

Additional information:

BC Parks

Web: www.env.gov.bc.ca/bcparks

CHAPTER 22

Big White Ski Resort

Statistics	For map, see page 113 and page 116
Distance:	55 kilometres from Kelowna
Travel Time:	45 minutes to an hour from Kelowna
Condition:	Paved road to resort
Season:	Mid-November to mid-April
Topo Maps:	Christian Valley, BC 82 E/10
Communities:	Kelowna

Big White Ski Resort is both big and white. It's Canada's largest totally ski-in / ski-out resort village with more than 15,000 on-site beds. The village is at an elevation of 1,768 metres and boasts an annual average snowfall of 750 centimetres (24.5 feet!), so it's white from November through April.

Priding itself on dry, light, champagne powder skiing, Big White offers world-class skiing and snowboarding, with a ratio of 18 percent beginner skiing, 54 percent intermediate, 22 percent advanced, and 6 percent extreme.

A recent addition is the $2.5 million TELUS terrain park which includes an Olympic-size 152-metre-long super pipe with 5.2-metre transitional walls that meet FIS World Cup and X Games standards; a standard half-pipe with 3.65-metre transitional walls, 122 metres in length; and a boarder / skier-cross course that can be tuned up

Snow Ghosts. *Photo courtesy of Big White Ski Resort, BC, Canada / Klaus Gretzmacher.*

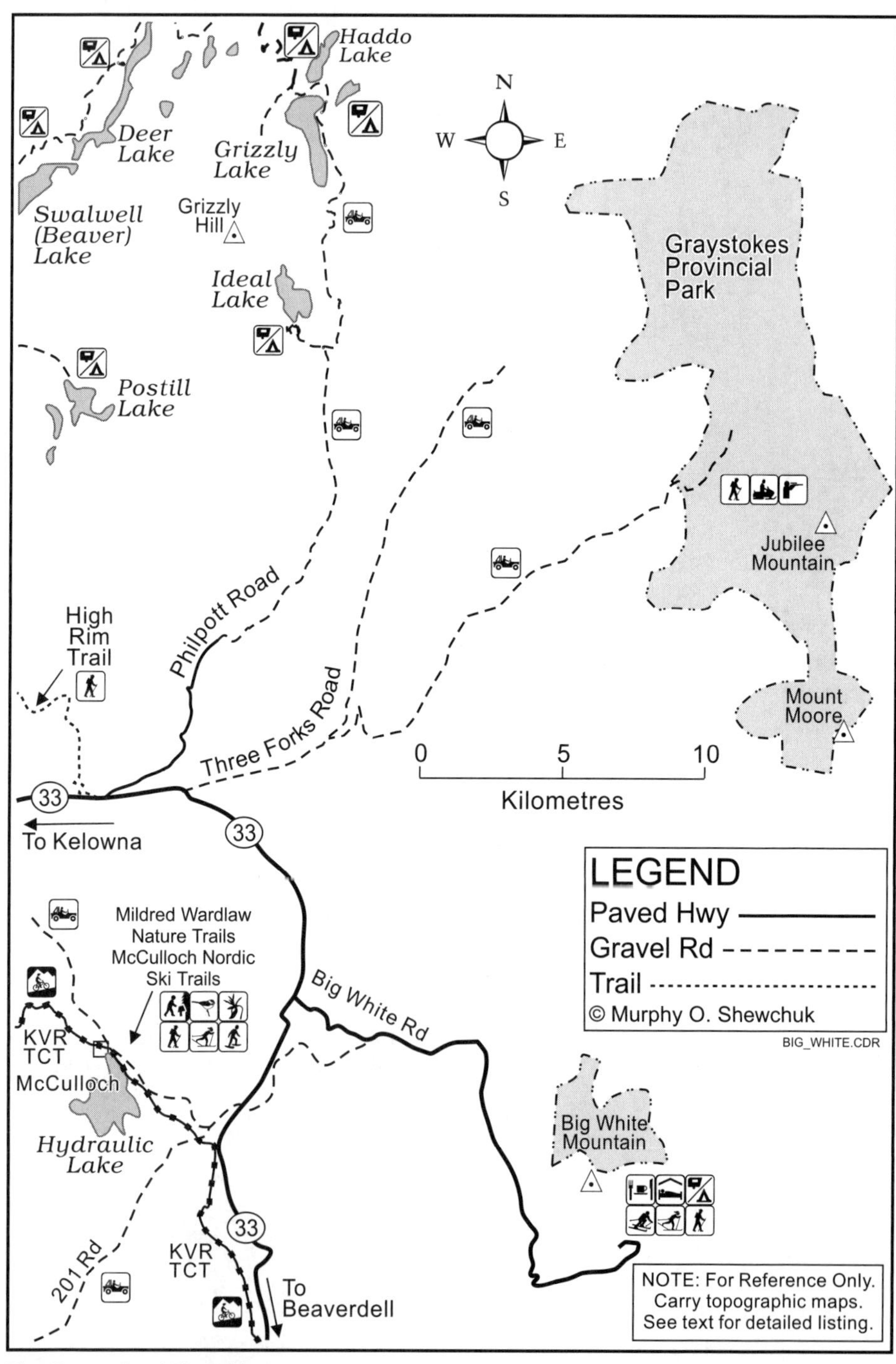

The Graystokes / Big White area

to run regional, national, and World Cup events. It features night lighting and snow-making equipment and is serviced by its own Doppelmayr double chairlift: 231 vertical metres, 596 metres long.

Another recent addition is a $1 million Cliff chair to access Big White's double-black diamond alpine terrain: 152 vertical metres, and almost 670 metres long. Six new runs on Gem Lake add 81 skiable hectares to the 1,115 existing patrolled hectares on the mountain.

In all, there are more than 118 runs, accessed by 16 lifts, including one eight-passenger express gondola, four high-speed quads, one four-passenger beginner chair, a triple chair, three double chairs, one T-bar, a children's magic carpet, a handle tow, and two tube lifts.

In addition to both day and night downhill skiing, there's the Mega Snow Coaster tubing park and 25 kilometres of alpine cross-country trails, an outdoor ice rink, and access to more than 100 kilometres of snowmobiling trails.

Modern Mountain Village

Big White was established in 1963 and has been growing rapidly since 1985. The modern village is mid-mountain and features breathtaking scenery overlooking the Monashee Mountains.

The Village Centre mall is where you'll find the guest services desk, along with the ski school, a gift shop, ski and snowboard shop, ski and snowboard rental and repair facility, Beano's coffee bar, and the QuickPix digital studio.

Big White has an impressive Kid's Centre, first-rate daycare, and children's lessons that have received many accolades from both international media and customers.

Accommodation ranges from hostels to luxurious hotels or condominiums. Most establishments offer either communal or in-suite hot tubs.

The eateries range from pubs to family restaurants to specialty offerings such as sushi, Italian food, or fine dining. Clubs and bars are part of the nightlife, and there is a grocery store and liquor outlet as well.

Get there from Kelowna by driving 32 kilometres along Highway 33 from Highway 97, then turning onto Big White Road at the marked turnoff and travelling a further 24 kilometres. — JS

Additional information:

BC Parks
Web: www.env.gov.bc.ca/bcparks

Big White Ski Resort
PO Box 2039 Stn. R.
Kelowna, BC V1X 4K5
Tel: 1-800-663-2772
Web: www.bigwhite.com

CHAPTER 23

West Kettle Route — Highway 33

Statistics For map, see page 120
Distance: 129 kilometres, Highway 33, Rutland to Rock Creek
Travel Time: Approximately two hours
Condition: Paved throughout, some steep grades
Season: Open year round
Topo Maps: Kelowna 82 E/NW
Penticton 82 E/SE
Grand Forks 82 E/SE
Communities: Kelowna and Rock Creek

Placer gold, fingers of silver, an abandoned railway, and a ski resort that rivals Europe's best may appear to be an unusual combination, but Highway 33 provides access to all of these and much more.

This 129-kilometre-long highway links the central Okanagan with the Boundary Region. On the way, it passes through the West Kettle River valley — a dry, timbered region rich in both scenery and history. This is a quiet part of the province, still largely unspoiled by modern hustle and bustle.

The north end of Highway 33 begins at its junction with Highway 97 in Rutland, a Kelowna community. (Just a word of warning, the next gasoline service station is at Beaverdell, 79 kilometres down the road.) It ends at Rock Creek, at the junction with Crowsnest Highway 3 near the Canada-U.S.A. boundary, 52 kilometres east of Osoyoos.

Follows Mission Creek

Highway 33 passes through the heart of Rutland before beginning a steady southeast climb out of the Okanagan Valley. Rangeland, scrub brush, and pine

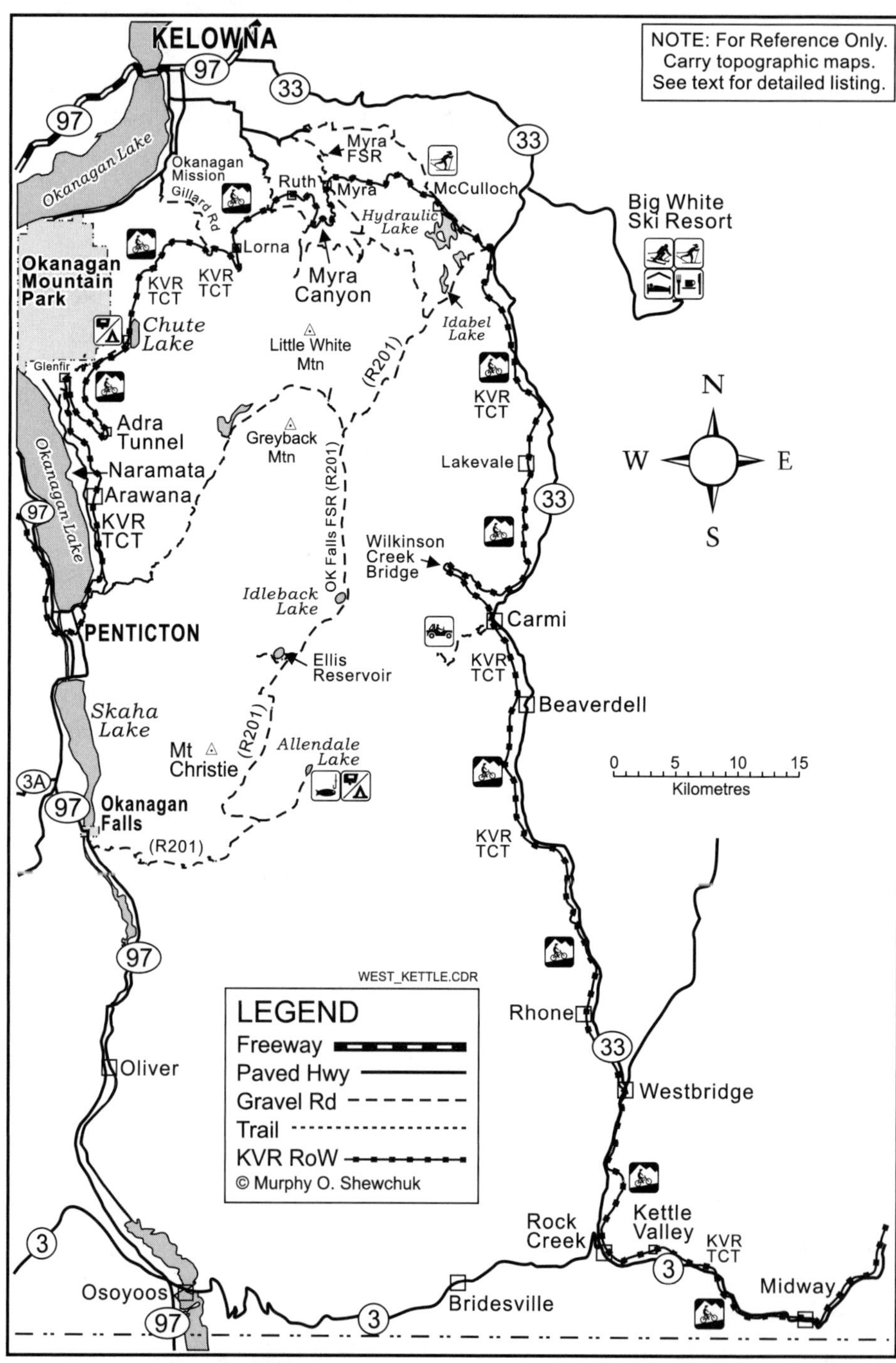

Highway 33 – the West Kettle route.

forests gradually replace the orchards that have helped make the Okanagan Valley famous.

After allowing one last glimpse of the sprawling city below, the road opens to a view of the timber-lined canyon of Mission Creek. Originally named Riviere L'Anse du Sable by the fur traders, Mission Creek was a busy gold placer creek for a short time in the mid-1870s. According to historian N.L. "Bill" Barlee, a man named Dan Gallagher, the last of the old prospectors, eked out a living on the creek until the 1940s.

Approximately 24 kilometres east of Kelowna, the highway crosses Mission Creek and enters the Joe Rich Valley. During the period between the two World Wars, the remarkably rich black soil of the valley supported a lettuce market gardening industry. E.O. MacGinnis started the lettuce farming and made a fortune before everybody got into it, says one old-timer. The Joe Rich Community Centre marks the heart of the former market gardening enclave.

Big White Ski Resort

Less than 10 minutes beyond the Joe Rich Valley community centre, a junction marks the paved road that leads 24 kilometres east and up to Big White Ski Resort. From a start in the early 1960s, Big White has become the closest a westerner can get to a European ski experience. It is a ski village in the mountains, equipped with private chalets, condominium style apartments, and a hotel complex with ski-to-your-door accommodations. A choice of restaurants, discos, lounges, and a grocery store help round out the facilities. Oh yes! Chair and T-bar lifts, numerous downhill runs, plus cross-country ski trails on top of 7.5 metres of average snowfall all help complete the requirements for a memorable ski holiday. See *Big White Ski Resort* for more information.

West Kettle Valley

Just beyond the Big White junction is the Rock Creek—Kelowna Summit. At an elevation of 1,265 meters it marks the divide between the Okanagan and West Kettle drainage basins. The summit also marks a change in the scenery from the narrow valley of Mission and Joe Rich creeks to a broader, drier valley, lightly timbered with aspen and pine.

Five kilometres past the summit, there is another major junction, this time to the right. The well-maintained Okanagan Falls Forest Service Road continues south past Idabel Lake to Okanagan Falls (see *Okanagan Falls FS Road*). A secondary road parallels the former Kettle Valley Railroad bed as far as McCulloch Station before the railbed strikes across the mountainside to Penticton and the

The Kettle River Valley, north of Rock Creek. *© Murphy Shewchuk*

road winds down the mountainside to Kelowna. (See *McCulloch Road* for details.)

Kettle Valley Railway

Under the direction of Chief Engineer Andrew McCulloch, construction of the Kettle Valley Railway (KVR), a Canadian Pacific Railway subsidiary, was begun in the summer of 1910. By the end of 1913, tracks had been laid from Midway in the Boundary region to Mile 83, a short distance west of McCulloch Station. This long-awaited Coast-to-Kootenay railway was finally completed through the Coquihalla Canyon (north of Hope) on July 31, 1916.

Steam buffs will undoubtedly remember the KVR as one of the last bastions of "real" railroading. With speeds that varied from 25 kilometres per hour (15 mph) on the tortuous mountain grades to 90 kilometres per hour (55 mph) on the flat valley floors, steam led the way. The Mikados, the Consolidations, and a few old Ten-Wheelers pulled passengers and freight over some of the most difficult terrain in North America. In its heyday, the steam-driven cylinders powered the eastbound Kettle Valley Express from Vancouver through Hope, Penticton, Rock Creek, Midway and on to Nelson in 23 hours. In another five hours, the "Express" had arrived at Medicine Hat, Alberta.

A large washout permanently closed the Coquihalla section of the KVR in 1959 and the last passenger run from Penticton to Midway took place in 1964. Since then, despite protests and suggestions that the route could be operated as a tourist attraction, the tracks have been removed on the Penticton-Midway section, as well as the Coquihalla and most of the route between Okanagan Falls and Spences Bridge.

Arlington Lakes

Lakevale, the second KVR station southeast of McCulloch summit, was originally named Arlington Lakes in 1915 after the three lakes located three kilometres west of Highway 33. According to one source, it was soon renamed to Lakevale to avoid confusion with a station by the same name on the Esquimalt & Nanaimo (E&N) rail line on Vancouver Island.

If you are interested in fishing, camping, or cycling the KVR from a lakeshore base camp, watch for the "Arlington Lakes" sign on a gravel road on the west side of Highway 33, approximately 57 km south of the junction with Highway 97 in Kelowna. There is a supervised BC Recreation Site on the southernmost of the three lakes with a total of 23 vehicle access camping sites. Camping fees apply from mid-May to the end of October.

The old KVR grade goes through the recreation site. The remains of the water tank foundation are clearly visible and the old railway pump house was still there in June, 2011.

Carmi

Back on Highway 33, about 73 kilometres south of Kelowna, the paved road passes the remnants of the former community of Carmi. There is little left to indicate that, in 1914, Carmi had two hotels, two stores, a shoe shop, a resident policeman and jail, and a railroad hospital. The railway and a gold mine were the source of income in Carmi. When the mine closed in 1936, the town was dealt a severe blow. The closure of the railway finished it off.

Six kilometres south of Carmi, on the outskirts of Beaverdell, the East Beaver Creek Road begins a winding route eastward around Curry Mountain to Christian Valley. If you're interested in a little backcountry exploring, there is a network of logging roads and a dozen recreation sites in the mountains between Beaverdell and Christian Valley. The Boundary Forest District Recreation Map has the details.

There have been silver mines on Wallace Mountain, to the east of Beaverdell, since the 1890s. The first claim was staked on the mountain in 1889, but was apparently allowed to lapse. In 1896, a flurry of staking took place and the West Kettle River soon saw three new communities: Carmi, Beaverton and Rendell. Later Beaverton and Rendell, only a short distance apart, were united under the name of Beaverdell.

Several mines operated profitably during the first half of the twentieth century. The Bell Mine, for instance, produced 350,000 ounces of silver between 1913 and 1936. The Highland Bell Mine, the site of more recent activities, was formed in 1936 through the amalgamation of the Bell and the Highland Lass claims. The silver was in veins "like the fingers on my hand," remembered miner Charlie Pasco of the day in 1945 when he first came to work for the old Highland Bell.

Beaverdell Hotel

The Beaverdell Hotel, built in 1901, was one of the oldest operating hotels in British Columbia, and a museum piece until fire destroyed it in the early morning hours of Monday, March 28, 2011. It was certainly one of the more colourful places to visit in the community, particularly on a Friday or Saturday night. It was also undoubtedly the most photographed attraction along the West Kettle route.

Logging is the main industry of the West Kettle Valley today. The majority of timber harvested is pine and, according to one logger, most of it is hauled by truck to the mill at Midway.

Throughout the length of Highway 33 there are many spots where self-contained recreational vehicles can park for the night. However, the first privately operated roadside campground on the southward journey is the West Kettle Campground, 16 kilometres south of Beaverdell. It is an inviting location, laid out among the pines.

A kilometre or two farther south, a gravel road winds westward to Conkle Lake Provincial Park. See the *Conkle Lake Loop* section for details.

The West Kettle River and the Kettle River join at Westbridge. A secondary road follows the Kettle River northward, past the settlement of Christian Valley, eventually joining Highway 6 near Monashee Pass, east of Lumby.

Kettle River Park

A short drive south of Westbridge lays the Kettle River Provincial Park campground. Set in the pines at a bend on the west bank of the river, this picturesque spot contains 114 campsites, picnic tables, and an opportunity to swim, fish or cycle. The area is also ideal for the artist or photographer. In the summer

Fishing in the Kettle River, near Kettle River Provincial Park. *© Murphy Shewchuk*

months, the nearby irrigated hay fields are lush green, while outside the range of the sprinklers, the foliage is typical of the interior semi-desert plateau country.

Rock Creek

Rock Creek is the southern terminus of Highway 33 and the end of the 129-kilometre drive from Kelowna — plus side trips, of course. Rock Creek was also the best-known placer gold creek in the Boundary region of British Columbia. Discovered in 1859 by Adam Beam, the creek was worked extensively from 1860 to 1864. At the peak of activity, at least 500 miners scoured its gravels. Historians estimate that well over 250,000 ounces of gold — then worth $16 per ounce — were recovered from the creek before the paydirt played out and the miners moved north to the Cariboo. The creek saw limited action again during the recessions of the 1890s and 1930s. With the present price of gold there may again be prospectors searching for the elusive Mother Lode.

Today, Rock Creek is the centre of a busy agricultural community. Patient ewes and prancing lambs liven up the fields in the spring, while the yellow arrow-leaved balsamroot brightens the open slopes.

Midway, 19 kilometres east of Rock Creek on Crowsnest Highway 3, is well worth the visit regardless of your ultimate direction. The Kettle River Museum is an excellent source of information on the history of the Kettle Valley.

The West Kettle Route — Highway 33 — seems left out of the hustle and bustle of today. But, if you are interested in a skiing holiday, or a camping, fishing or backcountry exploring vacation, this may be an advantage — not a disadvantage. — MS

Additional information:

BC Parks
Web: www.env.gov.bc.ca/bcparks

CHAPTER 24

BC's Trans Canada Trail & The Kettle Valley Railway

An Overview

The Historic Kettle Valley Railway

The Kettle Valley Railway (KVR), a subsidiary of the Canadian Pacific Railway (CPR), was constructed between 1910 and 1916 to provide an all-Canadian railway route between the Kootenay Mining Region in the southern interior of British Columbia and the BC coast near Vancouver. The 500-kilometre-long railway commenced at Midway, at the western terminus of the CPR's Columbia and Western Railway. It ran westward across three mountain summits (the Monashee Mountain Range, the Interior Plateau, and the Cascades Mountains), and

Cycling across the Bellevue Trestle on the Trans Canada Trail. © Murphy Shewchuk

through three deep valleys (the Okanagan, the Tulameen and the Coquihalla), to the Fraser River Valley. It established an uninterrupted rail communication from the Kootenays to the Coast by connecting with the CPR mainline in the Fraser River Valley near Hope.

In running westward from Midway, the KVR passed through the mining centres of Beaverdell and Carmi; crossed over the Okanagan Highlands to Penticton in the Okanagan Valley; over Trout Creek Canyon to West Summerland; and then crossed the Thompson Plateau to Princeton in the Similkameen Valley. It then ascended the Tulameen and Otter valleys through Coalmont and Tulameen to Brookmere and Brodie Junction in the North Cascade Mountains. At Brodie, the rail line first branched northwards down the Coldwater River Valley to Merritt where it joined an existing CPR branch line (the Nicola Branch). From Merritt the grade led westward to the CPR mainline at Spences Bridge in the Thompson River Valley. At Brodie, the railway was also built southwards along the Coldwater and Coquihalla Valleys to connect, via the narrow Coquihalla Pass, with the CPR mainline at Odlum in the Fraser River Valley, near Hope. The KVR headquarters was at Penticton in the Okanagan Valley.

The KVR served the Kootenay Mining Region of the southern interior of British Columbia for 60 years, and for much of this time operated both as a freight and passenger railway. The KVR served the Okanagan and Similkameen for another 16 years before freight service ended in 1989 in the face of severe competition from trucking companies. Sections of the railway were abandoned piecemeal as freight traffic declined: the Coquihalla section in 1961, following a severe washout; the Midway to Penticton section, in which the Myra Canyon is located, in 1978; and the last operating section, Penticton to Merritt, in 1990. After each abandonment, the railway tracks, a number of the steel bridges, and most of the ancillary railway structures (stations, section houses, freight sheds, engine houses and turntables, tools sheds, and the telegraph line, etc.) were demolished, and the rail yards and sidings obliterated. Earlier, following the dieselization of the KVR in 1953-54, the coaling towers and almost all of the water tanks from the steam locomotive era were removed. However, a large number of the most significant bridges, tunnels, trestles, rock cuts and embankments, and the railbed, with many short gaps, survive today within the former right-of-way of the 500-kilometre-long railway.

(Adapted with the permission of Parks Canada from the Historic Sites and Monuments Board of Canada report prepared by Robert W. Passfield, Historian, Parks Canada Agency.)

The Trans Canada Trail – History in the Making

Canadians have always been a nation of trail builders. Native peoples used waterways and woodland trails for trade and travel. And our modern nation was forged by a railway ribbon of steel linking the frontier west coast with the great seaports of eastern Canada. Building the Trans-Canada Highway further cemented our national identity, bonding us together into one great country. Following history's path we meet the new breed of trail builders, conserving and preserving our natural grandeur for all Canadians to enjoy — now and beyond tomorrow.

The Trans Canada Trail (TCT) was conceived by the Canada 125 Corporation in 1992. The organization, which is now defunct, was set up to celebrate Canada's 125th year of Confederation. In December of 1992, it was provided with $580,000 in seed funding to help establish the Trans Canada Trail Foundation. Subsequently, the Trails Society of British Columbia (Trails BC) was formed in early 1994 (and became a registered society in 1995). Since then, Trails BC has worked closely with all levels of government, industry, and private landowners to develop the 1,750 kilometres Trans Canada Trail across southern BC.

In BC's southern Interior, the Trans Canada Trail's primary route follows the abandoned rail grades of the Columbia and Western Railway, and the KVR. In the following descriptions, we have chosen to follow the east-to-west direction of the KVR. — MS

For additional information on the KVR, refer to the following books:

Sanford, Barrie. **McCulloch's Wonder, The Story of the Kettle Valley Railway.** West Vancouver: Whitecap Books, 1977.

Sanford, Barrie. **Steel Rails and Iron Men: A Pictorial History of the Kettle Valley Railway.** Vancouver: Whitecap Books, 1990.

Smuin, Joe. **Canadian Pacific's Kettle Valley Railway.** Port Coquitlam, BC, 1997.

Smuin, Joe. **Kettle Valley Railway Mileboards: A Historical field guide to the KVR.** Winnipeg, MB: North Kildonan Publications, 2003.

Turner, Robert D. **Steam on the Kettle Valley Railway: A Heritage Remembered.** Victoria: Sono Nis Press, 1995.

Turner, Robert D. **West of Great Divide, An Illustrated History of the**

Canadian Pacific Railway in British Columbia, 1880-1986. Victoria: Sono Nis Press, 1987.

Williams, Maurice. **Myra's Men: Building the Kettle Valley Railway.** Myra Canyon Trestle Restoration Society, Kelowna, BC, 2008.

For additional information on the Trans Canada Trail, refer to the following books:

Langford, Dan & Sandra. **Cycling the Kettle Valley Railway.** Rocky Mountain Books, Calgary, AB, 1997, 2002, 2010.

Obee, Bruce. **Trans Canada Trail: British Columbia.** Whitecap Books, North Vancouver, BC, 2008.

Cyclists on Myra Canyon Trestle #11. *© Murphy Shewchuk*

CHAPTER 25

The TCT — Midway to Penticton:

The KVR Carmi Subdivision

Statistics	For map, see page 120
Distance:	213 kilometres — Midway to Penticton
Travel Time:	Variable
Condition:	Variable
Season:	With appropriate transportation and clothing, all
Topo Maps:	Greenwood, BC 82 E/2
(East to West)	Osoyoos, BC 82 E/3
	Beaverdell, BC 82 E/6
	Wilkinson Creek, BC 82 E/11
	Kelowna, BC 82 E/14
	Summerland, BC 82 E/12
	Penticton, BC 82 E/5
Communities:	Midway, Rock Creek, Beaverdell, Carmi, Kelowna, Naramata, Penticton

A Critical Period in British Columbia History

The late 1800s and early 1900s were a period of intense railway competition and laying of track in BC's Boundary District. However, it wasn't until June 1910 that construction began on the Kettle Valley Railway under the stewardship of Chief Engineer Andrew McCulloch. The rails reached Beaverdell in July 1912 and Hydraulic Summit (McCulloch Lake) in December 1913. In the meantime, construction started at the Penticton end of the grade in September 1912. By the end of 1913, most grading work was complete. Work continued on the Adra (Spiral) Tunnel and the numerous trestles of the Myra Canyon throughout 1913 and 1914. According to Barrie Sanford in *McCulloch's Wonder: The Story of the Kettle Valley Railway*, "… on October 2, 1914, not far from the 4,178 foot summit of the railway, the last spike on the Penticton-Midway section was driven at West Fork Canyon Creek bridge." The steel rails had met at what is now known as the Pooley Creek Trestle in the heart of the Myra Canyon.

The TCT — Midway to Penticton

Note that the following KVR mileage references were adapted from a CPR grade book dated "6/73."

REFERENCE	DISTANCE (km)	KVR MILEAGE	ELEVATION (metres)
Midway KVR Station	0	0	575
Rock Creek Fairground			
Jim Blaine Memorial Park	17	10.5	600
Rock Creek Station	18.8	11.7	
Kettle River Park Trestle	25	15.5	610
Westbridge	33	20.5	626
Rhone (Cyclists Rest)	40	24.7	650
Bull Creek Canyon	47	29	704
Bull Creek Canyon Trestle (West Kettle River)	48	29.8	705
Taurus Water Tank Foundation	50.7	31.5	716
Tuzo Creek	61.5	38.2	762
Dellwye	63.6	39.5	770
Beaverdell (Welcome Kiosk)	68	43	790
Downtown Beaverdell	69	n/a	787
Carmi Information Kiosk	74.2	46.1	
Carmi Station	74.7	46.4	
Wilkinson Creek Bridge	81.3	50.5	908
Lois Speeder Shed	86.9	54	951
Lakevale Stn – Arlington Lake	98.2	61	1060
Cookson Speeder Shed	113.7	70.6	1182
Road 201 Crossing	118.7	73.8	1240
Summit Lake Gazebo	121.2	75.3	1248
Rec Site	122.2	75.9	1260
McCulloch Lake Resort	122.5	76.1	1260
McCulloch Station	123.1	76.5	1256
Myra Station / Myra FSR	135.2	84	1258
See *Myra Canyon Bypass* for more information.			
Ruth Station	146.8	91.2	
Little White FSR	148	92	
Bellevue Trestle	155	96.3	1226
Lorna Station	156.9	97.5	
Gillard Creek	158.7	98.6	
Gillard FSR	159.4	99	
Lebanon Lake	166.4	103.4	
Old Chute Lake Road	169.2	105.1	1202
Chute Lake Resort	171.4	106.5	1192
Rock Oven # 11	180.3	112	
Elinor Lake FSR	180.6	112.2	
Water Tank Foundation	181.7	112.9	
Adra Tunnel Bypass	182.9	113.7	
Adra Tunnel	183.5	114	
Rock Ovens	186.5	115.9	
Glenfir Loop – Chute Lake Rd	192	119.3	
Naramata (Little) Tunnel	196.3	122	
Arawana water tank (gazebo)	202	125.5	
Hillside Estate Winery	208	129.2	
McCulloch Trestle (Randolph Cr)	209.6	130.2	
Vancouver Place (Penticton)	212.2	131.9	
Vancouver Avenue	212.4	n/a	
TCT Pavilion – Rotary Park	213.2	n/a	

The Trans Canada Trail

Today the Trans Canada Trail follows much the same route as the former KVR, except for a detour around the Pope & Talbot sawmill in the western outskirts of Midway and around some development near Rock Creek. While the grade ascends up the Kettle River Valley between Midway and Rock Creek, the climb is minimal as the trail winds through farms and ranches and along the river. Be prepared to dismount to open and close gates and use caution when crossing cattleguards. Also be prepared for a few rough sections, although plans are underway to clean up the rail grade.

From Rock Creek, the grade swings north up the West Kettle River. The climb increases slightly, occasionally reaching 0.8 percent as it winds through forest parkland and the occasional farm. The valley narrows at Westbridge and forest parkland becomes more predominant. The grade gets a bit steeper, regularly reaching 1.0 percent on the steady climb to Beaverdell.

A couple of missing bridges near Rhone mean that the trail traveller is forced to take Blythe-Rhone Road for about seven kilometres before returning to the rail grade. The distance change is minimal and there is the benefit of being able to take a break at Paul Lautard's cyclist's rest stop. Paul often comes down from his nearby house to greet travellers and fill them in on the history of the region. He has also provided a sizable picnic shelter, toilets, water, and a weatherproof shelter built like a

Bull Creek Canyon, seven kilometres north of Rhone. © *Murphy Shewchuk*

Paul Lautard on his Caboose at his Cyclist's Rest Stop in Rhone. *© Murphy Shewchuk*

caboose. Don't forget to sign the guest book, which Paul uses to figure out how many travellers use the trail.

Bull Creek Canyon, seven kilometres north of the rest stop, is one of the more spectacular canyons on the West Kettle River. In September, the pools are like mirrors, but in May or June, you can hear the roar long before you see the canyon. The rail grade crosses the river on a steel bridge a few hundred metres up from the canyon mouth. Note the "M 29.8" and "16-10-56" marks on the southeast side of the bridge, with the M indicating the mileage out from the Midway KVR Station, and the date perhaps signifying the last time the bridge was painted.

About one kilometre north of the bridge the rail grade becomes a logging road, although there are efforts to limit motorized traffic. Kilometre markers will signal your northward progress as the steady climb continues. On one trip along the route, I cycled from Rock Creek north to Beaverdell and found my energy beginning to flag on the steady straight sections.

Beaverdell

The railway grade disappears under a gravel road and it is difficult to determine where it is on the final approach to Beaverdell. Finally the route is blocked by industrial development. The only way through is to go right (east) on Beaverdell Station Road for a couple hundred metres to a Y-junction marked by a wooden kiosk and information signs. If you are continuing north without a stop in Beaverdell, take the rough road north through the trees. If, however, it is time for a break, follow the pavement as it loops southeast to Highway 33 and into the heart of the community.

There are restaurants, a grocery store, and accommodations in Beaverdell.

Wilkinson Creek Loop

North of Beaverdell, the railway begins a steady one percent grade that takes it through Carmi and up Wilkinson Creek to a yellow steel bridge. The original railway bridge was removed from the site after the rails were lifted in 1979. The gap remained for over 20 years, forcing trail users to make a long detour or ford the creek — a particularly dangerous activity in high water. As part of a major rail-trail improvement project, the bright yellow 24-metre prefabricated steel span was lifted into place by a crane in November 2001.

The rail grade makes a 10 kilometre loop up Wilkinson Creek before returning to the West Kettle River Valley a hundred metres higher than when it started. The grade continues north along the west side of Arlington Mountain, past the Lakevale station and the Arlington Lakes. There is a recreation site on Lower Arlington Lake and the foundation of a large water tank adjacent to the rail grade.

The Cookson speeder or tool shed at Mile 70.6 (km 113.7) is one of the few remaining buildings along the route. It and a similar building near Wilkinson Creek make good photo subjects in the afternoon sun.

Okanagan Highland

The relentless one percent climb continues to Mile 74.7 (km 120.2) before levelling off at Summit Lake. If you are keeping track, this amounts to 50 kilometres of steady climbing (over 450 metres of elevation gain) since the outskirts of Beaverdell — ample reason to consider doing this section in the reverse direction.

The grade is now making a steady arc as it passes north of McCulloch Lake and starts its southward passage to Penticton. However, if you are expecting a downhill coast, you will be disappointed. The elevation difference between Summit Lake and Chute Lake (Mile 106.5 or km 171.4) is a mere 56 metres.

The KVR and the Myra Canyon

The details are covered in the *Myra Canyon* and *Myra Canyon Bypass* section, but here is a quick review. The CPR's KVR carried freight and passengers through the

Myra Canyon from 1915 until passenger service ended in 1964 and the last scheduled train went through the canyon in 1973.

In June 1973, the KVR section in the Myra Canyon, with its wood-frame trestles, tunnels, rock cuts, and awe-inspiring mountainous terrain, was used by the Canadian Broadcasting Corporation (CBC) as a location for filming a segment of Pierre Berton's National Dream television film, which focused on construction of the CPR through the mountains of British Columbia.

The province purchased the rail corridor from the CPR in 1990. The Myra Canyon Trestle Restoration Society, established in 1992, has been instrumental in leading the restoration and maintenance of the corridor and trestles. Hundreds of volunteers have worked to cover the open trestle ties and timbers with boardwalks and to install railings to make the route safe and accessible for all ages and abilities. As a result, the trestles became a cornerstone of the Provincial Rails to Trails network, a vital link along the Trans Canada Trail, as well as a significant tourism asset that attracts as many as 50,000 visitors a year.

Myra-Bellevue Protected Area was established on April 18, 2001 as part of the Okanagan-Shuswap Land and Resource Management Plan (LRMP). In January 2003, the Myra Canyon section (from Mile 84.5 to Mile 90.5) of the Kettle Valley Railway was designated a National Historic Site. In May of 2004, the Protected Area was reclassified as a Provincial Park.

Okanagan Mountain Park Fire

The summer of 2003 was one of BC's worst forest fire seasons in recent history. In mid July, a wild fire raced up the side of Anarchist Mountain near Osoyoos, destroying timber and threatening numerous homes.

Early in the afternoon of July 30, a grass fire broke out at McLure, north of Kamloops, rapidly spreading northward, destroying timber, homes, and businesses in its path. By that time, BC had experienced 921 fires. Of these, 198 were still burning and nine were considered major fires.

While it appears that the McLure Fire was human-caused, nature was already preparing its worst with 40°C weather and steady winds. On August 16, two weeks after the McLure Fire, an early morning lightning strike in Okanagan Mountain Park set off a fire that was to blacken 26,000 hectares and consume 238 homes before it burned itself out. The initial strike occurred south of Kelowna. The prevailing winds quickly carried the resultant fire into the city and up the mountainside. After veering away from the Myra Canyon trestles, the firestorm shifted direction and, on September 3rd, it raced up the super-heated canyons, taking with it 12 wooden trestles and damaging two steel bridges.

Myra Canyon Trestle #10 in 2010. *© Murphy Shewchuk*

On August 26, 2004, just over a year after the infamous lightning strike, Premier Gordon Campbell and Senator Ross Fitzpatrick jointly announced a $13.5-million federal-provincial grant to rebuild the trestles. Work started on Trestle #18 in October 2004. Reconstruction was completed in 2008 and the new trestles were officially opened on June 22, 2008.

Bellevue Trestle

After a convoluted set of loops through the Myra Canyon, the KVR grade crosses Bellevue Creek Canyon over one of the longest bridges in the system. According to Joe Smuin in *Kettle Valley Railway Mileboards,* the 65-metre-high, 238-metre-long (almost 800-foot) steel bridge was constructed in 1946-47, replacing an even longer 270-metre wood frame trestle. Due to the hard work of firefighters and the vagaries of the fire storm, this trestle escaped the Okanagan Mountain Park Fire unscathed.

Unfortunately, the same can't be said for the rest of the rail grade to Chute Lake. While wildflowers, grass, and shrubs are rapidly growing out of the charcoal and ash, the reminder of the summer of 2003 will remain visible for a long time. I don't want to suggest that this should be viewed in a negative way, for the new growth brings back wildlife such as deer that had very little forage in the old-growth environment; and it also opens up panoramic views of the Okanagan Valley.

Chute Lake Resort

Chute Lake Resort barely escaped the conflagration that devoured much of Okanagan Mountain Park. That it still stands to serve trail travellers and those escaping the heat of the valley is a testament to the persistence of the water bomber pilots. Chute Lake also marks the end of the relatively flat crossing of the upland plateau and the beginning of a steep (by railway standards) 44 kilometre descent to Penticton. With much of the grade rated at 2.0 to 2.2 percent, extra engines were needed to climb it and good, working brakes were a definite asset on the way down.

Rock Ovens

The KVR grade initially cuts across the mountainside on a southwest direction before gradually swinging south and then southeast. Signs mark the start of Rock Oven Regional Park approximately nine kilometres from Chute Lake. According to several sources, including Bob Gibbard of nearby Glenfir, these ovens were used by railway construction camp cooks during 1912 and 1913, when baking for the hungry, hardworking crews. The regional park was established to protect these unique relics of our past. Although we only managed to find a few complete ovens on our trips down the KVR, the signs suggest that there are nearly a dozen such locations between Chute Lake and Naramata.

Watch for the foundation of a railway water tank near km 181.7 (Mile 112.9), and the extra wide right-of-way of the passing track of Adra, before reaching the 489-metre (1,604-foot!) Adra Tunnel. The tunnel carves a 217-degree curve within the mountain. A weak spot in the roof near the mid-point is slowly caving in. At last check, the tunnel had been barricaded and a hiking / biking trail bypasses it. The Elinor Lake Road, near km 180.6, can also be used to get down to the next level of the right-of-way.

After the tunnel bypass, the right-of-way now traverses the mountainside in a northwesterly direction. Watch for a wide spot in the grade near km 186.5 just before it enters a rock cut. If you've found the right wide spot, you'll have lots of room to get off the grade and follow a fairly well-used trail up the hillside to several fine rock oven specimens that once served railway construction crews. (If you

Rock ovens such as this fine example are found at several locations between Naramata and Chute Lake. *© Murphy Shewchuk*

bypassed Adra Tunnel via Elinor Lake Road, back-track a few hundred metres up the railway grade.)

Little Tunnel

A little more than five kilometres farther down the hill, the KVR grade makes another switchback loop at Glenfir. There is an opportunity here to take Chute Lake Road up or down the hill. There is also a pit toilet near the trail. Although the scenery has been quite spectacular, it becomes even more so as the grade edges southward along the cliffs. The Naramata (Little) Tunnel, at Mile 122 (km 196.3) is one of the most photographed landmarks on this section of the KVR. The view to the south takes in Naramata, Penticton, Okanagan Lake, and Skaha Lake.

Smethurst Road, approximately 4.5 kilometres south of the tunnel, is your next opportunity to leave the rail grade. If you are interested in a break much closer to the KVR, there is a short trail down to the Hillside Estate Winery at km 208. The grade crosses Naramata Road a few hundred metres later and then winds through the orchards to McCulloch Trestle across Randolph Draw.

McCulloch Trestle

According to Joe Smuin, Randolph Creek was originally spanned by a 91-metre-long timber frame trestle. This was later replaced by a concrete culvert and still later, due to unstable soil, a steel culvert. The steel culvert was removed some time after the trains quit running, leaving a 90 metre wide gap in the grade. In keeping with the traditional railway trestles in this region, the local community decided to build a timber bridge over the valley. Unlike the original heavy timber trestles, which relied on abundant quantities of large timbers, this new bridge was built from glued-laminated Douglas-fir and state-of-the-art technologies, including computer numerically controlled (CNC) machining and high strength connectors. Because the new bridge did not need to carry the weight of a freight train, the new design, coupled with the reduced load, meant much less timber was required.

Downtown Penticton

The Trans Canada Trail (KVR grade) skirts the west side of Mount Munson as it continues through the orchards and vineyards. It enters Vancouver Place at km 212.2 and, a couple hundred metres later, Vancouver Avenue. A right turn down Vancouver Avenue and another right turn on Lakeshore Drive should take you to the Trans Canada Trail pavilion in Rotary Park. If my calculations are correct, you will have travelled approximately 213 kilometres since leaving Midway (plus any diversions.—MS

Additional Information:

BC Parks
Web: www.env.gov.bc.ca/bcparks

Chute Lake Resort
c/o Gary and Doreen Reed
797 Alexander Avenue
Penticton, BC V2A 1E6
Tel: (250) 493-3535
E-mail: info@chutelakeresort.com
Web: www.chutelakeresort.com

Regional District of Central Okanagan
1450 KLO Road
Kelowna, BC
Tel: (250) 763-4918
Fax: (250) 763-0606

E-mail: info@cord.bc.ca
Web: www.regionaldistrict.com

Regional District of Okanagan-Similkameen
101 Martin St
Penticton, BC V2A 5J9
Toll-free:1 877 610-3737
E-mail: info@RDOS.bc.ca
Web: www.rdos.bc.ca

Trails Society of British Columbia
Tel: (604) 737-3188
E-mail: trailsbc@trailsbc.ca
Web: www.trailsbc.ca

Glen Carlson at Myra Canyon Trestle #11. *© Murphy Shewchuk.*

CHAPTER 26

TCT — Penticton to Princeton:

The Princeton Subdivision

Statistics	For map, see page 144 and page 146
Distance:	113 kilometres — Penticton to Princeton.
Travel Time:	Variable
Condition:	Variable
Season:	With appropriate transportation and clothing, all
Topo Maps:	Penticton, BC 82 E/5
(East to West)	Summerland, BC 82 E/12
	Bankier, BC 92 H/9
	Hedley, BC 92 H/8
	Princeton, BC 92 H/7
	Tulameen, BC 92 H/10
	Aspen Grove, BC 92 H/15
Communities:	Penticton, Summerland, Faulder, Princeton, Coalmont, Tulameen and Brookmere

Wars at Home and Abroad

The construction of the rail grade from Penticton to Princeton was one of many skirmishes, most of which were, fortunately, political. Andrew McCulloch and the Kettle Valley Railway (KVR) had difficulties satisfying land owners and communities along the route. The KVR was also competing with the Great Northern Railway (GNR) for the right to lay tracks into Princeton and through the Coquihalla Canyon. To compound the problem, the First World War almost forced a total halt to railway construction.

According to Joe Smuin in *Kettle Valley Railway Mileboards*, the first construction work on the Princeton Subdivision started in Penticton in 1912. Grading work started in Summerland shortly afterward while the famous Trout Creek Trestle was under construction. The Penticton to Osprey Lakes section was approved for operation in September 1914, and Osprey Lakes to Princeton in May 1915. The section from Princeton to Coalmont had already been constructed by the GNR. The tracks finally reached Brookmere in May 1915 as a joint KVR-GNR operation.

The Trans Canada Trail

Note that the following KVR mileage references were adapted from Kettle Valley Railway Mileboards, the Reid-Crowther Report on the KVR, and personal observation. Your actual trip distances will vary somewhat due to detours and distractions.

REFERENCE	DISTANCE (km)	KVR MILEAGE	ELEVATION (metres)
Penticton Waterfront	0	0	345
Trout Creek Trestle (Summerland)	11.8	7.3	
West Summerland	15.3	9.5	
Faulder Road Crossing	25.6	15.9	680
Crump Water Tank base	32.8	20.4	
Trout Creek Bridge	37.7	23.4	850
Kirton	41.4	25.7	
Altamont (Demuth)	44.9	27.9	
Thirsk	52.1	32.4	1038
Trout (Kathleen) Creek Bridge	59.6	37	1080
Princeton-Summerland Rd	61.3	38.1	
Osprey Lake Station	62	38.5	1100
Osprey Lake Trestle	63.3	39.3	1098
Link Lake	65.6	40.8	
Bankier – Three Lakes Store	66.5	41.3	
Princeton-Summerland Rd	66.7	41.4	
Jellicoe Stn B&B	70.6	43.9	
Jellicoe	73.5	45.7	1027
Siwash Creek	77.9	48.4	985
Spukunne Creek Bridge	81.1	50.4	
Erris Tunnel	88	54.7	975
Jura Water Tank (Gazebo)	95.9	59.6	925
Princeton-Summerland Rd	98	60.9	
Separation Lakes	100	62.1	
Princeton-Summerland Rd	100.4	62.4	
Belfort	104.9	65.2	
Princeton-Summerland Rd	107.3	66.7	
Rainbow Lake Road	108.6	67.5	
Old Hedley Road	111.6	69.3	
Tulameen River	112.5	69.9	
Bridge Street - Princeton	113	70.2	638

While there were no World Wars to contend with at the time of writing, there was still much to be settled regarding the exact long-term route of the Trans Canada Trail between downtown Penticton and Faulder.

Using the Trans Canada Trail pavilion at Rotary Park as your starting point, you can follow Lakeshore Drive and Riverside Drive west to Highway 97 (Eckhardt Ave. W.). After crossing the Okanagan River Channel on Highway 97, you can continue north on Highway 97. Or you can leave Highway 97

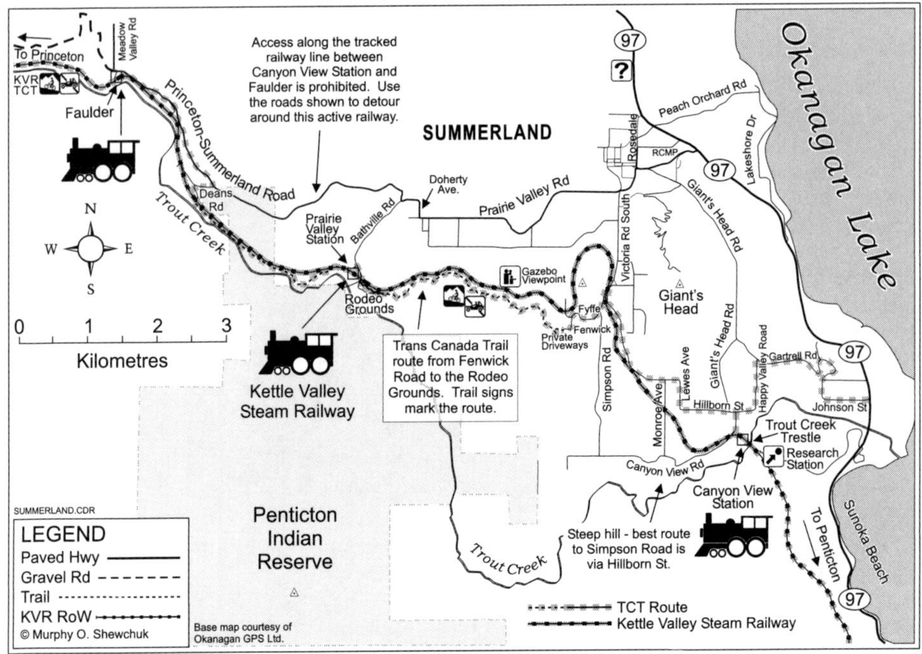

The Kettle Valley Steam Railway route and the Trans Canada Trail through Summerland.

immediately west of the bridge and cycle about one kilometre up West Bench Drive, past the golf driving range, to Moorpark Drive. You can then climb the embankment to the old KVR railbed and continue north approximately 8.5 kilometres to the Trout Creek Trestle.

The Penticton Indian Band permits trail users on the railbed north to Summerland, however they discourage use of the grade south of the West Bench Drive crossing. As a courtesy, groups planning to cycle the route from Penticton to Summerland are asked to notify the Penticton Indian Band at (250) 493-0048.

If you decide to continue north along Highway 97 and Okanagan Lake to Summerland, do not take the road up the hill at the Pacific Agri-Food Research Centre. There isn't any public access to the rail grade or the newly decked and railed Trout Creek Trestle from the research centre. Instead, continue a few hundred metres farther north to the traffic light at Johnson Street and then turn left (west) off Highway 97. Continue up Johnson Street to Fir Avenue, then turn north, following Fir as it becomes Gartrell Road. Follow Gartrell up the hill to Happy Valley Road, then turn south to Hillborn Street and west to Canyon View Road.

If you have made arrangements for a Kettle Valley Steam Train ride, go south on Canyon View Road to the KVR Canyon View Station. (Even if you haven't made arrangements for a trip, this is a good opportunity to view the world-famous Trout Creek Trestle.)

Trout Creek Trestle

The 188-metre-long, 73-metre-high Trout Creek Trestle is considered by many the highest on the KVR and one of the highest in North America. According to Joe Smuin, the original Trout Creek Trestle was approximately 314 metres (1,031 feet) long, but the approaches were filled in when the crossing was rebuilt in 1927 and 1928.

After the CPR quit running, the rails were removed from most of the bridges and trestles on the former KVR. One exception was the Trout Creek Trestle. With the rails still in place, it was difficult to install a walking deck and safety railings. The result was a hazardous crossing that was braved by some and avoided by others until an unfortunate accident on October 15, 2002 prompted the community to launch fundraising efforts to reduce the risks.

The present safety improvements to the Trout Creek Trestle are testament to what a family can do when the community rallies behind it. From the tragic death of Mark Ricciardi — who fell over 60 metres from the bridge to his death in

The Kettle Valley Steam Train winds through the grasslands above Summerland.

© Murphy Shewchuk.

October 2002 — arose a push to make the historic bridge safer so others and their families could be spared such tragedy. It took two years to raise the funds and do the necessary engineering and construction, but on October 15, 2004, the community celebrated the official re-opening of the bridge. Unfortunately, the fundraising didn't cover the complete cost of the work and more money is required to pay all the bills.

Donations for the project can be made at Summerland Municipal Hall, 13211 Henry Ave., Summerland, V0H 1Z0. Tax receipts will be issued for donations over $20.

Cheques should be made payable to the District of Summerland (Trout Creek Trestle / Bridge Project).

The Kettle Valley Steam Train

The Kettle Valley Steam Railway offers a unique one and a half hour journey on one of BC's few remaining fully operational steam railways. Here, passengers can enjoy a tour along a preserved 13-kilometre section of the original KVR. The locomotive, a 1924 Shay steam engine, pulls two 1950's passenger coaches and the Kettle and McCulloch Kars (open air). Friendly, informative guides bring the his-

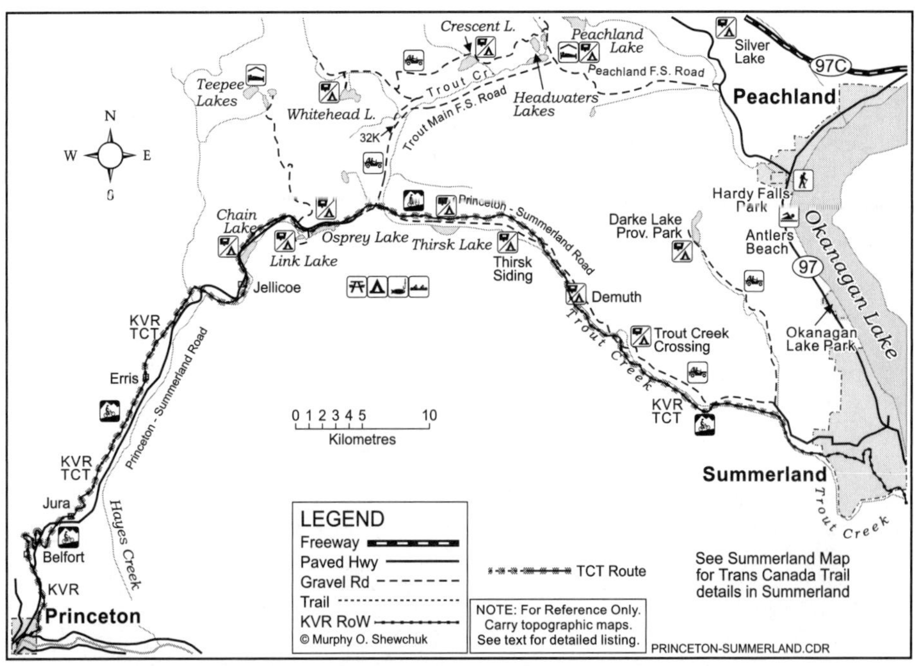

The Trans Canada Trail parallels the Princeton-Summerland Road.

tory of the railway alive as the train rolls along hillsides overlooking beautiful Okanagan orchards and vineyards. At the time of writing, adult round trip fares were $17.00 and one-way fares for cyclists were $14.00. Seniors, students and family rates were also offered. Contact the Kettle Valley Steam Railway (information below) for reservations and up-to-date information.

Summerland's Trout Creek Trestle is one of the highest in North America. © Murphy Shewchuk.

More Options through Summerland

The Summerland Trans Canada Trail Society has constructed a trail that parallels the KVR for much of the distance between the Trout Creek Trestle and Faulder. If you didn't ride the railway to Faulder, then consider taking the trail. Access is off Fenwick Road, approximately three kilometres northwest of the Trout Creek Trestle — as the crow flies. Unfortunately, in mountainous country neither railways nor streets run particularly straight so the route to the trailhead is convoluted to say the least. If you are at Canyon View Station, go north on Canyon View to Hillborn and continue west on Hillborn to Lewes Avenue; north on Lewes to Victoria Road South, west then north to the railway crossing at Simpson Road. Then go south on Simpson Road to Fyffe Road, then west to Fenwick Road and the trailhead.

If you don't want to tackle the new trail, continue north on Victoria Road South to Prairie Valley Road, then west to Doherty Avenue, and north to Bathville Road. After a short jog west on Bathville Road, take the right turn (north) on the Princeton-Summerland Road. After a bit of climbing, it winds westward to Faulder where you can then get on to the KVR grade.

Climbing to Osprey Lake

Faulder marks the end of the steam train run and the start of a steady climb up Trout Creek to the Osprey Lake summit. The elevation difference in the 36-kilometre climb is 420 metres, and the average grade is over one percent with some sections noticeably steeper. The first significant distraction is a new bridge across Trout Creek at KVR Mile 23.4. The CPR removed this 58-metre-long bridge in 1995, before the right-of-way was turned over to the province. Trout Creek Bridge # 2, as it is known locally, was rebuilt early in 2005. Trout Creek Bridge # 3 at Mile 37 was rebuilt a few years later.

There is a recreation site near the highway bridge across Trout Creek, a few hundred metres above the missing (?) railway bridge. If you are equipped for camping, there are several places along the route suitable for a tent, including recreation sites at Thirsk Lake and Link Lake.

Cyclists at the Erris Tunnel. © Murphy Shewchuk

Downhill Grade

From the Osprey Lake summit, the KVR grade begins a rather gentle descent toward Princeton, dropping about 70 metres in the 10 kilometres to Jellicoe. It drops another 100 metres in the next 25 kilometres to Jura — and then the fun (or work, if you are climbing eastward) begins. On the way to Jura, you'll cross over the Spukunne Creek Bridge and through the 91-metre-long Erris Tunnel. The tunnel is wide open to natural light so you shouldn't need your headlamp.

The Jura (Belfort) loops (starting at km 98) provide a railway version of a slalom course across the grassland mountainside on the descent to the Allison Creek valley and Princeton. The rail line descends 287 metres in the 17 kilometres to downtown Princeton – an average of nearly 1.7 percent.

Pusher engines were required on the climb out of the valley in the railway days. Today, it is a welcome coast into town after a long day on the trail. If you are climbing east, it is well worth starting the climb at first light and spending the heat of the afternoon relaxing at your lakeshore campsite. If you are considering camping in Princeton, the Princeton Castle Resort, adjacent to the rail grade near Rainbow Lake Road (km 108.6), is well worth investigating.

Princeton to Brookmere

It is a little over 60 kilometres from Princeton to Brookmere. Along the way the KVR grade passes through Coalmont and Tulameen, both with limited services. As this section is out of the geographical area of this book, we will end our description at Princeton. Coquihalla Trips & Trails (I.S.B.N. 978-1-55041-353-3) covers the KVR from Princeton to Hope and many more routes in the region between Hope, Spences Bridge, Kamloops, and the Okanagan. — MS

Additional Information:

Kettle Valley Steam Railway
PO Box 1288
18404 Bathville Road
Summerland, BC V0H 1Z0
Tel: (250) 494-8422 or 1-877-494-8424
Fax: 1-(250) 494-8452
Reservations: reservations@kettlevalleyrail.org
Information: information@kettlevalleyrail.org
Web: www.kettlevalleyrail.org

Pacific Agri-Food Research Centre
4200 Highway 97
Summerland, BC V0H 1Z0

Penticton & Wine Country Visitor Centre
553 Railway Street
Penticton, BC V2A 8S3
Tel: (250) 493-4055
Fax: (250) 492-6119
Toll free: 1-800-663-5052
Email: visitors@penticton.org
Web: www.tourismpenticton.com

Princeton Castle Resort
5 Mile Road, RR1, S1, C10
Princeton, BC V0X 1W0
Tel: (250) 295-7988
Fax: (250) 295-7208
Toll free: 1-888-228-8881
E-mail: info@castleresort.com
Web: www.castleresort.com

Princeton, Town of
169 Bridge Street
PO Box 670
Princeton, BC V0X 1W0
Tel: (250) 295-3135
Fax: (250) 295-3477
Web: www.town.princeton.bc.ca

Summerland Visitor Info Centre
15600 Highway 97
Box 1075
Summerland, BC V0H 1Z0
Tel: (250) 494-2686
Fax: (250) 494-4039

Trails Society of British Columbia
Tel: (604) 737-3188
E-mail: trailsbc@trailsbc.ca
Web: www.trailsbc.ca

CHAPTER 27

Myra Canyon KVR Corridor

Statistics	For map, see page 158
Distance:	12.8 kilometres, Myra FSR to Little White FSR
Travel Time:	About four hours (hiking) from Myra to Ruth station
Condition:	Trail level and well-maintained
Season:	Spring, summer and fall
Topo Maps:	Kelowna, BC 82 E/14
Communities:	Kelowna

Prior to the devastating Okanagan Mountain Park Forest Fire of 2003, more than 50,000 people from all over the world hiked and cycled through Myra Canyon annually. The historic Kettle Valley Railway (KVR) corridor, just 40 minutes from downtown Kelowna, was a major attraction and a major part of the Trans Canada Trail.

Steel tracks were built through this steep-walled rocky canyon in the early 1900s, and the line was completed in 1914. They were removed in the 1980s because the railway was no longer used. However, the intricate steel and wooden trestles spanning creeks and cuts in the canyon remained behind, a legacy of the visionaries who created this transportation link. Those historic artifacts were considered engineering marvels in their day, and are still absolutely awe-inspiring, with the highest reaching 55 metres from its base to the wooden ties. In all, there are 18 trestles — 16 wooden and two steel — and two tunnels in this 12-kilometre stretch of old railway bed.

In 1993, following both death and injury to persons falling from the trestles, the community formed the Myra Canyon Trestle Restoration Society. The members coordinated an upgrading of the trestle crossings and construction of 1.2-metre-high handrails to prevent people from falling to the rocks far below. Within two years, there were donations of thousands of metres of lumber, an estimated 80,000 nails, and more than 10,000 hours of volunteer labour. Volunteers constructed a

Myra Canyon Trestle #17 in 2010. © Murphy Shewchuk

one-metre-wide board walkway, complete with handrails, across each of the trestles. From corporations to kids, everyone got involved to create a safe walking and cycling corridor at the 1,250-metre elevation of Kelowna's southeast slopes.

Myra-Bellevue Protected Area was established on April 18, 2001 as part of the Okanagan-Shuswap LRMP. In January 2003, the Myra Canyon section (from Mile 84.5 to Mile 90.5) of the KVR was designated a National Historic Site. In May of 2004, the Protected Area was reclassified as a Provincial Park.

Early on Saturday morning, August 16, 2003, a bolt of lightning struck a tree near Squally Point in Okanagan Mountain Park. An extremely dry summer and plenty of fuel, coupled with high winds, quickly spread the fire into the city of Kelowna. It destroyed over 230 homes before spreading up the mountainside to the former KVR right-of-way. On September 3, the Okanagan Mountain Park wildfire entered the Myra Canyon area and, despite heroic efforts by firefighters and water bombers, destroyed 12 wooden trestles and damaged two steel trestles.

Soon after the fire was put out, various politicians announced intentions to rebuild and, on August 26, 2004, Premier Gordon Campbell and Senator Ross Fitzpatrick announced a $13.5-million federal-provincial partnership created to rebuild the historic Myra Canyon trestles. Work began on Trestle #18 in October 2004 and was completed by year-end. The rebuild was completed three years later and the trestles officially reopened in June 2008.

Getting There

Access to the north end of the Myra Trestle section is via Myra Forest Service Road. Although rough in places, the 8.5-kilometre gravel road from McCulloch Road to the rail grade is suitable for two-wheel drive vehicles. The parking lot near the old Myra Station location also includes pit toilets. To reach it from Highway 97 in Kelowna, turn south off that highway onto Gordon Drive at the Capri Hotel, continuing south to KLO Road. Turn east (left) and follow KLO, then McCulloch Road until you reach the turn-off to the Myra Forest Service Road, between crossings of KLO Creek and Hydraulic Creek. (See the *McCulloch Road* section for more information.)

Workers rebuild Trestle #18 in December, 2004.

© Gordon Bazzana

An alternative, but rougher-surfaced route is the Little White Forest Service Road, reached via June Springs Road, which accesses the KVR at the Ruth Station end of Myra Canyon, instead of the Myra Station end. Take the same route from Highway 97, but turn off McCulloch Road just past Gulley Road, onto June Springs. It is 4.6 kilometres along the Little White Forest Service Road to the KVR.

Myra Canyon Trestle and Tunnel Statistics

1	Length 78 m - Height 15 m
2	Length 110 m - Height 15 m
3	Length 82 m - Height 9 m
4	Length 131 m - Height 37 m
5	Length 23 m - Height 3 m
6	Length 220 m - Height 55 m (Steel trestle)
7	Length 71 m - Height 25 m
8	Length 73 m - Height 21 m
9	Length 111 m - Height 48 m (Steel trestle)
10	Length 59 m - Height 9 m
T	Tunnel Length 84 m
11	Length 132 m - Height 24 m
T	Tunnel Length 114 m
12	Length 24 m - Height 10 m
13	Length 87 m - Height 15 m
14	Length 73 m - Height 12 m
15	Length 46 m - Height 12 m
16	Length 27 m - Height 8 m
17	Length 27 m - Height 8 m
18	Length 55 m - Height 10 m

Myra Canyon trestle statistics prepared with information from the Myra Canyon Trestle Restoration Society.

For additional information on the Trans Canada Trail on either side of Myra Canyon, review the *TCT - Midway to Penticton* section. – JS & MS

Additional information:

BC Parks
Web: www.env.gov.bc.ca/bcparks

Myra Canyon Trestle Restoration Society (MCTRS)
PBC Box 611
Kelowna, BC V1Y 3R7
E-mail: mctrs@telus.net
Web: www.myratrestles.com

Trails Society of British Columbia
Tel: (604) 737-3188
E-mail: trailsbc@trailsbc.ca
Web: www.trailsbc.ca

Myra Canyon Trestle #11 in 2008. . *© Murphy Shewchuk*

CHAPTER 28

Myra Canyon Bypass

Statistics	For map, see page 158
Distance:	15 kilometres, Myra FSR to Little White FSR
Travel Time:	2 to 2.5 hours (bicycling) from Myra Station to Little White FSR and the KVR
Condition:	Gravel surface can be rough and muddy in places; some challenging sections.
Season:	Four seasons, with appropriate clothing and transportation
Topo Maps:	Kelowna, BC 82 E/14
Communities:	Kelowna

Trails BC, with the valuable help of the Myra Canyon Restoration Society, began searching for a viable route around the destroyed trestles in September 2003. After a couple of exploratory trips, a route was identified that could use existing logging roads, the South East Kelowna Irrigation District ditch road, and a steep trail through a fireguard.

However, fears of water supply contamination and safety hazards on the steep trail ruled out this route. Research continued during the winter, and in May 2004, an alternative route was identified that was shorter, lower in elevation and below the domestic water ditch. After obtaining permission from the BC Forest Service and BC Parks, work began on the new trail under the supervision of Stacey Harding of the Regional District of Central Okanagan. Wet weather and wet slopes prompted several delays; however, work was completed on a basic trail by October 2004.

The bypass trail uses approximately 12 kilometres of existing logging roads, and three kilometres of newly constructed or rehabilitated road and trail, to complete a 15 kilometre route between the Myra Forest Service Road, and Little White Forest Service Road crossings of the former Kettle Valley Railway grade.

East to west description (Myra Station to Little White FSR crossing):

East to West	Description
0	KVR Grade at Myra Forest Service Road
0.5	Junction: keep right (older road)
2.5	Joel's Knob Viewpoint
2.9	Junction: Grassy cutoff "shortcut" to right
3.8	Junction: Keep right - bottom of grassy shortcut
4.6	85 km marker (from Okanagan Falls via 201 Road)
7.4	Start of newly constructed trail
8.3	Pooley Creek Bridge
9.0	Junction: Little White Forest Service Road
15.0	KVR Grade at Little White FS Road

The bypass route follows Myra Forest Service Road east for a hundred metres before swinging south as it climbs away from the rail grade. Keep right at the first junction, taking an older road that winds nearer the edge of the canyon.

At 2.5 kilometres from the KVR, you should see a short road leading down the hill to the right. Some of the timber was removed from the edge of the cliff during the Okanagan Mountain Park fireguard building. When we first explored the area shortly after the fire was extinguished, a penned marker on a plastic sheet declared this rocky outcrop "Joel's Knob." At the point of publication, we still hadn't determined who Joel was, but the name seemed an appropriate reminder of those who risked their lives to contain the blaze.

Ken Campbell of the Myra Canyon Trestle Restoration Society stands on the cliff-top "Joel's Knob" viewpoint overlooking the KVR. *© Murphy Shewchuk*

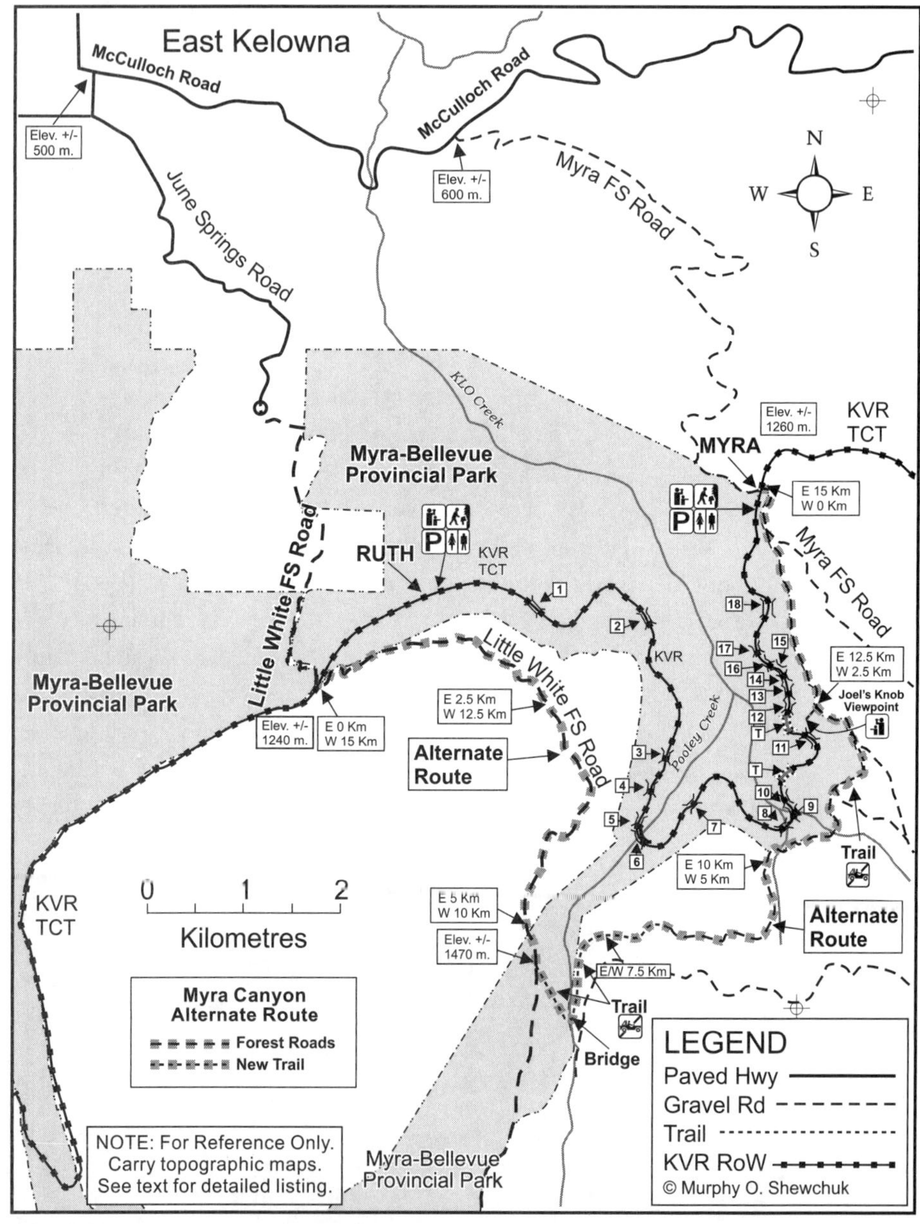

The Myra Canyon Bypass or alternate route.

A junction to the right at km 2.9 leads fairly steeply down the hillside to join up with new roads put in after the fire. If you are packing a load or are concerned about your safety, continue south for about 1.3 kilometres to another junction where you can then follow the forest road down the hill. The shortcut joins the forest road at a wide corner at the foot of the shortcut and then continues down a grade for about 500 metres to KLO Creek.

After crossing KLO Creek, the route begins a steady climb southwest to Pooley Creek. After crossing Pooley Creek, the route climbs through Myra-Bellevue Park to Little White FS Road at km 9.0. Once on the forest road, it is a fairly steep descent (over five percent in places) to the KVR grade.

West to east description (see above for details):

West to East	Description
0	KVR Grade at Little White FS Road
6.0	Junction: Keep left - start new Myra Bypass Trail
6.7	Pooley Creek Bridge
7.6	End of newly constructed trail
10.4	85 km marker (from Okanagan Falls via 201 Road)
11.2	Junction: Keep left - bottom of grassy shortcut
12.1	Junction: Keep left - top of grassy shortcut
12.5	Joel's Knob Viewpoint
14.5	Junction with Myra FS Road – keep left
15.0	KVR Grade at Myra Forest Service Road

Special thanks go to the people of Kelowna for their support in the construction of the bypass trail. They are too many to list here, but details are on the Trails BC website at www.trailsbc.ca. — MS

Note: Information on the bypass route has been kept as the route continues to serve equestrians because of safety issues on the trestles.

Additional Information:

BC Parks
Web: www.env.gov.bc.ca/bcparks

Trails Society of British Columbia
Tel: (604) 737-3188
E-mail: trailsbc@trailsbc.ca
Web: www.trailsbc.ca

CHAPTER 29

Chute Lake Loop

Statistics	For map, see page 87 and page 161
Distance:	77 kilometres, Highway 97, Kelowna to Highway 97, Penticton
Travel Time:	Two to four hours
Condition:	Some rough gravel sections; may be closed in winter
Season:	July through October
Topo Maps:	Kelowna, BC 82 E/14 Summerland, BC 82 E/12
Communities:	Kelowna, Naramata, and Penticton.

The Kettle Valley Railway (KVR) right-of-way, between Gillard Forest Service Road and the south end of Chute Lake, is one of the few sections of the former KVR where, at the time of publication, there were no restrictions against vehicles. Although it has been designated as part of the Trans Canada Trail, logging trucks and industrial equipment are / were using this route, posing a hazard for any unwary self-propelled traveller. The hazards, however, have done little to discourage cyclists from making the long, scenic run from Myra Canyon to Penticton.

Ups and Downs

From a lazy man's perspective, the most enjoyable direction in which to follow the KVR route is from high above Kelowna, down to Penticton, particularly if you are on bicycle. With the junction of Highway 97 (Harvey Avenue) and Pandosy Street as your kilometre 0 reference, follow Pandosy Street south, continuing on as it becomes Lakeshore Road. Leave Lakeshore Road where it makes a right turn at the traffic light at km 9. Follow Chute Lake Road up the hill for 1.7 km, past the Summerhill Pyramid Winery. Just before Chute Lake Road turns sharply to the right, turn left on Upper Mission Drive and continue straight 0.3 km to a "Y" junction. Stay left and you should be on Gillard Forest Service Road.

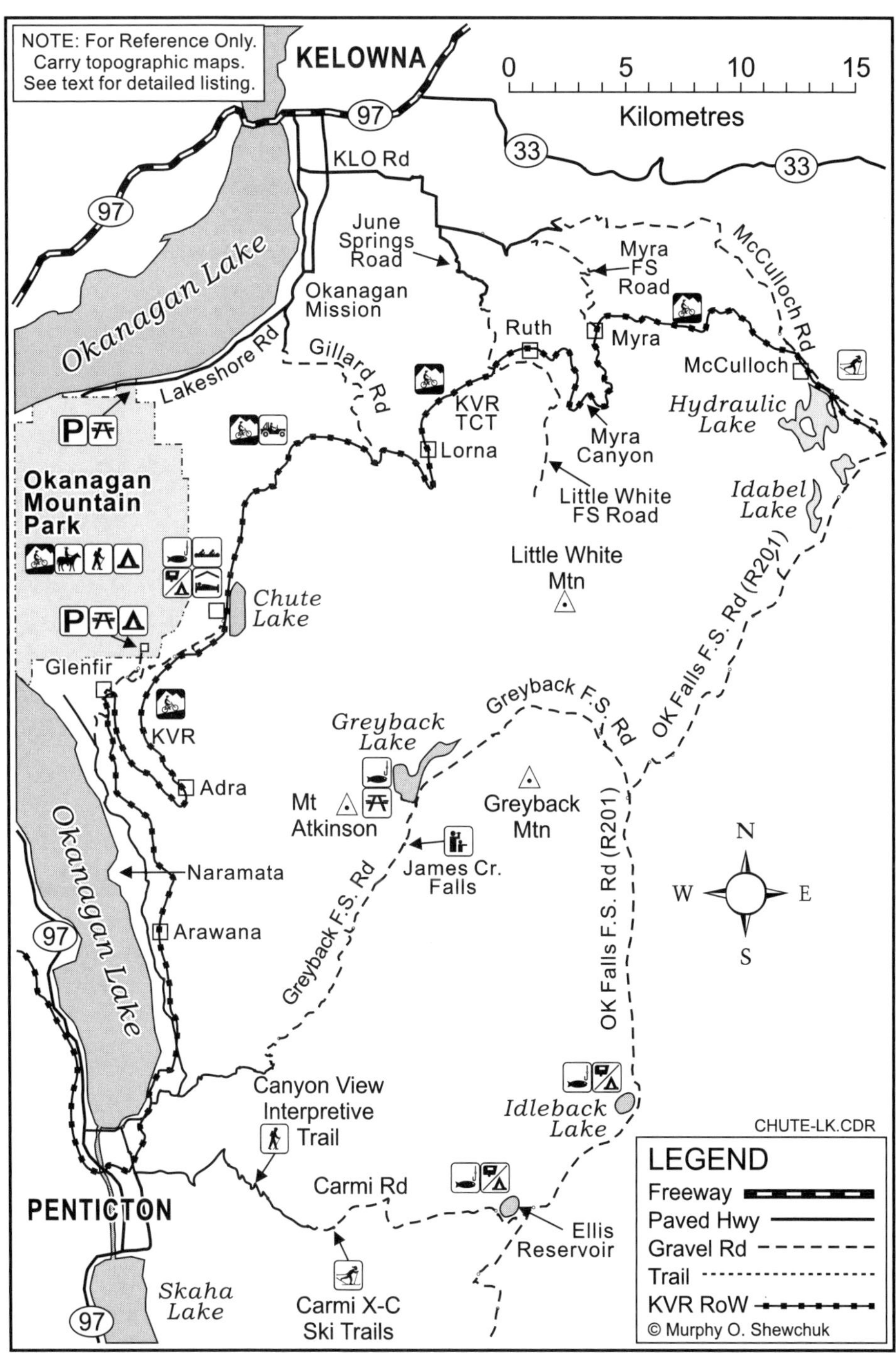

The Okanagan Highlands, east of Okanagan Lake.

Gillard Road is a well-used forest access road. Although steep and dusty, with a few switchback turns and narrow sections thrown in for excitement, it should pose few difficulties in dry weather. As a safety precaution, it might be smart to leave the road to the logging trucks on weekdays.

At one time, the regular route from Kelowna to Chute Lake was via the old Chute Lake Road, but by summer of 1991, it was virtually blocked by a major washout 8.5 kilometres from the junction with Lakeshore Road. A bypass had been chewed around the washout, but it was too steep for two-wheel drive vehicles and many normal 4x4's.

North to Myra Canyon or South to Chute Lake?

After climbing approximately 700 metres in the 8.8 kilometres from Chute Lake Road to the KVR right-of-way, the time comes to make a decision. If you're planning a bicycle trip to Myra Canyon, you can follow the right-of-way east (up the track) for a few hundred metres to a wide, safe parking area near the old Gillard Creek trestle, and begin your cycle touring. If you decide to continue left (east), the tall, curved steel Bellevue Creek trestle is about 4.5 kilometres east of the Gillard Road / KVR junction and is well worth a visit. A network of logging roads and trails lead from the east side of the trestle southeast past Crawford Lake to the 2,137-metre summit of Little White Mountain. It's about 9.5 kilometres from the trestle to the summit. Information on this and other hiking trails in the area can be found in the *Crawford Hiking Trails* section.

If you choose to go right (west) at the Gillard Road / KVR junction you'll begin the nearly level run to Chute Lake before the steady descent to Naramata and Penticton. The right-of-way is fairly narrow with little room to pass a cyclist, let alone a logging truck or another vehicle. Fortunately, visibility is generally good and there are frequent wide sections where you can pull over.

Lebanon Lake, approximately 26 kilometres from downtown Kelowna (Highway 97), is the first major landmark on the now-southward descent. The rough road to the west near the south end of the lake is the continuation of the old Chute Lake Road. If you are riding a mountain bicycle or a 4x4 with excellent clearance, you could consider returning to Kelowna via this route, but there are no guarantees the road will be easy, or even passable.

The KVR right-of-way continues south another 5.9 kilometres to the Chute Lake Resort at the former site of the Chute Lake station. At an elevation of 1,160 metres, Chute Lake can be a cool oasis in a hot Okanagan summer, or a snowmobiling haven in a dry Okanagan winter.

Chute Lake Resort

Gary and Doreen Reed have operated the Chute Lake Resort since 1975, catering to fishermen, hunters, snowmobilers, cross-country skiers, and just plain vacationers who want to get away from the city for a weekend. Chute Lake, says Gary Reed, is high enough and cool enough to keep the rainbow trout firm and tasty year round. To make it easier for the drop-in angler, the resort offers log cabins, lodge accommodation, campsites, and a licensed dining room, if you aren't into cooking. Gasoline- and electric-powered motorboats, canoes, and rowboats as well as fishing tackle are also available.

Bring up the subject of hunting, and Gary Reed will show you snapshots of the # 3 and # 5 record Boone & Crockett whitetail bucks taken in the nearby mountains. According to Gary, George West of Victoria took the # 3 buck (a B&C score of 173) in 1987. Fred Metter, also of Victoria, took the # 5 buck that same year with a B&C score of 169 points. He will also tell you about the herd of elk that is attracting plenty of attention. Moose, once a scarcity this far south, are now thriving in the upland marshes.

The junction at the south end of Chute Lake is a place for decision making. If you are in a vehicle, you can follow the steep, winding gravel road for about 11 kilometres down to Naramata Road and a further 20 kilometres south to downtown Penticton. If you are a cyclist, you can follow the steady grade of the KVR as it snakes down the mountain, passing two tunnels, rock ovens, and spectacular viewpoints before reaching Naramata and Penticton. Cyclist should review the *TCT – Midway to Penticton* section.

Chute Lake Road

With the Chute Lake Lodge as your km 0 reference, Chute Lake Road offers a spectacular descent to Okanagan Lake — with the opportunity to detour into Okanagan Mountain Provincial Park.

The generally winding, downhill run picks up steam near km 4.2 with an excellent view of Okanagan Lake — and a series of tight switchback turns that will keep your foot on the brake. A junction at km 6.1 marks the start of Gemmill Lake Road, a rough gravel road into Okanagan Mountain Park. The parking lot and the Mountain Goat trailhead (to Divide Lake) are about 1.6 kilometres up the road. There is also a picnic site, but no vehicle campground at the trailhead.

Back on Chute Lake Road, there is another access to the KVR right-of-way at Glenfir (km 7.6). The steep descent continues until you reach another junction and pavement at km 10.7. Go left (south) to Naramata and Penticton. The road to the north ends at a ranch gate.

You'll pass several excellent viewpoints along the way as you continue south. Depending on the season, you may find the bird watching or wildflower photography worthwhile. You should see the junction to Smethurst Road near km 17.2 and the route to downtown Naramata at 17.7. As you continue south, your route winds through orchards and vineyards. Watch for the sideroad to Munson Mountain Lookout near km 28.3 — this may also be a good spot to check out the birds and wildflowers.

The road changes names several times before it reaches downtown Penticton, approximately 31 kilometres from Chute Lake. — MS

Additional information:

Chute Lake Resort
c/o Gary and Doreen Reed
797 Alexander Avenue
Penticton, BC V2A 1E6
Tel: (250) 493-3535
E-mail: info@chutelakeresort.com
Web: www.chutelakeresort.com

CHAPTER 30

Okanagan Mountain Provincial Park

Statistics	For map, see page 166
Distance:	20 kilometres, Highway 97, Kelowna to north entrance; 27 kilometres, Highway 97, Penticton to south parking lot
Travel Time:	Approximately one half hour from highway
Season:	South entrance may be closed in winter
Topo Maps:	Peachland, BC 82 E/13 Summerland, BC 82 E/12
Communities:	Kelowna, Peachland, and Penticton

Fire Changed Okanagan Mountain Provincial Park

The Okanagan Mountain Park Fire began with a lightning strike around 01:55 on August 16, 2003 at a point about 200 metres above lake level, just north of Wild Horse Canyon in Okanagan Mountain Provincial Park. The fire was on the east side of Okanagan Lake in an area of the park that is inaccessible by road.

By the time the shifting firestorm had burned itself out in early September, it had destroyed over 230 homes and had scorched 25,912 hectares of mountainside from the lakeshore to well above the former KVR right-of-way. It cost over $33 million to fight the fire. The total cost of the resulting damage will never be known.

One park supervisor likened the devastation to that of an atom bomb explosion with vegetation and topsoil completely wiped out by the fire. In some areas the trails are still visible while in others it is difficult to determine the actual path that had been worn down by hundreds of travellers. Many of the landmarks and facilities are gone, never to be replaced. Others have been rebuilt in the original or new locations. This is a continuing process that will take years to complete.

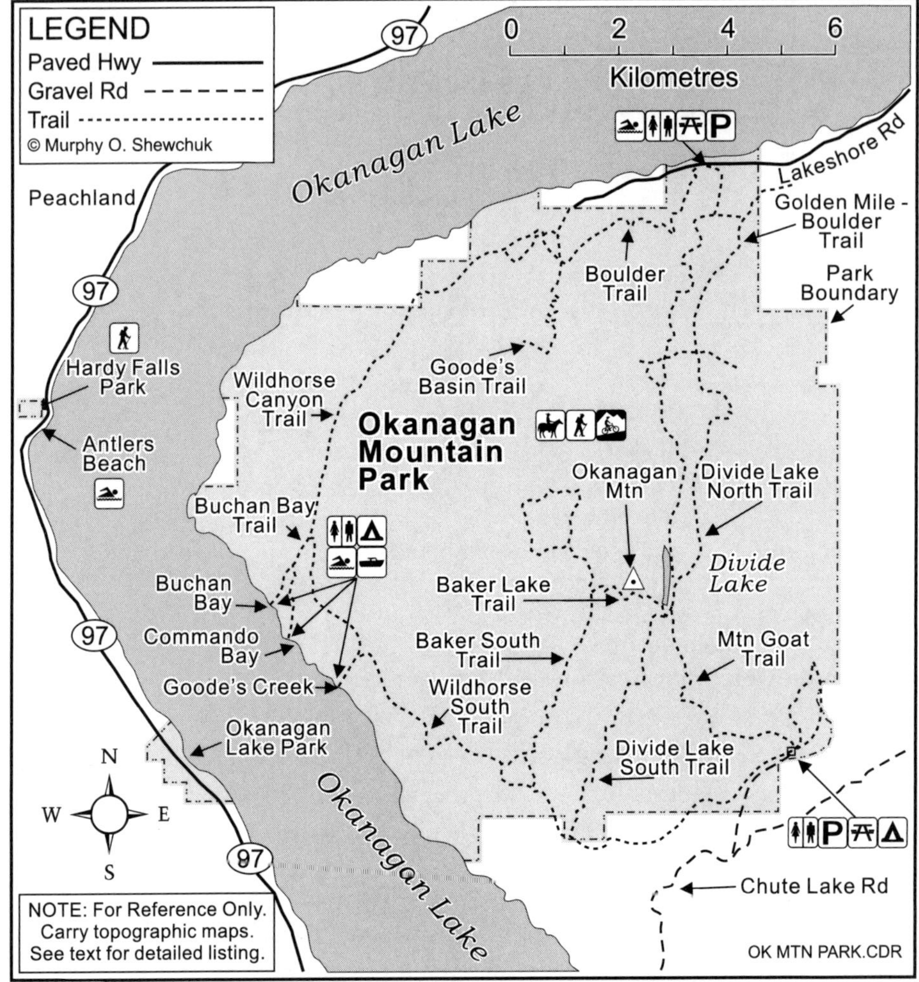

Okanagan Mountain Provincial Park.

Bird Numbers Increasing

Central Okanagan Naturalists, South Okanagan Naturalists and others held a bird count in Okanagan Mountain Park on May 28 & 29, 2011 as part of an ongoing survey of the results of the fire. According to their report, 39 participants on 14 routes counted 104 species in total.

"Birds that do particularly well in post-fire habitats are doing fantastically. House Wren numbers have been increasing yearly and were at 172 this year, compared to an average of 2.6 per year before the 2003 fires. Black-backed Woodpeckers only showed up after the 2003 fires, and were still around (6 counted including a nest). Both species of bluebirds were pretty much absent before the fires, but this year we counted 13 Western and 19 Mountain Bluebirds. Spotted Towhee and Orange-crowned Warbler numbers have tripled, Warbling Vireos and Dusky Flycatchers have doubled, and Song Sparrows have increased tenfold. All that, and no breeding bird species has disappeared from the park-meaning overall species diversity has increased."

Okanagan Mountain Park

Okanagan Mountain Provincial Park offers you a truly diverse spectrum of outdoor pursuits. Because of its large landmass and wide elevation range — 1,200 metres between lakeshore and mountain summit — the park contains a wide variety of ecosystems. A semi-desert wilderness on the lakeshore headlands blends into lush, green forest in the subalpine plateau.

Secluded coves and sandy beaches highlight the park's Okanagan Lake shoreline, with six marine camping areas for overnight boat camping. Inland are the spectacular Wildhorse Canyon and Goode's Creek Canyon, cutting deeply north and south through the mass of Okanagan Mountain. More than 24 kilometres of connecting trails suitable for hiking, mountain biking, and horseback riding lead through the canyons and into four spring-fed mountain lakes located along forested upper mountain ridges. You might see mule deer, elk, and black bear, and even an occasional mountain goat and cougar. Ospreys build massive aeries in the tall trees near Norman, Baker, and Divide lakes.

Established in 1973, after years of lobbying by the Okanagan Similkameen Parks Society, the park encompasses 10,462 hectares of wilderness on Okanagan Mountain and the spectacularly rugged Okanagan Lake foreshore.

Fascinating Cultural Diversity

Okanagan Mountain Provincial Park has a fascinating cultural history as well. Aboriginal pictographs can occasionally be found on canyon walls and outcrops. Early missionaries, fur traders, cattlemen, and miners travelled a series of now overgrown Okanagan Mountain trails more than a century and a half ago. Scattered old homesteads are evidence of the various attempts to settle this rugged landscape. Horse-logging was common up until the 1930s, and cattle are still grazing on the eastern boundary of the park. Despite all the human activity, the park remains a relatively undisturbed wilderness area.

Access from Kelowna and Penticton

The northern boundary of Okanagan Mountain Park can be reached from

Kelowna by turning south off Highway 97 (Harvey Avenue), a few blocks from the floating bridge, onto Pandosy Street (km 0). Pandosy Street soon becomes Lakeshore Road as you follow it through Okanagan Mission, keeping right at the light at the junction of Lakeshore and Chute Lake Road (km 9.0). If you are planning to spend a day or two in the hills, consider stopping for refreshments at the Cedar Creek, St. Hubertus, or Summerhill Estate wineries near km 13. (Visit www.thewinefestivals.com/ for details.)

Divide Lake Trail

Rimrock Road, near km 15, provides access to the start of the Divide Lake trailhead. This 10-kilometre route follows an old microwave site access road to Divide Lake and the peak of Okanagan Mountain. A gate two kilometres up Rimrock Road bars vehicles from using the microwave site access road; and parking is limited to only a few vehicles.

About two kilometres farther along Lakeshore Road is a parking lot and entrance sign to Okanagan Mountain Park. There are toilets, a horse loading ramp, and a swimming beach nearby, but no overnight camping.

Wildhorse Canyon

After passing through several small subdivisions, Lakeshore Road ends at km 20 in a wide cul-de-sac. Parking here is also limited, but a very rough, enticing trail angles down to the lake. A few hundred metres before the end of the road, a sign on the hillside marks the start of the ancient trail into the upper end of Wildhorse Canyon. The trail, though wide and easily navigated on foot or mountain bicycle, climbs steadily, gaining about 200 metres in two kilometres before levelling off. Near the crest it is joined by portions of the Boulder Trail and Goode's Basin Trail. An up-to-date map, available from BC Parks, and topographic maps (see the chapter header for details), are essential before heading too far into the north end of the park.

Okanagan Mountain Park has approximately 25 kilometres of unobstructed shoreline with ready access to the trail system at Buchan Bay, Commando Bay, and Goode's Creek. The south-facing slopes surrounding these access points are classic examples of the dry environment that is said by some to be a northern extension of the Sonoran Desert found overlapping Arizona, California, and northern Mexico. Sagebrush, bunchgrass, prickly-pear cactus, ponderosa pine, and poison ivy eke out an existence wherever moisture gathers. Pacific rattlesnakes are frequently sighted along the trail but, given a wide berth, they tend to be wary of humans.

Commando Bay on the east side of Okanagan Lake. *© Murphy Shewchuk*

Commando Bay

The Commando Bay trail, across the slopes and into the foot of Wildhorse Canyon, is an easy, picturesque walk that is best tackled in early morning before the sun turns the sheltered draws into one big bake-oven. The canyon trail offers a pleasant hike along an old road that was once promoted as the ideal route for a highway from Kelowna to Penticton. Wilderness lovers should be thankful that saner heads prevailed.

Several trails offer access to the southern part of the park from Penticton and Naramata via Naramata Road and Chute Lake Road. With the five-way junction of Main Street, Westminster Avenue, and Front Street in downtown Penticton as km 0, follow Front Street northeast to Vancouver Avenue, then follow the signs to Naramata. Continue past Naramata to Chute Lake Road (km 20), then follow the steeply climbing Chute Lake Road for another five kilometres to the Gemmill Lake Road (marked with a sign to Okanagan Mountain Park). A narrow road winds through the evergreens for another 1.6 km to the South Parking Lot and a tenting campground near Chute Creek.

Mountain Goat Trail

The Mountain Goat Trail, in the southeast sector of Okanagan Mountain Park, is aptly named. It starts off at the south parking lot, accessible from Chute Lake Road, and climbs steadily through semi-open timber to Divide Lake, just east of Okanagan Mountain summit. In keeping with the park's goal to conserve habitat and provide wilderness experience, the trail has no gravelled pathways and no toilets along the way. It is unsuitable for mountain bicycles and a challenge to skilled equestrians on skilled horses. It is a steady climb up and around granite bluffs, over boulders and between trees.

The BC Parks map shows that the trail is 4.7 kilometres long and a three-hour hike one way. Add another half an hour if you're over 40. You can also count on one half to three quarters of that time for the return trip.

Carry Plenty of Drinking Water

Although Divide Lake is a cool, clear spring-fed lake at an elevation of 1,500 metres, carry plenty of water. For a mid-summer jaunt up the Mountain Goat Trail, plan on carrying at least one litre of water per hiker. There are no trustworthy creeks along the way. In fact, most of the creek beds are likely to be bone dry. Because of the wildlife in the park, the water is also likely to be unsafe even if it is flowing.

If you haven't been frightened off by this preamble, you'll probably enjoy the hike. Among the reasons to consider taking it are: the relatively short distance from your vehicle to the heart of the park, plus the opportunity for a cool, private swim in an upland tarn. An additional reason to make the climb is the relatively easy access to Baker and Norman lakes. Both lakes have excellent fishing for pan-sized trout and are downhill from Divide Lake.

From a naturalist's or photographer's perspective, getting there is half the fun. The trail starts off in a damp upland environment with evergreens, alder, and vine maple shading queen's cup, thimbleberry, and star-flowered Solomon's seal. Oregon grape grows profusely at all elevations along the trail. As you climb away from Chute Creek, the growth reflects the drier climate. White bunchberry blossoms, columbine, and lupines add colour to the slopes in early summer, and are later replaced by red bunchberries and black huckleberries that could serve as a dainty addition to your bannock.

Not everyone thinks of food when they hike, poor souls. If scenic views turn you on, you'll be able to catch a few glimpses of Giant's Head Mountain and the south end of Okanagan Lake. But Divide Lake is the real beauty up here. It is a steep-sided mountain crevice filled with cool, clear green water. It will take you about 15 minutes to walk the length of it, skirting the six-metre cliffs that make up the east shore. You may find a few ledges suitable for sunbathing or fishing, but you won't find a beach. You may, however, find a few picnic tables and a pit toilet nearby. — MS

Additional information:

BC Parks
Web: www.env.gov.bc.ca/bcparks

CHAPTER 31

Rose Valley Trails

Statistics	For map, see page 173
Distance:	Varies
Travel Time:	Varies
Condition:	Varies
Season:	Year-round
Topo Maps:	Peachland, BC 82 E/13
Communities:	West Kelowna, Kelowna

A spring-fed pond alive with the call of birds, and a larger water reservoir tucked into the valley in a fold between two hills — these are the two main features of a fairly new park between Kelowna and West Kelowna. There are two types of trails in this 250-hectare Rose Valley Regional Park.

A short, easy walk takes you around the pond which is home to dramatically-coloured yellow-headed blackbirds, red-winged blackbirds, and a great variety of other shorebirds and waterfowl. Take your binoculars, bird book and bug repellent.

From there, the more ambitious hiker can strike off uphill on a trail through the forest toward the ridge that separates the residential area from its water supply. Be prepared: this is an undeveloped wilderness park with trails marked by usage rather than by signs. But there are some tremendous views.

Canoe, Fish, Hike or Bird Watch

To reach the pond, take Westlake Road off Highway 97, west at the traffic lights. Travel 2.9 kilometres up Westlake Road and park in a small parking area to the left off the road. The trail that takes you around the pond begins here, and the longer hike heads up to the ridge from the parking area.

The latter hike is steep, but provides worthwhile views out over Rose Valley Reservoir and later over Okanagan Lake. It's not a loop, so you have to retrace your steps, but there are a number of routes you can chose from.

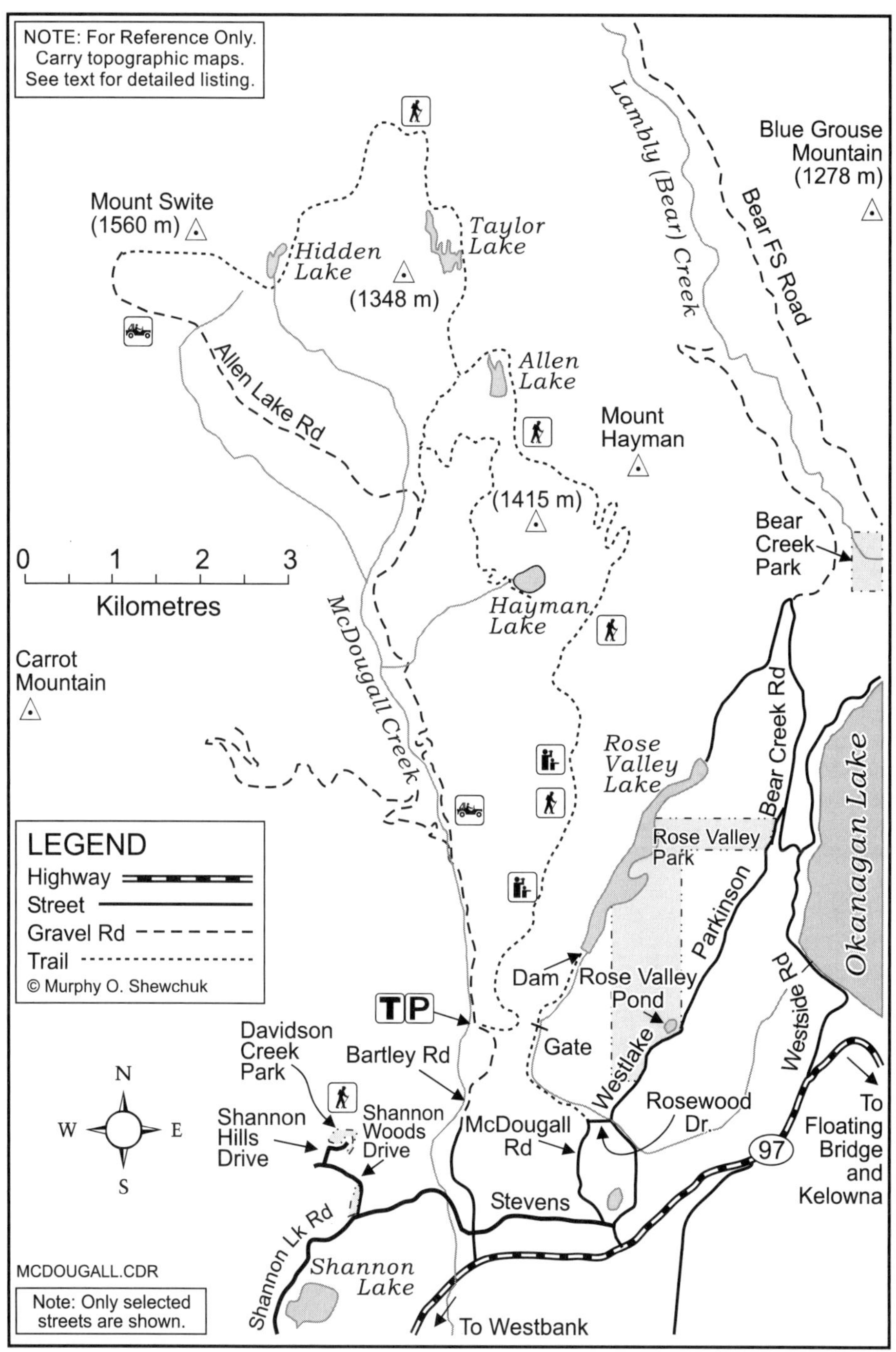

Upland parks and trails in the West Kelowna area.

Aside from the usual jays and swallows, watch for golden eagles, Clark's nutcrackers, and black swifts.

Another trail into the Rose Valley Reservoir watershed begins at the end of West Kelowna Road, west off Westlake Road, immediately past Rose Valley Elementary School, which is adjacent to the pond.

From here, it's not marked, but the old roads to your right take you onto private property (which probably will eventually be developed), while the trails to the left take you into the park. One steep trail takes you down to Rose Valley Reservoir where the variety of waterfowl might include ruddy ducks, loons, buffleheads, and shorebirds.

The upper trails take you along the rocky ridge high above the reservoir. Looking across the lake, notice the volcanic cliffs marked by caves, believed to have been created by large air bubbles in the lava.

To reach the dam at the south end of the lake, take Westlake Road west off Highway 97, then turn left onto Rosewood Drive. Go through a new subdivision to the end of the road. Here, there is a chain across the road. Park off the road and walk in to the dam from here.

There's another gate along the road before you reach the dam. This road provides access for irrigation district staff that maintains the water storage facility — so don't block it. It is an easy two- to three-kilometre walk in to the lake. Remember that this is the source of water for thousands of homes below, so enjoy the area with respect for those users. There's fishing on the lake, but only electric boat motors are permitted.

Lots of History

Rose Valley Reservoir was created when an earth-filled dam was built to block a glacial meltwater channel. The dam was built in 1949 and completed in 1951, when the Lakeview Irrigation District was incorporated. It holds water diverted from Lambly (Bear) Creek in what was once just a spring-fed marshy area between the hills. The project was part of larger efforts to provide local services that would facilitate the re-settlement of World War II veterans.

This goal involved clearing the forest over what is now Lakeview Heights, and subdividing the land into parcels for farming. Water would then be provided to the new settlers under the Veterans' Land Act. The reservoir and park was named after the Rose family, who were Kelowna-area pioneers. Local oral history includes a story about one of the Rose brothers who built a cabin on property in what is now the park, with the intent of settling there with his young bride. However, when the young woman realized how isolated it was, she refused the move. She stuck to her

A hiker pauses to look out over Rose Valley Reservoir. *© Judie Steeves*

guns and never moved to the property.

More recently, in the early 1990s, area residents marshalled forces when the small pond was about to be filled in and developed for housing people, instead of birds. Residents lobbied and raised funds and finally purchased the property containing the little wetland. This special place was the seed of public land from which a larger wilderness park did grow.

The Central Okanagan Regional District now has a Crown lease on the land uphill from the pond, over the ridge that separates it from Rose Valley Reservoir. The District intends to apply for a Crown grant for parkland. There is also a move to extend that parkland to include more of the watershed around Rose Valley Reservoir. — JS

Additional Information:

Regional District of Central Okanagan
1450 KLO Road
Kelowna, BC
Tel: (250) 763-4918
Fax: (250) 763-0606
E-mail: info@cord.bc.ca
Web: www.regionaldistrict.com

CHAPTER 32

McDougall Rim Trail

Statistics	For map, see page 173
Distance:	12-15 kilometres of trail
Travel Time:	Three to five hours
Elev. Gain:	800 metres
Condition:	Varies seasonally
Season:	Spring, summer and fall
Topo Maps:	Peachland, BC 82 E/13
Communities:	Kelowna, West Kelowna

Sweeping views of the Okanagan Valley and of Rose Valley Reservoir, tucked in a fold in the hills far below, are the reward for a steep initial climb on the McDougall Rim Trail. It's more than a 600-metre (2,000-foot) climb in altitude from the trailhead parking area on Bartley Road to where this trail finally levels out. Here you can catch your breath, where the view really is spectacular. That first hour (longer if you have to stop to breathe), offers an excellent example of the open dry hillsides typical of the Okanagan Valley.

During this part of the hike you are vulnerable to quick changes in weather. One spring while hiking the trail, we experienced hot sunshine, a quick shower, a hailstorm, wind and cooler temperatures as we moved higher, until we hit muddy patches of snow.

Although this is the most popular section of the trail, it does continue along the canyon rim above Rose Valley Reservoir and Lambly and McDougall Creeks. On the way, you hike through marshy areas, grassy meadows, heavy timber, and must pass around small ponds and lakes.

Getting There

To reach the trailhead, leave Highway 97 at Bartley Road, about halfway between the communities of Kelowna and Westbank. Drive west past Bylands Nurseries through a gravel mining operation to where you'll see private property signs nailed to trees. Drive slowly and respect the fact that this narrow road winds through a small farming community. The road becomes gravel 1.5 kilometres from the highway. You should reach the trailhead at three kilometres, just past a cattle guard. Park off the road in the small cleared area in the trees and head uphill along the trail.

Breathtaking Views

In spring these hillsides are marked by patches of brassy yellow spring sunflowers, or arrow-leaved balsamroot (Balsamorhiza sagittata). In summer you'll likely find clumps of shy pink bitterroot (Lewisia rediviva), with their delicate tissue-like flowers, clinging to the slopes. When the shimmering summer sun beats down on this southeast-facing hillside, the pines give off a distinctive, pungent odour. As the trail winds around the hill, views of the McDougall Creek canyon far below open up, and there's sometimes a whiff of cool dampness from that very different environment.

The creek below was named after Westbank pioneer John McDougall, who once travelled with the Hudson's Bay Company horse brigades. In *A Bit of Okanagan History,* author Dorothy Hewlett Gellatly writes that McDougall's sons held reputations as excellent and dependable guides and hunters.

Higher up this trail, as you hike along the rocky Westside cliffs, both the terrain and the scenery change. Not far after, the trail levels off and a short diversion to the east leads to a spectacular, panoramic viewpoint. Don't get too close to the edge. In places it's straight down. Below is Rose Valley Lake, Lakeview Irrigation District's water reservoir, trapped in a fold in the hills. Farther off, Okanagan Lake spreads out between higher hills. The floating bridge and City of Kelowna are front and centre. Shift your eyes to the north where Vernon is almost visible, and to the south Rattlesnake Island, across Okanagan Lake, juts out from Okanagan Mountain Park.

A Ferry Captain

The trail continues along the ridge line past a marshy area to an old road which will take you to Hayman Lake. This body of water was named after a pioneer family whose patriarch, Captain Len Hayman, was skipper of the ferry on Okanagan Lake before the floating bridge was built between Westside and Kelowna.

The trail crests at 1,415 metres, topped in the area only by Mount Swite to the northwest, and Carrot Mountain to the west.

The Road Back

The most popular hike is a shortened version, from the trailhead to the spectacular viewpoints at the top of the cliffs over Rose Valley Lake, about a 12-kilometre return hike. Your second option is available when you reach the swampy area: watch for an old road on your left that will take you in to Hayman Lake. From there you can carry on down an old road that's badly washed out, to the main McDougall Creek logging road on which you began your hike. It's about six kilometres, and a further six down the logging road after you turn left for the hike back to your car.

Whichever route you take, you should hike on by the swampy part to reach the rocky cliffs on your right, from where there are panoramic views up and down the valley, over Rose Valley Reservoir and Okanagan Lake. From there your third option is to continue on up the trail about six or seven kilometres, around Allen Lake, then make your way back to the McDougall Creek logging road. Then it's another six or seven kilometers along the logging road to your car. —JS

From the MacDougall Trail you can look out over Rose Valley Reservoir in the foreground, Rose Valley Regional Park adjacent, then Okanagan Lake and the City of Kelowna beyond.

© Judie Steeves

CHAPTER 33

Davidson Creek Trail

Statistics	For map, see page 173
Distance:	A 10-12 kilometre loop
Travel Time:	Two to three hours to the falls and back; double that for the loop
Condition:	Un-maintained, so unpredictable
Season:	Late spring through fall
Topo Maps:	Peachland, BC 82 E/13
Communities:	West Kelowna, Kelowna

The steep trail that criss-crosses Davidson Creek in a ravine above the Shannon Lake area, between West Kelowna and Kelowna, was actually built partly in the undeveloped Davidson Creek regional park, and partly on Crown land, by one of the developers of the subdivision just below it.

Sherwin Goerlitz spent countless hours carving this trail out of the hillside, down which little Davidson Creek tumbles each spring. However, Sherwin has since left the area, and at last check, the trail hadn't been well maintained.

In summer, sections of the little creek sometimes run underground, but even then in the quiet, you can often hear its song.

Because it's in a shadowed ravine, this difficult hike features some of the Okanagan's more unusual wildflowers: the ones that don't have any love for the arid, open slopes so characteristic of this valley.

You'll find the delicate blue clematis, mountain arnica, shooting stars, Hooker's fairybells, Indian paintbrush, and chocolate lilies in spring and early summer. Watch out though: there are also stinging nettles and poison ivy, so keep an eye out for those telltale "leaves of three."

It's about an hour's steep and winding hike up to a 45-metre waterfall where a bench was created for a peaceful moment of contemplation.

This trail makes a nice return hike that will take two to three hours to complete.

Poison Ivy (Rhus radicans) grows on the drier slopes and rocky benches. © Murphy Shewchuk

But you should be in good shape to hike it. Be sure to wear good, sturdy shoes with soles that grip. This is a pebbly path that can be slippery when it's dry.

You can carry on up the trail to an intriguing log into which Sherwin carved steps. This might help you avoid having to climb the steep shale hillside. However, the log is beginning to rot, so it's six of one and half a dozen of the other.

The log is only about half way to the top of the hill, which is a shoulder of Carrot Mountain.

Alternatively, you can hike up along an open ridge, instead of hiking in the ravine, to reach this hilltop. You then turn south to reach the top of this trail, then hike down it to do a loop. Allow at least four hours for the loop.

To Get There

From Highway 97, turn west at Bylands Nursery, onto Bartley Road, then left onto Shannon Lake Road after passing the Lakeview Irrigation District yard.

After crossing a bridge over McDougall Creek, continue along to Shannon Woods Drive and turn right.

You're in a subdivision now and headed toward the hills above it, which is where the Davidson Creek trail begins. Turn right onto Shannon Hills Drive, then left onto Shannon Heights Place and park to begin your loop on the ridge instead of in the ravine. It's about three kilometres from the highway.

There's a paved walkway between two houses that leads to a gravel path that will take you to the ridge north of Davidson Creek.

However, to take the ravine hike up the creek, continue on to the end of the cul de sac on Shannon Heights Place, park and strike off on foot behind the houses to your right, crossing over the cement reservoir at the mouth of the ravine to start your hike.

Be aware: bears and other wildlife are likely in the area.

Shannon Lake

The location of peaceful little Shannon Lake Regional Park is a jealously held secret by many, with its delightful little treed lakeside spot and picnic tables, pathways, and benches.

The Westbank First Nation, part of the Okanagan Nation, knew Shannon Lake as Tenas Lake, meaning small lake. It's now better known after Shannon Marshall, a Westbank pioneer. Shannon Lake's first school opened in 1897 and a post office called Westbank opened on May 1, 1902 on the west side of Shannon Lake.

The lake provides water for Marshall and Marlow springs via underground aquifers downslope. These aquifers were also the source of water for the Tsinstikeptum First Nation in the early twentieth century.

The south end of Shannon Lake was established as a Regional Park in 1977. The entrance is farther south along Shannon Lake Road past the Shannon Lake Golf Course. Watch for a parking area and sign on your left just past the lake. Park and walk in to the park itself. — JS

Additional Information:

Regional District of Central Okanagan
1450 KLO Road
Kelowna, BC
Tel: (250) 763-4918
Fax: (250) 763-0606
E-mail: info@cord.bc.ca
Web: www.regionaldistrict.com

CHAPTER 34

Kalamoir Regional Park Trails

Statistics: For map, see page 183
Distance: More than 5 kilometres of trails along Okanagan Lake
Time: Depends where you enter and exit the trails
Condition: Good
Season: Closed in winter
Topo Maps: Peachland, BC 82 E/13
Communities: West Kelowna, Kelowna

This long, narrow, 27.6-hectare lakefront park features a typical sagebrush-dotted Okanagan hillside in its natural state, except for a fine network of trails which will take you from near the Okanagan Lake Floating Bridge to Sunnyside, a West Kelowna residential neighbourhood. Kalamoir is a Central Okanagan Regional District Park that offers spectacular views of Okanagan Lake over its entire length.

The park drops about 200 metres in elevation from the top of the rocky hillside to the lake, so the trails are steep in places. However, the hiking is neither long nor difficult. You should be able to circle the park in less than two hours.

Through Lakeview Heights

Access is to the south along Campbell Road, just before the Okanagan Lake Floating Bridge, off Highway 97, to Casa Loma Resort. Park there and follow the signs to the beginning of the trail. Alternatively, you can access the park from farther south along Highway 97, by turning east at the Boucherie Road intersection, travelling up the hill 1.9 kilometres to Anders Road where you turn left, then right on Thacker Drive, just over a half kilometre along. The first road to the left is Collens Hill Road which will take you down into the park, 3.9 kilometres in all from the highway. It's about another half kilometre down to the lake.

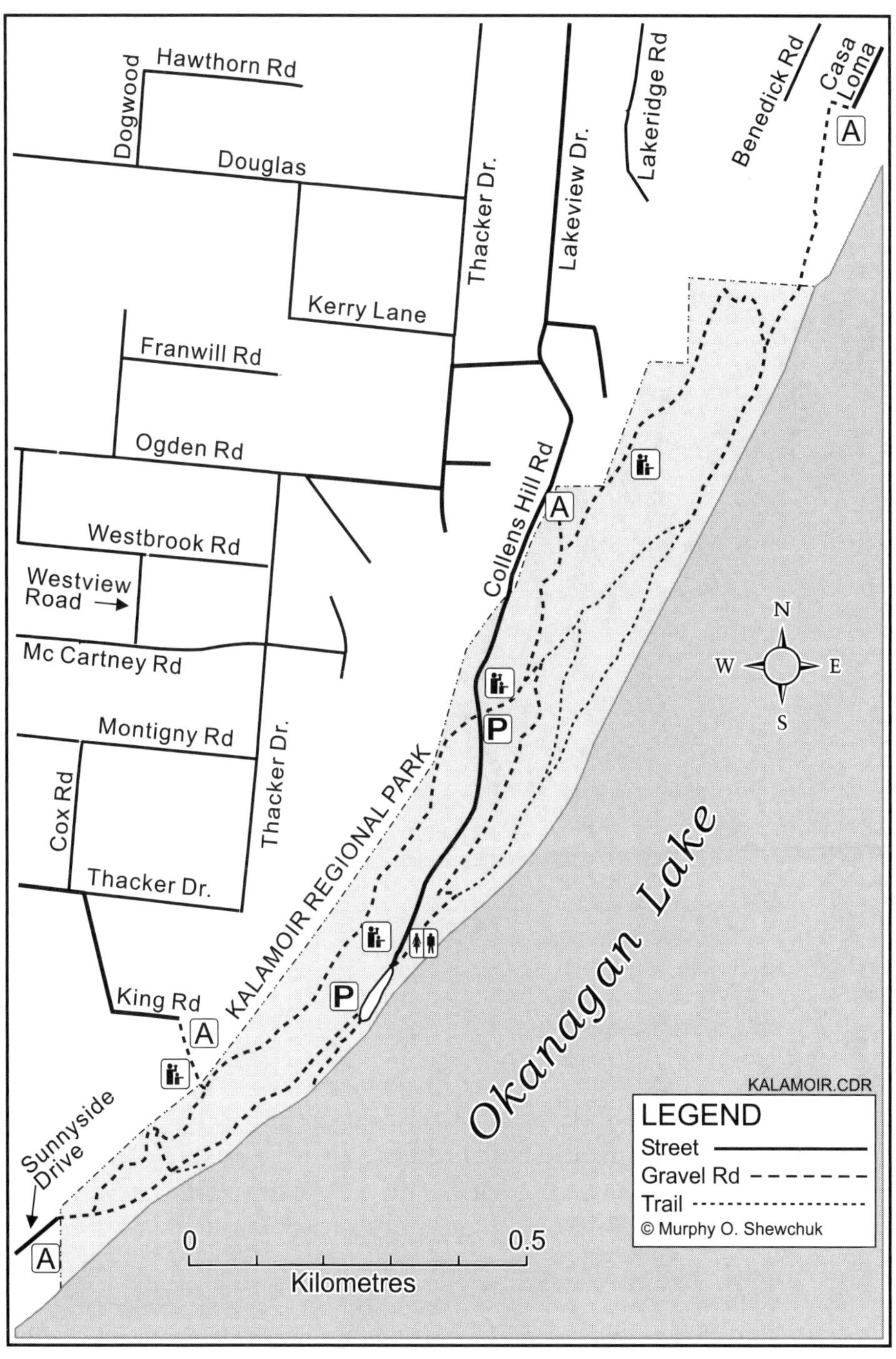

Kalamoir Regional Park and the southeast Westbank area.

Kalamoir Park provides a scenic loop trail. *© Judie Steeves*

Parking is available off Collens Hill Road at either the upper or lower parking areas, with lake views from each. Trails begin at each of the parking areas, heading both north and south along the length of the park, ending either at Sunnyside Drive in the south, or Casa Loma in the north. However, instead of leaving the park, you can loop back, taking the upper or lower series of trails instead of the same one you first took, so you don't have to retrace your steps. There are also access points, without much parking, at the end of Sunnyside Drive and also at the end of King Road off Thacker Drive, where there's also a viewpoint.

Classic Okanagan Habitat

Bright yellow patches of arrow-leaved balsamroot or spring sunflowers herald the arrival of early spring in the Okanagan, cheering the hillsides with their beautiful blooms. Hidden among them, the careful observer will find single stems of graceful yellowbells, a native plant belonging to the fritillaria family. In summer, the delicate mariposa lilies dot these hillsides, often protected among patches of spiny prickly pear cactus, which literally seem to jump from the ground with the sole purpose of planting themselves in your bare calf. In June or July, the prickly pear sport delicate, tissue-like yellow flowers that belie the spines underneath. In fall, red sweeps of sumac brighten the brown grass hillsides as their leaves change colour with each cold night.

Many of the trails are exposed, so it's a relief during summer days when one occasionally branches off down to a rocky beach where you can cool off in the lake. A bit of local history sits at the corner of Boucherie Road and Sunnyside. Here Quails' Gate Estate Winery's boutique and tasting room is housed in the historic Allison family log homestead, which was called Sunnyside. The structure dates from 1873 when John and Susan Allison became the first European settlers on the west side of Okanagan Lake.

Just south on Boucherie Road, then right on Mission Hill Road, is the Mission Hill Family Estate Winery, famous for its award-winning Chardonnay and its recent $40 million reconstruction. Today, the breathtaking hilltop structure boasts a panoramic view, terrace restaurant, tasting room, outdoor amphitheatre, and lush gardens. Wines are aged in an awesome cellar, located under the bell tower and carved out from the cliff's solid rock.

North along Boucherie Road is Volcanic Hills Estate Winery plus Little Straw Vineyards, on Ourtoland Road, and Mount Boucherie Estate Winery, on Douglas Road on the other side of Boucherie. — JS

Additional Information:

Regional District of Central Okanagan
1450 KLO Road
Kelowna, BC
Tel: (250) 763-4918
Fax: (250) 763-0606
E-mail: info@cord.bc.ca
Web: www.regionaldistrict.com

CHAPTER 35

Gellatly Nut Farm and Gellatly Heritage Regional Parks

Statistics For map, see page 187
Condition: Well-maintained
Season: All
Communities: West Kelowna

The recreational opportunities in the historic Gellatly Nut Farm Regional Park take you back in time, to when the pace of life was much slower, transportation more difficult, tools more primitive, and people were closer to the land that provided their food.

Gellatly is a four-hectare working heritage nut farm which celebrated its 100th anniversary in 2005. For the occasion, the Gellatly Nut Farm Society (GNFS), the group of volunteers that operate the farm for the regional district, held a party in early fall and opened the park permanently, after three years of preparing the site for public use.

Gellatly was purchased in 2002 through a grassroots community effort that initially generated $240,000 to reserve the property for future purchase. The final full price was $3.4 million, which was raised by the regional district, with help from the GNFS.

Along with the heritage buildings and ancient nut trees, there's a 150-metre pebble beach, washrooms and caretaker's home.

Visitors can come in the fall to harvest nuts from the ground, to wander through the magical old trees in the nut orchard, or use the beach and walk the shoreline. Over time, a museum featuring artifacts related to the nut orchard and century-old Okanagan farm will be established in some of the buildings on site.

At Gellatly Nut Farm there is a barn that was constructed of hand-hewn, squared poplar logs, each dovetailed at the corners. There is also a farmhouse built of the same hand-hewn, squared poplar logs, but arranged vertically and hidden

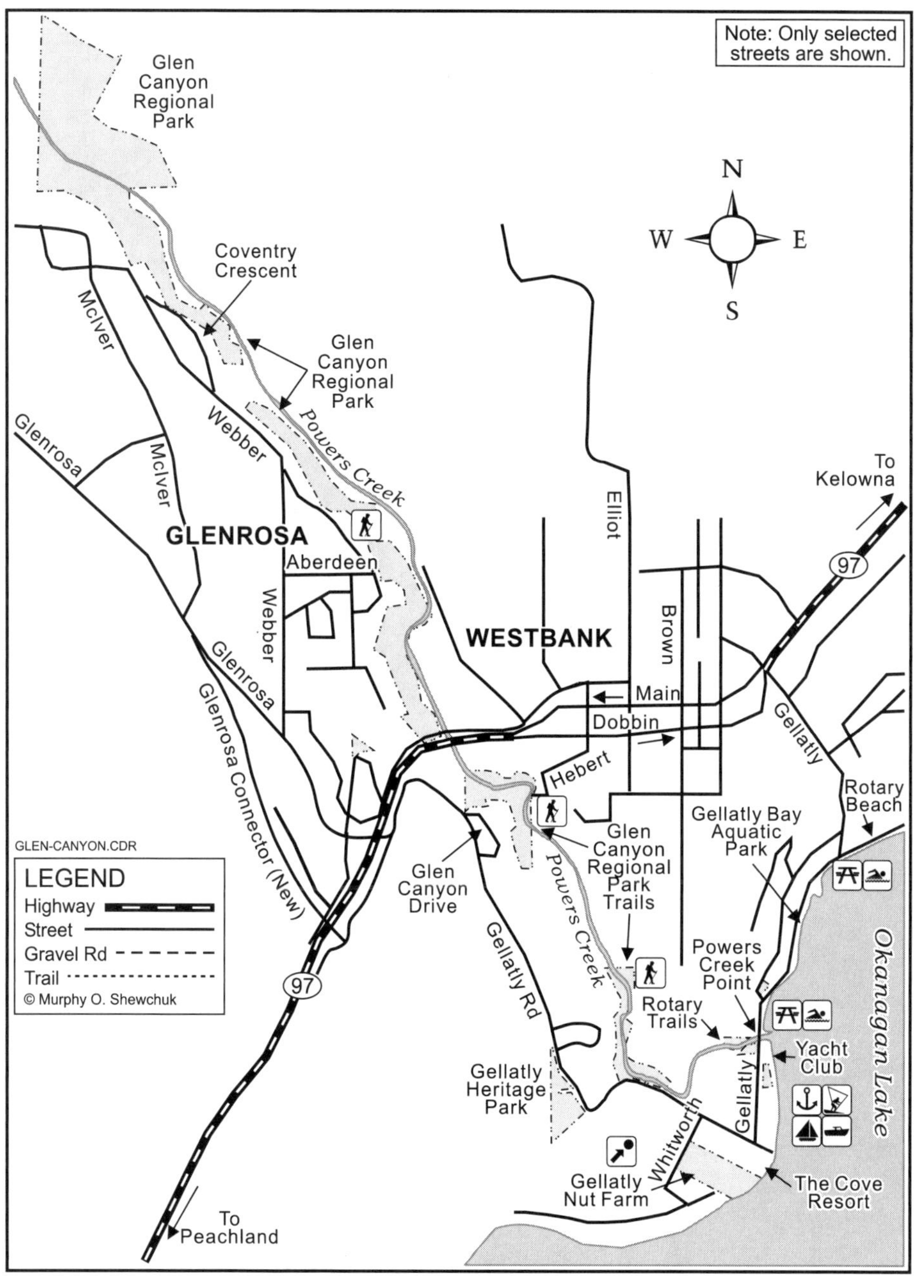

The Powers Creek area of Westbank

The old Gellatly nut drying shed. *© Gordon Bazzana*

under years of plaster.

There's a 1920s-era shed or changing house on the beach, a circa 1944 home called the Pilot House nestled in a grove of hazels, a cottage built around 1945, and the nut-drying shed sporting a host of primitive equipment.

The nut orchard itself includes a wide variety of walnuts, chestnuts, hazelnuts, butternuts, buartnuts, heartnuts, filberts and trazels, some on trees soaring 18 metres in the air. Most were bred by brothers Jack and David Gellatly, sons of David Erskine and Elizabeth Ure Gellatly. According to *Fintry: Lives, Loves and Dreams,* by Stan Sauerwein with Arthur Bailey, the Gellatlys came to Canada in 1883, first to Ontario for a decade before making their way west. At first David worked as a carpenter for two years in Vernon, but he felt the urge to grow things, and leased land at what was then called Shorts' Point, later called Fintry. By 1897 he was selling tomatoes and potatoes from his farm. However, without warning, Shorts' Point changed hands and the new owner wanted the Gellatly family out immediately, which led to a legal dispute that had to be settled by an umpire. Apparently, the Gellatlys lost. They moved 50 kilometres down the lake with their nine children, settling on Powers' Flat near Westbank. There, Gellatly became known as the Tomato King for the tonnes of tomatoes he grew and shipped around the province each year.

This unusual park combines examples of the Okanagan's unique agricultural heritage with recreation, tourism and education. In the coming years it will be further developed to preserve and restore Gellatly's distinct features for public use and enjoyment.

To Get There

From Highway 97 just north of downtown Westbank, turn east onto Gellatly Road, where the full gamut of fast food outlets should satisfy your appetite. Travel nearly a kilometre downhill to the lake and turn right. Follow Gellatly Road along the lake, across the bridge at Powers Creek and pass the Westbank Yacht Club. Continue for nearly a kilometre farther, turning right where the road ends, then turn left onto Whitworth Road and watch on your left for signs for the park entrance.

For details and event listings, go to the website at www.gellatlynutfarm.ca.

Gellatly Heritage Regional Park

Just up Gellatly Road is a public park which is related to the nut farm by history. It includes a restored log barn and home built by Billy Powers circa 1888 (which the Gellatly family lived in until 1908), a short interpretive trail, picnic area, and the century-old Gellatly family cemetery.

This is a small 2.6-hectare park that's open year-round. It was developed in partnership with the Gellatly family and the regional district, in an effort spearheaded by descendant Ferne Jean.

Visitors will find the short interpretive trail engaging; and the sweeping views out over Okanagan Lake, the Byland family's nursery, and the Gellatly Nut Farm are all quite awesome.

A heritage tea is held here each spring. Interpretive programs can be arranged for school or community groups interested in learning about the local environment and cultural history.

Dogs are permitted on leash only, and owners are expected to clean up after them. There are no open fires permitted, or camping.

Use only designated trails.

To reach this park, continue along Gellatly Road, past the turnoff to the nut farm, turning left and heading uphill for a short distance. The park is on your left.

Otherwise you can reach it from Highway 97 at the Glenrosa interchange. Turn south, following Gellatly Road to the park, which will be on your right. — JS

Additional Information:

Regional District of Central Okanagan
1450 KLO Road
Kelowna, BC
Tel: (250) 763-4918
Fax: (250) 763-0606
E-mail: info@cord.bc.ca
Web: www.regionaldistrict.com

CHAPTER 36

Lower Glen Canyon / Gellatly Aquatic Park

Statistics	For map, see page 187
Distance:	Varies
Travel Time:	Fragmented trail sections so far
Condition:	Well-maintained
Season:	Year round
Topo Maps:	Peachland, BC 82 E/13
Communities:	West Kelowna

Raised, rustic wooden walkways protect not only walkers' feet, but also the rare Okanagan ecosystem deep in the glen along Powers Creek in Glen Canyon Regional Park. Because of the shade in this deep canyon, and the extra moisture provided by a year-round stream, the plants that grow here are quite different from those that frequent the arid hillsides above.

If you can climb stairs, these shady trails, with and without the wooden walkways, won't be too much of a challenge for you.

And the prize: from Powers Creek Falls Bridge you'll have a fabulous view of the rushing creek 24 metres below. Here the little creek exerts its surprising power where, over the centuries, it has worn through the rock, creating deep undercuts in the canyon walls as it sped its way to the big lake.

To the Glen Canyon Trails

Access this trail network by turning east off Highway 97 at the Glenrosa / Gellatly junction. Head downhill for a half-kilometre on Gellatly Road. Park off Gellatly Road at a cluster of mailboxes, near the signed entrance to Glen Canyon subdivision. Look for stairs leading down into the canyon.

This walk probably won't take you more than an hour — even if you smell the

From the pedestrian bridge over Powers Creek in Glen Canyon Regional Park, you can look far down into the canyon below where the creek has carved deeply into the rock. © Judie Steeves

flowers along the way. In late summer, you might pass a few wild blackberries to snack on, a rare treat in this dry valley climate.

This route will also have you treading in the footsteps of pioneers. The historic Hudson's Bay Company Brigade Trail, which carried trappers and traders through the Okanagan in the early 1800s, followed a portion of the route through this shady glen.

On foot, you can exit at downtown Westbank on Hebert Road (behind the Dairy Queen) if you follow the pathway up toward the highway from this park. Conversely, you can also enter the trail from this same spot.

To More Trails

For a pleasant and easy lakefront walk followed by a bit of birding, begin by turning southeast from downtown Westbank at the major intersection of Highway 97 and Gellatly Road. This is the intersection where you're bombarded by signs catering to those fast food urges.

Drive down Gellatly Road toward the lake, and to dine outdoors, turn left at the bottom to Rotary Beach. Here picnic tables on a grassy stretch between the paved parking lot and the beach provide a pleasant setting for a meal. Sun yourselves on the adjacent beach, or have a swim before embarking on a 1.2-kilometre walk along the lakeside paths to the Rotary Trails.

On the way, you'll pass under ancient willows and cross Smith Creek. When you reach the Gellatly Aquatic Park docks, you might see youngsters diving from the pilings into the lake. Your stroll will take you to a sandy beach at Powers Creek Point where the creek empties into the lake.

Rotary Trails

Here the local Rotary club created a kilometre-long network of trails and bridges around a calm, heavily treed portion of the creek, where birding is a treat. The West Kelowna Yacht Club (formerly the Westbank Yacht Club) and a public boat launch are across the road. The clubhouse is located in the historic Pendozi. According to Bill Chubb, a former member of the West Kelowna Yacht Club, the Pendozi "was originally built as a ferry for crossing from Kelowna to the Westside. It was built in Victoria, taken apart and rebuilt in Kelowna. The Pendozi was diesel-powered and had four propellers, two on each end."

Horses and History

From your walk around Rotary Trails, you can either walk back for the car, or carry on in the opposite direction, past the Flying Horse Farm, where R.J. Bennett raises thoroughbred horses. The Bennett family is inextricably linked to the political history of this province. Russell (R.J.) Bennett is the son of a long-time premier of BC. Kelowna hardware merchant W.A.C. Bennett was premier from 1952 to 1972. His son Bill Bennett, Russell's brother, was elected BC premier in 1975.

Nearby is historic Gellatly Nut Farm, which was purchased by the community and transformed into a regional park. For details, see the *Gellatly Nut Farm* chapter.

Stroll up the Creek

Powers Creek winds its way through Flying Horse Farm, which Gellatly Road parallels for another half kilometre to the southwest. There, the new and imposing Cove Beach Resort has been built on the lakeshore adjacent to the Gellatly Nut Farm Regional Park.

Gellatly Road turns to the right (left takes you to the lake and the entrance to the resort), so follow it past Whitworth Road, which, incidentally, will take you to the entrance of the Gellatly Nut Farm park.

A total of three kilometres from where you turned off Highway 97 amid the burger restaurants, you'll reach another turn in the road. Here, a new 1.4 kilometre section of the Glen Canyon Regional Park Trail begins. It will take you across a little wooden bridge, through the woods along the creek to a set of 105 steps that wind their way up the cliff. On your hike up there are some rest stops with benches and excellent views.

At the top is a bench dedicated to the memory of Chuck Ashbee. Ashbee was a member of the Gellatly Aquatic Park Society, the group of visionary community members who created this park bordering the lake and Powers Creek. Here you'll not only see Okanagan Lake far below, but on the other side of the cliff you can look deep into Powers Creek canyon and see the amazing rock formations that were created in its rush to the lake.

Returning to Gellatly Road, continue another third of a kilometre along the road, up the hill to the Gellatly Heritage Regional Park (on your left) where the pioneer family's cemetery is located. (See the *Gellatly Nut Farm* chapter for more information.)

Another 1.4 kilometres along Gellatly Road, you'll pass another entrance to the Glen Canyon Regional Park Trails. After a total drive of 5.8 kilometres, this loop drive will take you back to Highway 97, on the opposite side of West Kelowna from where you began.

Additional Information:

Regional District of Central Okanagan
1450 KLO Road
Kelowna, BC
Tel: (250) 763-4918
Fax: (250) 763-0606
E-mail: info@cord.bc.ca
Web: www.regionaldistrict.com

CHAPTER 37

Upper Glen Canyon Trails

Statistics	For map, see page 187
Distance:	More than 4 kilometres of trails in Glen Canyon Regional Park
Travel Time:	It's up to you
Condition:	Well-maintained
Season:	Year round
Topo Maps:	Peachland, BC 82 E/13
Communities:	West Kelowna

Come summer it's delightfully cool on the hiking trails along Powers Creek in Glen Canyon Regional Park. In all, this 74-hectare park features more than four kilometres of trails over a great variety of terrain and changing wildlife habitat on both sides of Highway 97. You can take a short after-dinner constitutional or a day-long hike on the Glen Canyon network. The creek flows through a deep canyon separating the downtown community of Westbank from the newer residential area of Glenrosa, perched on the hillside to the southwest.

The Powers Creek canyon is not only an oasis of cool air on a hot summer day, it also forms the route for this rapidly growing community's life-giving water supply. Originally, this water was brought down from such high-elevation storage reservoirs as Jackpine Lake and Lambly (Bear) Lake, dammed in the 1920s by the Westbank Irrigation District. The water passed through a system of laboriously built wooden flumes, and then flowed to the first orchards and farms.

Today, water is carried through a system of underground pipes and into the thousands of homes now sprouting up along the fertile benchlands above Okanagan Lake. Portions of the old flumes still cling to the cliffsides along creeks throughout the Okanagan. They are a reminder of simpler times when the valley was sparsely populated, and a less sophisticated, above-ground water supply was all that was needed.

Const. Neil Bruce Memorial, near Aberdeen Road. *© Judie Steeves*

The Central Okanagan Regional District maintains a still-growing network of trails along Powers Creek.

Access from Glenrosa Road

The upper canyon trails can be reached from a number of access points in Glenrosa. Turn west off Highway 97 onto Glenrosa Road, then take the first road to the right. Drive along Webber Road to Aberdeen Road, which comes into Webber on the right. Turn right and follow Aberdeen Road the few blocks to its end where you can park.

Another trail into the canyon can be reached from the cul-de-sac between Aberdeen and Dunbarton Road. You could also continue farther up Webber Road and turn onto Coventry Crescent to take either one of two trails down to the main creek trail. Another option is to go farther up Glenrosa Road, then turn right onto Gates Road at the West Kelowna Firehall. Follow Gates Road to Salmon Road and turn left. At Canary, turn right until Bluejay. Turn left and park to enter the canyon, or right to McLeod Road, then left and park, for another entrance to the trails.

Most of the main trail leads you right along the winding creek, which gives off cool whiffs of misty dampness as it burbles along over the rocks. Powers Creek is critical to survival of the dense canopy of old cottonwoods, aspens, birch and maple trees that grow along the canyon floor.

Higher up the canyon walls, ponderosa pine and Douglas-fir are more common, along with such dryland vegetation as the bright brown-eyed Susans, Saskatoon bushes and spiny Oregon grape.

Cliffs and Hoodoos

You can see the weather-worn 100-metre-high cliffs across the canyon and bizarre-shaped columnar rock formations called hoodoos near the trail, south of the Aberdeen Road entrance to the canyon. Geologist Murray Roed, an editor of Okanagan Geology, explains the hoodoos were likely formed during torrential discharge and abrasion of Powers Creek at a time when average rainfall far exceeded that of present day.

On the other hand, Roed suggests, the hoodoos could also be the result of meltwater flooding during a late stage of deglaciation, making the hoodoo, in geologists' terms, a glaciofluvial erosional remnant.

Whatever the case, water partially eroded the sandstone, leaving behind the more resistant rock and isolating it from its surroundings.

The most direct route to view these fantastic sites is by entering the canyon from Aberdeen Road, beginning at the Bruce Memorial. This stone memorial was established to honour Constable Neil Bruce, an RCMP officer who was fatally wounded in April 1965 while attempting to arrest a suspect holed up in a nearby cabin.

A "hoodoo" rock formation in Upper Glen Canyon. © *Judie Steeves*

You may hike downstream to Highway 97 near Westbank's

town centre, or upstream for a more ambitious workout and some spectacular views. In fact, you may continue on Crown-owned land upstream from Glen Canyon Regional Park to Black Canyon and beyond, but only the park trails are well marked. Eventually, there may be a looping trail up the creek to a wilderness campsite, then across the creek and back down on the rim of the canyon along the historic Westbank irrigation pack trail. This trail leads up to the Lambly Lake reservoir. Also known as Bear Lake, it can be reached by Bear Road from either Bear Creek Park or from Highway 97C. See the *Bear Forest Service Road* chapter for details.

The canyon is home to more than 100 species of birds ranging from colourful woodpeckers and western tanagers to sparrows, crows, and chickadees. You might also see a variety of mammals and reptiles, including the Pacific tree frog, garter, gopher and rattlesnakes, squirrels, skunks, mice, chipmunks, bear, deer, cougar, coyotes, and porcupines.

Respect the Park

Follow regional district park regulations by keeping your dog on a leash and cleaning up after it. Use only designated trails and do not pick flowers. The use of motorized vehicles on trails is not permitted. Fires and camping are also banned.
—JS

Additional Information:

Regional District of Central Okanagan
1450 KLO Road
Kelowna, BC
Tel: (250) 763-4918
Fax: (250) 763-0606
Email: info@cord.bc.ca
Web: www.regionaldistrict.com

CHAPTER 38

Crystal Mountain / Telemark

Statistics	For map, see page 200
Distance:	11.5 kilometres, from Hwy 97 in downtown Westbank
Travel Time:	One half hour
Condition:	Paved, with gravel sections
Season:	Year round; may need chains in winter
Topo Maps:	Peachland, BC 82 E/13
Communities:	Kelowna, West Kelowna and Peachland

Alpine Skiing

Crystal Mountain ski area (formerly Last Mountain), located 11.5 kilometres north west of Westbank, is geared to serve the family-oriented market. With only 20 percent of the ski mountain rated as difficult and 30 percent rated easy, it's a good place to learn, practice technique or get back in shape to tackle the more demanding Okanagan ski mountains.

With a normal late-December to late-March season, Crystal Mountain offers skiing Thursday to Sunday 9 a.m. to 3:30 p.m. Spring skiing starts early at Crystal Mountain — why not give it a try this February?

Crystal Mountain Statistics	
Peak Elevation	5001 ft / 1535 meters
Base Elevation	3940 ft / 1200 meters
Top of Chair	4590 ft / 1400 meters
Vertical Drop	650 ft / 200 meters
Lift Capacity	3000 people /hour
Runs & Acreage	21 runs, 470 acres of trails
Glades & Trees	25 acres
Terrain Park	Centennial
Average Snowfall	310 cm / 122 inches
Average Temperature	-4° C / 25° F
Slope Rating	30% easy 50% intermediate 20% difficult

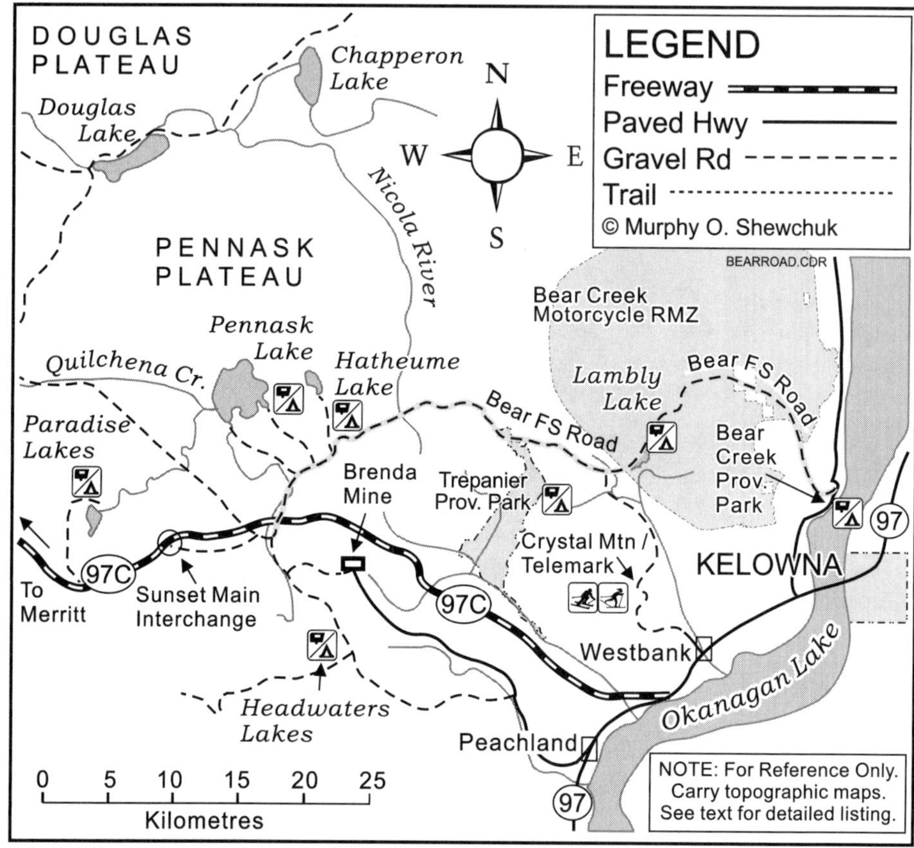

Bear Forest Service Road and the West Kelowna area.

Cross-country Skiing

Telemark X-C Ski Trails are also located near Crystal Mountain. Access from Highway 97 is via Glenrosa Road on the southwest outskirts of downtown Westbank, with the large parking area nine kilometres from the highway. Telemark has over 50 kilometres of marked trails, groomed for classic and freestyle skiing. The area also has 3.5 kilometres of lit track for night skiing to 9:00 p.m.

A comprehensive ski school program has been very popular with thousands participating every year. This volunteer club also has a strong racing program and a new biathlon program.

In summer the trails are used for hiking and mountain biking.

Backcountry Exploring

Summer can also be an interesting time in the area. You can continue northwest up Powers Creek for another 10 kilometres and then west for five kilometres into Jackpine Lake. Here a recreation site can be your base for a little fishing, boating or camping. You can also continue farther north to Bear Road for further backcountry exploring. (See the *Bear Forest Service Road* chapter for details.) — MS

Cross-country skiing is an excellent winter activity.

© Murphy Shewchuk

Additional Information:

Crystal Mountain Resort Ltd.
Box 26044
West Kelowna, BC V4T 2G3
Tel: (250) 768-5189
Fax: (250) 768-3755
Snowline: (250) 712-6262
E-mail: info1@crystalresort.com
Web: www.crystalresort.com

Telemark Cross-Country
Ski Club
Box 26072,
West Kelowna, BC V4T 2G3
Tel: (250) 768-1494
Fax: (250) 768-1493
E-mail: tccsc@telus.net
Web: www.telemarkx-c.com

CHAPTER 39

Lacoma Lake Trail / Trepanier Park

Statistics	For map, see page 202
Travel Time:	Allow at least 2-3 hours to hike each way, plus time at the lake; it's a 22-kilometre round trip
Condition:	Trail is well marked and easy to follow
Season:	Spring (but it can be very wet), summer and fall
Topo Maps:	Peachland 82 E/13
Communities:	Peachland

Lacoma Lake is an oasis of pristine wilderness caught in the cup formed by steep surrounding hillsides. The lake can be reached by an 11-kilometre hike along a sun-dappled trail through the forest adjacent Trepanier and Lacoma Creeks. This trail has an elevation gain of about 200 metres.

Vibrant with wildlife, this serene little spot is a long but not difficult hike from Peachland, on a trail that was upgraded by the Canadian EarthCare Foundation in 1997, with a grant from Forest Renewal BC. Workers installed pit toilets at the trailhead, at the half-way point, and at the lake. Primitive level campsites were also established at these spots.

On April 18, 2001 a 2,884-hectare provincial park was established which includes this walk through the Trepanier Creek drainage. The park was the result of years of community negotiations which resulted in an agreement on a Land and Resource Management Plan for Okanagan public lands.

Trepanier Provincial Park includes Cameron (Cameo) Lake, reached via Bear Main Forest Service Road (see that chapter for more information). The park also includes Lacoma Creek down from Cameron Lake, to Silver Creek, near Highway 97C, which flows into Trepanier Creek.

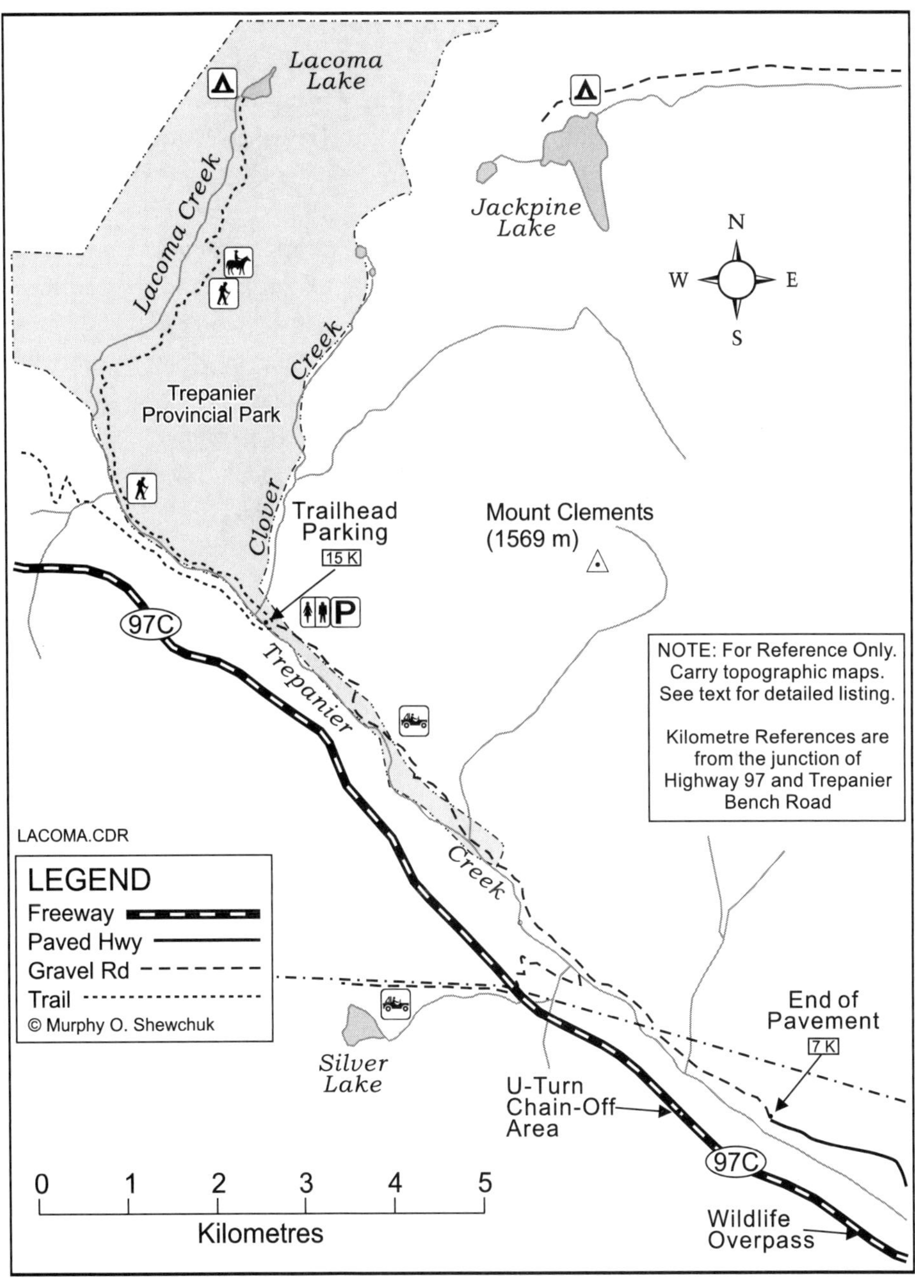

Lacoma Lake / Trepanier Park area.

Lacoma Lake Trail. *© Judie Steeves*

Getting There

The trailhead to Lacoma Lake can be reached by turning west off Highway 97 onto Trepanier Bench Road, past Hainle Vineyards Estate Winery, then along Cousins Road to Trepanier Road. You can also take Highway 97C from the Okanagan, and then turn off at the Trepanier Road exit.

Follow Trepanier Road as it twists and turns through rural acreage, finally changing from pavement to a rough gravel road about seven kilometres from Highway 97.

Continue to follow this road to a cul-de-sac at its end, about 18 kilometres from Highway 97, or about 8.5 kilometres from the end of the blacktop. The road can be rough and puddly in spots after heavy rains or in spring, particularly the last few kilometres, which can be difficult going for a low-slung vehicle.

Here, a bridge once crossed Trepanier Creek until it was removed. This is the trailhead for the hike into Lacoma Lake. You'll find a pit toilet about 100 metres back from the end of the road. The first trail markers are high on the trees on the boulder-strewn road that parallels the last bit of the road to the cul-de-sac. The trail is not maintained.

Bird Haven

A great blue heron spread its enormous wings and soared over the little lake as we reached it. The call of the loon told us there were fish in this water as we parted the undergrowth and first set eyes on our goal. While we watched the wild scene before us, a belted kingfisher hovered over the water, plunged, and then flew to the nearest branch with its breakfast. The loon danced atop the water, then dove, with a tremendous splash, and disappeared from the still surface. Waxwings, warblers, flickers, sparrows, chickadees, a sparrow hawk, a flock of swallows, some ducks, and several chipmunks all appeared in just the first few minutes.

Lacoma Lake is 945 metres above sea level. On the dam built by Peachland pioneer families in the 1920s there are now three campsites and a firepit for use by hikers.

"Lacoma," the name attached to this little lake and creek, comes from the combination of three family names: Law, Coldham, and Morshe. These pioneer families built a crude log and rock dam which stored water in the early years of the 20th century. The dam was needed to hold the spring runoff for use during the later dry summer months. The latent gravitational power held in this new body of water allowed the "Lacoma" families to irrigate their holdings far downstream on the dry bench above Okanagan Lake.

It's believed Okanagan First Nations people created this trail while travelling to powwows with the Nicola bands on the North Douglas Plateau. There is an Aboriginal trail marked here on the Archibald McDonald map of 1827, and called Indian Road. It reached Okanagan Lake at "squ-ha," which meant "the bend," where the lake takes a bend around the rocky promontory in Okanagan Mountain Provincial Park.

Native people were followed in later years by European Peachland pioneers searching for a source of water they could control to keep their farms productive through the dry Okanagan summers. The first stretch of trail into the lake incorporates the remnants of a road that provided dam access for horses and vehicles. The road narrows after a time and clings to the edges of hillsides in places.

Other sections are boggy from spring-fed Trepanier Creek tributaries. There's a great viewpoint where the Lacoma Creek valley enters the Trepanier Creek valley. From there you can look far down the valley and across the creek and the Okanagan Connector, Highway 97C, to the flat face of the tailings dam at Brenda Mine.

As you come closer to Lacoma Lake, you hike through huge patches of devil's club and false Solomon's seal. In late summer, you can spot the distinctive deep blue berry of the queen's cup or alpine beauty, which blooms here in early summer.

Prepare Properly

Before embarking on this hike, make sure you have adequate drinking water, comfortable hiking boots, and something to eat. At this altitude the weather can change suddenly, so be prepared. Don't travel alone and allow at least five to seven hours for the return trip.

In addition, you should allow for an opportunity to take the goat trail, which goes part way around the east side of the lake. When at Lacoma Lake, try spending some time enjoying the peace, tranquility, and wildlife.

Remember that this lake is a source of drinking water for Peachland residents and also, a pristine wilderness area — so pack out every single scrap you pack in.

Stay on the trails and obey signs. — JS

Additional information:

BC Parks

Web: www.env.gov.bc.ca/bcparks

CHAPTER 40

Hardy Falls Park

Statistics	For map, see page 146
Distance:	29 kilometres, Kelowna to Hardy Falls Park 4 kilometres, Peachland (Princeton Ave.) to the park
Travel Time:	Approximately one-half hour from Kelowna
Hiking Time:	One-half to one hour
Condition:	Paved highway (Highway 97)
Season:	Year round
Topo Maps:	Summerland, BC 82 E/12
Communities:	Peachland

Hardy Falls Park, on Peachland (Deep) Creek in south Peachland, is a cool oasis in what can sometimes be a hot landscape. A pleasant walking trail begins at a parking lot and picnic site on Hardy Street, just off Highway 97 on the southern outskirts of Peachland. The kilometre-long trail, complete with seven footbridges, leads to a splendid little falls hidden away at the head of a narrow canyon. Allow one-half to one hour to make the trip to the falls.

In April, the sunflower-like blossoms of the arrow-leaved balsamroot brighten the slopes and the yellow flowers of the Oregon grape add splotches of colour to the underbrush. Kokanee, rainbow trout, and carp spawn in the creek in season, while in spring a dipper nests in a crevice part way up the waterfall. In October, the Oregon grape fruit turns a dusty blue while crimson kokanee dart about in their spawning beds in the creek.

Although the Hardy Falls Park sign was once marked with a "1972" date, the park had already gone through several incarnations by that year. It started off as an Order-in-Council setting aside 15.4 hectares in October 1949. The BC Parks Branch established Antlers Beach Park in 1955, taking in Okanagan Lake waterfront and the creekside property. At the time of writing, the park had been transferred to the Regional District of Central Okanagan.

Hardy Falls on Peachland (Deep) Creek. *© Murphy Shewchuk*

Harry Hardy Arrived in 1884

According to Stella (Gummow) Welch in Peachland Memories (Volume II), "It was the fall of 1884 that Harry Hardy came down through the Okanagan Valley for the first time, and on New Year's Day, 1885, he got his first glimpse of what was later Peachland."

The same Harry Hardy soon "got a job with Bob Lambly. The Lambly Brothers had bought out the squatter, Bill Jenkins, at Trepanier and pre-empted District Lot 220, and Harry Hardy was sent down to look after the stock. Peachland became his home from that time on and he thus became the first permanent settler."

Irrigating with water from Trepanier Creek, Harry Hardy planted the first peach orchard in the Okanagan Valley in 1885. "In 1891 Hardy pre-empted land where the Gorman Bros. Lumber Ltd. mill now stands, its southern boundary being Hardy's Lake, known to old timers as the Turtle Ponds. At this property he planted about 200 fruit trees, one of the first orchards in the Westbank area."

The First peaches at "Peachland"

According to Stella Welch: "it would seem he cared for the two properties at the same time.

The first peaches that ripened on the young orchard at Trepanier Creek inspired visions of a new venture in the mind of energetic mine promoter J.M. Robinson. He had earlier induced a number of prairie farmers to invest in mining claims, and a little cluster of homes housed these venturing pioneers. But no ore was ever taken out, and Mr. Robinson's first taste of a delicious peach, which Mr. Hardy declared was nine inches around, opened up a whole new prospect. J.M. bought up pre-emptions in and around Peachland, paying Harry $600 for a pre-emption that extended from the lakeshore to the top bench, D.L. 1184. He subdivided this land into 10-acre plots, and went down to Winnipeg to sell them. As a result, John Gummow arrived with his young family from Winnipeg in December 1899, and the first land planted on the south side of the village came to fruition. His first crop of huge potatoes grown on this new and fertile land, with the aid of a plowed furrow as an irrigation ditch, inspired the disgruntled miners to buy up land for orchards, and the new settlement took form as a fruit-growing community."

"But," continues Welch, "Harry Hardy, in the meantime, left the Lambly Ranch to do a little prospecting on his own. After several disappointing years spent prospecting, Harry Hardy bought 10 acres of his own pre-emption back

One of the many bridges on the trail to Hardy Falls. *© Murphy Shewchuk*

from J.M. Robinson, and started an orchard of his own. This was later sold and Harry spent the last years of his life in his little home in town. He passed on quietly March 21, 1947 at the age of 89 years."

Antlers Beach

Across Highway 97 from the entrance to Hardy Falls Park is Antlers Beach Regional Park. This usually quiet beach offers beautiful views of Okanagan Lake to the north and the south as well as a natural swimming beach with ponderosa pines shading the picnic area. — MS

Additional Information:

Regional District of Central Okanagan
1450 KLO Road
Kelowna, BC
Tel: (250) 763-4918
Fax: (250) 763-0606
Email: info@cord.bc.ca
Web: www.regionaldistrict.com

CHAPTER 41

Bear Creek Provincial Park

Statistics	For map, see page 212
Distance:	Nine kilometres from Kelowna
Travel Time:	A 15-minute drive from Kelowna
Condition:	Paved and well-maintained
Season:	All
Topo Map:	Peachland, BC 82 E/13
Communities:	Kelowna and West Kelowna

One of the busiest camping destinations in the Okanagan Valley is Bear Creek Provincial Park, located across from Kelowna on the west shore of Okanagan Lake. This 178-hectare park is open from April to October with camping fees in effect throughout the season. To reach Bear Creek Provincial Park, turn west off Highway 97, two kilometres south of the Okanagan Lake floating bridge, and follow Westside Road north for seven kilometres. To get to the park from Highway 97 near O'Keefe Ranch, northwest of Vernon, follow Westside Road south for 57 kilometres.

Wild Canyons to Waterfront

Westside Road serves as the boundary between two quite different natural environments that comprise a natural diversity worth exploring. To the west, Lambly (Bear) Creek has cut a spectacular steep-walled canyon in its final descent from the rugged 1,800-metre-high Pennask Plateau. In the process, the rushing water has created a fan-shaped delta in Okanagan Lake, to the east of Westside Road.

Above and on either side of the canyon, ponderosa pine and Douglas-fir dominate the dry, rocky hills. Juniper, bunchgrass, Indian paintbrush, arrow-leaved balsamroot, Oregon grape, and prickly-pear cactus compete for the area's meagre rainfall. Below, in the shady confines of the canyon, moistened by the mist rising

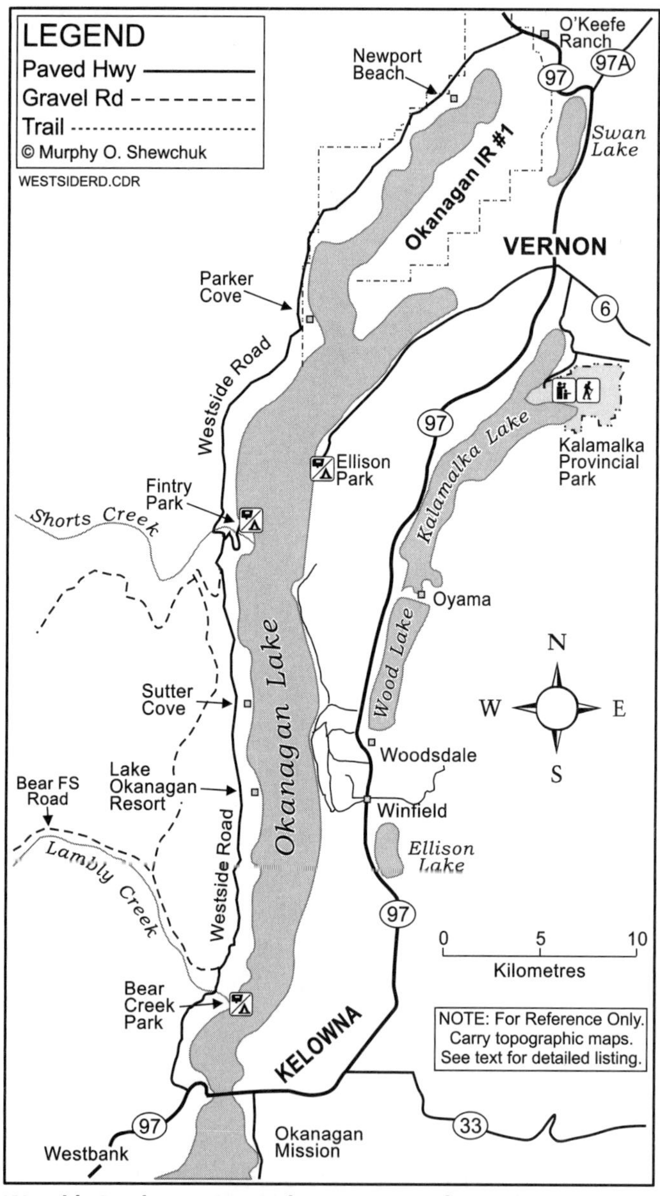

Westside Road area, West Kelowna to O'Keefe Ranch.

from the waterfalls, is yet another world. It is one of maple and birch, of Saskatoon and chokecherry, of wild rose, horsetail and moss.

Swallows glide gracefully through the canyon, red-tailed hawks ride warm afternoon updrafts high above, and owls hoot the night away. Tree-frogs are noisiest in spring; the crickets click in the summer; and the coyote's song occasionally drifts down from the hills.

A network of trails encircles the lower canyon, with parking available near the Lambly Creek bridge, west of Westside Road. Note that there are some very steep cliffs along the canyon walls. For safety reasons, stay on the trails when hiking. A loop hike on the mid-canyon trail to the canyon rim and then upstream to the footbridge presents an excellent example of typical north-slope environment in desert country. The walk back down the north side of the canyon is much drier. Watch for the remnants of an old irrigation ditch near viewpoint #5. Because of the west-east

A footbridge across Lambly Creek in Bear Creek Park. *© Murphy Shewchuk*

flow of Lambly Creek, early to mid-morning is usually the best time to photograph the waterfalls from the canyon floor.

Allow about an hour for the five-kilometre hike, unless you pause to enjoy some of the benches set at strategic locations that look out over Okanagan Lake, the canyon, or the creek.

Once a Working Ranch

The park campground, day-use picnic area and boat launch facilities are on the delta of Lambly (Bear) Creek. Once an integral part of Bear Creek Ranch, the S.M. Simpson Sawmill Company purchased the site from the ranch for its logging activities, and later sold it to Crown Zellerbach Canada Limited. In 1981, the British Columbia government purchased the land from Crown Zellerbach for a provincial park. As a condition of sale, Crown Zellerbach maintained the rights to continue its booming activities north and south of the main beaches.

When Bear Creek Park originally opened in the early 1980s, it contained 80 campsites, but a recent expansion added another 42 plus associated facilities. There are now 122 campsites, plus showers and washrooms with flush toilets. In addition to the canyon trails, there are lakeshore trails and over 400 metres of sandy beach. At the amphitheatre, a park interpreter provides interesting programs from mid-June to early September. Note that this park accepts reservations. Call 1-800-689-9025 or 604-689-9025 in Greater Vancouver. Reservations can also be made online at www.discovercamping.ca. — MS

Beach scene at Bear Creek Provincial Park.

© Murphy Shewchuk

Additional Information:

BC Parks

Web: www.env.gov.bc.ca/bcparks

CHAPTER 42

Fintry Provincial Park

Statistics: For map, see page 212
Distance: 32 kilometres from Kelowna
Travel Time: A 45-minute drive from Kelowna
Condition: Paved and well-maintained
Season: All; campground closed in winter, but trails open all year
Communities: Kelowna, Vernon, West Kelowna

The history of the Okanagan, its reliance on the lake for transportation links, its orchards, eccentric pioneers, and its natural beauty are all illustrated in miniature at Fintry, one of the earliest settlements on the west side of Okanagan Lake.

Fintry is reached via Fintry Delta Road, off Westside Road, 34 kilometres south of Highway 97 near Vernon, or north of Highway 97 across the bridge from Kelowna, 34 kilometres along Westside Road.

Today, the old settlement is a provincial park that includes a 360-hectare historic estate, cherished for its preservation of representative, rare Okanagan ecosystems. As well, the park preserves the Okanagan's pioneering heritage and, not missed by visitors, an invaluable Okanagan Lake shoreline stretching more than two kilometres. The province purchased the Fintry estate in December 1995 for $7.48 million, including a $2 million contribution from the Central Okanagan Regional District. Fintry Provincial Park was officially designated on April 30, 1996.

On April 18, 2001, a 523-hectare upland area was added to the park. The new addition encompasses the steep canyon walls through which Shorts Creek rushes, and the rocky highlands which shelter remnants of the historic Shorts Creek California bighorn wild sheep herd. The herd has been augmented in recent years with sheep transplanted from the Kamloops area, after habitat enhancement work opened up the underbrush to help protect the animals from predators and improve browse.

The additional upland also improved the ecological viability of the park by creating a ribbon of protected land from lakeshore to high above the valley. It's a spectacular canyon, with hiking and wildlife viewing opportunities far above the delta.

Natural History for Visitors

On the Shorts Creek delta itself, there are now 100 campsites, a group campsite, new shower rooms, and flush toilets as well as a picnic site. The campground is open from April 1 to Oct. 31 every year.

The remainder of the park is undeveloped except for the historic buildings on site, and a new, solidly built 400-step stairway that leads to awe-inspiring views of the lake and a great shot of the 24-metre (100-foot) waterfall in Shorts Creek Canyon. At the top are remnants of a historic water intake that was used for both irrigation and the generation of electricity. (Electricity was generated through the rotation of a Pelton wheel, which rotated when water was directed across the many cups that extended from along its circumference.)

The waterfall on Shorts Creek creates a humid micro-climate that provides a home for ferns, cedar trees, and other plants not usually found in the arid Okanagan. While the ecosystem surrounding the falls is atypical of Okanagan Valley's natural heritage, the dry hillsides, deep canyon, and the alluvial fan at the mouth of the creek present excellent examples of what is more common in this valley.

Preservation of the wilderness corridor along the creek is also part of the park's value. It is essential to ensure a natural link for wildlife, including the remnants of a bighorn sheep herd, which need to migrate from the lakeshore to the rocky bluffs with minimal interference from humans. Deer winter on these south-facing slopes and bears den up among the rocks above. Kokanee and rainbow trout spawn in the creek.

Members of the Central Okanagan Naturalists' Club sighted 57 species of birds in just a few hours. They expect there are more than 100 species here year round. The group also reported that there were at least three rare plants on the delta.

Although the campground is closed in winter, hikers can access the waterfall staircase and delta year round. Park by the "Welcome" sign near the barn.

Okanagan History in a Capsule

Captain Thomas Dorling (T.D.) Shorts, the first white settler on the delta, was co-owner and master of the first powered freighter to ply Okanagan Lake. In partnership with Thomas Greenhow, T.D. Shorts launched the Mary Victoria

Greenhow on April 21, 1886. Unfortunately, the coal-oil-burning two-horsepower engine was much too small for the 32-foot-long (9.75-metre) ship. The craft's maiden voyage to Penticton turned out to be a comedy of errors that cleaned out the Valley's supply of lamp coal oil.

Shorts later retired to Hope, BC where he died in 1921 at the age of 83. After Shorts, the delta land was owned, in succession, by the Honourable John Scott Montague and the Viscount Ennismore, Sir John Poynder Dickson, and the Honourable James Dunsmuir, who was lieutenant-governor of BC from 1902 to 1906. Dunsmuir later gave the land to his daughter, Sarah Audain, who then sold it to Captain J.C. Dun-Waters in 1909.

Waterfall on Shorts Creek in Fintry Provincial Park. *© Murphy Shewchuk*

David Erskine Gellatly became the first farmer there when he leased the property in 1895. He later moved to Westbank with his wife Eliza and their nine children in 1899. (See the Gellatly chapter for more details.)

Dun-Waters changed the name of his new property from Shorts Point to Fintry, after the family estate near Stirlingshire, Scotland.

His first interest was in establishing an orchard on the delta, and according to Stan Sauerwein, author of Fintry: Lives, Loves and Dreams, Dun-Waters constructed an elaborate irrigation system of flumes and pipes carried by suspension bridges to get water from Shorts Creek to the apple, crab apple, and soft fruits he planted on the delta.

According to Angus Gray, manager of the estate for 24 years, two European engineers looked at the irrigation system spanning the gorge and said it was "impossible." They were absolutely amazed at the ingenuity of Dun-Waters' system.

The Scottish-born Dun-Waters became known as the Laird of Fintry because of his aristocratic style of hunting and his palatial Manor House. In fact, the Laird had envisioned a Garden of Eden on the Fintry delta and so built — between 1910 and 1911 — a five-bedroom manor house constructed of local granite. Although it was gutted by fire in 1924, the trophy room was saved and the interior was rebuilt that year.

The Manor still remains and is located adjacent to the campground. In summers, visitors can tour the grand home, which is being refurbished as a museum by the volunteer Friends of Fintry Society. Inside, visitors will find some of Dun-Waters' original hunting trophies, including his famous Kodiak bear.

In 1924, Dun-Waters embarked on an ambitious foray into raising Scottish Ayrshire dairy cattle. For the purpose he constructed a unique octagonal dairy barn designed by Vancouver architect John J. Honeyman. (It has been partly restored by the Friends of Fintry and is often open to visitors for guided tours.)

Honeyman also designed Burnside, now called the Stuart House, at the mouth of Shorts Creek, which is currently leased out to the Baileys, former owners of the property.

In July 1938, Captain Dun-Waters, then in his 70s, donated this self-contained estate to the Fairbridge Farm Schools. He would die of colon cancer five years later.

Fairbridge Farm Schools were part of a philanthropic scheme aimed at strengthening the British Empire and improving conditions for underprivileged British children. The scheme was conceived by Kingsley Ogilvie Fairbridge (1885-1924), a South African-born reformer who was raised in Southern Rhodesia. As a result of the donation, Fintry was used by the Duncan, BC school as an agricultural training ground. The school ran the orchard and managed the herd of Ayrshire cattle during summers. The school closed in 1950.

Arthur W. Bailey arrived in the Okanagan Valley in 1961, with the intention of developing Fintry into a California-style resort community. He concedes that he was "a little bit premature," but he did add seven bedrooms with attached bathrooms to the attic of the Manor House.

As part of his efforts, Bailey also outfitted the Fintry Queen to carry his clients to the resort before Westside Road was paved. The Fintry Queen was originally built as a diesel-powered car ferry, a sister ship to the Pendozi, but it was retired from service when the Okanagan Lake Bridge was opened in 1958.

In addition to conducted tours, the Friends of Fintry hold special events here throughout the year. For up-to-date information visit their website at: www.fintry.ca. —JS

Additional information:

BC Parks
Web: www.env.gov.bc.ca/bcparks

Friends of Fintry Society
7655 Fintry Delta Rd.
Kelowna, BC V1Z 3V2
Tel: (250) 542-4031
E-mail: info@fintry.ca
Web: www.fintry.ca

The Manor at Fintry Provincial Park. *© Photos by Gordon Bazzana, Kelowna Capital News*

CHAPTER 43

Bear Forest Service Road

Statistics	For maps, see page 200 and page 228
Distance:	71 kilometres, Westside Road to Sunset Main Interchange on Highway 97C
Travel Time:	Two to four hours
Elev. Gain	1200 metres, Westside Road to Sunset Main Interchange
Condition:	Some rough gravel sections. West end be closed in winter
Season:	July through October
Topo Maps:	Peachland, BC 82 E/13
(1:50,000)	Shorts Creek, BC 82 L/4
	Paradise Lake, BC 92 H/16
Communities:	Peachland, West Kelowna, Kelowna and Merritt

Bear Forest Service (FS) Road begins (or ends, depending on your direction of travel) at its junction with Westside Road approximately 8.5 kilometres north of Highway 97 and 1.7 kilometres north of the Bear Creek Provincial Park main gate.

Note: Do not confuse Bear Forest Service Road with Bear Creek Road further south, but also off Westside Road.

Bear FS Road climbs steadily as it cuts a wide arc northwest and then southwest up to the Pennask Plateau. The upper terminus is at its junction with Sunset Main Road near the Pennask Creek overpass on the Okanagan Connector of the Coquihalla Highway. Although the junction is within sight of the freeway, the nearest access to the Connector (Highway 97C) is at the Sunset Main Road interchange approximately 6.5 kilometres to the west. (See *Sunset Main to Summerland* for details.)

The elevation where it passes under the Connector (Highway 97C) is 1,600 metres so Bear FS Road may not be passable until mid or late June. But when

Jackpine Lake, north of West Kelowna. © Murphy Shewchuk

open, it is a pleasant, though sometimes bumpy, alternative to the freeway — an alternative that allows access to several recreation sites and some of the finest trout lakes in the BC interior.

Bear FS Road is an industrial forest road and should be approached with caution, particularly on weekdays between 6:00 a.m. and 6:00 p.m. Although it is generally wide enough for you to pass an oncoming vehicle, the sharp turns and dust can severely reduce visibility.

Roadside kilometre markers, used by radio-equipped logging trucks, can also serve as a reference to you when exploring the region. One important point to consider should you stray off the main roads: the markers usually count down to the nearest highway or mill yard. In this case, "0K" appears to be the log dump at the shores of Okanagan Lake, a short distance north of Bear Creek Provincial Park. If you are unsure of which way to find civilization, following the decreasing numbers is a safe bet.

Dry and Dusty

Bear Road initially climbs northwest as it clings to the benches along Lambly (Bear) Creek Canyon. There are a few wide areas where it is safe to pull over and enjoy the view down the canyon to Okanagan Lake. Depending on where you choose to stop, you may notice a network of dirt bike trails through the pines on the benches below.

Access to the main Bear Creek OHV Trail System is to the north at Terrace Road near the 8K marker. The 150 kilometre trail network is supported by the Okanagan Trail Riders Association. In 2011, the new Aspen Trailhead was built just above the Lower Pits, on Terrace Mountain Main FS Road, with a Learner's Loop for new riders to practice riding. A number of rustic campsites have also been built on the site, along with a large gravel area for off-loading bikes.

Off Highway Vehicle (OHV) riding is not permitted on Bear Main Road, or in streams, wet areas, bogs or the marshy perimeter of a stream or lake.

More information and a map are available at www.okanagantrailriders.com.

Bald Range Road (kilometre 9.8) and Esperon Road (kilometre 12) present opportunities for fishing and other diversions into the plateau to the north and west. Keep left at all three junctions, following the Bear Road signs as your direction gradually changes to southwest.

Bear Lake

The first major fishing opportunity is at Lambly (Bear) Lake, near the 23K marker. There is a private resort and a recreation site on this lake, which also serves as a water reservoir for the District of West Kelowna (DWK). At an elevation of 1,158 metres, the 74-hectare lake should be high enough to sustain rainbow trout fishing well into the summer, and it's been unofficially stocked with perch as well.

Lambly Lake takes its name from the Lambly brothers, a trio of pioneer settlers who came to the Okanagan Valley in the 1870s. According to an article in Peachland Memories (Volume II), the Lamblys were natives of Megantic County, Quebec, an area settled by United Empire Loyalists.

Robert Lambly, the first to arrive in the Okanagan, tramped in from the coast over the Hope Trail and initially settled in what is now the Enderby district. A year later his brother Thomas who took up land nearby joined him. Charles Lambly followed his brothers westward in 1878 and obtained work as a civil engineer in northern British Columbia. A decade later, Charles moved into the Enderby area to work on the construction of the Shuswap and Okanagan Railway. Charles soon entered the service of the Provincial Government, first as Assessor, and later as Mining Recorder, Gold Commissioner, Stipendiary Magistrate and still later,

Government Agent. His first post was Enderby, as the young town at "Lambly's Landing" was later christened, but soon he was off to Rock Creek, where he spent the rest of his life.

The other Lambly brothers, Thomas and Robert, continued to live in the Enderby area until 1894. Some years earlier they had acquired land on the west side of Okanagan Lake at Trepanier Creek, with extensive range north and west of present-day Peachland.

The brothers had bought out William Jenkins who had located at Trepanier Creek in 1886, and on March 1, 1887 a pre-emption for D.L. 220 was registered to Charles A.R. Lambly, the first pre-emption in the district. Charles also purchased D.L. 490 in 1893, and his brother, Tom, bought D.L. 449 the same year. These properties all fronted on Okanagan Lake, and gave the brothers five kilometres of lakeshore. On the lakeside property at Trepanier they experimented with fruit growing, and pioneered the growing of soft fruits in that area.

"This was not the brothers' only activity in the area," reads the article in Peachland Memories. "While ranging the horses and cattle on the hills they had done some prospecting, and had become the possessors of a number of likely-looking mining claims."

This, however, led to tragedy.

"Tom Lambly contracted a severe cold while doing some development work on claims west of Trepanier. This turned into pneumonia and he was taken across the lake to Kelowna for treatment, but to no avail, and he died there on Nov. 24, 1897."

Following the death of his brother, Robert Lambly moved back to Enderby after selling off part of the Trepanier holdings. A short time later he moved with his wife and family to Alberta, where he operated a stock ranch in the foothills of the Rockies.

Jackpine Lake

Jackpine Forest Service Road, between 26K and 27K, winds down through the Powers Creek Canyon to West Kelowna, passing sideroads into Jackpine Lake and the Crystal Mountain ski area. See the *Crystal Mountain / Telemark* chapter for more information.

Cameo Lake

Bear FS Road continues to climb — now westward — reaching Cameo (Cameron) Lake near the 38K marker. There is a small recreation site on the rock outcropping at the west end of the lake and usually someone out doing a little fishing. This is the top end of a new provincial park that encompasses the drainage of Trepanier Creek, above Peachland. See Chapter 39 on Trepanier Park. Beyond Cameo Lake, forest roads lead into the headwaters of the Nicola River and several small lakes, including Windy Lake, near the 44K marker. Windy Lake also has a recreation site.

Beyond the 49K marker, the road markers begin a countdown to the junction with the Trout Main Road near the Headwaters Lakes. The 20K marker is about 52.3 kilometres from Westside Road.

Hatheume Lake

Hatheume Lake Road, near the 17K marker, presents another opportunity to explore the backcountry and enjoy camping, fishing or a wilderness resort experience. Although, at 134 hectares, Hatheume Lake is considerably smaller than nearby Pennask Lake, it too has a widespread reputation as a source of fighting rainbow trout. There are medium-sized recreation sites on Pinnacle Lake, the south side of Hatheume Lake, and a resort on the northeast shore.

If you reset your odometer, and take the road north, you will pass Pinnacle Lake recreation site near km 2.5 and reach a junction near km 3.4. The road to the right leads less than a kilometre to the Hatheume Lake recreation site while the road to the left partly circles the lake, reaching Hatheume Lake Resort in another 4.6 kilometres.

Both recreation sites and the resort have been upgraded considerably in recent years.

Pennask Lake Provincial Park

Your next possible detour is north to Pennask Lake. At 1041.29 hectares it is one of the larger lakes in the upland region. At an elevation of 1,402 metres, it is also one of the highest. Check the latest fishing regulations, but at the time of writing, Pennask was a fly-only lake yielding prize rainbow trout up to three quarters of a kilogram (1.5 pounds).

The very rough six-kilometre-long public road into Pennask Lake leaves Bear FS Road about 4.4 kilometres southwest of the access to Hatheume Lake.

Be forewarned. The BC Parks Pennask Lake Park website reads:

- The last 6 km takes about half an hour or longer
- Vehicles must have high clearance for the last 6 km. As well, if there have been heavy rains the road will have very large and deep puddles, as much as 40 feet long and 2-3 feet deep

Canoeing on Pennask Lake. *© Murphy Shewchuk*

There is a 28-vehicle / tent campground on the southeast corner of the lake. Facilities also include a day-use / picnicking area, boat launch, and pit toilets. No fee is charged and reservations are not available.

The public area was first established as a Class A Park on May 2, 1974, but was downgraded to a Recreational Area early in 1975. There were several reasons for the change: the new status would allow ranching interests to keep their cattle in the area; limited resource development would be allowed if it would not damage recreational values; but probably most important, it would limit park development and any consequent pressures on Pennask Lake, which is the province's most important source for rainbow trout eggs. While facilities are still limited, the recreation area was recently upgraded to a park.

The construction of Coquihalla Highway Phase III — now known as the Okanagan Connector — prompted some serious soul searching on the part of BC Parks. The present rough access road limits the number of visitors to the recreation site, but with a major highway only a short distance away, pressure will certainly be felt to improve access and facilities at the lake.

Pennask Lake Lodge

Pennask Forest Road, near the 13K marker, leads north into the plateau with a sideroad into a private lodge on the west shore of Pennask Lake.

James D. Dole, whose name is synonymous with the Hawaiian pineapple, first visited Pennask Lake in September 1927, where he camped for a week. He was accompanied by his wife, Belle, two employees, and three friends who then managed the lodge at Fish Lake (Lac Le Jeune) near Kamloops.

Author Stanley E. Read notes in *A Place Called Pennask,* that James Dole was in search of a dream — to be part of a fishing club that could control its surroundings. He wanted a perfect fishing lake in a region teeming with attractions, which he and his friends could call their own. He found it in Pennask Lake and moved quickly to gain control.

In a memorandum dated October 26, 1928, Dole wrote, "We believe that by controlling the land at shore-front we can maintain good fishing in this lake for a long time to come, and it is hoped that it will be kept as a fly-fishing lake solely and not be dredged ... with tin shops and worms."

The Pennask Lake Club was established in 1929, and officially incorporated in June 1930 as the Pennask Lake Company, Ltd. Membership was limited to 50 at a fee of $1,000 per member. Several prominent U.S. citizens joined the club (including California agriculture pioneer James Irvine and New York investment banker John M. Hancock), but the Great Depression dealt a series of setbacks before Dole's plans could materialize. The new lodge was under-utilized, resulting in deficits that Dole dealt with from his own pocket. It was not until the late 1940s, when the Pennask Lake Fishing and Game Club was formed, that new financial life was breathed into the operation — and this time the club fell under Canadian control.

Three-way Junction

After passing under Highway 97C, Bear FS Road ends at a junction with Sunset

Lake and Sunset Main roads. If you continue straight ahead (south), you can visit Brenda or McDonald lakes, and descend to Peachland or Summerland, or go there via the Headwaters Lakes area. See the *Sunset Main to Summerland* chapter for details.

The road to the right (west) offers access to Highway 97C at the Sunset Main interchange, about 6.5 kilometres from the three-way junction. If neither Peachland or Summerland or the freeway suits your fancy, you can always go back the way you came — looking downhill all the way, which will make the scenery just that much different. — MS

Additional Information:

BC Parks
Web: www.env.gov.bc.ca/bcparks

Hatheume Lake Resort
PO Box 490
Peachland, BC V0H 1X0
Tel: (250) 767-2642
Web: www.hatheumelakeresort.com

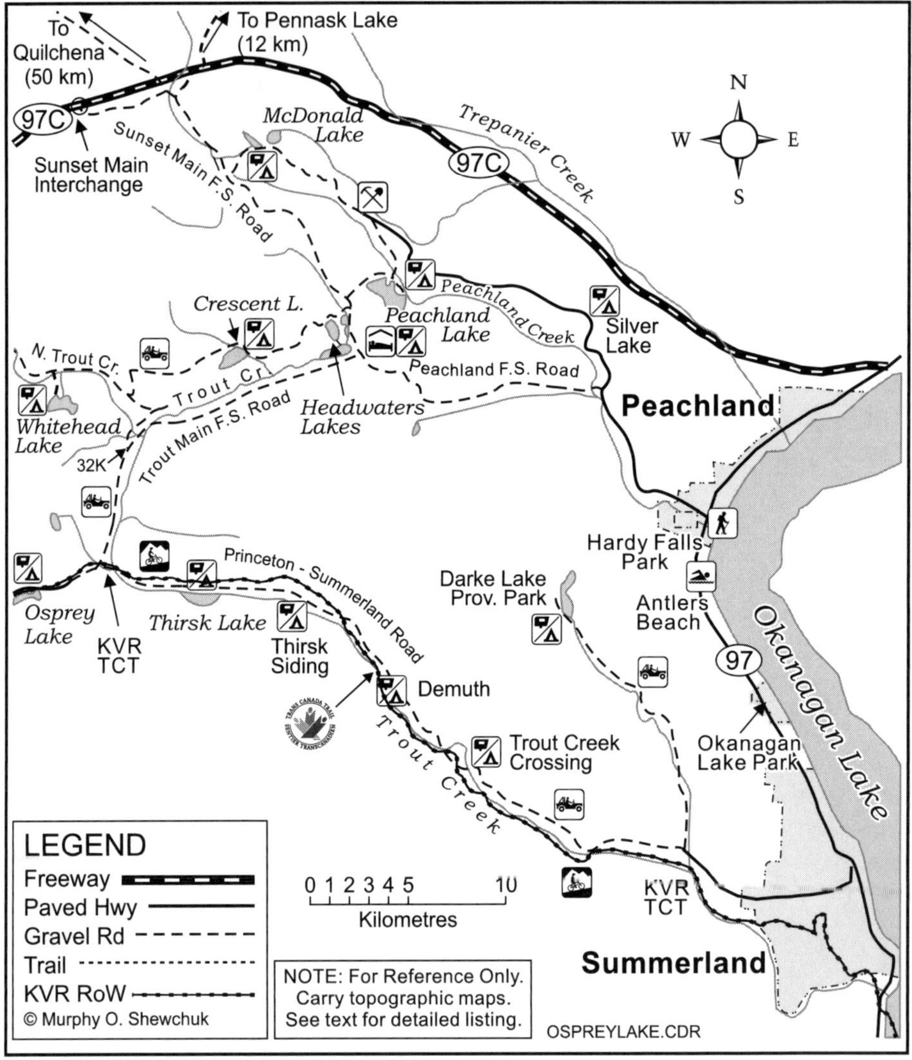

The west central Okanagan area.

CHAPTER 44

Sunset Main to Summerland

Statistics	For map, see page 228
Distance:	90 kilometres, Sunset Main Interchange to Summerland
Travel Time:	Approximately three hours
Condition:	Mostly gravel, some paved sections
Topo Maps:	Paradise Lake, BC 92 H/16
	Peachland, BC 82 E/13
	Bankier, BC 92 H/9
	Summerland, BC 82 E/12
Communities:	Merritt, Peachland, Summerland.

There are as many reasons for backroad exploring as there are backroad explorers. The seasons often influence what you'll discover or what will interest you. However, if you're like me, as the snow retreats from the high country, you're off looking for whatever may be around the next corner. Sometimes what is around the next corner is an impassable washout or a snowdrift that still hasn't been melted by the sun.

We've all spent time proving that mud holes or snowdrifts really are deeper than we expected. However, when we discover a brightly lit field of wildflowers or a grazing deer and fawn, we understand why we risk life, limb, and the family sedan for a spring drive in the country.

The high country that surrounds the Okanagan Valley is a backroad explorer's and wildflower lover's delight. Getting away from the city scene can be as simple as taking a walk in a park, but to get away from civilization and people involves a wee bit more effort.

If your base is in the central Okanagan, here is one way to enjoy a scenic tour and photograph the wildflowers. It involves half an hour's drive on the Okanagan Connector of the Coquihalla Highway and half a day or more of backcountry exploring. Although this trip includes active logging roads, some steep grades, and

Fishermen at MacDonald Lake, west of Peachland. *© Murphy Shewchuk*

loose gravel sections, it is often quite passable by ordinary car come late May or early June. It is probably safest to travel it on weekends and from a west to east (downhill) direction.

Sunset Main Road

For this Okanagan adventure, head 45 kilometres west of Peachland on the Connector (Highway 97C) and take the Sunset Main Road exit about 10 kilometres west of the summit. Reset your odometer at the cattleguard on the south side of the underpass and then head east along a gravel road that parallels the freeway.

Your first opportunity for diversion is near the 1K marker on the Sunset Main Forest Service Road. Look closely for an unmarked trailhead and an undeveloped parking area on the south (right) side of the road.

Although unmarked, the trail into Sunset Lake is well used and easily wide enough to portage a canoe or drag a car-top boat. And it's only a few minutes' walk. Game trails circle the lake, but you'll need a good set of gumboots and a sturdy walking stick to probe the mud holes. In addition to the lupines that do remarkably well here, you're likely to find ground dogwood and a host of other shade-loving plants that have adapted to the short season at this elevation (1,600 metres or 5,250 feet). Wildlife is also plentiful in the area. If you are early and quiet, you may see a mule deer browsing along the lakeshore.

As you continue following the gravel logging road eastward, it swings away from the freeway through a clear-cut that is quickly regenerating. Depending on when you get around to making the tour, you may find the lupine still in blossom or fields of fireweed swaying in the wind. In late summer, the flowers may be a secondary attraction to rich, black huckleberries. The lush foliage also attracts natural residents. Don't be too surprised to see white crowned sparrows, yellow bellied marmots and black bears foraging near the road.

Pennask Creek

Several sideroads lead off to new logging cuts and the high voltage power line, but the first major diversion is just before the Pennask Creek crossing near the 6K marker. A little-used road to the left crosses under the freeway near the creek and swings northwest along the north side of the freeway. This was once the main road across the plateau. Although rough, you could follow it westward to Quilchena or Douglas Lake, but now a missing bridge across Quilchena Creek makes it impassable.

Back on Sunset Road, a short climb past the creek crossing will bring you to another junction. Bear Road, to the left (north), could take you past Pennask and

Hatheume lakes and down to Okanagan Lake near Bear Creek Provincial Park. For now, swing right and continue southeast on Sunset Lake Road.

The timber in this area is older and the undergrowth a little different. Lupine, arnica, wild strawberries, and columbine grace the roadside slopes. Watch for the potholes, washouts, and washboard gravel surface as too little caution and too much speed can be disastrous.

Brenda and MacDonald Lakes

A junction near the 11K marker offers a chance to do a little fishing and get a different view of the Okanagan Valley. To the left lay Brenda and MacDonald lakes, and a few sideroads above the now-closed Brenda open pit mine.

To the right, Sunset Lake Road climbs over a saddle and skirts a box canyon that is the head of Peachland Creek. You may catch glimpses of the craggy cliffs of the canyon before you start the winding descent to the Headwaters Lakes area. There are signs of recent logging in this area and also signs that mark still more diversions.

A signpost near the 23K marker indicates a short detour into Peachland Lake. About half a kilometre farther along, another post marks the route to Whitehead Lake via Peachland Forest Service Road. There are small recreation sites at Peachland, Crescent, and Whitehead lakes. Many of the lakes in the area have been developed or enhanced to hold irrigation water for the orchards and communities of the Okanagan Valley. These are no exception, but Whitehead Lake shows the least sign of water control work.

If you're not an altogether avid wildflower watcher, you may want to detour into one of these lakes to wet a few flies. If the roads are dry, the first two should be easily accessible, but unless there has been some maintenance done recently, the last two or three kilometres into Whitehead Lake could be a bit rough on the old family sedan. Here, a 4x4 pickup might be a better choice.

Regardless of your selection, if your timing is right, you could discover that the lodgepole pine stands near the Peachland Forest Service Road junction are carpeted in a solid mass of blue lupine.

Headwaters Lodge

Found the dusty road a little hard on your throat? You could detour into Headwaters Lodge for a cold pop. If you're interested in continuing your wildflower jaunt in the morning, you can rent a camping spot, a cabin, a boat or a mountain bike and take a break until the light is a little better for photography.

Meanwhile, back on the road, the next major junction is about 1.2 kilometres past the entrance to Headwaters Lodge. Peachland Road continues down to Peachland (no surprise here), while Trout Creek Road follows Trout Creek south for about 20 kilometres to the Princeton-Summerland Road. If you are looking for wildflower diversity, follow the Trout Creek route to Summerland (See *Princeton-Summerland Road* for details.)

The gravel road passes alternately through several clearcuts and old growth stands, with a corresponding variety of wildflowers. In addition to the plants I've already mentioned, look for fields of wild roses and Indian paintbrush, particularly near the 34K marker.

If you are heading to the southern Okanagan Valley, turn left at the Princeton-Summerland Road junction. As you continue past Thirsk Lake, you'll see a gradual change in undergrowth. The lower elevation and drier climate support semi-desert plants such as sedum and scarlet gilia. Lodgepole pine forests give way to scattered stands of ponderosa, and huckleberries are replaced by saskatoons.

When you break free of the confines of the valley and the upper reaches of Trout Creek, you'll discover that the road is narrow and dusty, with few places to enjoy the spectacular view of the Trout Creek Canyon. If you can find a safe spot to pull over, you may be surprised at the variety of wildflowers that survive the dry climate. The drying leaves of arrow-leaved balsamroot cover the slopes. Their yellow sunflower-like blossoms do their thing in April or early May. Closer to the ground lie the prickly pear cactus. You should consider yourself lucky to find one in blossom. You won't soon forget the delicate yellow-green-orange blossoms — or the sharp spines, should you sit down indiscriminately.

Your final journey to Highway 97 will be through the orchards of Summerland via Prairie Valley Road.

The total distance from the Connector to Summerland is about 90 kilometres, hardly more than a jaunt for today's Sunday traveller. However, if you are as easily sidetracked as I am, you should bring your lunch, drinking water, a full tank of gas, and plenty of film — and allow a full day of it.

Make it a lodgepole and lupine holiday. — MS

Additional Information:

Headwaters Lodge
PO Box 1358
Peachland , BC V0H 1X0
Tel: (250) 767-2400
E-mail: headwatersbc@yahoo.ca
Web: www.headwatersbc.com

CHAPTER 45

South Okanagan, Similkameen & Boundary

The South Okanagan, Similkameen and Boundary districts of BC have many similarities and many differences. At the lower elevations, the climate of all three is generally hot and dry in summer and moderate and dry in winter. Without irrigation water pumped from rivers or captured in the hills, the bottomland would be as dry and barren as the nearby sage-covered hillsides.

But it isn't dry and barren — and this makes for some of the most important attractions in the region. Where sprinklers cast their man-made rainbows, a virtual Garden of Eden flourishes. Cherries, apricots, peaches, and plums are harvested as the summer progresses. Apples and pears are cultivated in many varieties and follow in the soft fruit harvest. Grapes — raw material for the wine-making industry — grow on the slopes, row upon row.

What healthier form of recreation is there than fruit stand shopping?

Once you've filled your basket, head for the beaches of Okanagan, Skaha, or Osoyoos lakes — or one of the dozen other lakes on the valley floor or in the nearby hills. You can practice your swing at one of many golf courses, ride an inner tube down the Okanagan or Similkameen rivers, or bird watch in the riverside oxbows or sagebrush-covered hills. If you are really serious about hills, you can explore Apex Provincial Park, Nickel Plate Provincial Park, Cathedral Provincial Park or the south slopes of Okanagan Mountain Provincial Park. You're sure to bring back fine memories of the mountains.

If you choose not to hibernate in winter, the alpine region beckons. Strap on the slats and try skiing at the many ski resorts or cross-country trails. Penticton has many fine restaurants and an excellent Library / Museum centre, while Osoyoos features a Spanish theme to go with the nearby pocket desert. And Oliver, "The Wine Capital of Canada," is set halfway between Vaseux Lake and Osoyoos Lake.

Over Richter Pass, west of the Okanagan, lies the Similkameen, with more fruit stands per kilometre in Keremeos than probably any other place in Canada. Over Anarchist Mountain, to the east of the Okanagan, lies the Boundary District — and Doukhobor country. This narrow stretch of land has a heritage as rich as any in Canada.

The choices are many — and they're all yours.

CHAPTER 45

Okanagan Lake Park

Statistics	For map, see page 146
Distance:	25 kilometres, Penticton to Okanagan Lake Park
	35 kilometres, Kelowna to Okanagan Lake Park
Condition:	Paved highway, some four-lane sections
Season:	Year round, north park closed in winter
Topo Maps:	Summerland, BC 82 E/12
Communities:	Summerland, Peachland, and West Kelowna

Okanagan Lake Provincial Park is situated along the western shores of Okanagan Lake, a short drive north of Summerland and approximately 25 kilometres north of Penticton. Highway 97, continuing north to Peachland and Kelowna, passes directly through the park, dividing the terraced, developed campground sections below from the rocky hills above. The upper sections of the park typify the dry, semi-desert landscape for which the Okanagan Valley is famous.

Okanagan Lake Park was founded in 1955. Its planners created the park with the goal of creating a natural area that contrasted strikingly against the local vegetation. With this in mind, the first of more than 10,000 trees were planted in the foreshore area of the park in the latter part of the 1950s. Today you can set up your camp in the shade of any one of a dozen exotic tree species, including Manitoba, silver, and Norway maples, Russian olive, Chinese elm, Lombardy poplar, and red, blue and mountain ashes. In the hills above, natural stands of ponderosa pine and Douglas-fir continue to share the rocky landscape with sagebrush, bunchgrass, and cacti, as they have for centuries.

The extensive tree cover provides a haven for a tremendous variety of bird life. Many species, including cedar waxwing, quail, red-shafted flicker, western meadowlark, Lewis woodpecker, and several varieties of hummingbirds can be spotted

Okanagan Lake Park: A nearly deserted beach in the morning light. *© Murphy Shewchuk*

here with little difficulty. Along the many hiking trails in the dry upland areas of the park, you might well come across a harmless gopher snake sunning itself quietly on a rocky outcrop, or a colony of Columbian ground squirrels eyeing you suspiciously from the safety of their burrows.

Lakeshore Destination

The park's recreational activities focus on the warm, clear waters of Okanagan Lake. There is more than a kilometre of sandy beach, and the opportunities for wind-surfers, swimmers, sailors, fishers, water-skiers, picnickers, and sun worshipers are virtually limitless. Okanagan Lake Park is unusual in that it consists of two campgrounds instead of one.

The North Campground has 80 sites, including nine double sites, 56 of which are reservable from May 20 to September 6. The rest are available on a first-come, first-served basis. The campground is open from May 1 to Sept 30 (approximately), after which the gate is closed. This campground is laid out in a series of three terraces overlooking Okanagan Lake. The sites are large and well spaced with lawn and trees in between. In addition, the sites are located only on the lake side of the roads, which increases privacy and allows for better views of the water. The campsite pads are gravel and have fire rings and picnic tables. Wide, well-packed trails lead between the terraces and to pit toilets.

The South Campground has 88 sites, 60 of which are also reservable from May 20 to September 6, with the rest available on a first-come, first-served basis. The campground is open and staffed from April 1 to Oct. 31. There is a gatehouse at the entrance to the campground where guests must register. The gate is open year round though no services are provided outside the regular season.

The South Campground is very different from North Campground. All of the sites are at lake level and very close together though there is variation in site layout. The beauty of this campground is that all sites have easy beach access and there are large treed lawn areas shared by some of the sites. There is also a phone by the shower building.

In addition to the camping sites, there are day-use / picnic areas in both campgrounds, as well as change houses, showers, pit and flush toilets, and boat ramps.

Because Okanagan Lake Park is tremendously popular, it is on the reservation system during busy summer months. As is the case in many BC provincial parks, Okanagan Lake has a resident campground host / hostess to answer your questions and make your stay a pleasant and memorable one.

The boat ramp at Okanagan Lake Provincial Park is also a departure point for the marine campgrounds and trails on the west slopes of the 10,000-

hectare Okanagan Mountain Provincial Park. It is also accessible by road from either Kelowna or Penticton. (See the *Okanagan Mountain Park* chapter for details.) — MS

Additional information:

BC Parks General Information
Web: www.env.gov.bc.ca/bcparks

Okanagan Mountain panorama from Greata Ranch on the west side of Okanagan Lake.
© Murphy Shewchuk

CHAPTER 46

Giant's Head Mountain

Statistics	For map, see page 240
Distance:	Approximately 5 kilometres, Highway 97 to summit
Travel Time:	Allow 1 to 2 hours, including hike to top
Elev. Gain:	500 metres
Condition:	Mostly paved, very narrow and steep
Season:	Best in dry weather
Topo Maps:	Summerland, BC 82 E/12
Communities:	Summerland

One of the finest viewpoints in the south Okanagan is found in the heart of Summerland. Giant's Head Mountain, with a 360-degree perspective from 500 metres above Okanagan Lake, is the ideal point to get a true appreciation of the lay of the land.

Getting to the peak is relatively simple. If you are travelling along Highway 97 in upper Summerland, turn west on Prairie Valley Road, then south on Atkinson Road to Giant's Head Road. After a very short jaunt on Giant's Head Road, make a sharp turn to the right and head west on Milne Road. Watch for the signs and the stone gateway marking the start of the narrow switchback road to the picnic site near the top. Cars and smaller trucks should have little difficulty in dry weather, but leave your motorhomes, campers and holiday trailers at the parking area near the gate. From the parking area and picnic site near the top, several trails crisscross the ridge. The main route goes south and up with a switchback walking trail and a straighter route that has been gouged out of the mountain by errant 4x4s or ATVs.

Additional information on Giant's Head Mountain trails is available from the Regional District of Okanagan-Similkameen's website at www.rdos.bc.ca.

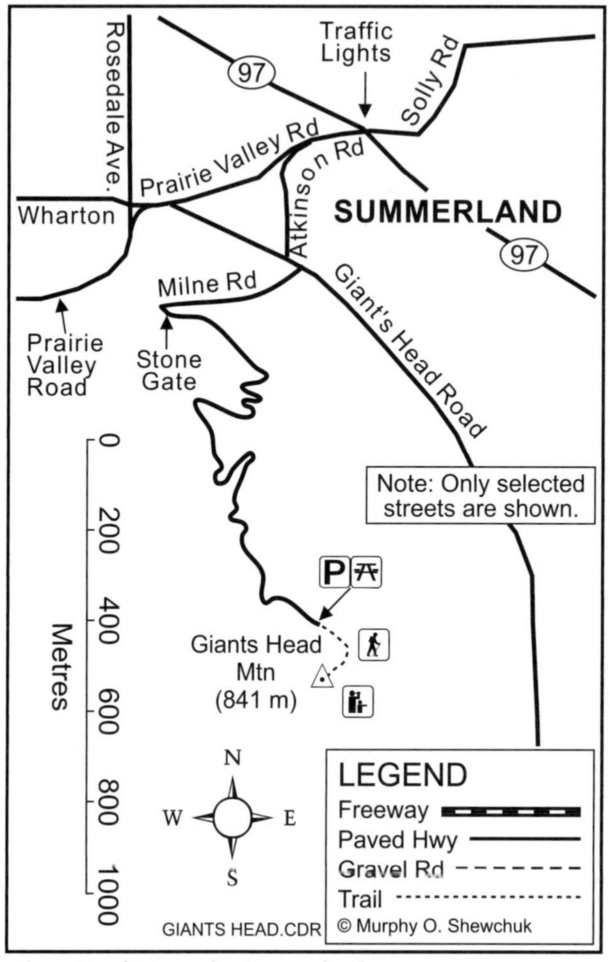

Giants Head Mountain, Summerland.

Excellent View of the South Okanagan

Many of the Okanagan's local landmarks are clearly visible from the peak of Giant's Head Mountain. Across the lake to the northeast is Okanagan Mountain and Okanagan Mountain Provincial Park. Across the lake to the east is Naramata, with several fine beaches. If you look carefully to the northeast, you may be able to pick out the twisting path of the Kettle Valley Railway right-of-way as it descends from Chute Lake on its way to Penticton. Just below you to the south is the community of Trout Creek and the Pacific Agri-Food Research Centre (formerly the Summerland Agricultural Research Station). Okanagan Lake, Skaha Lake, and Vaseux Lake lie progressively farther south. Nearer to the south and southwest, you should again be able to pick out the meandering path of the Kettle Valley Railway as it begins its steady climb out of the Okanagan Valley on its way to Princeton. With the Summerland, BC (82 E/12) topographic map as a reference, you may be able to visually follow Prairie Valley Road as it heads up Trout Creek.

If map reading doesn't enthrall you, you may be interested in the excellent variety of dry-country wildflowers and shrubs that cling to the mountain slopes. Yellow avalanche lilies and arrow-leaved balsamroot dominate the scene in April and May, but a closer look will reveal shooting stars, scarlet gilia and a host of other plant species. Saskatoon bushes thrust forth their white blossoms before most other plants bear any leaves, showing clumps of white on a drab brown slope. By early summer, the purple fruit attracts birds, chipmunks and anyone interested in a little variety in their berry pies. — MS

Additional Information:

Regional District of Okanagan-Similkameen
101 Martin St
Penticton, BC V2A 5J9
Toll-free:1-877-610-3737
E-mail: info@RDOS.bc.ca
Web: www.rdos.bc.ca

Summerland Chamber of Economic Development Tourism
15600 Hwy 97, PO Box 130,
Summerland, BC V0H 1Z0
Tel: (250) 494-2686
Fax: (250) 494-4039
Web: www.summerlandchamber.com

CHAPTER 47

Princeton - Summerland Road

Statistics:	For maps, see page 228 and page 146
Distance:	95 kilometres, Summerland to Princeton
Travel Time:	Two to three hours
Elev. Gain:	860 metres
Condition:	Mixed paved and gravel sections
Season:	Best in the dry months
Topo Maps:	Summerland, BC 82 E/12
	Bankier, BC 92 H/9
	Tulameen, BC 92 H/10
	Hedley, BC 92 H/8
	Princeton, BC 92 H/7
Communities:	Summerland and Princeton

Visit the Sumac Ridge winery, stock up at the local fruit stands, fill up with gasoline and groceries and prepare to head for the hills in search of some fine trout lakes, hidden recreation sites, and the last remnants of the famous Kettle Valley Railway (KVR).

The Princeton-Summerland Road follows much the same route across this section of the Interior Plateau as the former Kettle Valley Railway. Called Prairie Valley Road in Summerland, the eastern end of this upland backroad begins at a set of traffic lights on Highway 97 in upper Summerland. This backroad is paved for the first 13 kilometres and the last 45 kilometres, with some rough gravel sections in the Trout Creek Canyon area.

Using the junction of Prairie Valley Road and Highway 97 as your km 0 reference, follow the road as it winds through the village and out into an orchard-covered prairie that certainly isn't obvious from the main highway. Watch for the signs marked Osprey Lakes as you climb into the dry hills above Summerland.

Darke Lake Park

Bald Range Road, at km 11, is your first major junction. The road to the right continues up into the highlands, gradually getting narrower and rougher as it passes Darke Lake (Fish Lake). Bald Range Road, to the left, climbs away from the valley and up to a narrow bench high above Trout Creek. This is the truly scenic route to the Osprey Lakes and Princeton, and for the next 10 kilometres it offers several spectacular views of the Trout Creek Canyon and its arid rangeland. Wildflowers dominate the slopes in late April and May, but by July everything has a distinct brown look about it.

Brown gives way to green as the road crosses Trout Creek, near km 25, at the bottom of the Trout Creek valley. Forest Service campgrounds (basically a table or two and a pit toilet) have been established at several places along the creek for the cyclist, fisher, hunter, and itinerant tourist. The only service provided is the flat space among the trees. Carry in drinking water, fuel, and supplies, and carry out any garbage. These campsites do have their advantages — even in mid-summer, your solitude might only be breached by the yodel of a not-too-distant coyote and the gurgle of the stream.

Trans Canada Trail

A minute's drive beyond the Trout Creek Bridge, the road crosses the railbed of the former Kettle Valley Railway. The last train ran over the section from Spences Bridge to Okanagan Falls in May 1989. The twin steel rails have since been removed, with the province purchasing the railway right-of-way. At the time of writing, much of the KVR route from Brookmere to Midway had been designated part of the Trans Canada Trail.

Thirsk Lake, at km 42, is a reservoir maintained for the orchards and residents of the Summerland area, storing precious water for the hot summer months. Lake levels fluctuate significantly during the irrigation season as the water that begins in the Headwaters Lakes area is released via Trout Creek.

Trout Main FS Road, to the right at km 48.5, leads north to the Headwaters Lakes area with detour options east to Peachland, or northwest to Highway 97C and the Pennask Lake area. See the *Sunset Main to Summerland* chapter for more information.

Popular Fishing Lakes

Osprey Lake (at km 51), Link Lake, and Chain Lake form the popular Osprey Lakes chain near the summit of this backroad. The altitude allows for fine fishing throughout most of the summer. Your driving conditions will also improve since

The "Princeton Castle" is the remains of a pioneer cement plant. © Murphy Shewchuk

the road here to Princeton is now paved.

Switchback or hairpin turns are common on mountain roads, but not nearly so common on railways. After seriously considering a number of alternative routes to Princeton, KVR Chief Engineer Andrew McCulloch used the undulating grasslands to his advantage when he designed the line's descent into the Allison Creek Valley north of Princeton. From the Separation Lakes area, near km 87, the railway line makes four wide loops down the hillside as it follows Belfort Creek to the valley floor. The road crosses the railway right-of-way several times, offering glimpses of the switchback loops between the low rolling hills.

Princeton-Summerland Road joins the Old Hedley Road and Highway 5A on the northern outskirts of Princeton, near km 94. Directly across the highway, another sideroad leads to the old mining towns of Coalmont and Tulameen and Otter Lake Provincial Park, but that's another trip.

Princeton, a community of 4,000 at the junction of Highways 5A and 3 (at km 95), is the gateway to the dry interior for those travelling east on the Crowsnest Route. It was once known as Vermilion Forks because of the red ochre deposits nearby. More on the history of the region can be obtained from the museum and archives on Vermilion Avenue, near the Princeton city centre. — MS

Additional Information:

Princeton, Town of
169 Bridge Street
PO Box 670
Princeton, BC V0X 1W0
Tel: (250) 295-3135
Fax: (250) 295-3477
Web: www.town.princeton.bc.ca

CHAPTER 48

Green Mountain Road / Nickel Plate Road

Statistics	For map, see page 246
Distance:	60 kilometres, Penticton to Highway 3 near Hedley
Travel Time:	One to two hours
Elev. Gain:	1,640 metres
Condition:	Partly paved; some rough gravel sections
Season:	Nickel Plate to Hedley may be closed in winter
Topo Maps:	Penticton, BC 82 E/5
	Hedley, BC 92 H/8
Communities:	Penticton, Keremeos and Hedley

The backroad from Penticton to Hedley via Nickel Plate Mountain has historical significance that dates back to the late 1800s. In more recent years, the Penticton end has been the subject of Aboriginal land claims. Check the current status at the Penticton Indian Band administration office. If the road is signed or blocked, you might want to use the route from Highway 3A near Yellow Lake.

The description below is broken into three parts in order to take advantage of Forest Service kilometre markers and still provide a guide for the complete trip from Penticton to Hedley via Apex and Nickel Plate. The first part takes in part of the Green Mountain Road from Penticton to the junction to Apex Mountain Resort. The second part covers the route to the ski resort, and the last section describes the route from Apex past the Nickel Plate Mine to Hedley.

Green Mountain Road suffers from an identity problem, for it's called Fairview Road when it heads east off Channel Parkway (the Highway 97 bypass) in the heart of Penticton's riverside industrial area. For simplicity's sake, consider the junction with Channel Parkway km 0. The first dozen kilometres of this paved road pass through Penticton Indian Reserve. The stretch provides good opportu-

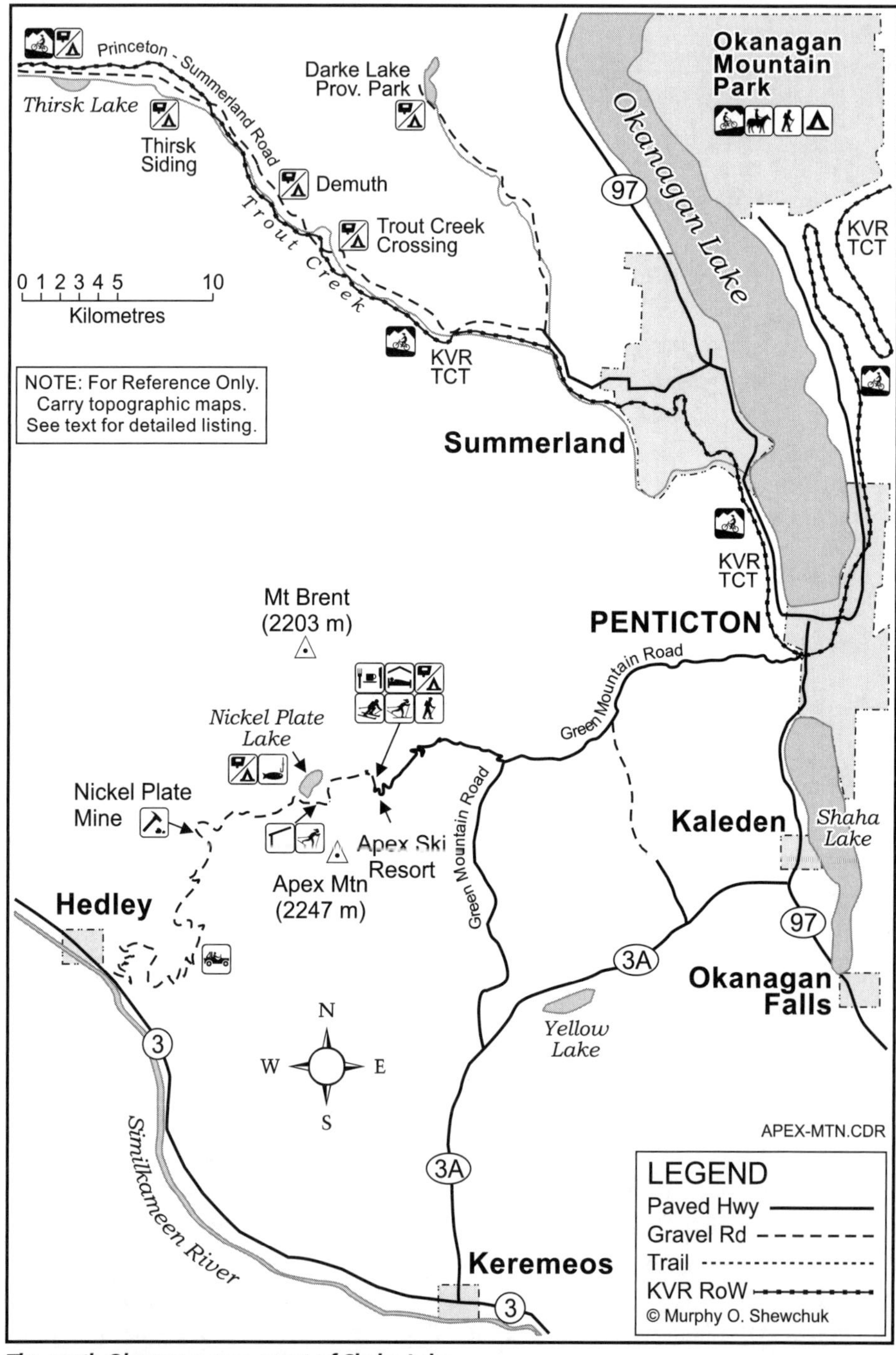

The south Okanagan area, west of Skaha Lake.

nities for backroads exploring to Farleigh Lake.

Marron Valley Road, at km 12.6, provides an alternative route to Highway 3A north of the Twin Lakes golf course, but at the time of writing, it was posted with "No Trespassing" signs. The term "marron" has French connections dating back to the fur brigade days. One sense of the word means "fugitive" or "wild" and could have been used to refer to the wild horses that once roamed the valley. But another sense of the word means "chestnut" which could also have referred to a horse, or perhaps the reddish-brown fall colours of the surrounding semi-desert hills. Word relationships such as this make the study of place names an interesting, but inexact science.

Marron Valley Road passes the T6 Ranch, then follows a switchback route up the hillside until it overlooks Aeneas Lake near km 5. From this midpoint, it follows a route apparently surveyed by the ubiquitous Sidehill Gouger until it joins Highway 3A approximately 11 kilometres southeast of Green Mountain Road.

Green Mountain House

It was near the junction of Green Mountain Road and the road to Apex Ski Resort that the first Green Mountain House (km 19.8) was built. Ezra Mills, the master carpenter of Keremeos, built this roadside stopping-house for Leonard Albert Clark. L.A. Clark was born in Vermont in 1840. After a stint with the Union Army ("the North") during the American Civil War, he began a westward trek. He married in Iowa, learned irrigation lay-out in Colorado, railroad grading in Washington State, and had a livery stable in Northport, Washington. By 1893, Clark and family were living in Calgary, where he installed an irrigation system. He later continued in the same line of work for the Coldstream Orchards at Vernon, BC.

After trying his luck in the Klondike in 1898, Clark returned to the Okanagan where M.K. Rodgers, of the Nickel Plate Mine, contracted him to build a road from Penticton to the mine. Clark and his crew began work August 10, 1900. Here, Leonard Clark faced one of the toughest challenges of his varied career as he surveyed feverishly to keep ahead of the construction equipment. But he succeeded, completing the rough wagon road by Christmas of that year.

His route left Penticton and wound up at the sand hills on the south side of Shingle Creek, joining the present route of Green Mountain Road about eight kilometres from the Catholic Church on the Indian Reserve. From that point to the mine, nearly 50 kilometres, the route has changed little — a credit to Clark and his crew, and their horse-drawn slip scrapers, hand tools, drill steel, and blasting powder.

Clark was not one to pass up an opportunity. He quickly recognized the potential of the area and, with his son Garry, pre-empted about 400 hectares (1,000 acres) of land in the Green Mountain District, named by him after his boyhood Green Mountains in Vermont. Green Mountain House was built and thrived with the steady traffic of freight wagons to and from the mine, and the thrice-weekly stage run over the soon-opened road to Olalla and points west in the Similkameen Valley.

Apex Ski Resort

The development of Apex Mountain Resort began in 1960. However, the original road to Beaconsfield Mountain (near Apex Mountain) proved woefully inadequate for the purpose and a new road was started. The road was mostly single-lane at first, but was steadily improved by the government until today where the road to the ski resort is now two-lane and paved.

The junction of the Green Mountain Road and the road to Apex — 21 kilometres southwest of Penticton — serves as the km 0 reference for the mid-section of this route. From the junction, the road climbs steadily toward the Apex ski area, passing Shatford Road near km 4. (Shatford Road winds north then northwest, providing access to the Sheep Rock trailhead near km 6.3 and the Mt. Brent trailhead near km 9.) At first, the timber is scattered, but fir and lodgepole pine soon dominate the view.

Hedley-Nickel Plate FS Road

Apex Village is reached at km 11.5. The junction to the Hedley-Nickel Plate FS Road is well marked at km 13. Apex Mountain Ski Resort first gained a reputation as a challenging, technical mountain. The first view of the ski runs from the day lodge will do little to allay a beginner's fears. However, on closer investigation, the hill holds appeal for both the recreational skier and the more serious racer looking for a greater challenge. For the cross-country skier, the Nickel Plate Nordic Centre maintains an extensive network of trails in the surrounding area.

Hedley-Nickel Plate FS Road begins in the upper levels of the Apex village (reset your reference to kilometre 0) and passes through an area marked for X-C skiers and snowmobiles at km 2. The Hedley Creek-Nickel Plate FS Road detours to the right, near the height-of-land and although it is very rough and boulder-strewn, it can be followed west to Nickel Plate Provincial Park on the north shore of Nickel Plate Lake. To get to the park beach, drive or walk west for about 2.6 kilometres and then turn south at a huge boulder. It's less than a kilometre from the boulder to the lake, but unless you are driving an ATV or a 4x4 with excep-

Nickel Plate Nordic Centre clubhouse. *© Murphy Shewchuk*

tional clearance, it is probably safest to park near the boulder and walk the rest of the way. The lake is at an altitude of 1,900 metres, so the fishing should stay good even during the summer. The swimming, however, is likely to be a bit on the chilly side.

A junction at km 5 offers a few options for hiking or backroads exploring. Although there have been recent changes, roads and trails lead south to Apex Mountain. Depending on the current state of the road and your vehicle, you can drive part of the way and walk the remaining distance to the peak of 2,247-metre Apex Mountain. The total distance is about four to five kilometres, so take drinking water, a lunch, and leave plenty of time. Other forest roads may end in log cuts or mud holes, so use caution.

The Nickel Plate Mine Road to the right has been variously marked by a "Mascot Gold" or "Corona Corporation" sign, but the best reference is the electric power line that leads to the open-pit mine site.

Nickel Plate Nordic Centre

Nickel Plate Nordic Centre, less than a kilometre down the gradual descent, is the focal point of a 56-kilometre network of groomed and track-set cross-country ski trails. A fine log building serves as a rendezvous and a warming hut for this relatively new operation. Work first started here in May 1989, and by fall, the trail clearing was well underway. Sale of the logs removed from the trail system helped finance the grooming and the cabin. The system opened in February 1990, in time for the Penticton Winter Games.

The Nickel Plate Nordic trails are rated as 70 percent easy; 20 percent intermediate; and 10 percent difficult. The club has also recently added 25 kilometres of snowshoe trails.

Nickel Plate Lake FS Recreation Site is less than two kilometres north of the junction near a creek crossing at km 7. Although not as attractive as the park at the north end of the lake, access is much easier. You will also discover some excellent fly-fishing. The Nickel Plate Road, keeping left, follows Cahill Creek southwest, descending across a lightly timbered mountain before reaching the open-pit Nickel Plate gold mine at km 12.5.

Nickel Plate Mine

The operation here is not new. In fact, the Nickel Plate Mine, 1,200 metres above Hedley, was one of BC's first successful hardrock mining operations. Except for a few short interruptions, the mine operated steadily from 1904 to 1956.

From 1900 to late 1909, when the Great Northern Railway reached Hedley, four-horse teams plied the Nickel Plate Road in regular procession, hauling heavy mining and milling equipment from Penticton to Nickel Plate. Once the mine began producing, the teams never returned to Penticton empty.

According to Geoffrey Taylor in his book Mining, "Every month two gold bricks came down to Penticton under special guard and were sent by Dominion Express to Seattle. Concentrates were sacked and hauled by horse-drawn wagon at $9 per ton to Penticton and from there by rail to the smelter in Tacoma. On the return journey the wagons would bring back supplies to Hedley at a contract rate of $20 per ton. The round trip usually took about a week."

The history of the Hedley Mascot operation also goes back to the turn of the century when the Mascot fraction, a triangular claim in the heart of the Nickel Plate ore body, was staked. The owners of the Nickel Plate mine were never able to come to suitable terms with Duncan Wood, owner of the Mascot fraction. In 1934, Hedley Mascot Gold Mines was formed to exploit the Mascot claim and neighbouring claims. The ore contained a variety of minerals. For instance, in 1941, Hedley Mascot produced 22,477 ounces of gold, 2,755 ounces of silver, 1.3 million pounds of copper and 2.25 million pounds of arsenic. In the first half-century of operation, the mines on Nickel Plate Mountain produced 1.5 million ounces of gold and 4 million pounds of copper, worth nearly $50 million at the time of production.

Mascot Gold Mine Tours

The Upper Similkameen Indian Band has recently been conducting tours of the now closed Nickel Plate Mine. The tour operates out of the old Hedley School near Highway 3 in Hedley. The tour buses take you 1,000 metres above the Similkameen Valley where you will get the opportunity to see the more modern mine workings as well as historic buildings that still cling to the mountainside.

"Reasonably good health" is one condition of the tour as you will be required to descend 100 metres by stair to the portal level of the mine where the tour guides explain all the workings.

Switchback Descent

To this point, the backroad has been descending steadily from a height near Apex Ski Resort. But after passing the mining operation, the descent gets serious. At first, the timber hides the steepness of the slope, but then the open hillside, dotted with aspen groves, makes the narrow, sometimes muddy switchback descent much more obvious.

A cattleguard and fence at km 21 mark a good spot to pull off the road, park and hike to the lip of a nearby rock bluff for an excellent view of the Similkameen Valley, both to the east and west. Caution is advised as there are no guardrails and a fall from the bluff means certain death.

Just beyond the viewpoint area, the road passes through a narrow rock cut and across a section of cliff face that is likely to convince even the bravest backroader to slow down. Once past the cliff, the road continues a steady switchback descent across a slope covered with sagebrush and bunchgrass. Visibility is good — and needed because the narrow road offers few places to safely pass oncoming vehicles. The Nickel Plate Road ends at Highway 3, 26 kilometres from the Apex Ski Resort and 60 kilometres from Penticton. If you're approaching it from the southwest, look for the road opposite St. Ann's Catholic Church, a few minutes' drive east of Hedley. — MS

Additional Information:

Apex Mountain Resort
PO Box 1060
Penticton, BC
V2A 6J9

Green Mountain Road / Nickel Plate Road

Tel: (250) 292-8222
Toll-free:1-877-777-APEX (2739)
Fax: (250) 292-8100
Web: www.apexresort.com

Mascot Gold Mine Tours
Tel: (250) 292-8733
Fax: (250) 292-8753
Web: www.mascotmine.com

Nickel Plate Nordic Centre
Tel: (250) 292-8110
Web: www.nickelplatenordic.org

Penticton Indian Band
200 Westhill Estates,
Penticton, BC V2A 6J7
Tel: (250) 493-0048

Chapter 49

Apex Mountain Resort

Statistics	For map see page 246
Distance:	32 kilometres from Penticton
Travel Time:	Less than an hour from Penticton
Condition:	Well-maintained
Season:	All
Topo Map:	Penticton, BC 82 E/5
Communities:	Penticton

Apex was initially developed in 1969, and is now the largest ski resort in the south Okanagan with over 60 runs served by a high-speed detachable quad, a triple chair, a T-bar, a platter, and a tube tow.

Apex Fast Facts

Peak Elevation	2,180 m
Vertical Rise	605 m
Downhill Trails	67
Skiable Terrain	450 ha
Base Elevation	1,575 m
Average Winter Temp	-4°C (23°F)
Longest Run	5 km
Average Annual Snowfall	600 cm (20 ft)

Apex Village features a range of accommodations, from The Inn with 90 rooms, hot tubs and a fitness room, to condominiums and the RV park. You can grab a quick bite to eat at the Longshot Cafeteria or dinner at the Rusty Spur; or kick back at the famous Gunbarrel Saloon. There's also a teen centre, outdoor hot tubs, Jacuzzi and sauna, childcare, ski schools, a skating rink, grocery store, liquor outlet, snowboarding, ski shop and rentals, snowmobile rentals, and tours and sleigh rides.

The village is at an elevation of 1,629 metres, while the peak reaches 2,180 metres. Just six kilometres away is the Nickel Plate Nordic Centre with over 50 kilometres of groomed trails and 25 kilometres of snowshoe trails. — JS

Additional Information:

Apex Mountain Resort
PO Box 1060
Penticton, BC
V2A 6J9
Tel: (250) 292-8222
Toll-free:1-877-777-APEX (2739)
Fax: (250) 292-8100
E-mail: info@apexresort.com
Web: www.apexresort.com/

CHAPTER 50

Old Hedley Road:

Princeton to Hedley (Similkameen Bridge)

Statistics:	For map, see page 256
Distance:	32 kilometres — Highway 5A to Highway 3 at Similkameen Bridge
Travel time:	One half to one hour
Elev. descent:	150 metres
Conditions:	Paved
Season:	Maintained year round
Topo maps:	Princeton, BC 92 H/7
	Hedley, BC 92 H/8
Communities:	Princeton and Hedley

The next time you're heading east (or west) along Crowsnest Highway 3 between Princeton and Hedley, consider a detour that will get you off the busy highway, but won't add much travel time or distance. The Old Hedley Road, on the north side of the Similkameen River, is a little more twisting and a little narrower and a whole lot more interesting than the main highway.

Route of Commerce

What is now the Old Hedley Road was once the main route of commerce in the upper Similkameen valley. First Nations used well-worn trails along the north side of the river as they travelled to trade the red ochre found on the banks of the Tulameen, a short distance upstream from Princeton. Edgar Dewdney constructed a mule trail along this route in a successful effort to help keep the Boundary District Canadian. And, from approximately 1903 until 1910 when the Vancouver, Victoria and Eastern Railway was completed to Princeton, this was the route of one of the last commercial stage coach runs in British Columbia. The Welby Stage operated three days a week, serving Princeton, Hedley, Keremeos, and Penticton.

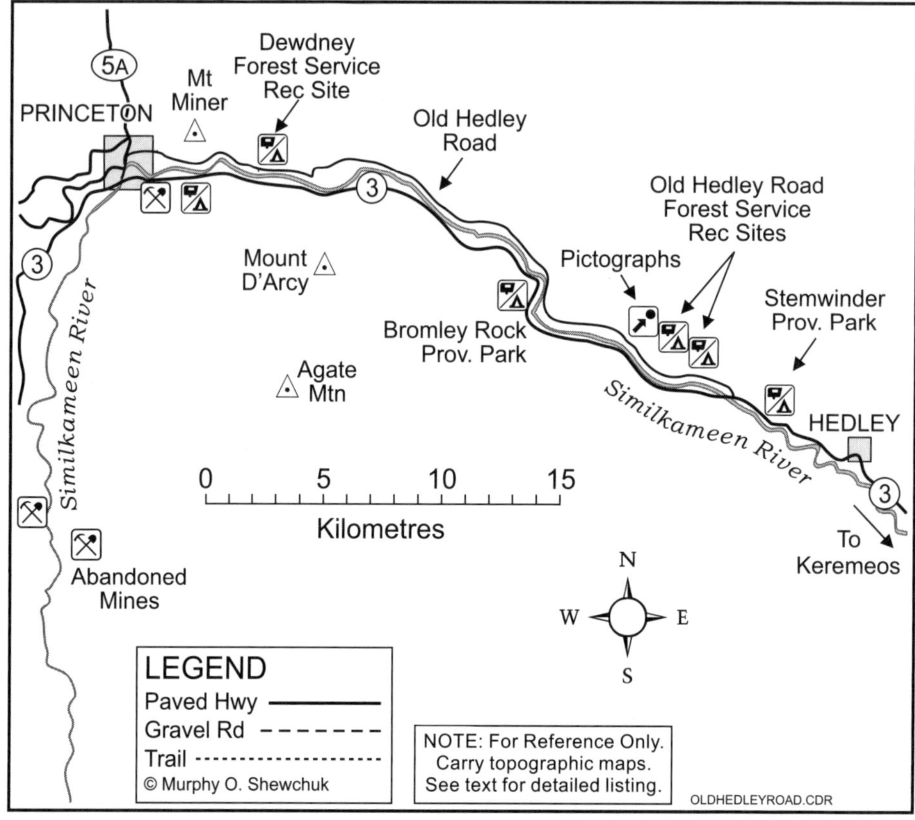

The Old Hedley Road leaves Highway 5A (the Princeton-Merritt route) less than a kilometre north of the Tulameen River bridge on the outskirts of Princeton. Using the junction with Highway 5A as km 0, Old Hedley swings wide to the right (east) before reaching a junction with the Princeton-Summerland Road and then continuing through the heart of Weyerhaeuser Canada's Princeton sawmill.

Princeton Castle

The Princeton-Summerland Road sign at km 0.3 marks a side trip that's well worth taking if you have a few hours to spare, or if you're looking for a place to camp for the night. Approximately 2.5 km up the Princeton-Summerland Road, and a short drive down Rainbow Lake Road, is an incredible stone ruin — all that remains of a massive undertaking that was once a masterpiece of engineering and stone masonry. It all began in 1909 with a grand scheme to build a Portland cement plant, a cement city to house the workers, and a powerhouse. The dream cost over a million dollars and the lives of several workers. It also involved hun-

Deer are a common sight inthe Princeton area. *© Murphy Shewchuk*

dreds of thousands of man-hours completed by skilled craftsmen, stonemasons, carpenters, and engineers. It took four years to finish, produced quality cement, had its official opening in 1913 — and closed a few months later.

The local dream had turned sour — and ended in a nightmare for the shareholders, many of whom came from the Princeton area. The mystery still lingers. Why did the cement plant close? Was it the result of a hoax, a blunder, a swindle?

In the mid-1970s, a new idea for the old cement city site took root and became a reality. Inspired by the sprawling castle-like ruins, Castle Enterprises Ltd. established "Princeton Castle Park," complete with an RV park, restaurant, and a trail through the remnants of dilapidated old cement city. Unfortunately, the new dream didn't last much longer than the original. A "For Sale" sign hung on the facility for several years before it was re-opened as Princeton Castle Resort.

Kettle Valley Railway (KVR)

Meanwhile, back on the Old Hedley Road, the pavement soon crosses the former KVR / CPR line from Spences Bridge to Penticton. The KVR first reached Princeton from Penticton in April 1915. According to Barrie Sanford ("McCulloch's Wonder"), there were actually two "last spike" ceremonies when the tracks reached town. The first took place on April 21, 1915 when track-laying superintendent Charles Taylor hammered home a spike and declared, "Well, the big stunt is done!" However, the switch that was needed to join the tracks of the KVR and Great Northern was still missing, and was not installed until two days later. It was then that Mrs. Griffith, the wife of a local minister, tapped home the second "last spike."

Weyerhaeuser Mill

John Nylund started Western Pines Lumber Co. Ltd. in 1957. Western Pines had a staff of over 100 men and was Princeton's biggest employer. It later became Northwood Mills, a Noranda subsidiary, and was expanded in 1970. Northwood sold out to Weyerhaeuser Canada Ltd. late in the fall of 1978. The operation is located at km 0.7.

Princeton Pioneer

Allison Creek, at km 2.7, and "The Allisons" Ranch at km 3, carry the name of one of the best-known pioneer families of the Similkameen district. John Fall Allison, considered by many to be the first European settler in the Similkameen Valley, was born in Leeds, Yorkshire, England in 1825. He travelled extensively and, following the California gold rush, landed at Victoria in August 1858. Here his goal was the golden horde said to lay amongst the gravel bottom of the Fraser River. Allison worked the gravel bars near Fort Hope, but gave them up to explore the Similkameen in 1860.

Gold diggings that paid Allison eight to ten dollars a day, a landscape that looked "more of a California ... than any other part of British Columbia I have seen," plus a government job and 160 acres of land — all this kept John Fall Allison firmly stationed in the Similkameen. He expanded his ranch, married Susan Louisa Moir, a "Pioneer Gentlewoman" from Fort Hope, and lived in the region until his death due pneumonia late in 1897. He was in his 72nd year.

After leaving the Weyerhaeuser sawmill, Old Hedley Road follows the base of skree slopes, occasionally squeezed between orange bluffs and the Similkameen River. Green irrigated fields contrast with the stark sage and pine-covered mountains alongside the river. In spring, sunflower-like arrow-leaved balsamroot spread their yellow blossoms across the slopes, while in June purple-blue penstemon cling to the rock bluffs.

Pioneer Engineer

The Dewdney Recreation Site, at km 6.2, is named after another important British Columbia pioneer. In order to maintain British control over gold rush

Native pictographs near the east end of Old Hedley Road. © *Murphy Shewchuk*

mining near Rock Creek and Vermilion Forks (now Princeton), Governor James Douglas decided to build a trail from Hope that ran north of what is now the United States-Canada border. On August 17, 1860, he gave the trail contract to Edgar Dewdney, a civil engineer. The trail route had been laid out by Sergeant McColl of the Royal Engineers earlier that year, but was changed somewhat because of rough going in the upper Tulameen canyon. In the end, after crossing the Cascade Mountains, Dewdney's "Similkameen Road" followed Whipsaw Creek down to the Similkameen River. It then followed the Similkameen to the Okanagan along the route generally followed today by Crowsnest Highway 3, except that from Princeton to Hedley it followed the north shore of the river. Portions of the old trail are still visible near the Old Hedley Road.

In 1861, Edgar Dewdney and Walter Moberly began improving the first few kilometres of the trail at the Hope end in an effort to make it into a wagon road. The Royal Engineers continued the trail improvement for the next 30 kilometres before abandoning work for the Cariboo Wagon Road.

Up to km 8.7, the road follows close to the river, but now it swings north toward the mountains. It crosses hayfields and, for the next three kilometres, winds eastward along the base of the bluffs, well away from the river. The road again swings closer to the river near km 16 where there are several openings in the trees allowing kayakers and river fishermen access to the Similkameen's whitewater rapids. Chokecherries and saskatoons grace the roadside with their flowers in spring and colourful berries in summer and autumn.

The pools at the base of Bromley Rock (km 21.4) attract swimmers in midsummer. Kayakers and canoeists brave the cold whitewater during high water in May and June. The main picnic site and campground of Bromley Rock Provincial Park are on the far side of the river, adjacent to Crowsnest Highway 3. There is some space for unorganized camping on the Old Hedley Road side of river.

Stage Road and Orchard

Remnants of the old stage road are visible through the trees on the flats north of the present route near km 23.4. Ancient fruit trees, sprawling with long neglect, stand in a rocky clearing where the birds and squirrels make a tasty meal out of the apples, crab apples, and pears. Deer are also a frequent sight in the Princeton-Hedley area, particularly at that time of the evening when driving visibility is at its worst. Use caution when driving this backroad and the main highway as these animals seem unable to comprehend the danger of fast-approaching vehicles.

Native Pictographs

This area boasts the largest concentration of Native rock paintings in the province. A rock bluff to the north of the road at km 27 also has some excellent examples of this lost and unexplained art. There are as many as two-dozen sets of pictographs in the vicinity, all of which are protected by law.

Recreation Sites

Several small recreation sites lie between the road and the river between km 28.4 and km 30.6. The key attraction of these un-serviced sites is their nearness to river fishing, kayaking, and canoeing. Old Hedley Road ends at km 31.7 at the junction with Crowsnest Highway 3, at the east end of the Similkameen River bridge, approximately 1.6 km west of Stemwinder Provincial Park. — MS

Additional Information:

Princeton Castle Resort
5 Mile Road, RR1, S1, C10
Princeton, BC V0X 1W0
Tel: (250) 295-7988
Fax: (250) 295-7208
Toll-free: 1-888-228-8881
E-mail: info@castleresort.com
Web: www.castleresort.com

Princeton, Town of
169 Bridge Street
PO Box 670
Princeton, BC V0X 1W0
Tel: (250) 295-3135
Fax: (250) 295-3477
Web: www.town.princeton.bc.ca

CHAPTER 51

Fairview Road

Statistics:	For map, see page 262
Distance:	8 kilometres, Keremeos to Cawston 24 kilometres, Cawston to Oliver
Travel Time:	Approximately 1 hour
Elev. Gain:	700 metres
Condition:	Narrow, some rough gravel
Season:	May be closed in winter
Topo Maps:	Keremeos, BC 82 E/4
Communities:	Keremeos, Cawston and Oliver

Fairview Road, linking Cawston in the Similkameen Valley and Oliver in the Okanagan Valley, provides a glimpse of the colourful mining history of the region. The western end of the road can be approached from several points between Keremeos and Cawston. In the following description, I have followed Upper Bench Road from Highway 3A because of the special attraction of the historic Keremeos Grist Mill. This route also usually has light traffic, and the scenic contrast of the orchards below the stark mountainside presents some interesting photographic opportunities.

The junction of Highway 3A and Upper Bench Road, one kilometre north of the junction of Highways 3 and 3A, makes a good starting point (km 0) for a leisurely trip over Orofino Mountain. Upper Bench Road parallels the valley eastward, cutting a path through the orchards and along the barren cliffs.

Grist Mill at Keremeos

The Grist Mill, less than a kilometre from Highway 3A, is the first stop along the way. Keremeos Creek gurgles through the sheltered vale, providing motive power for the giant wheel and a welcome reason to meander around the site. This grist mill is the only nineteenth-century mill in British Columbia that

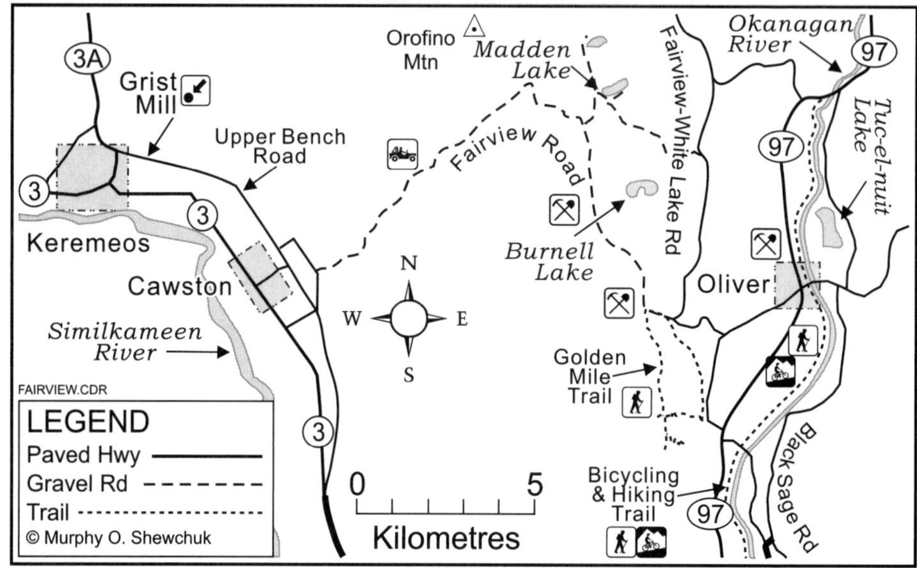

The South Okanagan - Similkameen area.

still has most of its machinery intact. This includes the original flour mill, a Eureka buckwheat screen, grain chute, and a corn grinding machine.

The original mill was built in 1877 by Barrington Price, who had pre-empted land near Keremeos in 1873. The water-powered mill was operated by John Coulthard after 1885, and served the needs of the Similkameen Valley for almost 20 years before stiff competition from larger mills forced its closure.

In 1974, the mill and adjacent log building were designated an historic site and restoration was begun. The Keremeos Grist Mill was officially reopened in 1985, and has since been steadily improved.

Beyond the grist mill, the road passes through the orchards and then along the base of the barren mountain. This country is too dry for timber at lower elevations, and all that thrives are the desert plants more common to the Cascade Mountain rain-shadow much farther south in Washington and Oregon.

Orchardists advertise fresh fruit and vegetables in season, and some of the best spring asparagus comes from Keremeos. Local beekeepers also sell orchard blossom honey and beeswax candles. Upper Bench Road continues east until it merges with Highway 3, east of Cawston. However, Lowe Drive, at km 7.7, marks the start of the mountain road to Oliver.

Closed in Winter

Because there is an option to leave Highway 3 at Cawston, the junction of Lowe Drive and Upper Bench Road has been chosen as km 0 for the backroad over Orofino Mountain. It is worth noting that the road may be closed in winter. It is not recommended for vehicles other than cars and pickups. And a four-wheel-drive vehicle is a valuable asset.

The pavement ends at km 1.2 and, not wasting any time getting away from the Similkameen Valley, the road quickly begins a northeast climb up Blind Creek. The desert environment, complete with ponderosa pine, sagebrush, prickly pear cactus, and sunflower blossoms of arrow-leaved balsamroot in spring, gives way to gullies lined with cottonwood and aspen.

As the surroundings get a little damper, the steep grade and tight corners give way to a wider road with an easier grade at km 3.7. The climate continues to change as the road reaches the height-of-land at km 10. Now the timber is Interior fir and vine maple bushes hang over the narrow road where it swings near the creek. Watch for cattle — they seem to believe they have the right-of-way by virtue of being there first.

The grist mill at Keremeos. *© Murphy Shewchuk*

Madden Lake

The road now swings southeast as it descends into the Okanagan Valley. A sideroad northeast marked Ripley Madden Lakes at km 12 offers a diversion for the backroad explorer. It is a convoluted two-kilometre drive to the recreation site on the north shore of Madden Lake with several locations where it is easy to get confused. Keep right at the junction approximately 400 metres from Fairview Road — the road to the left heads up to Ripley Lake. Keep left at the next two junctions as the road swings around a knoll. Ignore the kamikaze runways. When you spot the lake among the aspen, take the second entrance into the rec site. Just a note if you are now totally confused: I drove our pickup and Bigfoot camper the two kilometres into the rec site without any screaming from the passenger seat. If the road looks as though it may prompt a lot of hollering or stony silence, you may have taken a wrong turn.

Ripley, Madden, and Burnell (Sawmill) lakes are regularly stocked with rainbow trout. All three lakes have small recreation sites complete with car-top boat access.

Fairview Camp

Mill foundations, waste dumps, and open shafts at km 16.9 mark the location of the Fairview gold and silver mines. Karen Witte, in A Brief Historical Sketch of Fairview, writes that gold was first discovered in the area in 1887. Fred Gwatkins and George Sheenan staked what was later to become the discovery claim of the Stemwinder Mine, the primary impetus for the Fairview Camp. The Stemwinder interests were soon sold to an American and British syndicate and the two-decade first life of the mining camp began when the original Fairview Camp was established near the mine site in 1890.

On August 12, 1892, the first newspaper in Oro (now Oroville), Washington published the following account about Fairview: “This camp is in the same gold belt we are, and proves beyond a shadow of a doubt that this is the most extensive mineral belt in the known world.”

In 1893, the Golden Gate Hotel (later nicknamed the “Bucket of Blood”) opened for business. Quickly, residential buildings and other commercial developments, including the Miner’s Rest, the Fairview, and Moffatt’s Saloon, were built on the precarious slopes of the gulch.

But Fairview didn’t become a thriving community until the settlement moved down to the mouth of the gulch in 1897, at km 19, overlooking present-day Oliver. On July 1, 1899, celebrations marked the opening of the

Fairview Hotel (the Big Teepee), the most elegant hostel in the Interior.

The fire that destroyed the Big Teepee in 1902 signalled the end of Camp Fairview. The gold quartz veins became harder to work as the mine got deeper. By World War I, the only real activity left was the wrecking bar, as salvagers recovered the lumber and machinery from the townsite and mills.

The Fairview mines gained a new lease on life on January 31, 1934, when U.S. President Roosevelt raised the price of gold from $20.67 to $35.00 per ounce. Gold properties all over the continent saw renewed interest.

Robert Iverson worked at the Fairview Amalgamated Mines in 1938. "They had two horses in use pulling a train of five one-ton cars," wrote Iverson in the 48th Report of the Okanagan Historical Society. "My job was helping load and unload the train. Between 100 and 150 tons over two shifts were normal. Between 40 and 50 men were employed, including those employed at the mill."

The start of World War II forced the closure of the Fairview and Morning Star properties, but in the half dozen years of renewed operation, the land produced 14,000 ounces of gold and 152,000 ounces of silver.

A junction at km 18.2 marks a sideroad down to south Oliver while the main road keeps left to the junction of Fairview Road (350th Avenue) and Fairview-White Lake Road at km 19.3. (See the *Fairview-White Lake Road* chapter for information on the route to the north.) The gravel road gives way to pavement near the junction and the green orchards of the Okanagan Valley present a contrast to the stark grassland slopes dotted with sagebrush and greasewood in what some claim to be the driest part of Canada.

A nearby stop-of-interest sign offers a glimpse of Fairview's past:

FAIRVIEW GOLD

The 1890s held high hopes for the lode gold mines such as Stemwinder, Morning Star and Rattler. By 1902, when the Fairview Hotel or "Big Teepee" burned, the golden years were over. Fairview's population dwindled as miners left for more promising prospects. But some settlers, lured by the natural attractions of the Okanagan Valley, remained to profit from the lasting wealth of its abundant resources.

The "Big Teepee" was the centre of a community that included livery stables, offices, several stores and houses, a school, and a government building. Today all that remains of the original buildings is the jail which was moved and reassembled adjacent to the museum in downtown Oliver.

A concrete irrigation flume that passes under the street at km 23 deserves more than a passing glance, for in it is the real gold of the Okanagan Valley. Irrigation in the Okanagan grew out of necessity with techniques that were a carry-over from the water diversion techniques practiced by placer miners. Some of the first water licences in the Okanagan were recorded in the early 1870s, but serious irrigation didn't begin in the Oliver area until after World War I.

The South Okanagan Lands Project began in 1919, when the BC government bought out private holdings amounting to about 9,300 hectares. A gravity system was constructed to take water from Vaseux Lake. Water was carried across the valley through a siphon that had pipes large enough for men to work inside of. BC Premier John Oliver officially opened the dam and siphon in 1921, but it was not until 1927 that the project, with 100 kilometres of flumes and laterals, was completed and the first irrigation water served the whole area.

Without the foresight and determination of pioneer politicians such as "Honest John" Oliver, the beautiful green orchards and vineyards would still be "just the haunt of jack rabbits and rattlesnakes."

Golden Mile Trail

If you are interested in a closer look at both the man-made and the natural ecosystems, consider a hike on the 10-kilometre-long Golden Mile Trail.

No! This isn't a case of faulty metric conversion. The name refers to a narrowing of the Okanagan Valley at Oliver that has contributed to the desert microclimate. The three-to-four hour circle route extends from the Fairview townsite south to Road 7 (328 Avenue) and includes the desert hillside as well as orchards, vineyards, and three wineries. Extensions added in 1998 further the value of the interpretive trail network. There is a kiosk near the Fairview-White Lake Road junction that provides detailed directions.

Downtown Oliver

Fairview Road joins Highway 97 at km 23.6 in the heart of Oliver. If you are looking for more exercise, you could consider the 18.4-kilometre-long bicycling and hiking trail that extends south to Osoyoos Lake from the McAlpine Bridge on Highway 97, just north of Oliver. Across Highway 97 and the Okanagan River, you can continue an eastward trek to Mount Baldy and old Camp McKinney. North of the junction, Highway 97 continues on to Penticton while to the south lies Osoyoos and the U.S. border. — MS

Additional Information:

Keremeos Grist Mill
RR 1, Upper Bench Road
Keremeos, BC VOX 1N0
Tel: (250) 499-2888
Fax: (250) 499-2434

Oliver Visitor Centre
36205 - 93rd Street
Oliver, BC V0H 1T0
Tel: (250) 498-6321
Fax: (250) 498-3156
E-mail: info@winecapitalofcanada.com
Web: www.winecapitalofcanada.com

CHAPTER 52

Fairview—White Lake Road

Statistics:	For maps, see page 269 and 272
Distance:	32 kilometres, Oliver to Highway 97 near Kaleden
Travel Time:	Up to one hour
Condition:	Paved, with some gravel sections
Season:	Maintained year round
Topo Map:	Keremeos, BC 82 E/4 Penticton, BC 82 E/5
Communities:	Oliver, Okanagan Falls and Penticton

Historic Trail

Clothed in the history of the Okanagan, and of British Columbia, White Lake Road had its origins with the local Aboriginal population. It later became the path that David Stuart, of John Jacob Astor's Pacific Fur Company, followed in 1811 during the first European incursion into the valley. In 1821, it became part of the Hudson's Bay Company fur brigade trail between Fort Okanogan on the Columbia River and Fort St. James in northern British Columbia. The last fur brigade, with perhaps 200 loaded horses, their packers, families and dogs, the beaver-hatted factor and his piper in the lead, camped in the roadside meadows where Hereford cattle graze today.

The establishment of the Canada-U.S. boundary in 1846 led to the abandonment of the route as a brigade trail, but as the nineteenth century wore on, it became the route for gold-seekers and cattle drivers heading for the Cariboo. Along it Father Pandosy travelled on his way to establish the Church's presence at Okanagan Mission near Kelowna in the late 1850s. As the century closed, this Okanagan backroad echoed to the sounds of creaking wheels and snorting horses as freight wagons, loaded with supplies, headed for the gold camps of Camp McKinney and Fairview.

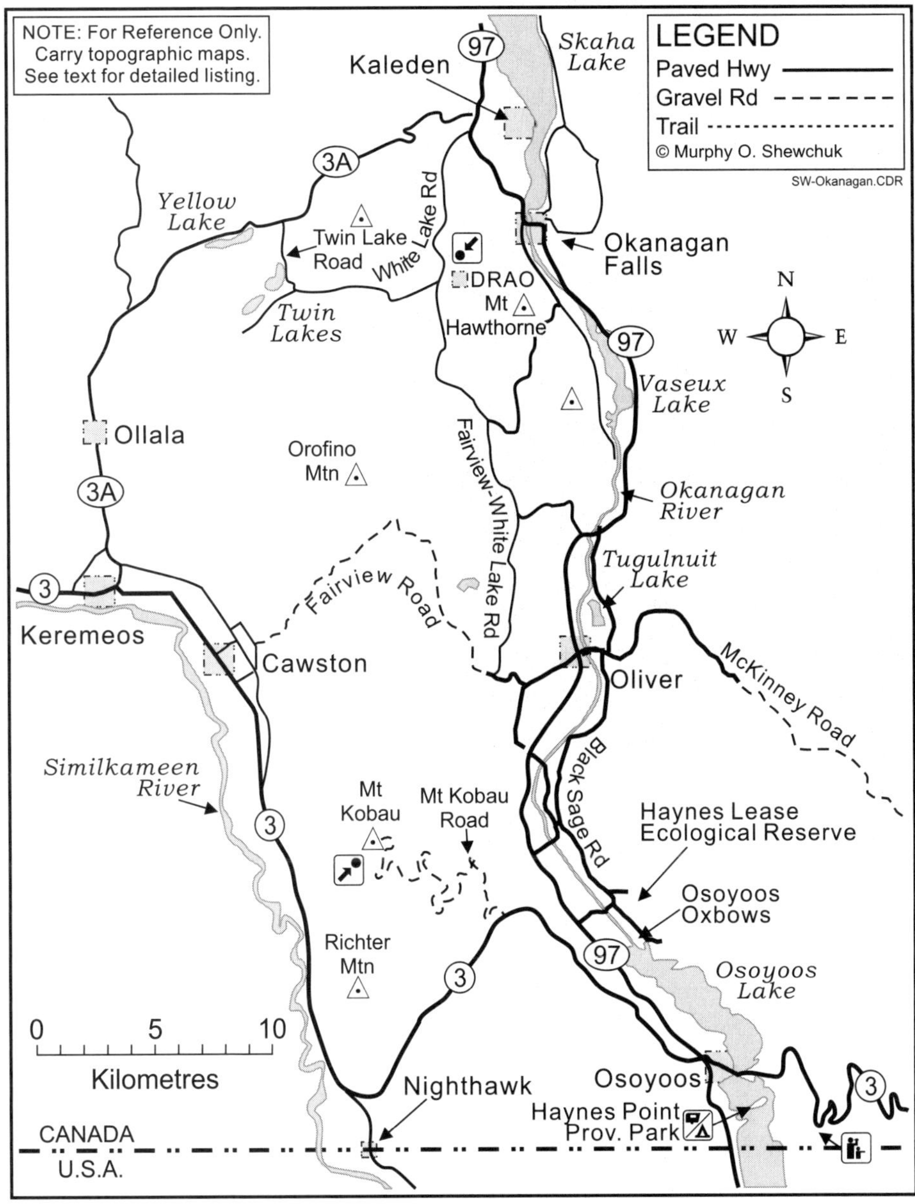

The Keremeos / Kaleden / Osoyoos area.

Vineyards and Orchards

With the main traffic light on Highway 97 in downtown Oliver as km 0, follow 350th Avenue as it climbs westward. Soon becoming Fairview Road, it leaves the village and orchards to continue up through the sagebrush and greasewood-dotted slopes. Irrigated vineyards cut into this greasewood domain, producing one of the Okanagan Valley's finest cash crops.

A stop-of-interest sign near the junction of Fairview Road and White Lake Road, km 4.5, provides a brief glimpse of the long-gone community of Fairview, spawned by the discovery of gold, the Okanagan's oldest cash crop, in a nearby valley. See the *Fairview Road* chapter for more information.

White Lake Road follows a dry bench northward, skirting stands of ponderosa pine, sumac bushes that turn flame red in autumn, and small ranches complete with children on horseback. Although paved, this backroad requires your full attention if you want to avoid domestic animals and other sightseeing drivers. The side valley begins to broaden, with homes nestled at the base of the cliffs. Another backroad, Secrest Road near km 12, winds down Park Rill to join Highway 97, north of Oliver.

Green Lake Road

Green Lake Road, km 16, marks the junction to yet another road down to the Okanagan Valley. After passing through the community of Willowbrook, it winds northeast around Mount Hawthorne, past Mahoney and Green Lakes as it descends to the Okanagan River near Okanagan Falls. Before joining Highway 97 at the bridge, it offers several excellent views of the valley and the highlands to the east.

White Lake Grasslands Protected Area

The White Lake Basin has long been a priority focus of conservation efforts in the Okanagan. The primary role of the protected area is to protect the very hot and dry grassland, open pine forest, and alkali ponds and rock outcroppings of the Southern Okanagan Basin ecosection. The protected area captures the full elevational gradient from lakeshore to mountaintop and provides important habitat for many of British Columbia's red-listed (endangered) and blue-listed (vulnerable) wildlife, plants and plant communities. White Lake Grasslands Protected Area is contiguous with other protected areas around Vaseux Lake, thereby forming a significant large conservation area.

White Lake Protected Area encompasses the height of land west of Okanagan Falls from Mount McLellan and Mount Hawthorne, wrapping around the vineyard, Green Lake and the community of Willowbrook as it continues down the west side of Vaseux Lake from Mount Keogan to McIntyre Bluff and over to Myers Flats. The eastern face of Mount Parker, overlooking St. Andrews Golf Course, is also protected. The protected area does not include White Lake itself or the lower elevations of the basin; these are managed by the Nature Trust of British Columbia. Access to the protected area is via Green Lake Road and Fairview-White Lake Road. See the White Lake map and the BC Parks website for more information.

Dominion Radio Astrophysical Observatory

Beyond the junction, the White Lake Road starts climbing gently at first, then more steeply as the road curves upward between the grassy hills and rock bluffs. Near km 22 the valley opens to a sometimes-dry pond (White Lake) and the

The Dominion Radio Astrophysical Observatory (DRAO) main building and one of the antennae. *© Murphy Shewchuk*

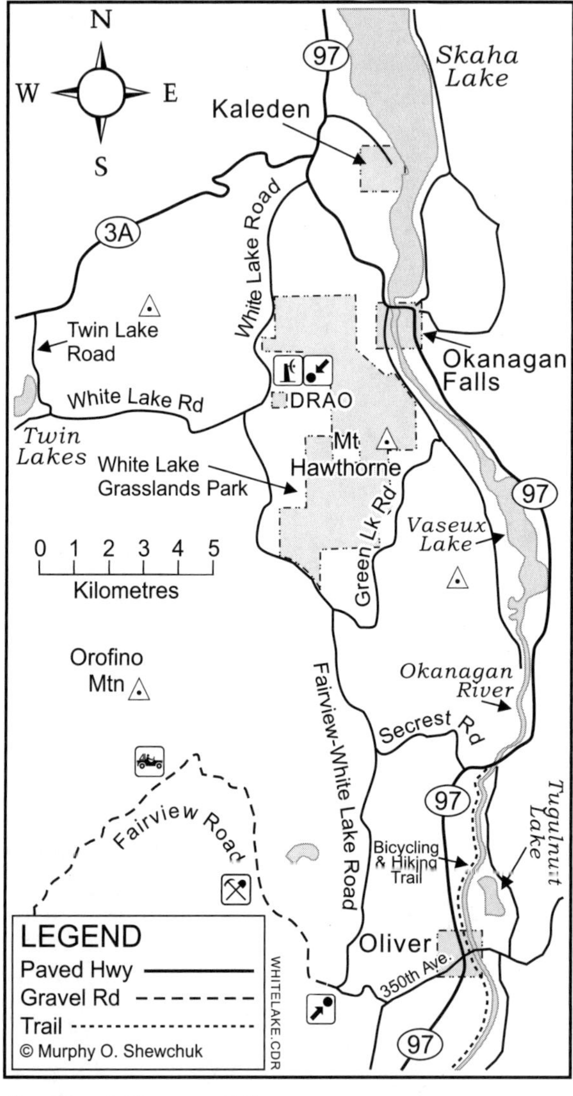

The Oliver / Okanagan Falls area.

antenna farm of the Dominion Radio Astrophysical Observatory (DRAO). The junction with Twin Lakes Road, km 24, presents the option of heading west to Olalla and Keremeos or continuing north to Kaleden. The road to the west (left) passes the Twin Lakes junction (eight kilometres) and joins Highway 3A near Yellow Lake, while the White Lake Road continues north, past the observatory.

The Dominion Radio Astrophysical Observatory can be an extraordinary sight when you first catch a glimpse of the group of giant parabolic antennae pointing skyward. Your questions can be answered at the visitor centre which is open daily.

Visitors are asked to park in the lot next to the White Lake Road, at km 25, and walk into the site so that vehicle ignition noise does not interfere with the sensitive radio receivers that are part of the operation. These receivers, coupled to the huge parabolic antenna and the pole-top antenna array, are used to study radio emissions from our own sun, moon and planets as well as distant nebulae, supernovae (exploding stars), dark gas clouds and the Milky Way.

In addition to the computer-controlled receivers located at White Lake, computers further link the receivers here with those at the Algonquin Radio Observatory near Ottawa, Ontario. This simulates an antenna with a 3,074-kilometre baseline for studies of remote galaxies.

From the radio observatory to Highway 97, the road winds generally downhill with a few steep narrow sections for added excitement, particularly after a snowfall or heavy rain.

White Lake Road emerges from this side valley, at km 32, to join Highway 97 approximately one kilometre south of the junction of Highway 97 and Highway 3A near Kaleden. — MS

Additional Information:

BC Parks
Web: www.env.gov.bc.ca/bcparks

Dominion Radio Astrophysical Observatory
717 White Lake Rd.
PO Box 248
Penticton, BC V2A 6J9
Web: www.nrc-cnrc.gc.ca/eng/solutions/facilities/drao.html

Oliver Visitor Centre
36205 - 93rd Street
Oliver, BC V0H 1T0
Tel: (250) 498-6321
Fax: (250) 498-3156
E-mail: info@winecapitalofcanada.com
Web: www.winecapitalofcanada.com

Penticton & Wine Country Visitor Centre
553 Railway Street
Penticton, BC V2A 8S3
Tel: (250) 493-4055
Fax: (250) 492-6119
Toll free: 1-800-663-5052
E-mail: visitors@penticton.org
Web: www.tourismpenticton.com

CHAPTER 53

Mount Kobau Road

Statistics:	For maps, see page 269 and page 275
Distance:	20 kilometres, Highway 3 to Mount Kobau FS Recreation Site at summit
Travel Time:	Approximately 1 hour
Elev. Gain:	1190 metres
Condition:	Good gravel road, some rough sections
Season:	Closed in winter
Topo Maps:	Keremeos, BC 82 E/4
Communities:	Keremeos, Cawston and Osoyoos

Mount Kobau, roughly half way between Keremeos and Osoyoos, has what could be described as one of the finest "backroads" in the province. The $1 million gravel road to the summit was originally built to service a $22 million observatory project that was never completed.

German Origin

The name Kobau, according to An Historical Gazetteer of Okanagan-Similkameen, is believed to be of German origin. It appears on George Dawson's map of 1877, but the reason it was named so has not been determined. To the early settlers, the south slope was known as Richter Mountain, the north end as Old Timers' Mountain, and the high central cone as The Big Knoll. The local Native population called the cone, Nice Top.

Mount Kobau road leaves Highway 3 at the summit of 682-metre Richter Pass. The pass takes its name from Francis Xavier Richter, a pioneer cattleman who drove 42 head of cattle through it in 1864. Richter later settled near the pass where, in 1887, he built a comfortable home.

The first "road" was cut through the pass in 1865 as part of the Dewdney Trail.

It was later improved to wagon road status, but stagnated for a century until the southern route of Highway 3 was opened between Keremeos and Osoyoos in July 1965. The Honourable Frank Richter, son of the original pioneer, recalled in his ribbon-cutting speech all the great changes of the past century and the "fantastic" future that beheld the Richter Pass Highway and Mount Kobau.

He also spoke glowingly of the multi-million dollar Queen Elizabeth II Observatory planned for Mount Kobau. "In time, the observatory will become world famous for people from all over the world will flock to this installation ... "

Queen Elizabeth II Observatory Project

The Observatory project was originally announced on October 28, 1964. But despite the Queen's name and glowing support from local politicians, it was never completed. Less than four years later, on August 29th, 1968, the government announced it would scrap the $22 million observatory.

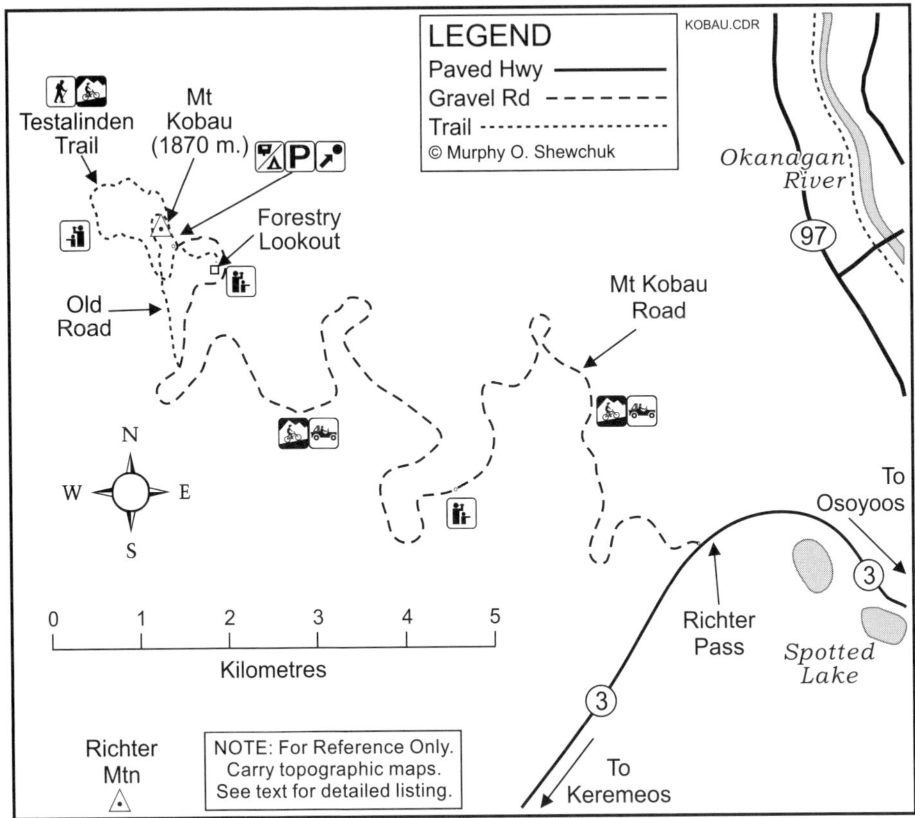

Mount Kobau Road.

According to a report in The Osoyoos Times of September 5, 1968, "Close to $4.5 million has now been spent on the project. One and a half million dollars was spent on the 150-inch blank that was cast in Corning, New Jersey. Over one million dollars was spent on the 11 miles of road built to the top of the 6,200-foot mountain. The balance was on studies and engineering."

Mount Kobau Star Party

The Mount Kobau Star Party, held every August near the dark-of-the-moon, has been attracting astronomers — amateur and professional — since 1984. Each year, over 150 dedicated deep-sky enthusiasts trek to the recreation site atop Mount Kobau, dotting it with tents, trucks, and telescopes.

As it is with most rec sites, this one has a "pack it in, pack it out" camping policy. Sky watchers who abide by this simple policy are rewarded with access to the clearest, steadiest of skies.

The Mount Kobau Star Party is geared to those who are prepared to "rough it" in pursuit of smog-free star watching. On Mount Kobau, city conveniences are exchanged for the necessary Spartan rigours familiar to serious observers: dim red lights at night, restricted noise during the morning sleep, limited amenities, and mountain-top isolation.

However, it isn't only a night-shift, eye-to-the-telescope experience. In the past, guest specialists have brought along displays of meteorites and presented various other programs during daylight and early evening hours. The nearby Dominion Radio Astrophysical Observatory is also a must see. (See the *White Lake Road* chapter for more details.)

Getting to the Top

The Kobau Lookout Forest Service Road leaves Highway 3 about 10.5 kilometres east of the Nighthawk junction. It is a wide gravel road with a few washboard sections and a few switchbacks. There are a number of excellent spots to enjoy the view of Osoyoos Lake and the south end of the Okanagan Valley.

For most travellers, the Mount Kobau rec site is the end of the road. However, it needn't mark the end to exploring. There is a one-kilometre walking trail to the Forest Fire Lookout. If you are fortunate, you may find Ken Bushey; Ken has been spending his summers on Mount Kobau watching for forest fires since the early 1990s.

Testalinden Trail

The four- to five-kilometre-long Testalinden Trail winds south and then west as it circles the summit of Mount Kobau. It offers some fine views of the Similkameen Valley before returning via the original road along the mountain-top. — MS

Additional Information:

Mt Kobau Star Party
E-mail: info@mksp.ca
Web: www.mksp.ca

Mount Kobau Astronomical Society
PO Box 20119 TCM
Kelowna, BC V1Y 9H2
E-mail: info@mksp.ca
Web: www.mksp.ca

CHAPTER 54

Haynes Point Park

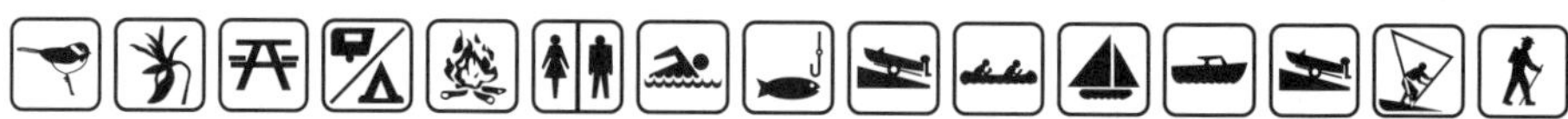

Statistics:	For map, see page 279
Distance:	Three kilometres, junction of Highways 3 and 97, to 32 Ave. 1.5 kilometres east from Highway 97 on 32 Ave.
Condition:	Paved access road; may be difficult to find
Season:	Year round
Topo Maps:	Osoyoos, BC 82 E/3
Communities:	Osoyoos and Oroville

Haynes Point Provincial Park is located at the extreme southern end of the Canadian portion of the Okanagan Valley, approximately 2.5 kilometres southwest of the town of Osoyoos. Haynes Point Provincial Park was established in 1962 on 15 hectares of unique and interesting parkland — a narrow sandspit in Osoyoos Lake and an adjacent marsh.

Judge J.C. Haynes

The park was named after Judge John Carmichael Haynes, a noted frontier jurist who brought law and order to the gold fields of Wildhorse Creek, near the present city of Cranbrook. The Haynes history in the Okanagan region goes back to the Rock Creek gold rush where, in 1860, John Carmichael Haynes was sent to assist the Gold Commissioner. Haynes was soon appointed Gold Commissioner as well as Customs Collector. His subsequent appointments included Member of the Legislative Council of BC and County Court Judge. Haynes acquired land at Osoyoos (then called Sooyoos) in 1866, and built a large home on the northeast side of the lake before his sudden death in 1888.

Hudson's Bay Company

The region around Haynes Point Provincial Park is also steeped in history. North

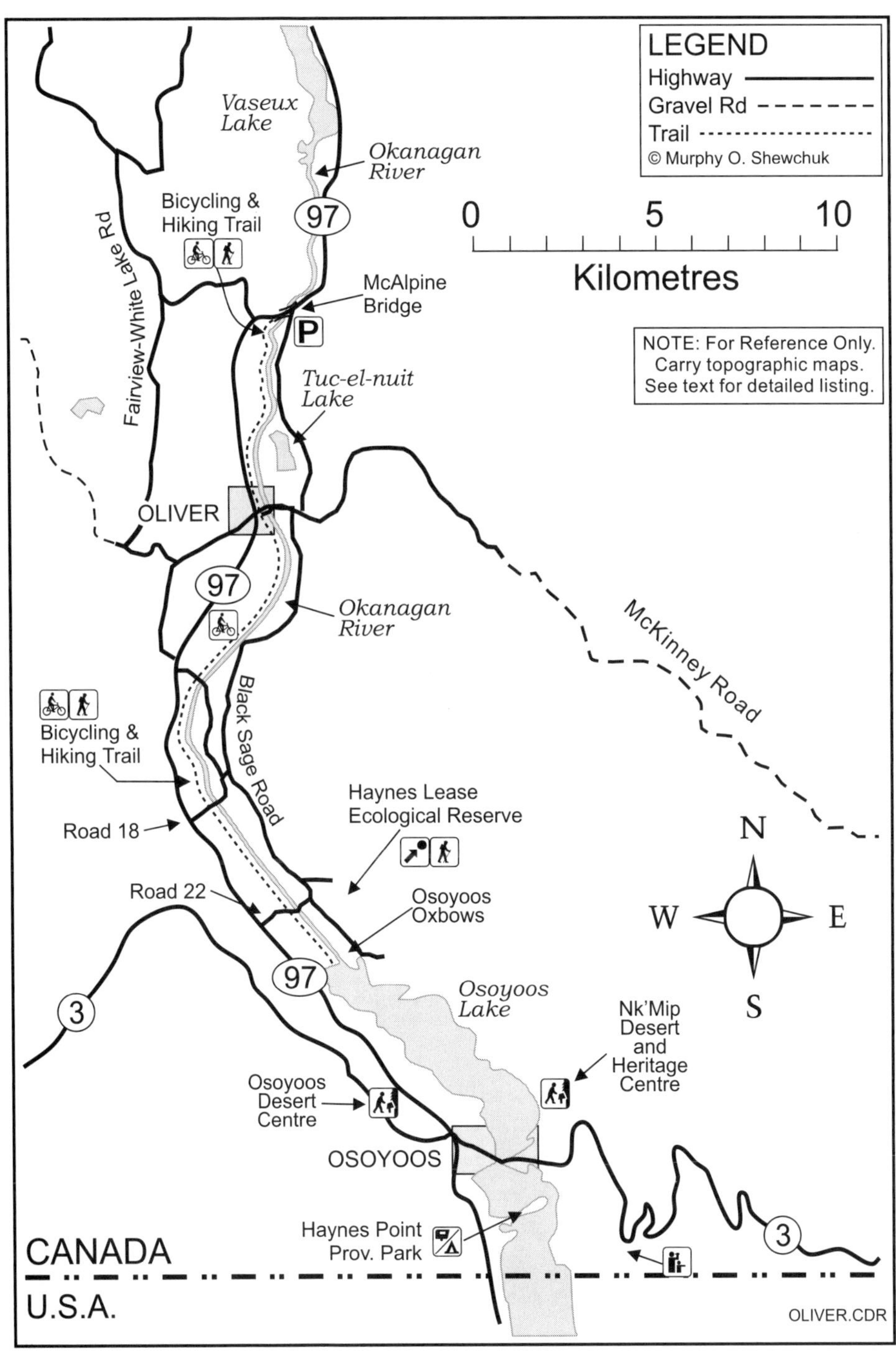

The Oliver / Osoyoos area.

Osoyoos as viewed from Anarchist Mountain. © Murphy Shewchuk

of the park, Highway 3 crosses a sandspit that was used by fur traders, explorers, miners, and First Nations people as a land bridge in their travels up and down the valley. The old Hudson's Bay Company Fur Brigade Trail passed through this very spot, nearly two centuries ago.

Okanagan Desert

Haynes Point Provincial Park is situated in an area which can boast Canada's only true desert. It receives less than 35 cm of rainfall per year, and enjoys long, sunny days and cool nights. The entire region is dominated by sagebrush, greasewood, prickly pear cactus, and ponderosa pine. As one might expect, much of the wildlife is exotic and some species are found nowhere else in Canada. The short-horned lizard and the desert night snake, for instance, have only been reported a few times this century. These two reptiles share their desert home with many other unusual creatures, such as the secretive spadefoot toad and the burrowing owl.

The bird life is exceptional and varied, especially in the marshes. A visitor might see canyon wrens, white-throated swifts, or red-winged blackbirds and, for those with eyes keen enough to spot them, those specks circling high above the valley floor could just be turkey vultures.

Osoyoos Lake is reputed to be the warmest lake in Canada, and visitors to the park are likely to have excellent weather for swimming, boating, picnicking, and sun-tanning. Additional activities include nature study and fishing — there are rainbow trout and bass in the lake. Haynes Point Provincial Park has long been a popular destination for visitors to the Okanagan. As a result the park is part of the new BC Parks reservation system.

Orchards, Vineyards, and Gardens

The desert isn't all sagebrush and cactus. Some of the Okanagan's finest orchards, vineyards, and gardens have been established where water can be pumped for irrigation. The Oliver-Osoyoos area has what is probably the highest number of fruit stands per kilometre of any area in Canada. From May to November, fresh fruit and vegetables are readily available direct from the producer almost anywhere along Highway 3 or Highway 97.

Osoyoos Historic Canal Walkway

Water pumps have replaced the gravity-feed canal system that originally served the Okanagan orchards. On the western outskirts of Osoyoos, the bank of an abandoned canal has become an interpretive trail. The 3.5-kilometre canal walkway, bisected by Highway 3, separates the Okanagan desert from the green orchard. — MS

Additional information:

BC Parks
Web: www.env.gov.bc.ca/bcparks

CHAPTER 55

Osoyoos Desert Centres

Statistics: For map, see page 278
Season: Summer months – check with individual centres
Topo Maps: Osoyoos, BC 82 E/3
Communities: Osoyoos

Sonoran Desert

North America's Sonoran Ecozone is an extensive desert ecosystem spanning three countries: Mexico, USA, and Canada. The northern boundary of the Great Basin Desert (one of the deserts within the Sonoran Ecozone) just barely stretches across the U.S.-Canada border into British Columbia's Okanagan Valley, thereby establishing the only desert in Canada.

The dryness of this southern interior landscape has a great deal to do with its geography. British Columbia's mountainous environment creates its own weather patterns. The Coast Range Mountains rob the prevailing winds of moisture, creating an ideal habitat for giant trees on the westward slopes and grasslands on the Interior Plateau. The Okanagan Valley cuts through the Plateau, further influencing the weather patterns and creating an "interior dry belt" running north to south.

The Osoyoos weather records tell part of the story:
Average July High: 30°C (86°F)
Average January Temperature: 0°C (32°F)
Annual Rainfall: 25 cm (10 in.)
Annual Snowfall: 40 cm (16 in.)

To complement this dryness, the sandy soils provide excellent drainage so that most precipitation quickly seeps away.

Spotted Lake, approximately nine kilometres west of Osoyoos. *© Murphy Shewchuk*

Sculpture at Nk'Mip Desert Cultural Centre.
© Murphy Shewchuk

The result is a unique desert. It receives more precipitation and cooler average temperatures than deserts to the south. Yet despite these conditions, desert habitats prevail and desert organisms persist. In the cool, damp winters, desert plants go dormant and many animals hibernate or migrate south. In the hot, dry summers, the desert life — including the Great Basin spadefoot toad, western rattlesnake, barred tiger salamander, and sun scorpion — survive in this, Canada's pocket desert.

This extraordinary habitat of international importance is home to one of North America's most fragile and endangered ecosystems. The Osoyoos Desert hosts one of the largest concentrations of species at risk in Canada, which include over 100 rare plants and over 300 rare invertebrates. Some 30 percent of British Columbia's endangered species (red-listed), over 50 percent of the province's vulnerable species (blue-listed), inhabit this ecosystem.

The region is also home to two desert centres.

Osoyoos Desert Centre

It took nearly a decade to secure the land and get the first section of boardwalk in place, but after its opening in 1999, the Osoyoos Desert Society has continued steady development and rehabilitation of a classic example of Canada's only natural desert.

The Desert Centre comprises a 26.8-hectare site located west of Highway 97 on 146th Avenue, about three kilometres north of Osoyoos. From May to October, a guided tour along the two kilometres of elevated boardwalk gives visitors the opportunity to learn about desert ecology, ecological restoration, and the conservation of endangered ecosystems in the South Okanagan. Tours through the antelope-brush ecosystem last about an hour. Self-guided and special tours are also available.

Nk'Mip Desert Cultural Centre

The Nk'Mip Desert Cultural Centre, a project of the Osoyoos Indian Band, is located on Rancher Creek Road on the western base of Anarchist Mountain. Access is off Highway 3 on the east side of Osoyoos via 45th Street. The Osoyoos Indian Band Development Corporation also operates a campground and award-winning Nk'Mip Cellars, North America's only Aboriginal winery.

Self-guided interpretive trails roll through over 20 hectares of sage grasslands and open ponderosa pine forests. The 1.4 kilometre wheelchair-accessible Village Trail includes interpretive signs, benches, and shady ramadas where visitors can relax and enjoy the spectacular views of Osoyoos Lake and the surrounding cliffs. The 2-kilometre Loop Trail includes some hilly sections. In all cases, visitors are advised to stay on the gravel trails and not wander through the delicate environment.

A teepee at the Nk'Mip Desert Cultural Centre walking trail.

© Murphy Shewchuk

An "artifact" near the Nk'Mip Desert Cultural Centre walking trail. © Murphy Shewchuk

One of the most interesting programs at the Nk'Mip Desert Cultural Centre is the Rattlesnake Research Project. Started during the summer of 2002, experts and apprentices take part in a special study of rattlesnake movement and denning patterns. Rattlesnakes are captured, measured, weighed, and receive tiny ID pit tags before being released back into the desert. Some are equipped with radio-transmitters so that researchers can study their movements in the wild. Researchers hope that knowledge gained from the project will help reduce the chances of conflict between rattlesnakes and people. — MS

Additional information:

Nk'Mip Desert Cultural Centre
1000 Rancher Creek Rd
Osoyoos, BC V0H 1V6
Tel: 1-250-495-7901
Fax: 1-250-495-7912
Toll-free in BC phone 1-888-495-8555
E-mail: nkmipdesert@oib.ca
Web: www.nkmipdesert.com

Osoyoos Desert Society
PO Box 123
Osoyoos, BC V0H 1V0
Tel: (250) 495-2470
Toll-free: 1-877-899-0897
E-mail: mail@desert.org
Web: www.desert.org

CHAPTER 56

Black Sage Road International Bicycling and Hiking Trail

Statistics	For map, see page 278
Distance:	12.6 kilometres, Oliver south to Road 22 8.0 kilometres, Osoyoos north to Road 22
Travel Time:	Approximately 25 minutes
Condition:	Paved highway
Season:	Year round
Topo Maps:	Osoyoos, BC 82 E/3 Keremeos, BC 82 E/4
Communities:	Oliver and Osoyoos

The dry benchlands and Okanagan River flood plain of the South Okanagan Valley have environments that are unique to British Columbia and Canada. In their natural states, these systems support abundant and varied plant and animal life that is not only valuable on its own accord, but also to us humans.

Important Bird Migration Route

The marshlands of the Okanagan River flood plain serve as one of the major migration resting areas and one of the few wintering areas for waterfowl in the interior of British Columbia.

According to a BC Ministry of Environment report: "Up to one million ducks, one hundred thousand Canada Geese and thousands of other aquatic birds migrate annually through the Okanagan Valley. These birds attract, in turn, a variety of the often more spectacular raptorial birds such as hawks, falcons, eagles, vultures and owls."

Many other birds also use this area to nest and rear their young. And many species of dryland plants and animals, some of which are rare or endangered, are found here and not elsewhere in BC or Canada.

We humans, unfortunately, have altered the natural state of the Okanagan environment to the detriment of the original inhabitants. The flood plain became the basis for extensive fruit farming and other agricultural pursuits. Then, when Nature persisted in its normal cycles, the Okanagan River was channelled to reduce flooding of the surrounding farmland. When most of the bottomland was taken up, agriculture, recreation and housing moved up to the benches, displacing the plants and animals that had adapted to the hot, dry environment.

Haynes Lease Ecological Reserve

Efforts are, however, under way to preserve segments of the desert environment that have not already been totally altered. The Haynes Lease Ecological Reserve, butting on the northeast corner of Osoyoos Lake, is one example of several steps being taken in the area. The reserve contains three distinct landforms; the Okanagan River flood plain; gently sloping terraces above the flood plain; and the steep, southwestern slopes of Inkaneep (Throne) Mountain. The southwest facing slopes, well-drained soils and the rain shadow effect of the Cascade Mountains combine to make this area the most arid in Canada.

The three definable physical zones result in 13 identifiable plant communities varying from cattail wetlands to sumac thickets on the mountain face. In between grow scattered ponderosa pine, fields of antelope brush, sage and rabbitbush, and prickly pear cactus, arrow-leaved balsamroot, and bluebunch wheatgrass.

The list of bird species, mammals, and insects that survive (and even thrive) in this harsh environment is too long to present here, but a few species on this list are worth mentioning. Rare birds include the canyon wren, sage thrasher, and burrowing owl. Rattlesnakes occur in rocky sites and, according to the Ecological Reserves Program report, "the western skink and short-horned lizard are expected to be present." The warm, weedy wetlands are home to largemouth and smallmouth bass and black crappies — fish not usually associated with BC.

International Bicycling and Hiking Trail

Access to the area is easy. Road 22 leaves Highway 97 on the west side of the Okanagan Valley approximately 12.6 kilometres south of downtown Oliver or eight kilometres north of the junction of Highways 97 and 3 in Osoyoos. It crosses the valley floor and then a bridge over the flood control channel at km 1.1. Although there are gates on the channel dikes, the east dike is open to traffic. The dike road to the south ends at Osoyoos Lake, 1.8 kilometres from the bridge, with several opportunities to watch waterfowl or osprey, or launch a car-top boat or canoe in the flooded oxbows.

The Haynes Lease Ecological Reserve, east of Black Sage Road. © Murphy Shewchuk

One of the series of control dams on the Okanagan River, south of Oliver.

The west dike also serves as the base for an 18.4-kilometre-long bicycling and hiking trail that extends south to Osoyoos Lake from the McAlpine Bridge on Highway 97, north of Oliver. The northern half of the trail through Oliver is paved while the southern portion is gravel.

Osoyoos Oxbows

Ducks Unlimited (DU) is involved with a program to re-water the Okanagan River oxbows that were left dry when the river was channelled in 1958. Working with the Ministry of Environment and other interested groups, DU built a weir and a control valve that feeds water into 48 hectares of former marshland in what has become known as the Osoyoos Oxbows.

Black Sage Road

Road 22 runs into Black Sage Road (71 Street) at km 1.6 near the historic Haynes Ranch House. This building dates back to the late 1800s, but time and vandals have taken their toll. Black Sage Road continues south for two kilometres to the Inkaneep Indian Reserve, and walk-through gates to the lower and upper sections of the ecological reserve. Vehicles aren't permitted and hikers should stay on the old roads to minimize damage to the fragile desert.

A signed road to the right, a few hundred metres to the north of the Haynes Ranch House on Black Sage Road, leads steeply up to a parking area and access to the upper section of the ecological reserve. Here you can walk south along an old road that takes you into the heart of the upper bench. Watch for cactus, grouse, and pheasants underfoot and burrowing owls on nearby fence posts.

Black Sage Road continues north to Oliver along the east side of the valley, joining Camp McKinney Road at km 14.4 and rejoining Highway 97 at km 15.5. (See *Mount Baldy Loop* for details.) — MS

Additional information:

Oliver Visitor Centre
36205 - 93rd Street
Oliver, BC V0H 1T0
Tel: (250) 498-6321
Fax: (250) 498-3156
E-mail: info@winecapitalofcanada.com
Web: www.winecapitalofcanada.com

The historic Haynes Ranch building near the junction of Road 22 and Black Sage Road. © *Murphy Shewchuk*

CHAPTER 57

Mount Baldy Loop

Statistics	For map, see page 293
Distance:	51 kilometres, Oliver to Highway 3 near Bridesville
Travel Time:	Two to three hours
Elev. Gain:	1,450 metres
Condition:	Gravel, rough in spots
Season:	Maintained all year-round, muddy in spring
Topo Maps:	Keremeos, BC 82 E/4
	Osoyoos, BC 82 E/3
Communities:	Oliver, Bridesville and Osoyoos

Backroads explorers are often forced to resort to armchair travelling when the snow closes in on the mountains of BC. This is usually the time to repair fishing equipment, overhaul the vehicle and sort the photographs taken on previous trips into BC's heartland.

There are exceptions, of course, and one is the McKinney Road - Mount Baldy Road loop through the Okanagan Highlands from Oliver to Bridesville. The attractions include BC's Okanagan desert, mountain climbing, and — the reason for year-round access — cross-country skiing at the Mount McKinney Nordic Ski Trails and alpine skiing at the Mount Baldy Ski Area.

Starts in the Heart of Oliver

The traffic light at 350th Avenue and Highway 97 in the heart of Oliver serves as km 0 and a suitable landmark for the start of this backroad trip into the highlands. Formerly Park Drive, 350th Avenue crosses the Okanagan River near the light. McKinney Road (362nd Avenue) swings right off 350th Avenue less than half a kilometre from the traffic light on Highway 97.

If you're hell-bent on heading for the hills, take McKinney Road. However, if it's hotter than Hades — as it can be in Oliver — continue straight ahead on 350th Avenue and 79th Street to 370th Avenue (formerly Harrison Way) and then take 370th Avenue and 81st Street to the public beach on Tuc-Ul-Nuit Lake. Also known as Tugulnuit Lake, this spring-fed swimming hole is a welcome break before tackling gravel and dust.

McKinney Road suffers from a minor identity problem with a sign at km 1.1 identifying it as Camp McKinney Road just before it crosses a concrete irrigation flume. At the junction with Sand Point Drive at km 1.9, the "Camp" is dropped.

Okanagan Desert

McKinney Road enters the Inkaneep Indian Reserve and as the paved road swings around a sandy knoll, sagebrush and ponderosa pine begin as you leave the fruit

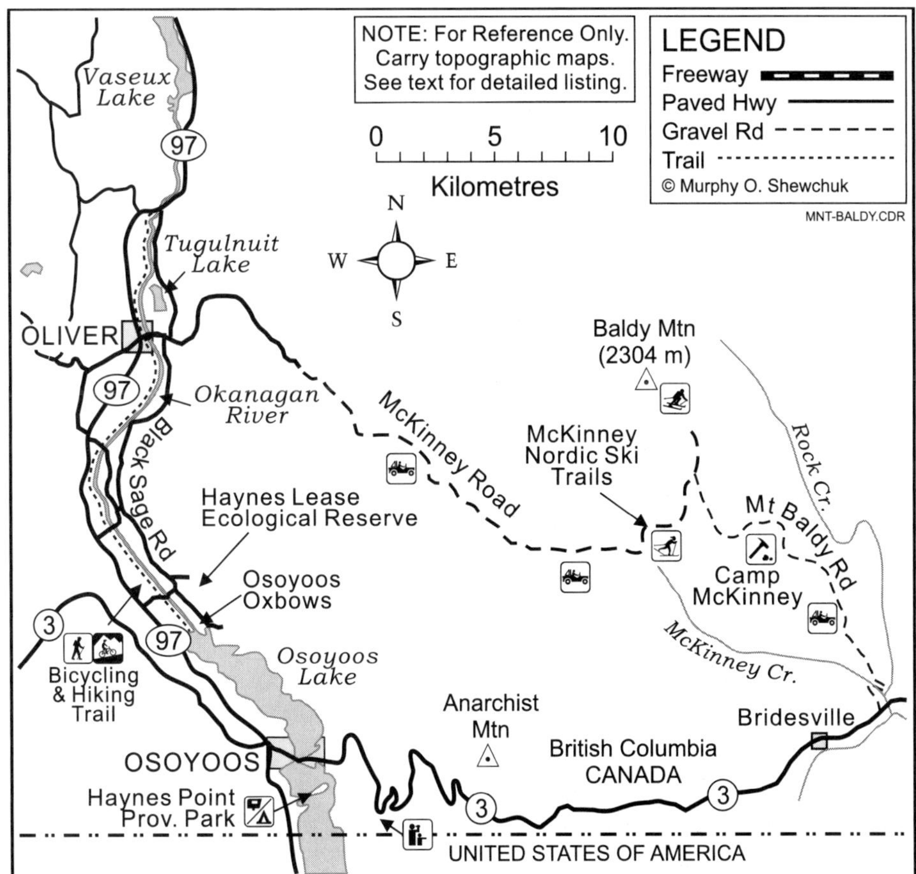

The Baldy Mountain / Anarchist Mountain area.

orchards behind. This land is typical of the desert that existed before irrigation turned the bottomland into orchards. It is barren, desolate and HOT. Greasewood, sumac and the occasional clump of bunchgrass cling desperately to the sand dunes that were once under an ancient glacial lake.

Farther up the road, the effects of water are again visible, with the desert on one side of the road and lush green hay fields on the other side, near Wolfcub Creek. Water makes the difference in this region, which is considered an extension of the Sonoran Desert that reaches into New Mexico.

The road continues to climb southeast into the highlands. Near km 8 the desert gives way to another symbol of the dry country — ponderosa pine trees. They are scattered all over the hillside among the clumps of bunchgrass, providing resting cattle with pockets of cool, green shade.

A small lake near km 16 (14K on the roadside markers) marks the end of the pavement. A close look at a detailed topographic map, or a view taken from a low-flying aircraft, will reveal countless small man-made lakes and ponds in southern British Columbia's high country. Some of these were originally developed to store water for gold mining operations. But most were built to collect the water from winter snows and June rains — the water needed for grazing cattle and hay fields when the hot, rainless summer winds sweep up from the American southwest.

Colourful Larch Trees

The stands of ponderosa pine gradually mix with interior Douglas-fir and then needle-shedding larch as the road climbs eastward up the slopes of the Okanagan Highland. In September and October, the larch changes colour, adding splashes of yellow to the background of evergreen forest.

A sharp corner near km 22 should be treated with respect — the loose gravel and occasional sand trap leave little room for mistakes. Although more than a bit dusty (depending on the season), McKinney Road is wide and well built.

McKinney Nordic Ski Trails

A sign on the south side of the road near km 27 marks the trailhead for the McKinney Nordic Ski Trail network. The 14-kilometre-long trail system, built on a network of old logging roads, is composed of a pair of stacked loops, each approximately seven kilometres in length. In addition to cross-country skiing, the trails are suitable for nature walks and equestrian use in the summer. The trails are groomed and track-set regularly by volunteer groomer operators using a Bombardier Snow Cat. There is an outhouse on site and a small shelter. Dogs are not allowed on the ski trails. Trail maps are posted at all junctions.

Mount Baldy Ski Hill

A junction near km 35 marks the last short leg of the trip to Mount Baldy. A short 2.6-kilometre drive up the mountain to the left (north) is the headquarters of the Mount Baldy alpine ski operation. According to Bill Hatton, a pioneer who has been in the region since 1920, Mount Baldy ski resort had its beginnings in the mid-1960s with the Borderline Ski Club. The Club was formed in 1939 and operated on nearby Anarchist Mountain before moving to the privately operated Mount Baldy in 1968. In his book, Bridesville Country, Hatton writes that a ski tow was set up on the Hedlund ranch on the east side of Anarchist Summit. The tow served local skiers for several years before they embarked on the ambitious project of developing Mount Baldy. It took hard work, but the sight of happy skiers on the sunny slopes using the T-bar tow and a dozen runs is an appropriate monument to their efforts.

In 1985, the club managed the popular ski races associated with the BC Winter Games held at Mount Baldy. This marked the peak of the resort's activity. It then slid downhill when operators ran into one of those low-snow years that plague all ski resorts. After closing for the 1986-87 season, Mount Baldy has re-opened with a flourish under the careful management of the Borderline Ski Club. At the time of writing, the Mount Baldy Ski Corporation was operating the facility.

The mountain serves skiers from the South Okanagan, Similkameen, and West Kettle districts. The mountain also attracts regular skiers from Washington State, south of the border. The main draw is the facility's friendly, family-oriented atmosphere — and every type of run for the beginner to the most advanced.

Halloween Trees

The "Halloween Trees," left over from a forest fire that gave the mountain its bald appearance, provide Mount Baldy with its trademark look. They also provide a challenging and interesting backdrop to glade skiing at higher mountain elevations. And when the mist rolls in, the "Halloween Trees" stretch out their grey arms in a way that triggers the imagination and further justifies the spooky name.

Mt. Baldy Road, to the right of the junction at km 35, was once the only access to the ski resort. It follows McKinney and Rice creeks down to join Highway 3 at the Rock Creek Bridge, a few kilometres east of Bridesville. The descent toward Highway 3 offers a number of excellent views of the Anarchist Mountain grasslands and the desert country far to the southwest.

Camp McKinney

Today, the Camp McKinney workings, five kilometres from the Mount Baldy junction, are a jumble of abandoned mine shafts, deep crevices, waste heaps, rusting mining equipment, and barbed wire fences. It's a dangerous place for stray man, woman, or beast — but it wasn't always so.

According to N.L. Bill Barlee in Gold Creeks and Ghost Towns, Camp McKinney was born in 1887 as one of the earliest lode gold camps in British Columbia. "By 1893," writes Barlee, "the camp was roaring on the strength of excellent assays from claims like the Cariboo, Amelia, Alice, Emma and Okanagan."

The Cariboo-Amelia claim later developed into the premier mine of the camp, even paying dividends to shareholders. By 1901, the population of the camp stood at 250, with hotels, stores, a school and a church among the amenities of the community. Three years later the Cariboo Mine closed and, within months, Camp McKinney became a ghost town.

Forest fires in 1919 and 1931 destroyed most of the original town. All that remains is a small, decaying log cabin of indeterminate age.

A mining structure at Camp McKinney, Sept. 1985. © Murphy Shewchuk

Gold, Silver, Lead, and Zinc

A short note in the BC Minister of Mines Report for 1943 states that two groups operating in the old Cariboo-Amelia claim mined 736 tons of ore, yielding 388 ounces of gold, 628 ounces of silver, 7,219 pounds of lead, and 5,381 pounds of zinc.

Beyond the mining camp, the gravel road continues its descent through stands of larch (tamarack) and lodgepole pine before emerging into the grasslands near the McKinney Creek crossing, approximately 51 kilometres from Oliver. A short drive farther and the road climbs up through a sand cut to the benchland high above the junction of McKinney Creek and Rock Creek.

The Oliver - Mount Baldy -

Bridesville loop joins Highway 3 at the western approach to the Rock Creek Bridge, one of the tallest bridges on Highway 3. From this point, pavement leads west to Osoyoos via Anarchist Summit or east to the community of Rock Creek in the Kettle Valley.

A provincial park at Johnstone Creek, a short drive to the east, can provide excellent campsites for those who want to continue backroads exploring in the area. If you are interested in camping a little farther off the highway, a gravel road near Johnstone Creek winds northward to Conkle Lake Provincial Park. See the *Conkle Lake Loop* chapter for details. — MS

Additional Information:

Mckinney Nordic Ski Club
Tel: (250) 498-8461
E-mail: info@mckinneynordicskiing.com
Web: www.mckinneynordicskiclub.com

Mount Baldy Ski Corporation
PO Box 1499
Oliver, BC V0H 1R0
Tel: 1 866 754-2253
E-mail: mail@skibaldy.com
Web: www.skibaldy.com

CHAPTER 58

Conkle Lake Loop

Statistics	For map, see page 299
Distance:	25 kilometres, Highway 3 to Conkle Lake; 21 kilometres, Highway 33 to Conkle Lake
Travel Time:	Up to one hour on each leg
Elev. Gain:	450 metres
Condition:	Rough gravel road
Season:	Best in dry summer weather
Topo Maps:	Osoyoos, BC 82 E/3 Beaverdell, BC 82 E/6
Communities:	Rock Creek, Beaverdell and Osoyoos

If you're looking for someplace to get away from it all, Conkle Lake Provincial Park, northwest of Rock Creek, is well worth exploring. Three-kilometre-long Conkle Lake, the dominant feature of the park, lies in a generally north-south direction, with an inviting, sandy beach at the north end. While the beach doesn't offer serious competition to the beaches at Skaha Lake or Okanagan Lake, it is for this very reason that Conkle Lake attracts repeat visitors. At an elevation of 1,067 metres, Conkle Lake is slow to warm in early summer, but when the beaches on the valley floor are sweltering hot, this upland lake can still be very pleasant.

Three Ways In — All Rough

There are three public routes to 124-hectare Conkle Lake — and all of them are best described as rough and not recommended for motor homes or vehicles pulling trailers. Judging by the number of motor homes and trailers at the park when we last camped there, however, this recommendation may mean little to those determined to "get away from it all."

What is probably the most used and least difficult route winds north from

Crowsnest Highway 3, 44 kilometres east of Osoyoos and approximately half way between Bridesville and Rock Creek. The signs on Johnstone Creek West Road warn of the difficulties, but the first few kilometres are merely steep, twisting and dusty. The transition from open grasslands to lodgepole pine and then to marshland and cedar-lined creekbeds is fairly quick. Signs mark the route to Conkle Lake at most of the junctions, particularly where much newer logging roads might create confusion. Much of the road is single lane with intermittent opportunities to pass oncoming traffic and virtually no opportunity to pass any slowpoke in front of you. Caution is essential and a good four-wheel-drive vehicle is a definite asset. A junction approximately 24 kilometres from Highway 3 marks the start of the last short, steep run up to the lake and Provincial Park. To the left is the park, while straight ahead is the backroad to Highway 33 near Rhone.

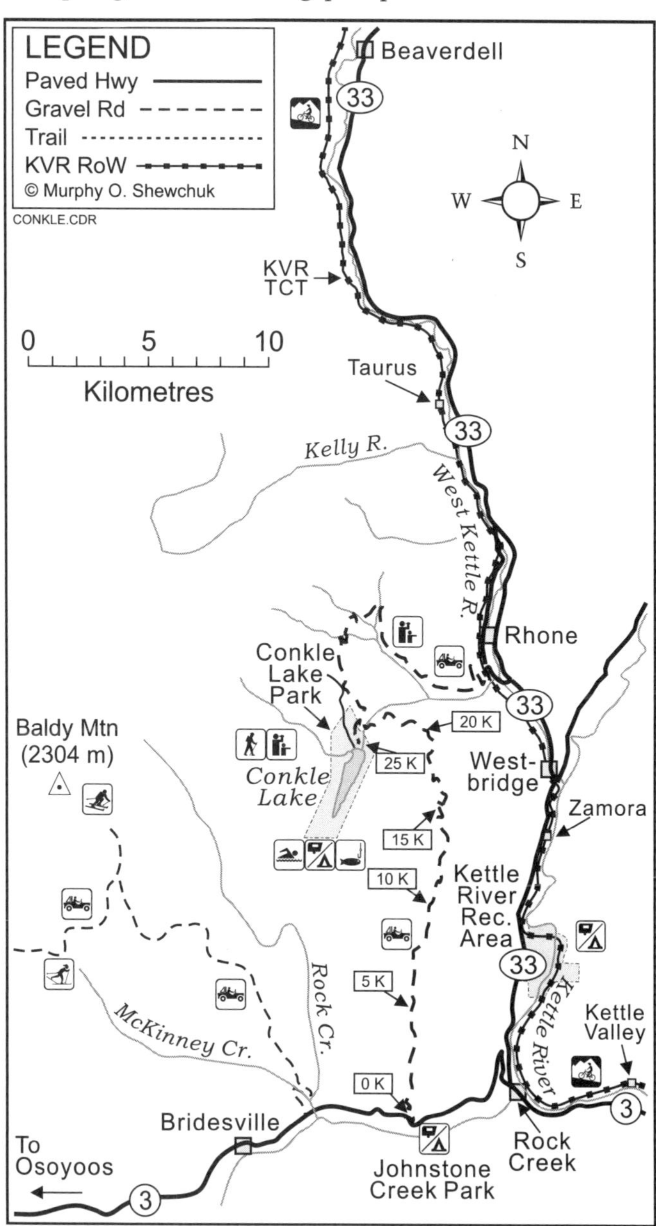

The Beaverdell / Rock Creek area.

Conkle Lake Loop

Tom Evans of Oliver has been fishing Conkle Lake almost every year since 1934. With his help and additional information from Jack Coates, another Oliver resident, I was able to piece together a bit of the puzzle that is the history of Conkle Lake.

Gold Nearby

According to these gentlemen, two trappers had cabins near the lake well before the 1931 Camp McKinney forest fire destroyed a vast tract of timber north of the Rock Creek Bridge. Sullivan and Ripperto were their names, it seems, and they were renowned for a private telephone line they had strung between their cabins. Tom Evans also remembers that Ripperto rawhided high-grade gold ore out of a mine he had on a nearby mountainside.

The original road into the lake was known as a corduroy road, made by laying poles of timber crosswise on a route cut through the upland marshes, put in from the south via Little Fish Lake.

"I've driven it, but it was a real tough drive," says Jack Coates, of Oliver. "It must have been put in way back in the teens or early 20s."

By 1945, the corduroy road had disappeared, flooded by beaver dams and over-

Conkle Lake looking south from the public beach. *© Murphy Shewchuk*

grown with timber and windfalls. In 1955, Frank Martin bought the land on the north end of the lake and started a fishing camp. He put in a road to the northeast end of the lake from the Johnstone Creek area. Later logging opened up access via the present route into the northwest corner of the lake. As part of his fishing camp, Martin built the two log cabins that now form part of the park maintenance facilities. Martin maintained the camp for three or four years before selling it to Jack Boicy.

Tamarac Lodge

Jack Boicy operated the camp as Tamarac Lodge for at least a decade. In the early 1970s, a group of speculators approached Jack. They wanted to buy and subdivide his property and build private homes or cottages. Feeling that the property should remain open to the public, Jack approached south Okanagan sportsmens' clubs and other groups such as the Okanagan Similkameen Parks Society for support. With their combined efforts, the provincial government purchased the land in 1972 and began turning it into a park.

Conkle Lake Provincial Park campground is set on benchland in a tamarack (larch) and lodgepole pine forest on the northwest corner of the lake. The vehicle sites are neatly arranged to offer privacy and utility. Services are minimal with no showers, flush toilets or corner store to distract from the backcountry camping experience. Make sure your food locker and fuel tank are both full before heading here. You may also want to plan your alternatives, should the park be full.

The beach, where tables and a boat launch are located to serve picnickers and fishermen, is only a short walk (or drive) from the campground. The sandy beach is a golden coloured weathered granite material and has a fairly steep drop-off — good for swimming, but not ideal for non-swimmers or small children.

According to local experts and the BC Ministry of Environment Guide to Freshwater Fishing, fishermen might expect rainbow trout up to two kilograms. Tom Evans has fished Conkle Lake since 1934. "We used to get a few big trout in those days," says Tom. "We could walk in there and spin cast off the shore or an old raft."

Waterfall Trail

Not only does this area offer fine swimming and fishing, but hikers will also find it a pleasure. An easy trail winds back into the hills to the west of the campground where a beautiful multi-tiered waterfall is hidden. It's about a half hour walk, if you're not in any rush, and the best time to get sunlight on the falls is in mid-

This waterfall on East Creek is well worth hiking up to. *© Murphy Shewchuk*

morning. A hiking trail is also being gradually developed around the lake.

With the park headquarters as km 0, the backroad to the north offers two options. Keep left at the junction at km 1.1 and follow the narrow road northwest through an even narrower canyon between km 3.5 and 4. A junction at km 5, marked R200 or Ripperto Forest Service Road, is the start of a 52-kilometre shortcut to Okanagan Falls. If you continue straight ahead, you should have a relatively uneventful trip down to the West Kettle River and Highway 33 at Rhone, about 15 kilometres to the northeast.

Backroad to Okanagan Falls

If the irresistible lure of the backcountry beckons, as it often does to us, you can swing west up Ripperto Creek and explore the maze of logging roads in the upland plateau. I certainly can't guarantee that they will be passable when you drive them, but we got through fine half a dozen years ago.

With the R200 sign as kilometre 0, we climbed steadily to the divide at km 6.3, keeping left at km 1.8 and right at a log landing at km 3.7. The divide, at about 1,750 metres, separates Ripperto Creek from the Kelly River drainage. With compasses at the ready, we switch-backed down to the Kelly River. After a leisurely lunch at an excellent recreation site, we continued west over the marshy divide into the headwaters of Vaseux Creek.

The logging roads got progressively better as we drove westward on R200 to a junction near kilometre 36, (12K on the roadside markers). Here we decided to take the steep winding road down the edge of Shuttleworth Canyon, and around the old Weyerhaeuser mill yard to Okanagan Falls and Highway 97.

If you have plenty of time, you can detour into Solco Lake "named after the South Okanagan Land Company," says Jack Coates. Or you can take the road to the right at the junction with the 12K marker and continue north on Okanagan Falls FS Road to Highway 33 near the Big White Ski Resort junction. (See *Okanagan Falls FS Road (R201)* for details.)

If you're looking for a backcountry getaway and a place to beat the summer heat — consider Conkle Lake Provincial Park. — MS

Additional information:

BC Parks
Web: www.env.gov.bc.ca/bcparks

CHAPTER 59

Ellis Ridge / Carmi Trails

Statistics	For maps, see page 113 and page 305
Travel Time:	Less than an hour to several hours
Condition:	Well-marked trails
Season:	All
Topo Maps:	Penticton, BC 82 E/5 Beaverdell, BC 82 E/6
Communities:	Penticton

The dark spires of burned tree trunks rise out of clouds of newly green bushes and undergrowth in the Ellis Ridge area east of Penticton — a stark reminder that a devastating forest fire here in 1994 claimed 5,500 hectares of forest land and 18 homes. The fire is a reminder that parts of this valley are virtually a desert in terms of annual rainfall. In the hot summer months a spark can set off tinder-dry grasses, quickly blackening a lush green mountainside. The foam of this bright green undergrowth, however, is also a reminder that new life springs from the ashes of a forest fire, and in fact, is sometimes dependent on fire.

Garnet Fire Interpretive Site

The force of fire and the wonder of water's effects in this ecosystem are the focus of two short trail systems created at the informative Garnet Fire Interpretive Site on the Ellis Ridge above Penticton. It's just a few kilometres from the Carmi Cross Country Ski Trails, 17 kilometres of well-marked trails used in winter for cross-country skiing, and in summer for hiking.

To Get There

From Main Street in Penticton, take Carmi Avenue east past Penticton Regional Hospital, through winding subdivisions, then uphill into acreage with an obvious

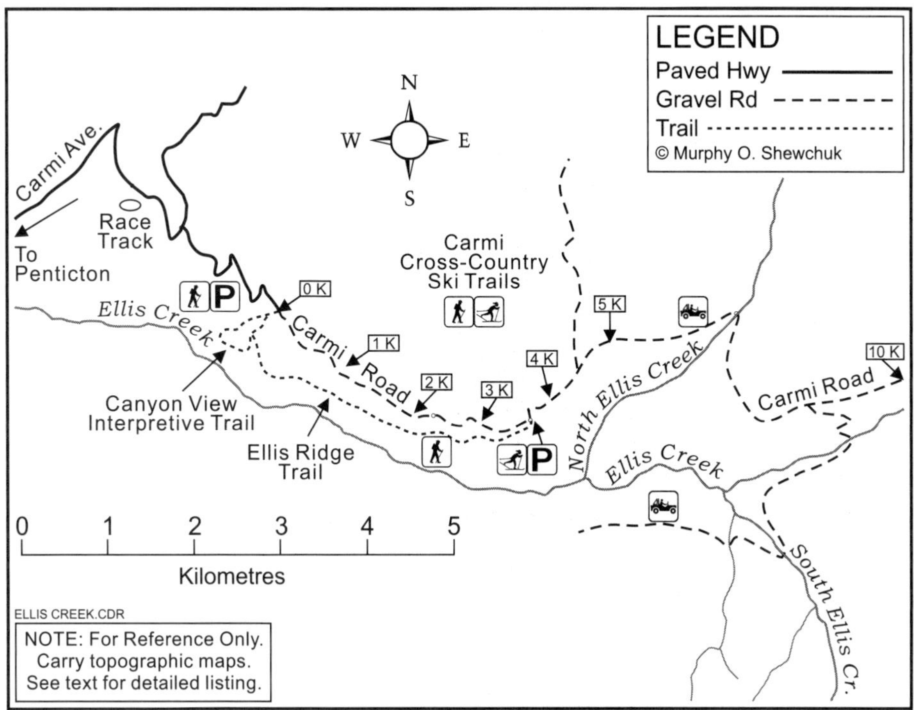

The Ellis Creek / Carmi cross country ski area, east of Penticton.

recent history of fire. It's nine kilometres from Penticton to the Garnet Fire Interpretive Site and 13 kilometres to the Carmi Cross Country Ski Trails and toboggan hill. This backroad continues on through to the Okanagan Falls Forest Service Road (see that chapter), and as the Carmi Creek Forest Service Road, ultimately to Beaverdell.

Canyon View Trail

The Canyon View Trail leads hikers through a forest recovering from a major wildfire, with spectacular views of the Ellis Creek Canyon (where the fire began), Penticton, and surrounding forest.

The Okanagan ecosystem is fire-dependent, where fire is a natural and relied upon event that changes and rejuvenates — a significant part in the organic maintenance of a healthy, sustainable forest. Historically this ponderosa pine and bunchgrass ecosystem burned every five to 10 years. These frequent natural wildfires quickly burned fuels on the forest floor, cleaning up dead and diseased plant debris, and leaving behind the ashes that provide mineral nutrients to nourish the soil. Every 100-150 years, even more devastating fires occurred.

The thick, layered bark of ponderosa pine and Douglas-fir trees protects the living tissues. Bunchgrass thrive on the mineral-rich, ash soil left behind by fire, while its deep root balls survive surface fires which actually enhance the seed development of other plants.

In recent years, humans have intervened in this natural process, preventing fire to protect both the timber resource and human communities. Ironically, this interference allows the build-up of fuels on the forest floor and ultimately endangers the human communities and timber we aim to protect.

The good news is that on the wildland side, the dead and dying trees now provide food sources, storage, shelter, nesting holes, hunting, and resting perches for wildlife. The fallen trees and branches provide nesting areas for mice, voles, and ground birds, while frogs, toads, salamanders, and skinks stay moist and cool in the shade. Insects are attracted to the weakened trees and woodpeckers, sapsuckers, and songbirds peck and drill into the wood for insects, ultimately excavating nesting cavities for themselves, as well as for bats and owls. Martens, squirrels and chipmunks use the cavities for nesting and food storage.

However, wildland-urban interface areas, where human homes butt up against wild ones, are now recognized as particularly potential threats because the proximity raises the possibility of fire moving easily from one type of home to the other. The consequences here could be catastrophic.

Ellis Ridge Trail

Water is a scarce and valuable resource in this ecosystem. The importance of this life-giving resource is the focus of the Ellis Ridge Trail, where hikers are shown how water sustains communities and maintains healthy forests.

In the Okanagan, snowfall is the main source of all the water used both for irrigation and domestic purposes, with 90 percent coming from the season's snowpack. Every 25 centimetres of snow equals 2.5 centimetres of water. In some parts of the Okanagan, the annual average precipitation is only 20 centimetres, while the provincial average is 150 centimetres. On the west coast of BC, on the other hand, the average ranges from 500 to 750 centimetres.

The trail takes walkers on a short trip with three scenic viewpoints, including community watersheds, lakeshore zones, and streamside and riparian areas. Contrasting with the dry forest high on the ridge, such gullies as Ellis Canyon boast riparian zones with green ribbons of life, including aquatic plants, shrubs, and trees filtering surface water before it reaches the creek. Stream corridors support a wider variety of plants and animals than any other habitat, and act as transportation corridors for some animals.

Returning to the main road — a further 3.5 kilometres will take you to the Carmi Cross Country Ski Trails, which include several scenic viewpoints over the length of the trails. — JS

Additional information:

Okanagan Shuswap Forest District
2501 - 14th Ave.
Vernon, BC V1T 8Z1
Tel: (250) 558-1700
Fax: (250) 549-5485
Toll-free (via Enquiry BC) 1-800-663-7867
Web: www.for.gov.bc.ca/dos

Penticton & Wine Country Visitor Centre
553 Railway Street
Penticton, BC V2A 8S3
Tel: (250) 493-4055
Fax: (250) 492-6119
Toll free: 1-800-663-5052
E-mail: visitors@penticton.org
Web: www.tourismpenticton.com

Regional District of Okanagan-Similkameen
101 Martin St
Penticton, BC V2A 5J9
Toll-free:1-877-610-3737
E-mail: info@RDOS.bc.ca
Web: www.rdos.bc.ca

CHAPTER 60

Okanagan Falls FS Road (R201)

Statistics:	For map, see page 113
Distance:	80 kilometres, Okanagan Falls to McCulloch Road
Travel Time:	Two to three hours
Elev. Gain:	860 metres
Condition:	Gravel industrial road, rough in spots
Season:	May be closed in winter
Topo Maps:	Penticton, BC 82 E/5
	Beaverdell, BC 82 E/6
	Wilkinson Creek, BC 82 E/11
	Kelowna, BC 82 E/14
Communities:	Okanagan Falls, Penticton, and Kelowna

The weekend wanderer may find the Okanagan Falls Forest Service Road (R201) to be a welcome break from the paved highways through the bottom of the Okanagan Valley. Coupled with the backroad through the Grizzly Hill / Dee Lakes area, R201 can form part of the route from Okanagan Falls to Lavington with only a short stretch of blacktop on Highway 33, near Joe Rich Valley.

Weekends are Safest

Weekend is the key word here. This is an industrial road and the logging trucks are wider and longer than normal. Expect tree-length loads between 4:00 a.m. and 4:00 p.m. weekdays with the usual lighter traffic during the off-hours and on weekends and holidays. Wherever you travel in the backcountry, it is wise to use extra caution on weekdays because of the logging-truck traffic.

Shuttleworth Creek

In an attempt to keep things as simple as possible and to allow you to join the route at one of several locations, I will use the Forest Service kilometre markers as a general reference with the old Weyerhaeuser mill scales as the 0K base. The simplest way to find the Okanagan Falls Weyerhaeuser mill is to start from the corner of Main Street (Highway 97) and 9th Avenue in downtown Okanagan Falls. Drive east to the end of 9th Avenue and turn right (south), then follow Maple Street south, watching for the mill on your left (east). Look for signs marked R201 on the road that skirts the main mill yard.

The first three kilometres of Okanagan Falls FS Road (R201) is an un-gated route through private land. Again, use caution and watch for industrial equipment. Beyond the mill, this route climbs steeply up the south side of Shuttleworth Creek. There are several opportunities to get a good view of the canyon and the Okanagan Falls area between 5K and 10K. A road to the right (south) near 12K can take you east to Solco Lake and, if you are really persistent, to Conkle Lake and the West Kettle Valley. The latter destination could require dry weather and a 4x4 vehicle.

Allendale Lake

Another junction to the right (this time to the east) near 18K and a bridge marks the start of the road to Allendale Lake. It is about six kilometres in, but the recreation site there may serve as a good base for some upland fishing. Beyond the Shuttleworth Creek Bridge, the road swings northwest, climbing less steeply for about four kilometres before levelling off at an elevation of about 1,525 metres. While there are a few side roads along the way, the next major diversion is near 37K where you have the opportunity to follow Carmi Road down Ellis Creek to Penticton. (See the *Ellis Ridge / Carmi Trails* chapter for more information.)

Idleback Lake

The next major diversion is at Idleback Lake, near 43K. The large recreation site here is an excellent base for fishing and canoeing. However, my wife, the swimmer, was not impressed with the cold water and soft bottom.

Greyback Road

If you are interested in a fine lake with a better bottom for swimming, consider detouring west to Greyback Lake. Greyback FS Road joins Okanagan Falls FS Road (R201) near the 57K marker. If you take this option, keep left at the Canyon Lakes FS Road junction and continue climbing west and then southwest to the height of land (1,675 metres) near 63K. Keep left at a gated junction near 65K and you should reach a narrow sideroad down to Greyback Lake near 69K. This is a

Penticton water reservoir, so be extremely careful with any pollutants.

Greyback FS Road continues southwest for about 17 kilometres to the suburbs of Penticton, but I would not recommend the last 15 kilometres for anything but a tough 4x4 pickup or an off-road vehicle. However, if you are interested in a bit more exploring, you might follow the road for about two kilometres to the James Creek Falls Trailhead. Here a wide trail winds through the trees for about 100 metres to a viewpoint. If you want a closer, more intimate look at the falls, you can climb down a rough trail through a natural rock cut to the valley floor. Mid to late

Idleback Lake, near Okanagan Falls Forest Service Road. *© Murphy Shewchuk*

afternoon will be the best time to see the falls lit by the sun.

Back on Okanagan Falls FS Road (R201)

North of the junction at 57K, Okanagan Falls FS Road (R201) crosses Wilkinson Creek and continues northeast across the uplands. You may want to stop to check out the granite quarry near 68K, or Myra FS Road at 70K. With a little luck, Myra FS Road could lead you across the ridge and down to the Kettle Valley Railway right-of-way (now part of the Trans Canada Trail). See the *Myra Canyon KVR Corridor* chapter for details. Beyond the KVR, Myra FS Road continues north and downhill to McCulloch Road and Kelowna.

If you are looking for a better class of accommodation than a recreation site, you might consider Idabel Lake Resort at 75K. You could also continue north to the junction with McCulloch Road at 78K and go west to McCulloch Lake rec site. And if a fishing resort isn't your style, you can take a short jaunt east to Highway 33 and continue on to Big White Ski Resort or down the hill to Rutland and Kelowna. — MS

Additional information:

Okanagan Shuswap Forest District
2501 - 14th Ave.
Vernon, BC V1T 8Z1
Tel: (250) 558-1700
Fax: (250) 549-5485
Toll-free: 1-800-661-4099
Web: www.for.gov.bc.ca/dos

CHAPTER 61

Pasayten Wilderness

Statistics:	For map, see page 313
Distance:	21 kilometres, Highway 3 to Pasayten River Bridge 35 kilometres to end of road
Travel Time:	One half to one hour
Condition:	Gravel road; some very rough sections
Season:	May be closed in winter
Topo Maps:	Manning Park, BC 92 H/2 Ashnola River, BC 92 H/1
Communities:	Hope and Princeton

"Wilderness" is an Appropriate Description

The Pasayten Wilderness, lying along the Canada-US border between Manning and Cathedral parks, is no place for the ill-equipped or inexperienced backcountry explorer. It borders on Washington State's 529, 477-acre (214,300-hectare) Pasayten Wilderness, made up of sections of the Mount Baker-Snoqualmie and Okanogan National Forests (it is spelled "Okanogan" in the U.S.). There is an abundance of wildlife here, including the largest population of lynx in the "Lower 48." There are no regular patrols and no cell phone coverage. Go prepared for adventure and heed the warning, "Use at your own risk!"

The Pasayten River Forest Service Road heads east off the Hope-Princeton Highway (Highway 3) approximately 50 kilometres south of Princeton or two kilometres northeast of Eastgate at the northeast entrance to Manning Park. With the junction at Highway 3 as your km 0 reference point, you will soon cross the Similkameen River and begin a switchback climb over the ridge separating the Similkameen from the north end of the Pasayten Canyon. Keep left at a junction near km 2.6 and right near km 2.8.

After about four or five kilometres, the road levels off and follows the Pasayten River Canyon south (upstream). The road has been carved into the timber on the

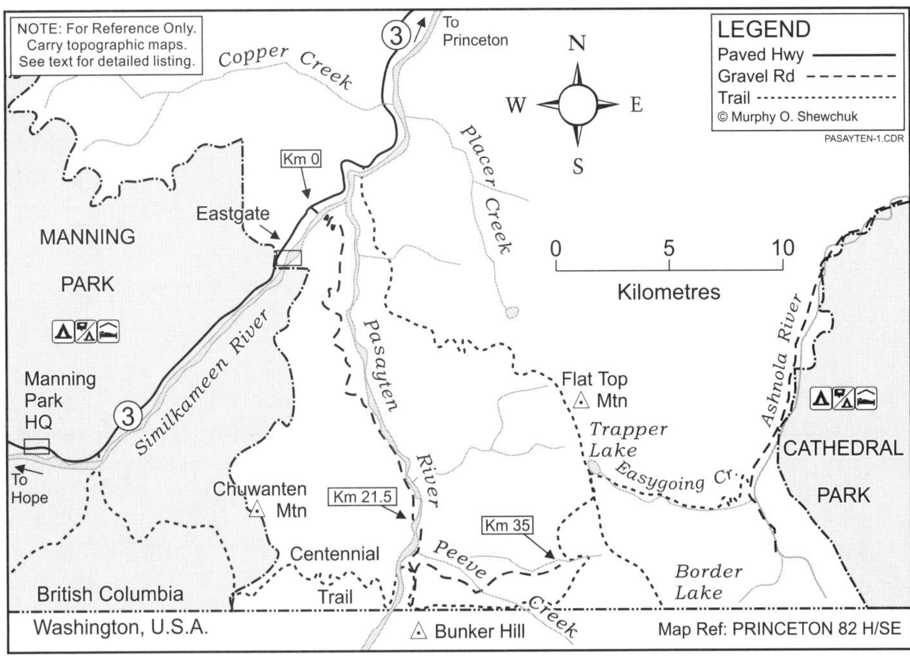

The Pasayten Wilderness lies between Manning and Cathedral provincial parks.

canyon wall, but there is a good viewpoint just past the 6K marker. At an elevation of about 1,300 metres and high above the river, you'll get a spectacular first look south toward the Canada-US boundary. The sun glistens off exposed sections of the river. On the southern horizon, 2,207-metre (7,240-foot) Bunker Hill pokes up above the surrounding timber.

A sign near the 9K marker indicates this is a "Wilderness Forest Service Road" that is not maintained.

After a gradual descent along the sidehill, the road meets the Pasayten River near km 17. Although there are no facilities, there are several excellent places for self-contained camping between km 17 and km 21.

Roads May be Closed

The Forest Road crosses the Pasayten River from the west to east side near km 21 where there is a corral and loading chute. There is a sign nearby warning that "Roads in the area may be closed without further notice."

The roads were not closed on our previous visits. However, the roads were "water-barred" near Peeve Creek, a short distance past the Pasayten River Bridge. As our truck and camper were a bit too long and heavy to comfortably cross these shallow ditches, we were unable to confirm the condition of the remainder of the road. A four-wheel-drive truck with a short wheelbase, a "Hummer" or an ATV may be the vehicles of choice for further exploring in this region.

On our first trip to the area, our southward journey ended at a blocked road near km 23. The original road to the border and the access to the eastward section of the Centennial Trail continued south. Fortunately, a switchback turn led us up and east into an old burn and the Peeve Creek drainage. Although steep in a few sections and very rough in a few others, we followed the path of least resistance to a turn-around and trailhead of sorts near km 35.

Spectacular Alpine Meadows

There were several vehicles parked there, and after a chat with a returning hunter, we tied on our hiking boots and scrambled up the tank-trapped fire break toward the distant alpine meadows. The elevation at the parking area reached about 1,875 metres and it took us about an hour to hike two kilometres to the flat-top ridge and meadows. Others who are not so easily distracted by birds, wildflowers, spectacular views, and breathing could probably climb the 200-metre elevation in much less time.

Moose enjoy the marshes and meadows. © *Murphy Shewchuk*

The tank traps along the fire break were there to stop (slow down?) vehicular access to the fragile alpine. It was obvious that they were little more than a challenge for some ATV drivers. Our stay on the ridge was cut short by the waning sun and cool breezes blowing in from the north. We retraced our steps to our van and headed back down the road to the Pasayten River. We camped that night, planning to return to the alpine in morning. The morning dawned grey — and we were socked in with alternating bouts of rain and snow. Rather than risk life, limb and vehicle, we headed north to Highway 3 and Thanksgiving dinner at home.

Since that Thanksgiving visit to the Pasayten Wilderness in 1994, we have done a bit of research and returned a number of times to hike various sections of the Centennial Trail.

Centennial Trail

The Centennial Trail was created in 1966-67 as part of an effort to have a national trail from the Pacific to the Atlantic. It was to commemorate the 1866 amalgamation of Vancouver Island and mainland British Columbia as a Crown Colony; the 1867 Canadian Confederation; and the 1871 entry of British Columbia into Canada.

The original trail ran from Victoria to Nanaimo and across (by ferry, I presume) to Horseshoe Bay where it linked with the Skyline and Baden Powell Trails. It then continued through Belcarra Park, Port Moody and up through the Fraser Valley to the Chilliwack River area. It only became serious wilderness trekking at the Post Creek area off the Chilliwack River Road. From the Chilliwack River to Manning Park, the original Centennial Trail is of dubious quality and has been obliterated by washouts, road construction, and in some place, logging.

The section through Manning Park to Monument 83 on the Canada - US boundary goes by a variety of different names, including Skyline II Trail, Skyline Trail, and Monument 83 Trail. Whatever the name, the section is generally passable. Near Monument 83, the trail leaves Manning Park and enters what is now the Cascades Forest District. The 11.5 kilometre descent to the Pasayten is relatively intact although there have been recent reports of numerous windfalls, and the cable crossing at the Pasayten has been out for several years. (See the *Centennial Trail: Monument 83 to Pasayten River* chapter for details.) A rough trail has been cut north to the Pasayten River Forest Service Road bridge near km 21. (See *Centennial Trail: Parson Smith Tree Trail.*) The trail then loops south to the boundary where it generally follows the boundary to the east end of the Say Fire burn before heading north to Trapper Lake. Unfortunately, the Say Fire (1984) and the earlier Bunkerhill Fire (1970) have both had a detrimental impact on parts of the trail.

Trapper Lake

From Trapper Lake, the trail follows Easygoing Creek to the Ashnola River where it then links up with the Wall Creek Trail into Cathedral Park. Here again park status and budget have helped keep it marked and passable. To add confusion, trails from the Trapper Lake area also lead north to Similkameen Falls and south to Border Lake.

The section of the Centennial Trail from Monument 83 to the Ashnola River goes through public land under the supervision of the Cascades and Okanagan Shuswap Forest Districts. This section, generally known as the Pasayten Wilderness, becomes the distant and forgotten cousin when it comes time to dole out funds from the meagre recreation budget.

Despite the lack of public funds, interest in this section of the trial has been relatively strong over the last three decades. However, North Vancouver's veteran hiker, the late Bob Harris, and groups such as the North Shore Hikers and the Back Country Horsemen, have not been able to raise the route's "political profile" high enough to warrant massive infusions of cash. Instead, such trail supporters have worked closely with other recreationists to gradually improve the trail system by themselves.

This is not to suggest that the route is impassable. A decade ago, Charlie Clapham, a Vancouver hiker, led a group of nine people on a series of hikes that covered the trail from Manning Park to Keremeos. Using four vehicles, they left two vehicles in Manning Park and moved the group and two vehicles ahead to the Pasayten. It is interesting to note that, travelling light, they were able to walk from the Pasayten River to the trailhead near Manning Park Lodge (an estimated 30 kilometres) in one day. After staying overnight in Keremeos, their second day of hiking took them from the Ashnola River up the Easygoing Creek trail to Trapper Lake and then down to their waiting vehicles at the Pasayten River — a distance, according to Charlie, of 26 to 27 kilometres. The hike through Cathedral Park was a little more complicated, but the details aren't essential to this chapter.

The Back Country Horsemen, with members throughout the province, have also been instrumental in maintaining the Centennial Trail. For a time the route was promoted as a potential part of the Trans Canada Trail system. After much discussion, the short season and long distance between communities prompted the decision to locate the Trans Canada Trail on the former Kettle Valley Railway right-of-way. See the *Trans Canada Trail* chapter for details.

While information on the Pasayten Wilderness and this part of the Centennial Trail is still limited, the work of Marg Anderson, a University College of the Cariboo co-op student working for the Ministry of Forests; Bob Harris, a noted historian and hiker; Jim McCrae of the Back Country Horsemen; and various other individuals and groups will serve as a foundation for a future detailed map / brochure. In the meantime, your best sources of information are the previously mentioned maps, personal contact with experienced hikers and horsemen, and books such as this one. — MS

Additional information:

Cascades Forest District
PO Box 4400
Merritt, BC V1K 1B8
Tel: (250) 378-8400
Fax: (250) 378-8481
Toll-free: 1-800-665-1511

Okanagan Shuswap Forest District
2501 - 14th Ave.
Vernon, BC V1T 8Z1
Tel: (250) 558-1700
Fax: (250) 549-5485
Toll-free: (via Enquiry BC) 1-800-663-7867
Web: www.for.gov.bc.ca/dos

Update: Wildfires in 2006 have damaged some of the trails in the southern Pasayten Valley. Be prepared for some changes to the descriptions in this book.

CHAPTER 62

Centennial Trail:

Monument 83 to Pasayten River

Statistics	For maps, see page 313 and page 318
Distance:	16 kilometres, Highway 3 in Manning Park to Monument 83; 11.5 kilometres, Monument 83 to Pasayten River at Monument 85
Travel Time:	One to two days
Condition:	Variable; some very rough sections with windfalls
Season:	Summer - July through September, depending on seasonal vagaries
Topo Maps:	Manning Park, BC 92 H/2
Communities:	Hope and Princeton

The Centennial Trail, as outlined in the Pasayten Wilderness section, was the precursor to today's Trans Canada Trail. It was also an attempt to establish a multi-purpose non-motorized travel route across British Columbia. Because of the short seasons at the higher elevations and significant distances between re-supply points, it did not attract significant numbers of hikers. The varying restrictions against horse traffic in the provincial parks also had a detrimental effect on rider usage.

Regardless of the low traffic density, the Centennial Trail between Manning Park and Cathedral Park does offer some interesting challenges and excellent scenic and wildlife viewing opportunities in a wilderness setting. The section within Manning Park, from the Castle Creek - Monument 83 parking area on Highway 3 to Monument 83, is part of an old fire access road to the US Forest Service Fire Lookout Tower. The trail is 16 kilometres one-way, with an elevation change of 850 metres and a suggested hiking time of five hours.

Cascades Forest District

Most of the trail from Monument 83 to the Pasayten River lies within the Cascades Forest District. With a small recreation staff and budget, trail maintenance has been largely left to volunteers such as the Back Country Horsemen and

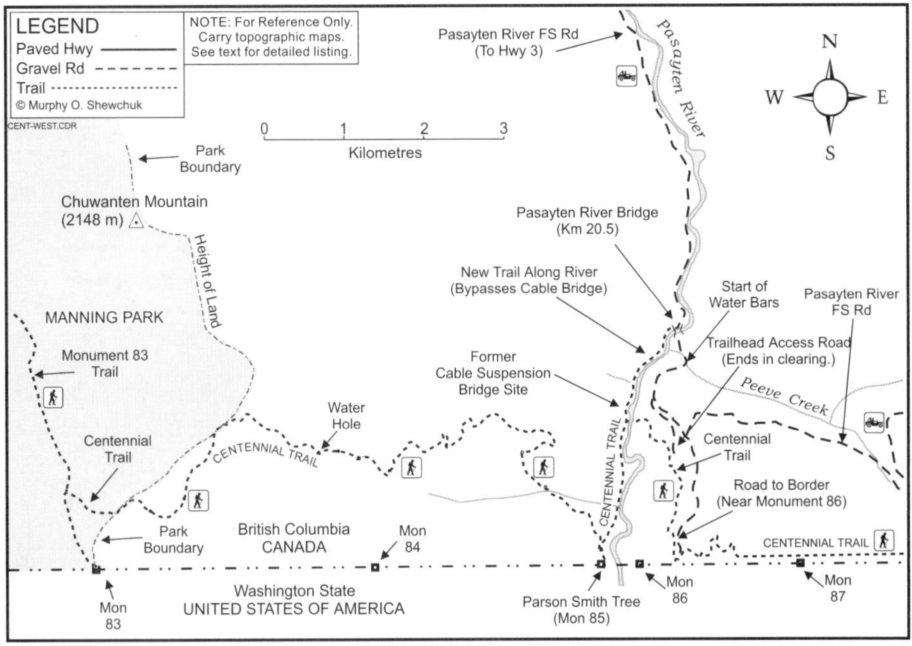

The Centennial Trail, Manning Park to Peeve Creek.

various hiking and cycling groups. The result: expect to encounter windfalls and some trail degradation. It is generally wide enough for an experienced rider and horse, and should be passable for experienced mountain bicyclists. If you are travelling on horseback, a small chainsaw may prove to be an extremely valuable tool.

The west-to-east (downhill) traverse of this route begins about 0.9 kilometres northwest of Monument 83 — elevation 1,981 metres — as a side trail off the old forest lookout road. In general, the first 1.5 kilometres of the trail winds through a stand of old-growth timber.

Limited Water

The trail then generally climbs across a semi-open hillside through the upper reaches of an old burn. At approximately 2.6 kilometres from the Monument 83 trail, the route begins a gradual descent toward the Pasayten River. For the next 2.4 kilometres the trail winds through small timber at or near the summit of a rounded ridge. Approximately mid-point along this ridge is a clearing suitable for tent camping. A pit has been dug in a boggy spring to collect ground water — one of the few places along this section of the trail where you can refill a canteen. A water purifying system will be essential if you aren't going to boil the water.

After leaving the ridge, the trail descends through mixed timber, crossing two

Monument 85, on the Canada - US boundary.
© Murphy Shewchuk

streams and several boggy hillsides. The streams were still flowing in a mid-August trip through the area, but water purification is still recommended. The trail emerges from the pines onto an aspen covered slope near the Pasayten River — elevation 1,190 metres, approximately 11.5 kilometres from Monument 83. Monument 85 and the International Boundary are about 200 metres to the south. There is a "Stop of Interest" shelter and an information sign near Monument 85. The sign provides background details about the Parson Smith Tree — a tree on which a poem was carved in 1886. The remains of the tree have been removed to a museum in Washington State. See the *Centennial Trail: Parson Smith Tree Trail* chapter for details.

The river marshes near Monument 85 are an excellent place for bird watching. These same marshes also block horse and foot traffic from continuing east along the boundary. Instead, anyone continuing east on the Centennial Trail must first detour north. The remainder of the route north to the Pasayten River Bridge is described in the *Centennial Trail: Parson Smith Tree Trail* chapter. — MS

Additional information:

BC Parks
Web: www.env.gov.bc.ca/bcparks

Cascades Forest District
PO Box 4400
Merritt, BC V1K 1B8
Tel: (250) 378-8400
Fax: (250) 378-8481
Toll-free: 1-800-665-1511

CHAPTER 63

Centennial Trail:

Parson Smith Tree Trail

Statistics: For maps, see page 313 and page 323
Distance: Approximately 3 kilometres, Pasayten River Bridge to Monument 85
Travel Time: One to 1.5 hours each way
Condition: Variable; some rough sections with occasional windfalls
Season: Summer - July through September
Topo Maps: Manning Park, BC 92 H/2
Communities: Hope and Princeton

Much of this trail is part of the Centennial Trail between Manning Park and Cathedral Park. However as the original Pasayten River cable crossing has succumbed to Nature and the trail has been extended north to the Pasayten River Forest Service Bridge, I've chosen to write this part up as a separate chapter. It also is an interesting day hike, lending itself to special consideration.

Access to the north end of the Parson Smith Tree Trail is from the Pasayten River Forest Service Road. This well-marked two-wheel-drive backroad leaves the Hope-Princeton Highway (Highway 3) approximately 50 kilometres south of Princeton (two kilometres north of Eastgate). See the *Pasayten Wilderness* chapter for more information.

Parking is available in a clearing on the west side of the Forest Service road immediately north of the Pasayten River Bridge, approximately 20.5 kilometres from Highway 3. There were no trailhead markers or other signs in place when we last visited the area.

Scramble and Ramble

Parson Smith Tree Trail begins at the southwest corner of the parking clearing, and after a short scramble up and around several large boulders, proceeds south-

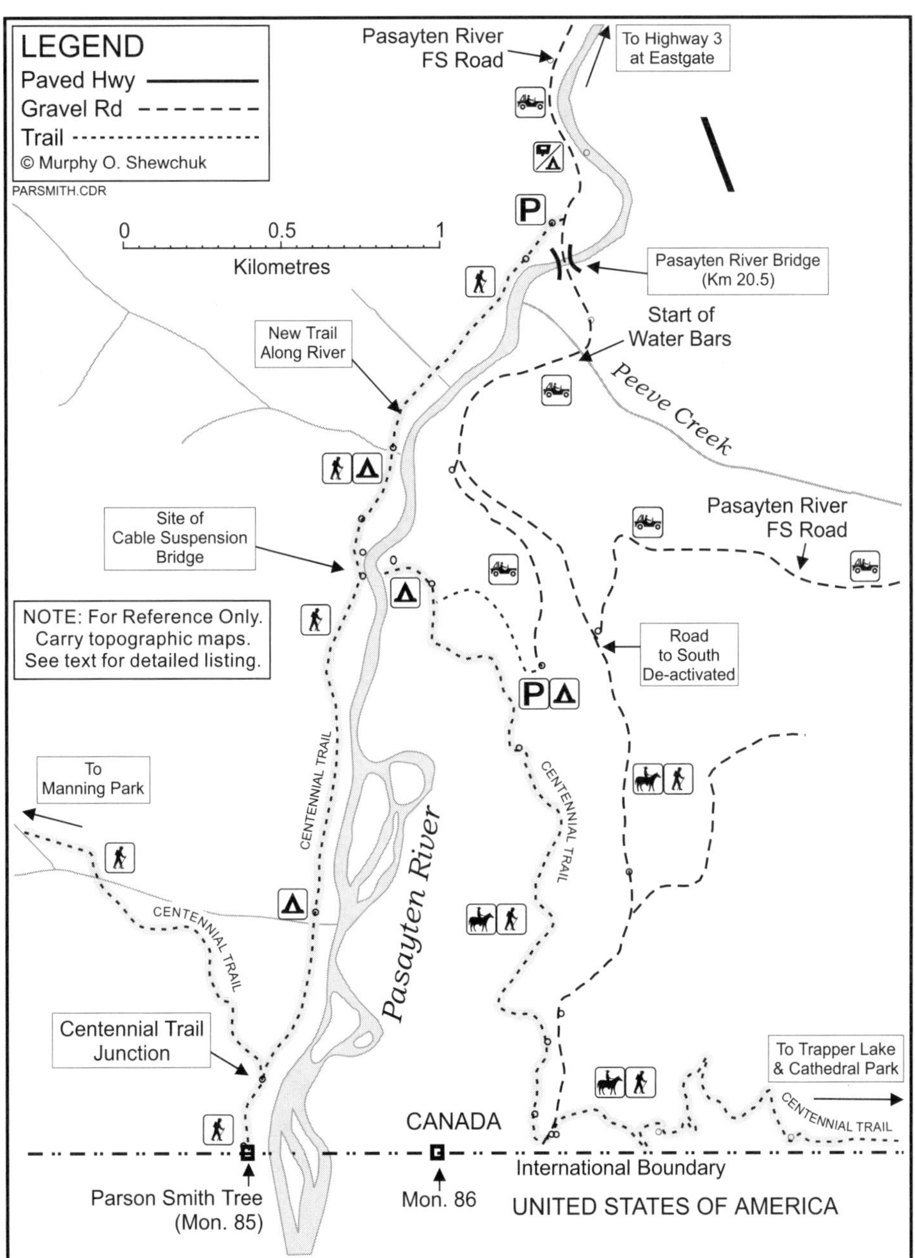

The Pasayten River, between Manning and Cathedral Parks.

ward, paralleling the Pasayten River upstream. The first 1.25 kilometres of the trail was recently cut through a stand of small timber. It is narrow in sections and will be difficult for a horse and rider until it is widened and the occasional windfall has

Hiking over a rock outcrop on the Parson Smith Tree Trail. *© Murphy Shewchuk*

been removed.

The trail generally follows the hillside or narrow benches well away from the river. However, it descends to the river edge at a creek crossing approximately 0.8 kilometres from the parking area. This location could be an excellent spot for a walk-in wilderness campsite.

This new section of trail joins the older BC Centennial Trail at the former cable crossing, approximately 1.25 kilometres south of the Forest Service Bridge. The former cable bridge across the Pasayten River was reduced to one weathered fibre rope by the late 1990s and had disappeared completely by September 2004. The remainder of the trail to Monument 85 is much older and wider. There are several locations suitable for wilderness camping, including another side stream approximately 1 kilometre south of the cable crossing.

The junction of the Centennial Trail to Monument 83 and Manning Park may be difficult to find. However, after you check out the "Stop of Interest" shelter and sign near Monument 85 on the International Boundary, you can back-track downstream about 100 to 200 metres. Here you should see a rough path angling up a clearing in the hillside to the west. Once out of the clearing, the path is much easier to follow. (To help make it easier to find the start of the trail, we cut back the branches blocking the old markers in late September 2004.)

Parson Smith Tree

The information sign provides details about the Parson Smith Tree — a tree on which a poem was carved in 1886.

One story suggests that "Parson" Alfred L. Smith was prospecting for white quartz (a common source of gold) with a partner near the Pasayten River in June 1886. The partner went back to Canada with an injury and Smith remained in camp. While waiting for his partner to return, Smith skinned off the outer bark of a lodgepole pine and carved the following bit of doggerel:

I've roamed in many foreign parts my boys
And many lands have seen.
But Columbia is my idol yet
Of all lands she is queen.
Parson Smith, June 1886.

Note that the state of Washington was known as "Columbia" at the time.

Parson Smith's partner never returned, leaving him to relay several hundred kilograms of supplies and equipment 65 kilometres south to his base camp near Winthrop, Washington.

Crews clearing the survey lines for the International Boundary discovered the tree in 1908. Various attempts were made to preserve it in place. However in July 1980 it was removed from the banks of the Pasayten River, chemically treated and placed in an airtight case at the Early Winters Visitor Center, Washington state, on the North Cascades Highway 20, located 29 kilometres east of Washington Pass.

Bring Camera and Binoculars

While you won't find the Parson Smith Tree here, you may discover that the river marshes near Monument 85 are excellent places for bird watching.

And as a sidenote: on a hike to Parson Smith Tree on the morning of September 25, 2004, we discovered dozens of varieties of fungi ranging in size from mere match heads to dinner plates. We photographed quite a few that morning, but by our return trip later that afternoon many had begun to fade away. — MS

Additional information:

Cascades Forest District
PO Box 4400
Merritt, BC V1K 1B8
Tel: (250) 378-8400
Fax: (250) 378-8481
Toll-free: 1-800-665-1511

Update: Wildfires in 2006 have damaged some of the trails in the southern Pasayten Valley. Be prepared for some changes to the descriptions in this book.

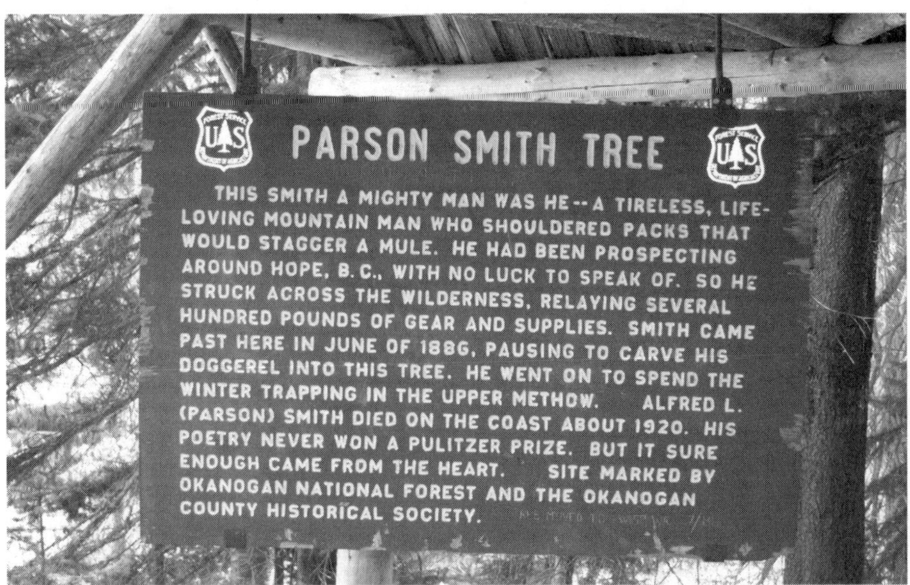

A US Forest Service stop-of-interest sign at the border near Monument 85.

© Murphy Shewchuk

CHAPTER 64

Centennial Trail:

Pasayten River Bridge to Ashnola River

Statistics	For maps, see page 313 and page 330 and page 328
Distance:	Approximately 26 kilometres, Pasayten River Bridge to Ashnola River
Travel Time:	One day minimum
Condition:	Variable; some rough sections with occasional windfalls
Season:	Summer - July through September
Topo Maps:	Manning Park, BC 92 H/2 Ashnola River, BC 92 H/1
Communities:	Hope, Princeton, and Keremeos

As it is with the Monument 83 to Pasayten River section and the Parson Smith Tree Trail, much of this trail forms part of the Centennial Trail between Manning Park and Cathedral Park. Some sections — such as the route from the Pasayten Bridge to Monument 86, the trail from the Say Fire to Trapper Lake, or the trail from the Easygoing Creek Road to Trapper Lake – offer interesting day hikes. However, hiking the complete trail from the Pasayten River to the Ashnola will require advance planning and a considerable degree of fitness.

Pasayten Bridge to Monument 86

Access to the north end of the trail from the Pasayten Bridge to Monument 86 is from the Pasayten River Forest Service Road. This well-marked two-wheel-drive backroad leaves the Hope-Princeton Highway (Highway 3) approximately 50 kilometres south of Princeton (two kilometres north of Eastgate). See the *Pasayten Wilderness* chapter for more information.

Parking is available in a clearing on the west side of the Forest Service road immediately north of the Pasayten River Bridge, approximately 20.5 kilometres from Highway 3. There were no trailhead markers or other signs in place during the fall of 2004. Parking is also available at the old trailhead clearing approximately 1.7 kilometres south of the bridge, on the benchland between the Forest Service

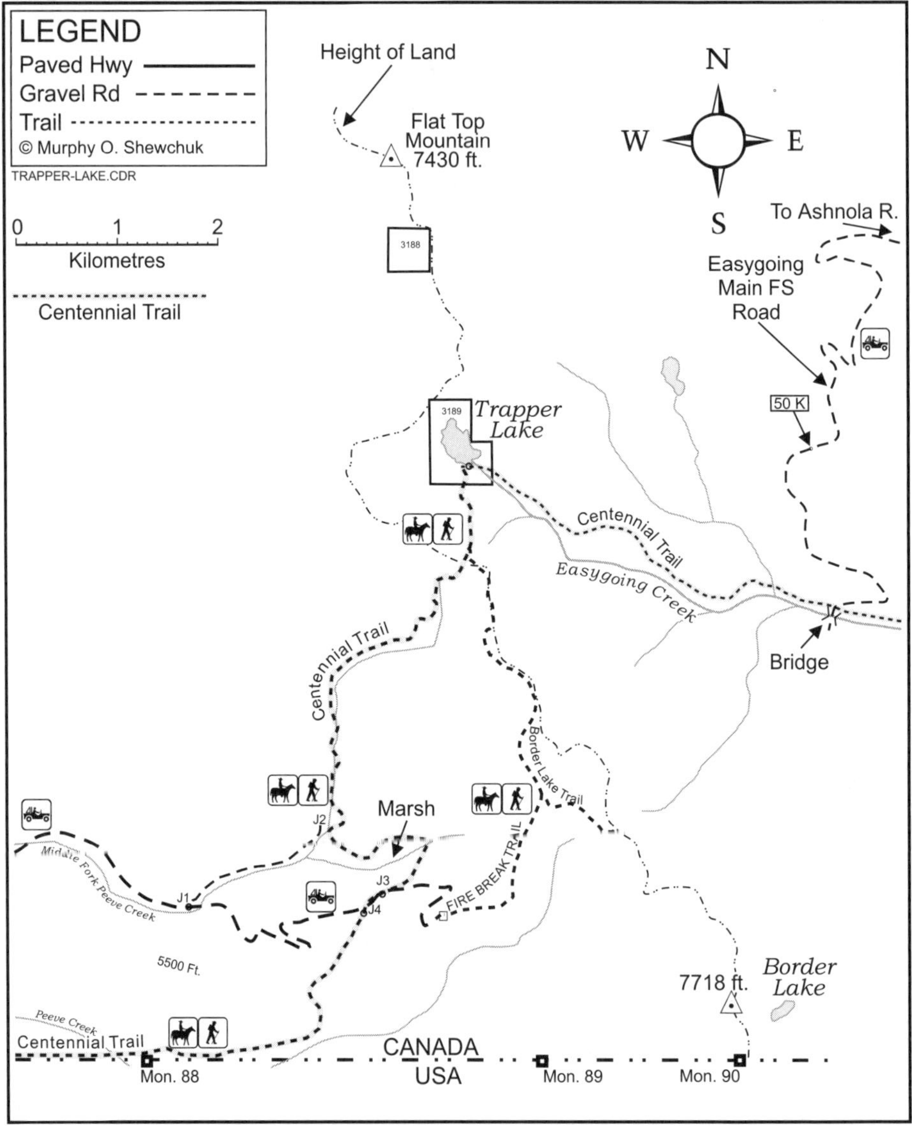

The Centennial Trail in the Trapper Lake area.

road and the Pasayten River. However, the road south of Peeve Creek was "water-barred" with vehicle access limited to four-wheel-drives or ATVs.

The original Centennial Trail crossed the Pasayten River at the cable crossing approximately 1.2 kilometres south of the present forest road bridge. It then wound through a grove of timber mixed with boggy sections for about 0.5 kilometres before beginning a steady climb southeast to the US border and the junction with the old fire access road. An old trail winds down to the river from the old trailhead clearing. Efforts have been made to cut a new trail directly south of the clearing so it will link up with the original Centennial Trail and avoid the boggy section near the river cable crossing.

Hikers at the Centennial Trail junction south of Trapper Lake. © *Murphy Shewchuk*

In general, the 2.1-kilometre trail to the border winds through a stand of old-growth timber. It is narrow in a few sections, but should not be difficult for an experienced horse and rider. There are a few boggy sections where the trail crosses creeks or springs and a few areas where windfall roots have torn up the trail.

The trail reaches the border clearing and then swings east and up a short incline to the old fire road, which also ends near the north edge of the border clearing. When we last visited, there was a picnic table at the end of the road. British Columbia Centennial Trail signs marked both the eastward continuation of the trail along the border and the northwest route back to the cable crossing.

Switchback Climb

From the end of the old fire road, the Centennial Trail climbs eastward away from the Pasayten River. It generally follows the boundary, sometimes swinging north a few hundred metres to ease the grade and avoid the very steep sections. We have climbed east from the end of the fire road to the summit, passing through a mixture of old growth and the younger trees that have filled in the Bunkerhill burn. We have not gone all the way through on this section, but usually reliable sources suggest that the trail continues east for a total of six kilometres before swinging north up a fork of Peeve Creek.

Say Fire to Trapper Lake

The Centennial Trail then crosses the remnants of the Say Fire and the salvage operation before continuing north to Trapper Lake. The trail through the burn can be confusing because of the network of roads and cattle trails and a marsh that is situated in the middle of the valley. The trail generally continues northeast to ford a creek just upstream of the grass marsh. It then swings west along the hillside and an old logging road for about a kilometre before disappearing into the timber 20 to 30 metres east of a creek flowing out of the north.

Access to the south end of the Trapper Lake Trail is also available from the Pasayten River Forest Service Road approximately 9.1 kilometres east of the Pasayten River Bridge — J1 on the map below. The main road follows the valley bottom at this point and a sideroad angles to the northeast. When we last visited the area, this sideroad had been partially de-activated and was barely passable with a four-wheel-drive vehicle. From J1 it is about 1.6 kilometres to the trailhead (J2 on the map) where the creek crossing had been completely excavated. As mentioned above, the trail started into the trees 20 to 30 metres east of the creek. Parking was also available at an old log landing at the junction (J1).

A view of the mountains of Cathedral Park from alpine meadows south of Trapper Lake in the Pasayten Wilderness. *© Murphy Shewchuk*

The Trapper Lake Trail climbs steadily north through old-growth timber with several creek crossings and mixed boggy sections for the first 1.5 kilometres. It then continues climbing on a drier semi-open hillside for about 1.9 kilometres before reaching the height of land at an elevation of about 1,980 metres.

There is a four-way junction a short distance north of the height of land. The trail to the north (straight ahead) leads for about one kilometre to Trapper Lake. The final 0.5 kilometres to the lake winds through a sub-alpine marshy area that will put most hiking boots to the test.

In general, the 4.5-kilometre trail to the east is narrow in a few sections, but should not be difficult for an experienced horse and rider. There are a few boggy sections, where the trail crosses creeks or springs, which should be approached with caution.

Trapper Lake to the Ashnola River

The Centennial Trail continues southeast of Trapper Lake. After crossing the creek a few times in the first kilometre, the trail follows the north side of Easygoing Creek for about three kilometres to where the trail crosses Easygoing Main Forest Road. This can be a suitable pick-up point for through hikers or an excellent parking and / or wilderness camping location for day hikers interested in exploring the Trapper Lake and Border Lake area. See the map on page 328 for an overview of the Keremeos - Cathedral Park - Trapper Lake area.

East of the road crossing, the Centennial Trail follows Easygoing Creek downstream for about a kilometre before beginning a zigzag descent northeast to the Ashnola River near the 40K marker on Ashnola Road. The trail crosses Easygoing Main FS Road about 1.5 kilometres from the Ashnola Road — if you hike or ride down the trail from Trapper Lake, look for the continuation of the trail about 100 metres north of where it emerges from the trees onto Easygoing Main Road.

Wall Creek Bridge

A new footbridge was built across the Ashnola River late in 1998 to access the Wall Creek Trail, a continuation of the Centennial Trail into Cathedral Park. It is located near the 38K point on the Ashnola Road, about two kilometres north of the junction of Easygoing Main and the Ashnola Road. — MS

Additional information:

BC Parks
Web: www.env.gov.bc.ca/bcparks

Centennial Trail: Pasayten River Bridge to Ashnola River

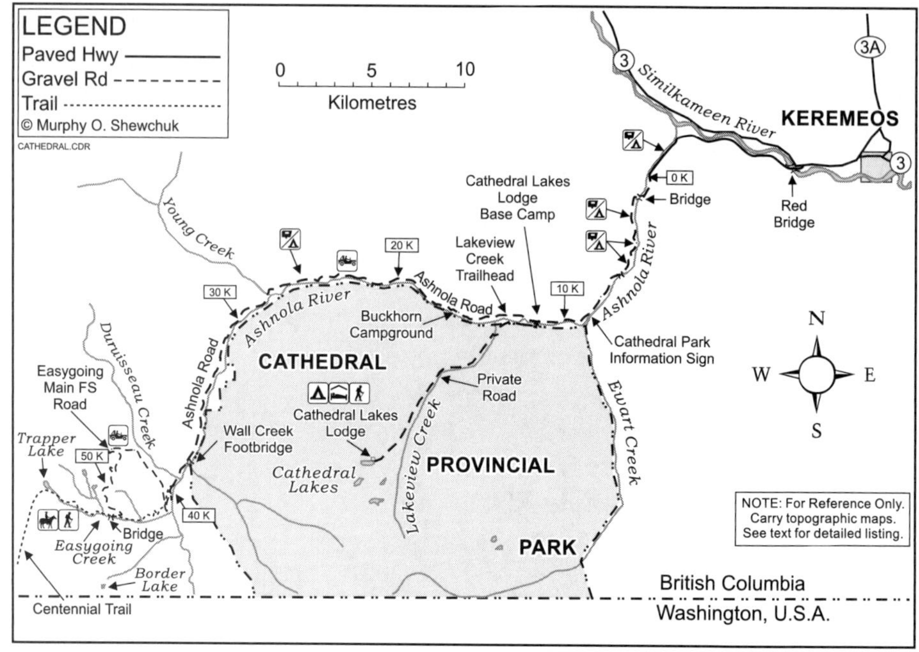

The upper Ashnola River and Cathedral Park area.

Cascades Forest District
PO Box 4400
Merritt, BC V1K 1B8
Tel: (250) 378-8400
Fax: (250) 378-8481
Toll-free: 1-800-665-1511

Okanagan Shuswap Forest District
2501 - 14th Ave.
Vernon, BC V1T 8Z1
Tel: (250) 558-1700
Fax: (250) 549-5485
Toll-free: (via Enquiry BC) 1-800-663-7867
Web: www.for.gov.bc.ca/dos

Update: Wildfires in 2006 have damaged some of the trails in the southern Pasayten Valley. Be prepared for some changes to the descriptions in this book.

CHAPTER 65

Ashnola Road

Statistics	For map, see page 328
Distance:	25 kilometres, Keremeos to Cathedral Base Camp; 73 kilometres, Keremeos to Easygoing Creek Bridge
Travel Time:	Two to three hours
Condition:	Paved, then gravel
Season:	Best in dry weather; may be closed in winter
Topo Maps:	Keremeos, BC 82 E/4 Ashnola River, BC 92 H/1
Communities:	Keremeos

Ashnola Road, although often associated with Cathedral Park, also provides access to a number of BC recreation sites. A Cathedral Lakes Lodge sign near Highway 3 marks the northeast end of the road, a few kilometres west of downtown Keremeos. After passing through the "Red Bridge" and following the south side of the Similkameen River westward for about eight kilometres, the road swings south and up the Ashnola valley. The pavement ends about 10 kilometres from Highway 3.

Forest Road

The end of the pavement and 0K of the Forest Service Road coincide with the foot of the Ashnola Canyon. A kilometre later, the road crosses over to the west side of the river and begins a steady climb upstream. There are several designated recreation sites and numerous unorganized sites along the river, some with toilet facilities and many without.

Cathedral Provincial Park

The main entrance signpost for Cathedral Park is on the right side of the road near km 19. The Cathedral Lakes Lodge base camp and parking area is across the

Kayakers launch in the lower Ashnola River. © Murphy Shewchuk

Ashnola River at km 22.2. See the *Cathedral Provincial Park* chapter for more information. For those interested in hiking up to the Cathedral Lakes area, the Lakeview Creek Trailhead and campground is another 1.6 kilometres farther up Ashnola Road. Buckhorn Campground is located alongside the river at km 26.7.

The road swings west near the Cathedral Park entrance signs and follows the river upstream in a gradual arc before heading in a southerly direction near the 30K marker. There are a number of "dispersed use" camping areas between the road and the river. Self-contained "pack it in - pack it out" camping is the rule in these areas since they are not maintained by the Forest Service.

Motorized Recreation Regulated Area

A map and information sign near km 43 set out the restrictions imposed in the "Placer Mountain to Border Lake Motorized Recreation Regulated Area." In general, all motorized recreation vehicles except snowmobiles must keep to designated routes to help protect sensitive alpine meadows, grasslands, and wildlife habitat. Additional information is available from the Okanagan Shuswap Forest District at (250) 558-1700 or 1 800 661-4099.

Wall Creek Bridge

A new footbridge was built across the Ashnola River near Wall Creek at km 49.1. It will serve as a much-needed crossing for hikers interested in using the Centennial Trail or the Wall Creek Trail. The main road forks near the 40K marker (km 50.9) with the old road continuing along the valley floor for another half kilometre. There is another rudimentary campsite near the fork; this shows signs of frequent horse traffic.

The Centennial Trail also joins the Ashnola Road at the junction. The trail can be followed southwest through the trees for about one kilometre before it crosses Easygoing Main FS Road. At last check, the crossing was not well marked. Look for the continuation of the trail 50 to 100 metres south (down the road) from where you first climb up onto the road. See the *Centennial Trail: Pasayten River Bridge to Ashnola River* chapter for more details.

The Wall Creek Bridge across the Ashnola River. *© Murphy Shewchuk*

Easygoing Main FS Road

From the junction near the 40K marker, the Forest Road climbs southwest and then northwest up Duruisseau Creek before swinging west and then south. If you keep left at the major junctions, you should climb up to the plateau and reach Easygoing Creek approximately 12.8 kilometres from the Easygoing Main / Ashnola Road junction. There are a number of steep, narrow sections on this route that make it tricky in wet weather — so use extreme caution.

There is ample room to park near Easygoing Creek Bridge. From here you can begin to explore the high country. The Centennial Trail leads west about 4.5 kilometres to Trapper Lake. If time permits, you can also explore the trail to Border Lake. — MS

Additional information:

BC Parks
Web: www.env.gov.bc.ca/bcparks

Okanagan Shuswap Forest District
2501 - 14th Ave.
Vernon, BC V1T 8Z1
Tel: (250) 558-1700
Fax: (250) 549-5485
Toll-free; (via Enquiry BC) 1-800-663-7867
Web: www.for.gov.bc.ca/dos

CHAPTER 66

Cathedral Provincial Park

Statistics	For map, see page 328
Distance:	25 kilometres, Keremeos to Cathedral Base Camp;
	15 kilometres, Base Camp to Cathedral Lakes Lodge
Travel Time:	Two to three hours, Keremeos to Lodge
Elev. Gain:	1,585 metres, Keremeos to Cathedral Lakes Lodge
Condition:	Paved , then gravel; private access to Lodge
Season:	Best in dry weather; may be closed in winter
Topo Maps:	Keremeos, BC 82 E/4
	Ashnola River, BC 92 H/1
Communities:	Keremeos and Princeton

British Columbia's mountain roads can put anyone's resources to the test, whether these are mental, physical, vehicular or all of the above. Steep grades, sharp turns, narrow bridges, muddy ruts and windfalls can take the fun out of backcountry adventure. These same conditions can also transform your family sedan into a creaky, muddy mess or worse – sometimes in a matter of only a few kilometres. For some of us, the choice is clear: buy a four-wheel-drive vehicle, stock it up with spare parts, maps and emergency supplies, and then boldly set out in search of backcountry roads to explore.

Cathedral Lakes Lodge

Cathedral Lakes Lodge, in Cathedral Provincial Park, offers a second choice. For a fee, lodge representatives will transport you and a limited amount of gear from their Ashnola Road base camp into the heart of one of BC's finest wilderness areas. The 15-kilometre trip, carried out in open-back Mercedes Benz Unimog trucks, takes about one hour and ascends over 1,500 metres, bringing campers within a five-minute walk of the Quiniscoe Lake campground. The round trip fee — check with the reservation office — applies only if you are camping at the park

The Giant Cleft near the south end of Cathedral Ridge. © *Murphy Shewchuk*

wilderness campsites. It is worth noting that the road is restricted to park-use permit holders so you will NOT be able to take your vehicle up to the lodge. Advance reservations are normally required, so plan ahead.

If you are staying at Cathedral Lakes Lodge, transportation is included in the accommodation fee. The lodge offers a variety of accommodations ranging from a log cabin built by Herb Clark when he first came to the Cathedrals in the 1930s, to a room in the two-storey "Bavarian Style" lodge. Also available are a variety of medium-size "family" cabins and "Tom's Cabin," a beautiful log home originally built for one of the owners in 1992.

Lodge and cabin rates vary from $200 to $300 per person per day, depending on season and length of stay. This includes all meals, plus use of canoes and hot tub. Small groups wishing to do their own cooking can also book Tom's Cabin at a special rate. Check with the lodge for current transportation and accommodation rates.

Cathedral Lakes wilderness, in the Okanagan Range of the Cascade Mountains south of Keremeos, has attracted nature lovers for nearly a century. Before the road was built, hikers and horsemen followed difficult trails through narrow mountain valleys and along windswept ridges to reach the heart of what is now Cathedral Provincial Park.

The rough trails didn't deter early adventurers from returning to this hidden paradise. Attractions included a cluster of half a dozen clear cool lakes – located at over 2,000 metres above sea level – which are surrounded by picturesque ridges and alpine peaks that reach up to 2,628 metres (8,622 feet). The present road and excellent trail system opened up the Cathedrals to a much broader range of visitors. Today seniors and youngsters can also reach the lodge or park campgrounds in the Quiniscoe Lake area where the options are many and all quite spectacular.

Hikers on the trail near Glacier Lake. *© Murphy Shewchuk*

Well-marked trails

"Trails are well marked so that even a novice hiker can reach these places without any danger," explained the late Chess Lyons, the man who, over 60 years ago, recommended that the park be created. "Whether it is a pleasant forest walk around the lakes or a climb to spectacular vistas and geological wonders, Cathedral Park has it all in a remarkably convenient area for the novice as well as the professional mountaineer."

Wildlife and wildflowers also make the park worth exploring. Chess Lyons' book, *Trees, Shrubs and Flowers to know in British Columbia,* has been the BC naturalist's bible for 40 years, and his descriptions and comments about the local plant life are well worth noting.

"Cathedral Park is in the dry interior where the weather is dependable. Towards the end of July and into the first week in August there is a very fine wildflower display. Meadows and swales are bright with lupine, Indian paintbrush, wood betony and veronica. Shrubby cinquefoil, a plant with flowers that look like buttercups, grows in dense masses on some of the slopes.

"White heather and red heather come into bloom just as the peak of the flowers is passing. On the higher elevations all of the plants are adapted to harsh weather and press close to the ground. Many have small hairy leaves to resist water evaporation. Willow grows only an inch or two high, yet in the spring it flaunts pussy willows that rival those growing on large shrubs."

High Mountain Lakes

According to local historians, Aboriginals who lived along the Similkameen and Ashnola Rivers knew of these high mountain lakes long before the arrival of European fur traders. They came here in summer to trap hoary marmots, from which they made valuable blankets. Then in 1860, an International Boundary Survey first recorded these magnificent mountains and sparkling lakes in detail. Cathedral Mountain, from which the area gets its name, was formally named in 1901 by Carl and George Smith because it looked "something like a big church."

Cathedral Lakes Lodge and the area that would become the provincial park owe their humble beginnings and preservation to two men with foresight and determination. Herb Clark of Keremeos fell in love with the land when he was a young man of 19. He then went to work in the mines to save money to purchase his dream. In 1934, with about $500 in savings, Clark purchased two parcels of land from the British Columbia government. One parcel was located on Quiniscoe Lake and the other between Glacier and Pyramid Lakes. Next he established a horseback guiding service.

Chess Lyons, then head of British Columbia's three-man Parks Branch, first visited the area about five years after Herb Clark bought his land: "Jim McKeen (Mt. McKeen), a schoolboy friend, swears I was in there in 1939, but I can't remember," writes Chess Lyons in a November 1991 letter. "I did go in with Joe Harris Herb's partner in 1941, had a good look around and recommended it for a provincial park. However, the Forest Service thought there was timberland involved and put a hold on it for many years.

A mountain goat on the ridge above Ladyslipper Lake. *© Murphy Shewchuk*

"About 1944, Herb and I rode in, climbed about everything in sight, and then made a packhorse trip into the backcountry. I took 16 mm colour film and much of it was used in various films I put together.

"Then Ruth Kirk and I did another trip and made a short film for CBC's Klahanie. The Gehringers were building the lodge at that time."

Herb Clark, with partners Tom Fleet and Karl and Helmut Gehringer, formed Cathedral Lakes Resort Ltd. in 1964. Work on a private road was completed in 1965 and construction was started on the present buildings.

Park Established in 1968

Cathedral Provincial Park was officially established in 1968, nearly 30 years after Chess Lyons' recommendations. According to Lyons, "Geologically, the park is fascinating and presents many facets. Except for the highest peaks, glaciers of the last ice age have rounded the mountain slopes. As the glaciers receded, the ice on the northern slopes lingered and created large bowls called cirques. This was done by a long process of water melting and then freezing in the rock beneath, breaking them apart. The volcanic nature of some of the mountains is demonstrated in the Devil's Fenceposts which are symmetrical columns now twisted and bent but resembling a huge piling of wood. In Stone City (or Hamburger City) there are most unusual formations of rocks shaped into massive discs. They are considered so unusual that a geologist did his Master's thesis on them. At the Giant Cleft you will find a split in the rock face of the mountain caused by some tremendous forces of the past. Geologists believe the erosion of an intrusion of softer rock caused the impressive cleft. Smokey the Bear is another impressive rock formation close by.

In silhouette, it appears as a gigantic replica of the forest-fire-fighting ursine complete with his forest ranger hat. It's a picture you can't duplicate."

Cathedral Provincial Park is indeed a picture you can't duplicate. It is a unique piece of British Columbia that offers those, unable to spend a day of hard slogging, the opportunity to explore this incredible wilderness region. Once at camp — whether at the lodge or the nearby park campgrounds — the irresistible draw of the Giant's Cleft, alpine wildflowers and turquoise lakes will beckon everyone. Go prepared to enjoy Nature at its finest and toughest. Don't forget your boots, warm clothing, slicker and water bottle. Above all, don't forget your camera. — MS

Additional information:

BC Parks
Web: www.env.gov.bc.ca/bcparks

Cathedral Lakes Lodge
Site 4, Comp 8
Slocan Park, BC V0G 2E0
Tel: (250) 226-7560
Reservations: 1-888-255-4453
E-mail: info@cathedrallakes.ca
Web: www.cathedrallakes.ca

INFORMATION SOURCES

Apex Mountain Resort
PO Box 1060
Penticton, BC V2A 6J9
Tel: (250) 292-8222
Toll-free: 1-877-777-APEX (2739)
Fax: (250) 292-8100
Web: www.apexresort.com

BC Recreation Sites & Trails
Web: www.sitesandtrailsbc.ca

BC Parks General Information
Web: www.env.gov.bc.ca/bcparks

Beaver Lake Mountain Resort
6350 Beaver Lake Road
Winfield, BC V4V 1T5
Tel: (250) 762-2225
E-mail: info@beaverlakeresort.com
Web: www.beaverlakeresort.com

Big White Ski Resort
PO Box 2039 Stn. R.
Kelowna, BC V1X 4K5
Tel: (250) 765-3101
Fax: (250) 765-8200
Web: www.bigwhite.com/

Cascades Forest District
PO Box 4400
Merritt, BC V1K 1B8
Tel: (250) 378-8400
Fax: (250) 378-8481
Toll-free 1-800-665-1511

Cathedral Lakes Lodge
Site 4, Comp 8
Slocan Park, BC V0G 2E0
Tel: (250) 226-7560
Reservations 1-888-255-4453
E-mail: info@cathedrallakes.ca
Web: www.cathedrallakes.ca

Chris Charlesworth
Avocet Tours
725 Richards Road
Kelowna, BC V1X 2X5
Tel: (250) 718-0335
E-mail: info@avocettours.ca
Web: www.avocettours.ca

Chute Lake Resort
c/o Gary and Doreen Reed
797 Alexander Avenue
Penticton, BC V2A 1E6
Tel: (250) 493-3535
E-mail: info@chutelakeresort.com
Web: www.chutelakeresort.com

Crystal Mountain Resort Ltd.
Box 26044
West Kelowna, BC V4T 2G3
Tel: (250) 768-5189
Fax: (250) 768-3755
Snowline: (250) 712-6262
E-mail: info1@crystalresort.com
Web: www.crystalresort.com

Dee Lake Wilderness Resort:
10250 Dee Lake Rd,
Winfield, BC V4V 1T5
Tel: (250) 212-2129

Dominion Radio Astrophysical Observatory
717 White Lake Rd.
PO Box 248
Penticton, BC V2A 6J9
Web: www.nrc-cnrc.gc.ca/eng/solutions/facilities/drao.html

Friends of Fintry
Provincial Park Society
RR7 S-12 C-61
Vernon, BC V1T 7Z3
Tel: (250) 542-3461
E-mail: info@fintry.ca
Web: www.fintry.ca

Friends of the South Slopes (F.O.S.S.)
Box 28011 RPO East Kelowna
Kelowna, BC V1W 4A6
E-mail: info@foss-kelowna.org
Web: www.foss-kelowna.org

Hatheume Lake Resort
PO Box 490
Peachland, BC V0H 1X0
Tel: (250) 767-2642

Headwaters Fishing Camp
PO Box 350
Peachland, BC V0H 1X0
Tel: (250) 767-2400

Keremeos Grist Mill
RR1, Upper Bench Road
Keremeos, BC VOX 1N0
Tel: (250) 499-2888
Fax: (250) 499-2434

Kettle Valley Steam Railway
PO Box 1288
18404 Bathville Road
Summerland, BC V0H 1Z0
Tel: (250)- 494-8422
or 1-877-494-8424
Fax: 1-(250)-494-8452
Reservations: reservations@kettleval
leyrail.org
Information: information@kettleval
leyrail.org
Web: www.kettlevalleyrail.org

Kingfisher Environmental Interpretive Centre
2550 Mabel Lake Rd.
Enderby, BC VOE 1V0
Tel: (250) 838-0004

Lumby & District Chamber of Commerce
1882 Vernon Street
PO Box 534
Lumby, BC V0E 2G0
Tel/Fax: (250) 547-2300
E-mail: lumbychamber@shaw.ca
Web: www.monasheetourism.com

Mascot Gold Mine Tours
Tel: (250) 292-8733
Fax: (250) 292-8753
Web: www.mascotmine.com

Mckinney Nordic Ski Club
Tel: (250) 498-8461
E-mail: info@mckinneynordicskiing.com
Web: www.mckinneynordicskiclub.com

Mount Baldy Ski Corporation
PO Box 1499
Oliver, BC V0H 1R0
Tel: 1 866 754-2253
or (250) 498-4086
Fax: (250) 498-4087
E-mail: mail@skibaldy.com
Web: www.skibaldy.com

Myra Canyon Trestle Restoration Society (MCTRS)
PBC Box 611
Kelowna, BC V1Y 3R7
Web: www.myratrestles.com

Nickel Plate Nordic Centre
777 - 650 Duncan Avenue West
Penticton, BC V2A 7N1
Tel: (250) 292-8110
Web: www.nickelplatenordic.org

Nk'Mip Desert Cultural Centre
1000 Rancher Creek Rd.
Osoyoos, BC V0H 1V6
Tel: 1-250-495-7901
Fax: 1-250-495-7912
Toll free in BC phone 1-888-495-8555
E-mail: nkmipdesert@oib.ca
Web: www.nkmipdesert.com

Kelowna Nordic Ski Club
E-mail: admin@kelownanordic.com
Web: www.kelownanordic.com

O'Keefe Ranch
PO Box 955, Highway 97
Vernon, BC V1T 6M8
Tel: (250) 542-7868
E-mail: info@okeeferanch.ca
Web: www.okeeferanch.bc.ca

Okanagan Shuswap Forest District
2501 - 14th Ave.
Vernon, BC V1T 8Z1
Tel: (250) 558-1700
Fax: (250) 549-5485
Toll-free (via Enquiry BC)
1-800-663-7867
Web: www.for.gov.bc.ca/dos

Oliver Visitor Centre
36205 - 93rd Street
Oliver, BC V0H 1T0
Tel: (250) 498-6321
Fax: (250) 498-3156
E-mail: info@winecapitalofcanada.com
Web: www.winecapitalofcanada.com

Osoyoos Desert Society
PO Box 123
Osoyoos, BC V0H 1V0
Tel: (250) 495-2470
Toll-free: 1-877-899-0897
E-mail: mail@desert.org
Web: www.desert.org

Pacific Agri-Food Research Centre
4200 Highway 97
Summerland, BC V0H 1Z0
Tel: (250) 494-7711
Fax: (250) 494-0755

Penticton & Wine Country Visitor Centre
553 Railway Street
Penticton, BC V2A 8S3
Tel: (250) 493-4055
Fax: (250) 492-6119
Toll free: 1-800-663-5052
E-mail: visitors@penticton.org
Web: www.tourismpenticton.com

Penticton Indian Band
200 Westhill Estates,
Penticton, BC V2A 6J7
Tel: (250) 493-0048

Penticton Museum and Archives
785 Main St
Penticton, BC V2A 5E3
Tel: (250) 490-2451
Fax: (250) 490-0440
E-mail: museum@city.penticton.bc.ca
Web: www.penticton.ca

Princeton Castle Resort
5 Mile Road, RR1, S1, C10
Princeton, BC V0X 1W0
Tel: (250) 295-7988
Fax: (250) 295-7208
Toll-free: 1-888-228-8881
E-mail: info@castleresort.com
Web: www.castleresort.com

Princeton, Town of
169 Bridge Street
PO Box 670
Princeton, BC V0X 1W0
Tel: (250) 295-3135
Fax: (250) 295-3477
Web: www.town.princeton.bc.ca

Regional District of Central Okanagan
1450 KLO Road
Kelowna, BC
Tel: (250) 763-4918
Fax: (250) 763-0606
E-mail: info@cord.bc.ca
Web: www.regionaldistrict.com

Regional District of North Okanagan
9848 Aberdeen Rd.
Coldstream, BC V1B 2K9
Tel: (250) 550-3700
Fax: (250) 550-3701
E-mail: info@nord.ca
Web: www.rdno.ca

Regional District of Okanagan-Similkameen
101 Martin St
Penticton, BC V2A 5J9
Toll-free: 1-877-610-3737
E-mail: info@RDOS.bc.ca
Web: www.rdos.bc.ca

Silver Star Mountain Resort
PO Box 3002
Silver Star Mountain, BC V1B 3M1
Tel: (250) 542-0224
Fax: (250) 542-1236
E-mail: star@skisilverstar.com
Web: www.skisilverstar.com

Sovereign Lake Nordic Centre
PO Box 1231
Vernon, BC V1T 6N6
Tel: (250) 558-3036
Fax: (250) 558-3076
E-mail: info@sovereignlake.com
Web: www.sovereignlake.com

Summerland Chamber of Economic Development Tourism
15600 Hwy 97, PO Box 130,
Summerland, BC V0H 1Z0,
Tel: (250) 494-2686
Fax: (250) 494-4039
Web: www.summerlandchamber.com

Telemark Cross-Country Ski Club
Box 26072, West Kelowna
West Kelowna, BC V4T 2G3
Tel: (250) 768-1494
Fax: (250) 768-1493
E-mail: tccsc@telus.net
Web: www.telemarkx-c.com/

Thompson Okanagan Tourism Association
1332 Water Street
Kelowna, BC V1Y 9P4
Tel: (250) 860-5999
Fax: (250) 861-7493
E-mail: info@totabc.com
Web: www.thompsonokanagan.com

Three Valley Lake Chateau Ltd.
Box 860
Revelstoke, BC V0E 2S0
Tel: (250) 837-2109
Fax: (250) 837-5220
Toll-free: 1-888-667-2109
E-mail: 3valley@revelstoke.net
Web: www.3valley.com

Trails Society of British Columbia
Tel: (604) 737-3188
E-mail: trailsbc@trailsbc.ca
Web: www.trailsbc.ca

Vernon Tourism
701 Highway 97 South
Vernon, BC V1B 3W4
Tel: (250) 542-1415
Fax: (250) 545-3114
Reservations only: 1-800-665-0795
E-mail: info@tourismvernon.com
Web: www.vernontourism.com

Allison-McDiarmid, Aurelia. *Letters and Reflections From the Life and Times of John Fall Allison.* Princeton, BC: 1977.

Barlee, N.L. *Gold Creeks and Ghost Towns.* Surrey, BC: Hancock House Publishers Ltd, 1988.

Barlee, N.L. (Bill). *Similkameen — The Pictograph Country: Simil Kameen* Summerland, BC: 1978. (Reprinted by Hancock House in 1989.)

Burbridge, Joan. *Wildflowers of the Southern Interior of British Columbia and adjacent parts of Washington, Idaho and Montana.* Vancouver, BC: University of British Columbia Press, 1989.

Christie, Jack. *Inside Out British Columbia.* Vancouver, BC: Raincoast Books, 1998.

Falk, Les. *Hiking Trails in the Okanagan.* Kelowna, BC: Mosaic Enterprises Limited, 1982.

Hatton, William J. *Bridesville Country: A Brief History.* Oliver, BC: Oliver Printing, 1981.

Hayman, Bob. *RMII - Memoirs of Bob Hayman.* Peachland, BC: Gordon Hayman, 1991.

Hill, Beth. *Exploring the Kettle Valley Railway.* Winlaw, BC: Polestar Press, 1989.

Langford, Dan & Sandra. *Cycling the Kettle Valley Railway.* Calgary, AB: Rocky Mountain Books, 1997, 2002.

Lyons, C.P. *Trees, Shrubs and Flowers to know in British Columbia.* Toronto, ON: 1952.

McLean, Stan. *The History of the O'Keefe Ranch.* Vernon, BC: Stan McLean, 1984.

McNeil, *Holly and Dona Sturmanis. Okanagan Secrets & Surprises.* Winfield, BC: Okanagan Editions, 1995.

Mussio Ventures & Trails BC. *Trans Canada Trail: The British Columbia Route.*

New Westminster, BC: Mussio. Ventures Ltd., 2001.

Nanton, Isabel and Mary Simpson. *Adventuring in British Columbia.* Vancouver, BC: Douglas & McIntyre, 1996.

Neering, Rosemary. *A Traveller's Guide to Historic British Columbia.* Vancouver, BC: Whitecap Books, 1993.

Peachey, Gordon. *The Okanagan.* Kelowna, BC: Gordon Peachey, 1984.

Peachland Memories, Volume One. Peachland, BC (Box 244, V0H 1X0): Peachland Historical Society, 1983.

Peachland Memories, Volume Two. Peachland, BC (Box 244, V0H 1X0): Peachland Historical Society, 1983.

Read, Stanley E. *A Place Called Pennask.* Vancouver, BC: Mitchell Press, 1977.

Reid Crowther and Partners Ltd. *"Kettle Valley Railway Evaluation."Report for the Ministry of Environment, Land and Parks.* Kamloops, BC: 1996.

Roed, Murray A. and John D. Greenough, (Editors). *Okanagan Geology: British Columbia.* Kelowna, BC: Kelowna Geology Committee, 2004. Distributed by Sandhill Book Marketing Ltd.

Roed, Murray A. and Robert J. Fulton, (Editors). *Okanagan Geology South: Geologic Highlights of the South Okanagan, British Columbia.* Kelowna, BC: Okanagan Geology Committee, 2011. Distributed by Sandhill Book Marketing Ltd.

Sanford, Barrie. *McCulloch's Wonder: The Story of the Kettle Valley Railway.* North Vancouver, BC: Whitecap Books, 1977.

__________. *Steel Rails and Iron Men: A Pictorial History of the Kettle Valley Railway.* Vancouver, BC: Whitecap Books, 1990.

Shewchuk, Murphy O. *Backroads Explorer Vol. 2 Similkameen & South Okanagan.* Surrey, BC: Hancock House Publishers Ltd., 1988.

__________. *Coquihalla Country: An Outdoor Recreation Guide.* Merritt, BC: Sonotek Publishing Ltd., 1990, 1998.

__________. *Exploring the Nicola Valley.* Vancouver, BC: Douglas & McIntyre, 1981.

__________. *Fur, Gold & Opals.* Surrey, BC: Hancock House Publishers Ltd., 1975.

Smuin, Joe. *Canadian Pacific's Kettle Valley Railway.* Port Coquitlam, BC, 1997.

__________. *Kettle Valley Railway Mileboards: A Historical field guide to the KVR.* Winnipeg, MB: North Kildonan Publications, 2003.

Stewart, Dave. *Okanagan Back Roads: Volume 2 North Okanagan - Shuswap.* Sidney, BC: Saltaire Publishing Ltd., 1975.

Surtees, Ursula. *Kelowna: The Orchard City. An Illustrated History. (Includes "Partners in Progress" by Mark Zuehlke).* Windsor Publications Ltd., 1989.

Turner, Robert D. *Steam on the Kettle Valley Railway: A Heritage Remembered.* Victoria: Sono Nis Press, 1995.

__________. *West of Great Divide, An Illustrated History of the Canadian Pacific Railway in British Columbia, 1880-1986.* Victoria: Sono Nis Press, 1987.

Vernon Outdoors Club. *Hiking Trails.* Vernon, BC: Vernon Outdoors Club, 1989.

Woolliams, Nina G. *Cattle Ranch: The Story of the Douglas Lake Cattle Company.* Vancouver, BC: Douglas & McIntyre, 1979.

See also Information Sources (343 to 347) and List of Maps (xi)

Index

Murphy Shewchuk

Judie Steeves

Murphy Shewchuk is a passionate wilderness explorer, award-winning photographer and author of numerous books about BC's and Western Canada's outdoors, including *Coquihalla Trips & Trails*. His writing and photographs have also appeared in such publications as *BC Outdoors, Canadian Geographic,* and *Field & Stream*.

Judie Steeves is an award-winning journalist whose writing has earned her a Federation of BC Naturalists's award for "outstanding contributions to the understanding and appreciation of the natural history of BC."